Beyond Reason

Beyond Reason

Postcolonial Theory and the Social Sciences

SANJAY SETH

OXFORD
UNIVERSITY PRESS

OXFORD
UNIVERSITY PRESS

Oxford University Press is a department of the University of Oxford. It furthers the University's objective of excellence in research, scholarship, and education by publishing worldwide. Oxford is a registered trade mark of Oxford University Press in the UK and certain other countries.

Published in the United States of America by Oxford University Press
198 Madison Avenue, New York, NY 10016, United States of America.

© Oxford University Press 2021

First issued as an Oxford University Press paperback, 2023

Library of Congress Cataloging-in-Publication Data
Names: Seth, Sanjay, 1961– author.
Title: Beyond reason : postcolonial theory and the social sciences / Sanjay Seth.
Description: New York : Oxford University Press, 2021. |
Includes bibliographical references and index.
Identifiers: LCCN 2020032020 (print) |
LCCN 2020032021 (ebook) | ISBN 9780197500583 (hardback) |
ISBN 9780197688953 (paperback) | ISBN 9780197500606 (epub)
Subjects: LCSH: Social sciences—Philosophy. |
Postcolonialism—Philosophy. | Knowledge, Theory of. |
Reasoning. Classification: LCC H61.15 .S49 2021 (print) |
LCC H61.15 (ebook) | DDC 300.1—dc23
LC record available at https://lccn.loc.gov/2020032020
LC ebook record available at https://lccn.loc.gov/2020032021

DOI: 10.1093/oso/9780197500583.001.0001

1 3 5 7 9 8 6 4 2

Paperback printed by Marquis, Canada

To Raju and Nishad

Contents

Acknowledgments   ix

Introduction   1

I. MODERN WESTERN KNOWLEDGE UNDER CHALLENGE

1. Unsettling the Modern Knowledge Settlement   21

2. Defending Reason: A Postcolonial Critique   52

II. POSTCOLONIALISM AND SOCIAL SCIENCE

3. The Code of History   87

4. The Anachronism of History   113

5. International Relations: Empire and Amnesia   145

6. Political Theory and the Bourgeois Public Sphere   175

   Epilogue: Knowledge and Politics   207

Bibliography of Works Cited   221
Index   245

Acknowledgments

This book has been a long time in the making, and I have garnered many debts along the way. The earlier phases of writing were facilitated by a research professorship at the Graduate School of Asian and African Area Studies of the University of Kyoto in 2013. I am grateful to Kazuya Nakamizo for the invitation, and to him and his colleagues for making my stay in Kyoto so pleasant and productive. Sabbaticals from my home institution, Goldsmiths, University of London, made it possible to continue research and writing in a sustained fashion. As the argument began to assume some shape, invitations to present my work afforded the opportunity to test out ideas and draft chapters before audiences across several continents: in Europe, Goldsmiths; All Souls College, Oxford; School of Oriental and African Studies; Sussex University; London School of Economics; Birkbeck; University College London; Birmingham University; Westminster University; Warwick University; Nottingham University; the Political Studies Association; Universidade NOVA de Lisboa; Universidade de Coimbra; Università degli Studi di Napoli "L'Orientale"; Kulturwissenschaftliches Institut Essen; Stiftung für Kulturwissenschaften, Ruhr-Universität Bochum; Helsinki Collegium for Advanced Studies; Université Paris 8; Royal Danish Academy of Art; Humboldt Universität, Berlin; Freie Universität, Berlin; and the University of Groningen; in Australia, the Australian National University; University of Queensland; University of Technology, Sydney; and the University of South Australia; in North America, the University of Chicago; in Asia, Habib University, Karachi; University of Kyoto; and Osaka University; in South America, Universidade de Brasília; Universidade Federal do Rio de Janeiro; Universidade Federal de Ouro Preto; and the Universidade de Buenos Aires. As I was completing my book, the Instituto de Ciências Sociais of the Universidade de Lisboa and the Faculdade de Ciências Sociais e Humanas of the Universidade NOVA de Lisboa convened a workshop in Lisbon where some of its arguments were subjected to questioning, to my great benefit. I am grateful to the organizers of all these talks for the invitations, and to the participants for their questions and comments.

Early in this project Barbara Herrnstein Smith was kind enough to make time to read my initial formulations and offer encouragement and sound advice. I am grateful to her, all the more so since we have never met, and her engagement with my work was purely an act of intellectual generosity. A number of friends and colleagues read and commented upon a part of the manuscript: my thanks to Amy Allen, Tarak Barkawi, Akeel Bilgrami, Francisco Carballo, Harriet Evans, Ian Hunter, Humeira Iqtidar, Leigh Jenco, Branwen Gruffydd Jones, Robert Manne, Hilary McPhee, Walter Mignolo, José Neves, Martin Savransky, and Ryan Walter; and to David Martin for suggesting the cover image. My thanks also to my editor Angela Chnapko, for steering this book through the acquisition and publication process with exemplary professionalism and courtesy.

I have been uncommonly fortunate that my affective and intellectual worlds overlap to a high degree. Dipesh Chakrabarty has been part of the life of this book, offering suggestions at the beginning, and then commenting upon chapters at the end. I owe him a special thanks for his counsel and insights and, more generally, for the unstinting warmth of his friendship over the last thirty years and more. My siblings, Vanita Seth and Suman Seth, fill my life with fun, laughter, conversation, and love; they have also read, commented on, and improved the arguments of this book, taking time out from their own academic work to do so. My parents, Sushil and Vimal Seth, always offered unqualified love and support; I owe them everything. My father continues to offer me encouragement and advice; it is a source of unremitting sadness that my mother is no longer here to cast her warm glow over her children.

As always, Rajyashree Pandey read every sentence in this book and offered serious, helpful, and sometimes challenging suggestions and criticisms. I could not have written this or any other book without her. To thank her and our son Nishad for all they have given me is something to be done in private; this book is dedicated to them.

Introduction

For over a century, scholars in the social sciences assumed that the intellectual presuppositions underlying their disciplinary practice and informing their various inquiries did not themselves require critical investigation. In the latter part of the twentieth century, for a variety of reasons, that began to change, and a knowledge that had once been seemingly secure came to be questioned in a sustained fashion. The "poststructuralist" and "postmodernist" discussions of the 1980s and 1990s were an important and productive expression of this, but the furious denunciations that followed, and the ensuing "culture wars," often generated more heat than light. Recently even the heat has gone out of these debates, not because they have been in any way "settled" one way or another, but because they have been inconclusive and because the passions that fueled them seem to have been largely exhausted.

It will be one of the arguments of this book that critical questioning of the foundations of our knowledge did not, however, disappear, but rather that it continued to take place, now on a different terrain. The evidence for this, to be discussed and developed in greater detail in the chapters to follow, is to be found, above all, in disciplinary debates and developments. For instance, the 1980s witnessed a curious trend in historiographical circles whereby one after another erstwhile social historians, many of whom had come of age in the 1970s, expressed doubts about the categories that had hitherto informed their work. Gareth Stedman Jones, Joan Wallach Scott, Patrick Joyce, Geoff Eley, William Sewell Jr., and others called into question the ontological solidity of the central concepts of social history (such as class and gender) and challenged the presumption that the actions and "consciousness" of those whom they studied had been determined, and thus could be explained, by "material interests" or by "experience." As this debate progressed, a few participants began to wonder out loud whether not just the categories embedded in the social, such as gender and class, but "the social" itself could be granted the unquestioned ontological status that it had been assumed to possess. Keith Michael Baker put it most directly and forcefully: "Society is

Beyond Reason. Sanjay Seth, Oxford University Press (2021). © Oxford University Press.
DOI: 10.1093/oso/9780197500583.003.0001

an invention not a discovery. It is a representation of the world instituted in practice, not simply a brute objective fact."[1]

At roughly the same time as social historians were questioning the solidity of "the social," the certainties hitherto surrounding "nature" and the study of it also came under challenge. Earlier, Thomas Kuhn's immensely influential *The Structure of Scientific Revolutions* had undermined the notion that the natural sciences produced knowledge that could be verified by comparing representations with the nature they "mapped." Soon after, the "strong program" in the sociology of science situated the production of scientific knowledge in its historical setting, and subsequently a host of studies showed how scientific inquiry, and the very idea of a "science" of nature, was embedded in historical and political circumstances. The objectivity and precision that had been thought to be the preserve of the natural sciences, and which scholars of the human sciences had usually been ready to concede—some because they hoped to emulate it, others in order to authorize different protocols for the study of "man"—were now put into question precisely by those charged with inquiring into the history of the production of scientific knowledge. But here too, as in the discussions among social historians, the debate moved on from questioning the status of the knowledge produced of its object, to questioning the object itself. Bruno Latour and some other historians and sociologists of science began to suggest that the existence of "nature," separate from society/man, was not a truth about the world that we moderns had discovered, but a distinction that modern, Western societies created and thereafter rigorously policed.[2]

These debates and others like them have been a feature of our intellectual life in recent decades. The debates and works in question come out of different disciplines (including history, the history of science, sociology, anthropology, and philosophy) and are animated by diverse ethical and political concerns. Though they are much less than a collective *project*, they have the collective *effect* of serving, in Judith Butler's description, to "parochialize a very specific . . . tradition within the West," by disinterring and challenging

---

[1] Keith M. Baker, "Enlightenment and the Institution of Society: Notes for a Conceptual History," in William Melching and Wyger Velema (eds.), *Main Trends in Cultural History*, Amsterdam: Rodopi, 1994, 114.

[2] See especially Bruno Latour, *We Have Never Been Modern*, translated by Catherine Porter, New York: Harvester Wheatsheaf, 1993, and his *Politics of Nature: How to Bring the Sciences into Democracy*, translated by Catherine Porter, Cambridge, MA: Harvard University Press, 2004; also Lorraine Daston, "Marvelous Facts and Miraculous Evidence in Early Modern Europe," *Critical Inquiry* 18:1 (Autumn 1991), 93–124 and "The Nature of Nature in Early Modern Europe," *Configurations* 6:2 (1998), 149–72.

"the various ways of organizing knowledge that are tacitly operating as the preconditions of various 'acts' of knowledge."[3] The preconditions or presumptions that underlie "modern Western knowledge"—I will elaborate on what precisely I mean by the marked terms later in this introduction— have been under challenge for some time now. This challenge can be loosely grouped into three currents, currents that provide the background intellectual conditions enabling this book.

The first current comprises a body of works that variously offer a critique of the "view from nowhere," insist on the "theory dependence" of observation, or provide a critique of "foundationalism." What these positions have in common is that they all insist that knowledge necessarily proceeds from presuppositions that are the basis, rather than the outcome, of facts and discoveries about the world. Terms bearing a strong family resemblance, including "conceptual scheme," "intellectual tradition," "paradigm," "social imaginary," "episteme," "knowledge culture," and "representational economy,"[4] all designate the presuppositions that necessarily ground any knowledge production, but which cannot themselves be grounded in facts or evidence, and which therefore do not have apodictic status. Since there have been multiple intellectual traditions, a direct implication of this intellectual current is that our knowledge begins to appear, precisely, as "our" knowledge, as a historically and perhaps culturally specific "tradition" or "episteme," rather than as knowledge tout court.

The second current comprises a growing number of inquiries that demonstrate the vicissitudes of time and place that went into the making of many of our intellectual categories. As a result, the emergence of modern knowledge

[3] Judith Butler, "The Sensibility of Critique: Response to Asad and Mahmood," in Talal Asad, Wendy Brown, Judith Butler, and Saba Mahmood (eds.), *Is Critique Secular? Blasphemy, Injury and Free Speech*, 2nd ed., New York: Fordham University Press, 2013, 116. Butler identifies three ways of doing so, slightly different from the three currents I identify: "through tracing internal contradictions, through comparing and contrasting alternative cultural lexicons for similar concepts, through offering historical account of how a set of cultural specific assumptions become recast as universal and postcultural" (116).

[4] See respectively Peter Winch, *The Idea of a Social Science and Its Relation to Philosophy*, London: Routledge and Kegan Paul, 1958; Alasdair MacIntyre, *Whose Justice? Which Rationality?*, Notre Dame, IN: University of Notre Dame Press, 1980; Thomas S. Kuhn, *The Structure of Scientific Revolutions*, 2nd ed., Chicago: University of Chicago Press, 1970; Charles Taylor, *Modern Social Imaginaries*, Durham, NC: Duke University Press, 2004, itself drawing upon Cornelius Castoriadis, *The Imaginary Institution of Society*, Cambridge: Polity, 1987; Michel Foucault, *The Order of Things: An Archaeology of the Human Sciences*, New York: Vintage Books, 1994; Margaret Somers, *Genealogies of Citizenship: Markets, Statelessness, and the Right to Have Rights*, Cambridge: Cambridge University Press, 2008; and Webb Keane, *Christian Moderns: Freedom and Fetish in the Mission Encounter*, Berkeley: University of California Press, 2007.

appears not as a story, as it has usually been narrated, of intellectual advance and progress, but rather of the historical contingency and arbitrariness that went into the making of that which we now deem to be obvious, fundamental, and universal. Foucault and those influenced by him have additionally shown that power is "not in a position of exteriority" in relation to knowledge, "but immanent in the latter,"[5] and thus that knowledge is not the formalization of methods of correct cognition, but rather, in Foucault's oft-quoted words, "Each society has its regime of truth, its 'general politics' of truth; that is, the types of discourse which it accepts and makes function as true."[6] The effects of these "genealogical" analyses, where they have been influential, have been to change the questions we ask of knowledges—not whether and why they are "true," but "how effects of truth are produced within discourses which in themselves are neither true nor false."[7] Some contemporary scholarship evinces a distinctly late-modern agnosticism, one that does not so much ask what is true and what is false, but instead interrogates how and why we came to see certain things as true, and what thoughts and practices these "truths" facilitate.

Both these currents have the effect of problematizing and also provincializing our knowledge, but the latter effect is only indirectly achieved. To see the social sciences as *a* knowledge tradition, rather than as knowledge as such, requires reference to something other that marks their specificity and distinctiveness. This can be done by contrasting the social sciences with the forms of knowledge that preceded them and that they replaced, or with non-Western knowledges. Where the latter tack is taken, these currents do not, by and large, engage with the other knowledge traditions and cultures that they invoke; the function of these is that of a generalized otherness, an "outside" that serves to demarcate the historical and cultural specificity of that which is being investigated. Thus when in *The Order of Things* Foucault tells the reader that his study of the classical and the modern epistemes that have dominated knowledge in the West since the seventeenth century arose out of the unease produced by his encounter with "a certain Chinese encyclopaedia," it is

---

[5] Michel Foucault, *The History of Sexuality: An Introduction*, translated by Robert Hurley, New York: Pelican, 1981, 94.

[6] Michel Foucault, "Truth and Power," in Colin Gordon (ed.), *Power/Knowledge: Selected Interviews and Other Writings, 1972–1997*, New York: Pantheon, 1980, 131.

[7] In full: "The problem does not consist in drawing the line between that in a discourse which falls under the category of scientificity or truth, and that which comes under some other category, but in seeing historically how effects of truth are produced within discourses which in themselves are neither true nor false" (Foucault, "Truth and Power," 118).

telling that the encyclopedia in question is a Borgesian invention. Derrida makes it very clear that his deconstructive critique of metaphysics is a critique of *Western* metaphysics—even if white or Western man mistakes this for "the universal form of that he must still wish to call Reason"[8]—but this gesture of delimitation does not signal an engagement with non-Western alterity: he characterizes deconstruction as "a product of Europe, a relation of Europe to itself as an experience of radical alterity."[9]

By contrast, the third intellectual current that provides the enabling conditions for this book, and which it draws upon most extensively and seeks to develop, consists of a range of different works, some undertaken under the sign of postcolonialism, that juxtapose concepts and categories of modern European thought with non-European histories and lifeworlds. These reflexive and theoretical works do not assume the adequacy of their categories and simply "apply" them, but are alive to the possibility that the presuppositions that undergird our knowledge may not, and sometimes do not, "travel" well to other times and places. Gayatri Chakravorty Spivak's *A Critique of Postcolonial Reason* provides a masterful discussion of some of the philosophical and historical complexities that arise when Western knowledge becomes the grounds of postcolonial critique in a globalized world.[10] In his study of culture and power in premodern India, Sheldon Pollock observes that the social sciences "have their origins in the West in capitalism and modernity and were devised to make sense of the behavior of power and culture under Western capitalist modernity. . . . These are the particulars from which larger universalizations have typically been produced, in association with the universalization of Western power under colonialism and globalization."[11] However, because the social sciences arose in association with "a historically very peculiar, temporally very thin, and spatially very narrow slice of human history," he finds that "the theory developed from that history fails to help us understand, and even impedes us from seeing, what did happen elsewhere and how this might differ."[12] The African philosopher and social theorist Achille Mbembe begins his important study of

---

[8] Jacques Derrida, "White Mythology," in *Margins of Philosophy*, translated by Alan Bass, Chicago: University of Chicago Press, 1982, 213.

[9] Jacques Derrida, *Learning to Live Finally: The Last Interview*, translated by Pascale-Anne Brault and Michael Naas, New York: Palgrave Macmillan, 2007, 44–45.

[10] Gayatri Chakravorty Spivak, *A Critique of Postcolonial Reason: Toward a History of the Vanishing Present*, Cambridge, MA: Harvard University Press, 1999.

[11] Sheldon Pollock, *The Language of the Gods in the World of Men: Sanskrit, Culture, and Power in Premodern India*, Berkeley: University of California Press, 2006, 33.

[12] Pollock, *Language of the Gods*, 564.

the African postcolony by noting that since social theory emerged "at the time of the first industrialization and the birth of modern urban societies," it is of limited value for his purposes: "By defining itself both as an accurate portrayal of Western modernity—that is, by starting from conventions that are purely local—and as universal grammar, social theory has condemned itself always to make generalizations from the idioms of a provincialism."[13] And the ethnographers John and Jean Comaroff argue that although we assume that the social sciences are rational and secular, in contrast to the "cosmologies" of earlier times and of contemporary non-Western others, they are in fact "our own rationalizing cosmology posing as science, our culture parading as historical causality."[14]

The social sciences had aspired to constitute a knowledge that, while it had developed in a particular time and place, transcended its origins, and was not limited by time and place. In Max Weber's words, uttered at the beginning of the twentieth century, the social sciences aspired to "be acknowledged as correct even by a Chinese."[15] That aspiration was achieved; for most of that century "Western" and "modern" were not taken to specify delimitations to the scope of this knowledge, but rather as descriptions of its origins that shed glory on those origins. That modern Europe had given birth to a knowledge that was properly scientifically etic rather than, as before, merely emic, reflecting the beliefs and prejudices of the time and culture that had produced it, was taken as testimony to the superiority of Europe and of modernity. Elites in the colonized world either accepted this description or, more often, characterized this knowledge as modern but as only accidentally rather than essentially European; in either case, they avidly sought to acquire it and put it to the service of their people.

Taken collectively, the three intellectual currents I have been referring to have given rise to the suspicion that a knowledge claiming to be "etic" is in fact modern, Western, and "emic"; that far from being free of any gross historical or cultural presumptions, it is in reality rooted in European histories and lifeworlds, and claims a *spurious* universality. In the 1990s, Immanuel Wallerstein and his collaborators observed that a growing number of "dissident voices" were claiming that "what the social sciences presented as

---

[13] Achille Mbembe, *On the Postcolony*, Berkeley: University of California Press, 2001, 10, 11.

[14] John and Jean Comaroff, *Ethnography and the Historical Imagination*, Boulder, CO: Westview Press, 1992, 6.

[15] Max Weber, "Objectivity in Social Science and Social Policy," in Edward Shils and Henry Finch (eds.), *The Methodology of the Social Sciences: Max Weber*, New York: Free Press, 1949, 58.

applicable to the whole world represented in fact the views of a minuscule minority within humankind," and that these social sciences had become dominant not because they were intellectually superior to all other possible ways of thinking, but "simply because the same minority was also dominant in the world outside the universities."[16] Or as Dipesh Chakrabarty put it a few years later, "There was a time when . . . the process of translating diverse forms, practices, and understandings of life into universalist political-theoretical categories of deeply European origin seemed to most social scientists an unproblematic proposition"[17]—but that this time had passed.

But although these currents overlap and influence each other, and evidence a degree of intertextuality, they are not animated by a collective or common intent. Moreover, the debates that give rise to these questions and doubts are often disciplinary ones, and their disquieting effects usually remain confined to the discipline concerned. In part because of this, the full implications of these arguments and such questioning, taken together, have not been adequately registered or explored. Arising at the confluence of these currents and drawing upon recent debates in diverse disciplines, this book argues that the nature and the status of the knowledge that we thought had discovered certain truths about the world have to be fundamentally rethought: that the social sciences do not transcend the historical and cultural specificities of their emergence and should instead be regarded as a parochial knowledge that nonetheless succeeded in becoming global.

Showing that the modern social sciences are a historically and culturally specific way of knowing and therefore being in the world, rather than a set of truths finally discovered, is important in and of itself, but it is also a necessary means to an end. For if the social sciences do not transcend their temporal and parochial origins, and are thus not explained and validated simply by the fact that they are "true," it becomes possible to ask what they *do*. The aim of this book is thus not to unmask our knowledge and to show it to be "false"—it is agnostic on the question of truth—but rather to unearth the presumptions that underlie and organize it, and to examine what intellectual effects these have. It seeks to show what these bring into view and what they obscure, what they make possible to think, and what they make difficult to think. This book also inquires into the "real-world" effects of these presuppositions,

---

[16] Immanuel Wallerstein et al., *Open Up the Social Sciences*, Stanford, CA: Stanford University Press, 1996, 51.

[17] Dipesh Chakrabarty, *Provincializing Europe: Postcolonial Thought and Historical Difference*, Princeton, NJ: Princeton University Press, 2000, 17.

recognizing that knowledge does not just "represent" or "cognize" a world that lies outside it, but has effects on the world it seeks to understand. For some time now scholars have drawn attention to the ways in which what were once only "our" versions of subjectivity and personhood, of agency, history, religion, and secularism, and so on and so forth, have replaced other, preexisting versions of these; or brought them into existence where they did not previously exist. Simply to unmask or denounce would be to miss what is most interesting and important: that in becoming globalized, modern knowledge has been a force in reshaping the world.

Since a defining feature of modern knowledge is that it is divided into disciplines, each with its own object(s) of inquiry and corresponding protocols (the presuppositions underlying modern knowledge in general are here supplemented by presumptions thought to be specific to the objects of the discipline in question), asking what our knowledge illuminates and what it obscures requires asking what *disciplines* "do"; what ways of understanding, encountering, and inhabiting the world they facilitate, and what they disallow. The contemporary disciplines of history and politics (or political science) serve as the sites for the elaboration of my argument. Anatomizing the presumptions that enable the practice of the disciplines of history and politics, I ask what representations and relations with the past, and with power and politics, they make possible and what possibilities they foreclose.

Modern, Western Knowledge

I have been referring thus far to modern Western knowledge without explaining why I use "modern" and "Western" to designate and delimit the knowledge this book engages with, and also without indicating what I mean when I refer to its "founding presuppositions." It is time to do so, and also to address the question of my own critical vantage point—from what knowledge position, space, or location I anatomize and critically evaluate modern knowledge.

Throughout this book I refer to the knowledge that is globally dominant in schools, universities, bureaucracies, government, and industry—the formal knowledge that is the subject of this book—as modern, Western knowledge: "modern" to indicate its historical provenance, and "Western" to draw attention to the geocultural specificity of these historical origins. This knowledge is modern in that it first begins to take shape in the early modern period, is further developed in the Enlightenment, and becomes formalized and organized—including by being divided into disciplines—in the nineteenth century. Of course, it displays intellectual continuities with what preceded it, but it also marks a sharp rupture, as observed by many of its champions, the best-known expression of which is perhaps Kant's claim that the Enlightenment marked "mankind's exit from its self-incurred immaturity."[18] The claim that a new, mature, and genuinely scientific knowledge was emerging was closely connected to the widespread perception that humankind, or a portion thereof, had entered a new age or epoch, marked (according to taste) by the transition from status to contract, feudalism to capitalism, enchantment to rationalization, Gemeinschaft to Gesellschaft: what we have come to call "modernity." Our knowledge is thus modern in a twofold sense: it is historically relatively recent and marks a break with the knowledges that preceded it and that it replaced; and it is closely tied to the phenomenon of modernity. Or as Wittrock, Heilbron, and Magnusson put it, in the eighteenth century, "A conceptual and epistemic revolution took place which was coterminous with the formation of the political and technological practices that we have come to associate with the world of modernity."[19]

Modern knowledge is also Western, inasmuch as it first emerged in Europe, tied to the processes and wider changes I have alluded to. Of course, Europe and the West are themselves historical products, and modernity and the knowledges associated with it were never an exclusively European affair. Why then call this knowledge "Western" at all? Indeed, for some time now scholars have been challenging the "diffusionist" account according to which capitalism, the modern state, and modern forms of social life are endogenous to Europe and were only subsequently exported to or imitated by non-Western peoples. These revisionist accounts have in common an insistence that the capitalist-modern was from the outset a global event, one that was made possible by the "discovery," conquest, and exploitation of the Americas, by the slave trade, and by Europe's colonization of Asia and Africa. Some have gone further and argued that it is not just capitalism and modernity that were "co-produced" by East and West, but that modern knowledge too is a joint inheritance, rather than "Western." In *Freedom Time*, taking issue with

---

[18] Kant, "An Answer to the Question: What Is Enlightenment?," in James Schmidt (ed.), *What Is Enlightenment: Eighteenth-Century Answers and Twentieth-Century Questions*, Berkeley: University of California Press, 1996, 58.

[19] Björn Wittrock, Johan Heilbron, and Lars Magnusson, "The Rise of the Social Sciences and the Formation of Modernity," in Johan Heilbron, Lars Magnusson, and Björn Wittrock (eds.), *The Rise of the Social Sciences and the Formation of Modernity*, Dordrecht: Kluwer, 1998, 2.

Chakrabarty's *Provincializing Europe*, Gary Wilder concludes that "if modernity was a global process, its concepts are a common legacy that already belong to all humanity."[20] The imperative of unmasking universalisms as covert
European particularisms that animated an earlier generation of scholars, and
that in Wilder's reading animates *Provincializing Europe*, vanishes once we
can see modern thought as "a common legacy": contra Chakrabarty, Wilder
announces that his "aim is not to provincialize Europe but to deprovincialize
Africa and the Antilles."[21] Also taking issue with Chakrabarty, Gurminder
Bhambra finds redundant his injunction that postcolonial thought cannot
avoid engaging with European categories, for, she argues, the concepts and
traditions in question "are not European; what is at issue is the claiming of
these concepts and traditions as European. It is this move that . . . places
Europe as the unique home of the innovative, the creative, the thoughtful,
and the active."[22] For Bhambra as for Wilder, modern knowledge, like modernity itself, was not globally diffused from a European origin, but was from
its beginnings forged in a "global context of socio-historical processes."[23]

In describing modern knowledge as Western I am, of course, rejecting
this claim. I am in sympathy with the argument that the historical origins
of modernity cannot be understood without according centrality to conquest, slavery, and colonialism.[24] But I do not think it follows that modern
knowledge was also an outcome of these global processes, and that it is the
joint product and inheritance, equally, of all peoples. There is no doubt, as
an ample scholarly literature attests, that modern knowledge drew upon
many sources,[25] and more generally, that cultures and knowledges are always hybrids or palimpsests. But the Enlightenment and the subsequent
development, systematization, and formalization of its fruits into the intellectual disciplines that characterize the formal intellectual inquiry that is

[20] Gary Wilder, *Freedom Time: Negritude, Decolonization, and the Future of the World*, Durham, NC: Duke University Press, 2015, 11.

[21] Wilder, *Freedom Time*, 10.

[22] Gurminder Bhambra, *Rethinking Modernity: Postcolonialism and the Sociological Imagination*, New York: Palgrave Macmillan, 2007, 146.

[23] Bhambra, *Rethinking Modernity*, 72.

[24] As long as it also remembered that the slaves, the indigenous, and colonized peoples who were part of the world-historical processes that created the modern were the unwitting "conscripts" rather than "volunteers" of modernity. See Talal Asad, "Conscripts of Western Civilization," in Christine Ward Gailey (ed.), *Civilization in Crisis: Anthropological Perspectives*, Gainesville: University of Florida Press, 1992, 333–51; and David Scott, *Conscripts of Modernity: The Tragedy of Colonial Enlightenment*, Durham, NC: Duke University Press, 2004.

[25] See, for instance, Simon Schaffer, Lissa Roberts, Kapil Raj, and James Delbourgo (eds.), *The Brokered World: Go-Betweens and Global Intelligence, 1770–1820*, Sagamore Beach, MA: Science History Publications, 2009.

my subject were principally European events. This formalized knowledge came to the non-Western world with trading ships and gunboats, often in association with European colonial rule. It became global, but it did so not because similar intellectual transformations were happening in the New World and Africa and Asia, but rather because it was imposed upon them through conquest and colonial rule. Even where it bore the marks of extensive borrowing that had been facilitated by prior contacts and exchanges with India, China, and elsewhere, modern knowledge did not arrive to these locales as a reworked version of what was already familiar, but as something new—and alien. How else are we to make sense of the ingenious—and sometimes anguished—debates of Chinese literati, Japanese intellectuals and bureaucrats, and Indian nationalists who sought to discover whether it was possible to borrow Western knowledge while preserving their "traditional" ways, and if so, how this was to be done? This knowledge came to be accepted by anticolonial nationalists not because of the "shock of recognition"—an embrace of that which was already familiar—but because, despite regarding it as alien and foreign, they also saw it as the source of European power and supremacy, and thus as something that must be acquired if their peoples were to become masters of their own fate.[26]

In short, it is possible to acknowledge that modernity was a global—if highly coercive and unequal—process, without drawing the conclusion that modern knowledge is a universal inheritance, and without thereby effacing the enormous differences between the knowledge traditions of the non-Western world and modern Western knowledge. The (dubious) benefit of according non-Western peoples credit for modern knowledge leaves unchallenged the presumption that this knowledge is universal and true, whence the issue of "credit" arises.[27] Earlier generations of anticolonial intellectuals accepted the superiority of modern knowledge and sought, variously, to selectively appropriate it, to find intimations of this knowledge in their own traditions, or to compensate by claims for the superior ethics or spirituality

[26] For a study of this with reference to India see my *Subject Lessons: The Western Education of Colonial India*, Durham, NC: Duke University Press, 2007, especially chapter 6.

[27] That a concern with according "credit" and acknowledging "contributions" is at issue is abundantly apparent. Wilder writes, "What is the analytic and political cost of assigning to Europe such categories or experiences as self-determination, emancipation, equality, justice, and freedom, let alone abstraction, humanity or universality? Why confirm the story that Europe has long told about itself?" (*Freedom Time*, 11). And Bhambra writes that the "connected histories" that she advocates "would provide a different understanding of modernity and the diversity of contributions to it," because they would encompass "both the contributions of non-European 'others' and the contribution of European colonialism" (Bhambra, *Rethinking Modernity*, 152–53).

of their own knowledge traditions. The revisionist historical account seeks to achieve a similar end, but now by denying that this knowledge is Western at all. But if we accept that knowledges are products of historically specific circumstances and contingencies, and none, including modern knowledge, escapes these contingencies such that it becomes unmarked and universal, then there is no longer any imperative to hunt down intimations and parallels for science, humanism, self-determination, autonomy, and so on in non-Western intellectual traditions; or to claim non-Western coauthorship for them. Once the superiority and universality of modern knowledge is no longer assumed or conceded, it becomes possible to give the historical record its due, and to recognize that a particular form of knowledge, forged in Europe, came to be globalized through the coercive agency of conquest and colonialism, and subsequently through its adoption and adaptation by anticolonial nationalists and postcolonial states.

Modern Western knowledge is immensely variegated, of course, and marked by numerous disputes; and it is in the process of constant change, as previously accepted positions are challenged and sometimes abandoned. Given this, is it even possible to speak about modern knowledge or "the" social sciences? I shall argue that it is, for notwithstanding all the diversity and dispute that characterize the social sciences, they share certain presuppositions, presumptions, or core categories, terms I will be using interchangeably. By these I do not mean specific propositions or ideas, which indeed are subject to constant revision, but what precedes propositions or ideas, "the preconditions that make thinking this or that idea possible";[28] not any specific intellectual position, representation, or practice, but the "foundational assumptions about what counts as an adequate representation or practice in the first place."[29] As Conal Condren observes, "Any statement takes something for granted, otherwise nothing can be said"; to work backward from statements and discourses to the presuppositions underlying and enabling them is "a matter of the imaginative mapping of a common ground between interlocutors, indicating the limits and conditions that enabled them to debate and differ."[30]

---

[28] Lorraine Daston, "Historical Epistemology," in James Chandler, Arnold Davidson, and Harry Harootunian (eds.), *Questions of Evidence*, Chicago: University of Chicago Press, 1994, 283.

[29] Mary Poovey, "The Liberal Civil Subject and the Social," *Public Culture* 14:1 (Winter 2002), 130.

[30] Condren goes on to explain that to identify "presuppositions" "is not to specify anything cohesive as a doctrine, a theory, a set of ideas, concepts, an ideology. . . . It is simply to suggest what is tacitly accepted at a given point in order that something might be said. Effectively, a presupposition comes to us as the contingent silence that helps structure the diversity of discourse." *Argument and*

The presumptions that provide the "common ground" of the social sciences are fundamentally different from those that informed the premodern knowledges of Europe, and they once had to be argued for and were contested. But they long ago became naturalized, such that we no longer think of them as the presuppositions of a certain way of encountering and knowing the world, but as necessary to encounter and know the world at all. These presuppositions, which I will outline and discuss in the chapters to follow, have become the common, and usually unexamined, ground that makes intellectual inquiry possible.

Modern knowledge is different from the medieval and Renaissance knowledges that it replaced not only and obviously in its content, but also in its "form." In contrast to the variegated and dispersed knowledges of earlier times, the modern period sees the emergence and consolidation of an educational "system" structured vertically in an ascending hierarchy—primary, secondary, and tertiary education.[31] This system of knowledge also came to be internally differentiated into "disciplines," a form of organizing knowledge that was novel and very different from, say, the trivium. Hence the importance of the university, an institution that predates this transformation, but which acquires a new function and importance, as the apex of a now unified educational pyramid, one that selects and certifies and distributes knowledges into different disciplines. "The eighteenth century," Foucault writes, "was the century when knowledges were disciplined . . . every knowledge became a discipline which had, in its own field, criteria of selection that allowed it to eradicate false knowledge or nonknowledge."[32] But the "eradication" of falsity no longer required the Index or other forms of censoring books and false claims, but rather the creation of a community of authorized knowledge producers who could in turn adjudicate what sorts of claims and underlying procedures could be granted the status of knowledge claims/acts,

---

Authority in Early Modern England: The Presuppositions of Oaths and Offices, Cambridge: Cambridge University Press, 2006, 3–4.

[31] On the emergence of educational systems see Andy Green, *Education and State Formation: The Rise of Educational Systems in England, France and the USA*, New York: Macmillan, 1990; and D. K. Muller, Fritz Ringer, and Brian Simon (eds.), *The Rise of the Modern Educational System*, Cambridge: Cambridge University Press, 1987. By contrast, in colonial India knowledges corresponded to class and occupational and other hierarchies and were disseminated accordingly—esoteric and restricted knowledges accessible only to some social groups such as Brahmins, more "practical" knowledges suitable for the children of trading and scribal castes, as well as knowledges that were more widely available. This riotous variety of knowledge practices was never conceived or organized as an educational "system" (see Seth, *Subject Lessons*, 34–39).

[32] Michel Foucault, *Society Must Be Defended: Lectures at the College de France, 1975–1976*, translated by David Macey, New York: Picador, 2003, 181.

and which ones could not. "We move," as Foucault puts it, "from the censorship of statements to the disciplinarization of enunciations."[33]

The knowledge that I engage with in this book is thus formal knowledge, the knowledge produced, authorized, and disseminated in institutions that exist for these purposes. In that regard, this book has a decidedly intellectualist bent: it is concerned with the knowledge produced, disseminated, and utilized in schools, universities, and state bureaucracies, rather than popular or quotidian knowledges. The formal knowledge that is my subject matter sometimes diverges from quotidian knowledges, but in much of the Western world there is also considerable overlap between the two, and even where they diverge, officially authorized and disciplined knowledge usually serves as the horizon of quotidian knowledges, and thus has a certain regulatory function in relation to them. That is less true in many parts of the non-Western world, where modern knowledge achieved its dominance in more recent times and has not effaced popular knowledges, and where quotidian knowledges continue to be strongly inflected by indigenous knowledge traditions. I seek to be attentive to this fact and, more generally, to the public role and function of the intellectual disciplines into which this knowledge is internally divided.

A project that seeks to anatomize and criticize the presuppositions of modern Western knowledge immediately raises a question regarding the vantage point from which such a project of anatomization and critique itself issues. This book is a critical study of modern knowledge from within that knowledge, not an external critique from the standpoint of, say, a Hindu *pandit* or an Australian indigenous elder, drawing upon their own knowledge traditions to engage with and refute a recent and arrogant competitor. Seeking to anatomize modern Western knowledge from within that knowledge gives rise to a number of paradoxes. For instance, in seeking to show the historical particularity—rather than the transhistorical universality—of modern knowledge, I draw upon conceptions of periodization and historicity that derive from the modern discipline of history, at the same time and even in the same breath that I subject this discipline to criticism. Such contradictions seem to me unavoidable—at any rate, I do not succeed in avoiding them. In a different but related context, Nietzsche pointed out the difficulties attendant on an enterprise such as this one: "A critique of the faculty of knowledge is senseless: how should a tool be able to criticize itself

[33] Foucault, *Society Must Be Defended*, 184.

when it can only use itself for the critique?"[34] But even if such an undertaking embroils one in paradoxes and contradictions, I wager that it is possible to work within a knowledge tradition and yet denaturalize it and by doing so, in Paul Rabinow's words, "to anthropologize the West: show how exotic its constitution of reality has been; emphasize those domains most taken for granted as universal; make them seem as historically peculiar as possible; show how their claims to truth are linked to social practices and have hence become effective forces in the social world."[35] That is what this book seeks to do.

The Structure of This Book

Chapter 1 outlines the core presuppositions that underlie and define the social sciences: that knowledge is a relation between a subject who represents and explains an object or a process; that nature and the social/cultural are two different domains, authorizing the distinction between the natural and the social sciences; and that knowledge must be secular, and thus that gods, spirits, and ghosts have no role in explanation. It then shows that these presumptions have been challenged and are coming undone. It does so not by focusing on sweeping challenges to our knowledge—such as Lyotard's claim in *The Postmodern Condition* that the grand narratives legitimating modern knowledge no longer command assent[36]—but rather on "local" or disciplinary debates and challenges, arising in the course of working within this knowledge and "applying" its presumptions. I seek to demonstrate that the questioning of our knowledge is not just something being undertaken by "postmodernists," "relativists," or other participants (real or imagined) in the culture wars, but by sober historians, anthropologists, sociologists, and scholars of science, often in the course of debates specific to their disciplines.

As the chorus of criticism increases in volume, the most sophisticated defenses of modern knowledge acknowledge the "impurity" of reason, yet seek to provide reasons why the presuppositions undergirding the social sciences nevertheless have a claim to transhistorical and transcultural validity. In chapter 2 I examine the most persuasive of such claims, which are

[34] Friedrich Nietzsche, *The Will to Power*, translated by Walter Kaufman and R. J. Hollingdale, New York: Vintage Books, 1968, 269.

[35] Paul Rabinow, *Essays on the Anthropology of Reason*, Princeton, NJ: Princeton University Press, 1996, 36.

[36] Jean-François Lyotard, *The Postmodern Condition: A Report on Knowledge*, translated by Geoff Bennington and Brian Massumi, Minneapolis: University of Minnesota Press, 1984.

anchored in transcendental arguments and indebted to Kant, and sometimes also embedded in a historical teleology. In the latter case, acknowledging the historical and cultural situatedness of our knowledge, such arguments nevertheless seek to show that occidental modernity is itself a privileged historical moment, one where previously inaccessible truths finally become available. Engaging with the defenses of Reason mounted by Habermas, Apel, and Rawls, chapter 2 concludes that these are not persuasive, as they presuppose the very ideas that they seek to validate or "ground." It further concludes that the social sciences are historically and culturally specific ways of knowing and being in the world, and that there are good reasons to doubt that they transcend these particularities.

The first part of this book draws upon and engages with debates in a variety of social science disciplines to show that the core presuppositions of the social sciences are not etic, that is, do not have warrant to be regarded as "true" and "universal." It is a defining feature of modern knowledge that it is divided into disciplines, each with its own object(s) of inquiry and corresponding protocols. The presuppositions underlying the social sciences in general are here supplemented by presumptions thought to be specific to the object(s) of the discipline in question. In the second part of this book I closely examine the presuppositions underlying the disciplines of history and politics. I show that these presumptions are not truths that must be presupposed in order to produce knowledge about the object concerned, but are rather ways of conceiving their object such that specific forms of representing and relating to it become possible. This allows us to ask what modes of understanding, encountering, and inhabiting the world these disciplines facilitate and what they disallow.

Chapters 3 and 4 are about history, the discipline that is assigned the task of attending to the past. In chapter 3 I suggest that the discipline of history does not simply "find" the past in the objects and texts it has left behind, but constitutes pastness in a particular way. History writing is a "code," and I explicate the elements of the code. Modern history treats past objects and texts as the congealed and objectified remains of humans who, like us, endowed their world with meaning and purpose, all the while constrained by the social circumstances that characterized their times; this time of theirs is dead, and it can only be represented, not resurrected; the past is only ever the human past, and it does not include ghosts, gods, spirits, or nature. In specifying the features that underpin the code of history, I engage with those forms of history writing—the history of art, music, and science—that do not always share all the elements of the code, but for that very reason, as I argue, illuminate all the more clearly what the discipline presupposes.

Chapter 3 demonstrates that the code of history came into being in the modern period in the West. But history as a discipline is thought to yield knowledge of *all* human pasts, including those that are premodern and non-Western. In chapter 4 I examine the paradox this gives rise to. It is a defining feature of "the historical sense" and of modern history writing that it avoids the sin of anachronism; and yet the application of the code of history to times and places where the presumptions that define it were/are not shared, and indeed before humanity emerged as an intelligible object, is itself anachronistic. What, then, does it mean to write histories of premodern and non-Western pasts? Are we producing genuine historical knowledge of these pasts, or are we translating them into our code? Furthermore, given that the discipline of history has a public life as well as a life in the university, what are the implications of my arguments? Where other relations to pastness still have some social salience—as in many parts of the non-Western world—the political and moral stakes of how we conceive knowledge of the past are sometimes very high. I conclude by examining one such example from India, and ask whether history writing can serve to ground our ethical and political choices.

Chapters 5 and 6 are concerned with the discipline of politics, or rather—because unlike history, politics or political science displays little disciplinary unity—with two of its subdisciplines, international relations and political theory. Despite the fanciful genealogies that international relations provides for itself, it is the youngest of the disciplines examined here. Although it has rightly been called an American, or an Anglo-American, discipline, its subject matter—the international and the global—is anything but parochial. And its starting point—an international order characterized by "anarchy," composed of nation-states without any sovereign entity standing over them—seems to take particularity and difference into account. Chapter 5 argues that this starting point, which entails naturalizing the nation-state form, willfully forgets or overlooks the form of political organization that was in fact dominant until very recent times—empire. The teleology built into the discipline's construction of its object (according to which the last few centuries saw the inevitable march of the nation-state to global dominance) has the effect of generalizing what is in fact a historically specific and parochial—if highly consequential—form of thinking and living political community. The result is that the discipline obscures, rather than illuminates, international politics.

History and international relations are disciplines that have an external object or referent (the "past" and "international politics" respectively) that they seek to provide knowledge of. Chapter 6 suggests that by contrast, political theory is knowledge "for" rather than "of," performance rather than representation. It argues that a recognition of this is key to understanding why and how it functions as it does: political theory is oriented toward, indeed is a mimicry in miniature of, the bourgeois, liberal, public sphere. It thus "performs" the liberal conviction that differing moral and political viewpoints are ineliminable, and must contend with each other in rational argument in a public sphere that is not itself marked by a commitment to any moral or political view. The parochialism of these presumptions, I suggest, is a major reason why political theory has not flourished in the non-Western world. Recognizing this, there have been attempts recently to "deprovincialize" political theory by extending its geographical and cultural remit through "comparative political theory." I critically assess the success of these endeavors.

Modern knowledge has not only served as a way of cognizing and representing the modern world, but also, I insist throughout this book, has helped constitute our global modernity, and has also anchored our moral and political convictions. The charges of relativism and irrationalism leveled against those who would parochialize it are in significant measure animated by the fear that the "project of modernity," and with it the grounds upon which our moral and political aspirations rest, is at issue. Conversely, those who see in the dominance of this knowledge little more than epistemic imperialism advocate a diversity or "ecology" of knowledges, arguing that epistemic equality is a necessary component of social justice. Disagreeing with those who see in contemporary challenges to knowledge the slippery slope of epistemological and moral anarchy, but also with those who denounce modern, Western knowledge and call for an "epistemology of the South," the epilogue assesses the ethical and political, as well as the intellectual, implications of the arguments advanced in this book.

PART I

MODERN WESTERN KNOWLEDGE UNDER CHALLENGE

1

Unsettling the Modern
Knowledge Settlement

In the early modern period in Western Europe, an intellectual transformation took place as a consequence of which we moderns are said to have discovered, among other things, that the world was not a cosmic order invested
with meaning and purpose. The "scientific revolution" played an important
role in this transformation, not because it facilitated the victory of Reason
over superstition—the relations between what we have come to call "religion"
and seventeenth-century natural philosophy are far too complicated for any
such simple opposition—but rather because it challenged and undermined
the hitherto dominant understanding, one that "offered an integrated understanding of the human and the natural, with a teleological idiom deemed
proper for interpreting both."[1] A defining characteristic of the new natural
philosophy was its rejection of explanations that "ascribed to nature and its
components the capacities of purpose, intention, or sentience."[2] Thomas
Hobbes declared that "scarce any thing can be more absurdly said in naturall
Philosophy, than that which is now called *Aristotles Metaphysiques.*"[3] The
explanations of the schoolmen were tautological, and moreover, assumed
that natural bodies were capable, like men, of intention: "The Schools will
tell you out of Aristotle, that the bodies that sink downwards, are *Heavy*; and
that this Heavinesse is it that causes them to descend: But if you ask what
they mean by *Heavinesse*, they will define it to bee an endeavour to goe to
the centre of the Earth: so that the cause of why things sink downward, is
an endeavour to be below: which is as much as to say, that bodies descend,
or ascend, because they doe . . . As if Stones, and Metalls had a desire, or
could discern the place that they could bee at, as Man does."[4] Boyle similarly
ridiculed the long-standing explanation that liquid rises up a straw when it

---

[1] Steven Shapin, *The Scientific Revolution*, Chicago: University of Chicago Press, 1996, 163.
[2] Shapin, *The Scientific Revolution*, 37.
[3] Hobbes, *Leviathan*, edited by C. B. Macpherson, New York: Penguin, 1985, 687.
[4] Hobbes, *Leviathan*, 694–95.

Beyond Reason. Sanjay Seth, Oxford University Press (2021). © Oxford University Press.
DOI: 10.1093/oso/9780197500583.003.0002

is sucked because "nature abhors a vacuum"; this explanation absurdly sup-posed "that a brute and inanimate creature, as water, . . . is withal so generous, as by ascending, to act contrary to its particular inclination for the general good of the universe, like a noble patriot, that sacrifices his private interests to the public ones of his country."[5] By the seventeenth century, Aristotelian explanations invoking teleology were not so much refuted as ridiculed— deemed to be unintelligible rather than simply mistaken.[6]

In denying the validity of teleological explanations of natural pro-cesses, the natural philosophers were, implicitly and sometimes explicitly, suggesting that the human world and the natural world were not cut from the same cloth. This was to undermine or directly challenge the organising presuppositions of almost all previous knowledges, which had sought "Understanding [of] the world in categories of meaning, as existing to em-body or express an order of Ideas or archetypes, as manifesting the rhythm of divine life, or the foundational acts of the gods, or the Will of God; seeing the world as a text, or the universe as a book."[7] Such ways of construing the world as a single order in which the natural and the human were connected, such that they resonated with each other and manifested a single underlying logic or a divine intention, now came to be regarded as a sign of immaturity: of confusing—as the schoolmen were alleged to have done—a human domain of purposes and meanings with a natural world of impersonal processes. In short, from the seventeenth century, natural philosophy began to constitute "nature" as a distinct object, separated from humans and their society.

Knowledge of nature was not, however, thereby disconnected from human purposes. As Francis Bacon was to observe, and as was to be endlessly re-peated thereafter, knowledge of nature could give humans the power to con-trol it, to their benefit. But knowledge of nature no longer offered any guide on how to live, or to organize society. How could it do so, once it was con-ceived of as devoid of meaning and as completely separate from the human and social worlds? By the mid-nineteenth century John Stuart Mill could assert, "Conformity to nature, has no connection whatever with right and wrong"; "we ought not to consider at all what nature does, but what it is good to do."[8] Half a century later, in "Politics as a Vocation," Max Weber told an

---

[5] Quoted in Shapin, The Scientific Revolution, 151.

[6] On this seen Peter Dear, The Intelligibility of Nature: How Science Makes Sense of the World, Chicago: University of Chicago Press, 2006.

[7] Charles Taylor, Hegel, New York: Cambridge University Press, 1975, 5.

[8] John Stuart Mill, "Nature," in Three Essays on Religion: Nature, The Utility of Religion and Theism, London: Longmans, Green, Reader, and Dyer, 1874, 62 and 31.

audience that only "big children" could "still believe that the findings of astronomy, biology, physics, or chemistry could teach us anything about the
meaning of the world."[9] In other words, it was impossible to deduce values
from the nature of the world, because the only values "out there" in the world
were those that we humans had created.[10] Metaphorically and sometimes
by analogy, the traffic between the natural and the human worlds continued
and indeed continues even today, in concepts like "natural laws" and "natural
justice." However this traffic is purely metaphorical, because long-standing
denunciations of deducing "ought" from "is" have made it impermissible to
draw any moral or political conclusions from the facts of nature.

If meaning or purpose was no longer to be found in nature, then where
did they reside, and who or what engendered them? An important part of
the intellectual transformation that produced modern knowledge was
that meaning and agency, having been wholly evacuated from the natural
world, were firmly relocated in the human subject, now seen not as part
of the world-as-text, but as the author of that text. Vico, Feuerbach, Marx,
Dilthey, Cassirer, and numerous other moderns asserted that art, music,
rituals, and so on were all "expressions" or "objectifications" of human subjectivity, whether of an individual or a collective subject. At the same time,
and often in the same breath, moderns discovered "society." A long-standing
tradition of making distinctions and typologies on the basis of political
arrangements—monarchy, aristocracy, and democracy—was discarded,
by Scottish Enlightenment thinkers, for instance, who explained such political forms as the outcome, frequently unintended, of a host of individual
choices and actions, rather than as origins to be traced back to a founder
or founding event. Adam Ferguson famously argued that "nations stumble
upon establishments that are indeed the result of human action, but not the
execution of any human design."[11] According to Ferguson, customs and laws
were not consequences of the will and founding acts of a lawgiver, but were
rather part of the "social"—a domain that included human will, action, and
desire, but was not reducible to any single element of these, because a host
of such interacting wills, actions, and desires produced effects beyond the
intentions of their authors. Adam Smith discovered this in the operations of

---

[9] Max Weber, "Politics as a Vocation," in *The Methodology of the Social Sciences: Max Weber*, edited
by Edward Shils and Henry Finch, New York: Free Press, 1949.

[10] Weber, "Objectivity in Social Science and Social Policy," in *Methodology*.

[11] Quoted in Christopher J. Berry, *Social Theory of the Scottish Enlightenment*,
Edinburgh: Edinburgh University Press, 1997, 40.

the market and the "hidden hand," and Kant in men's "unsocial sociability." A century later, Émile Durkheim was to insist that society was a discrete, thinglike object, and that the laws and customs characterizing a society "are not created deliberately but are engendered by causes that produce their effects quite unbeknownst to men."[12]

The separation of man and society from nature was not simply a new proposition or a new way of organizing knowledge; it was accompanied by a transformed conception of knowledge, that is, of what it means to know, and what counts as cognition. Knowledge became, from Descartes onward, a relation between a subject and an object, achieved when external things are accurately "represented" in the mind or consciousness. This conception of knowledge has been with us for so long that it is hard to think of what else knowledge could be. But earlier knowledges were not modeled on an idea of an external reality accurately represented in the mind or to consciousness: in the Aristotelian conception of knowledge—one that exercised enormous influence throughout the Middle Ages—"when we come to know something, the mind (*nous*) becomes one with the object of thought," in the sense that "they are informed by the same *eidos*."[13] To conceive of knowledge as a subject-object relation, with representation of an independent reality as its essence, is not something obvious or given. To do so signaled a fundamental change in the very conception of what knowledge is, one that begins in early modern Europe and was to result, as Richard Rorty describes it, in a conception of philosophy as the "mirror of nature." With this change epistemology assumed center ground in philosophy, in an unprecedented way.[14] Subject and object having been separated, the troubling question now became how to effect a hookup between them: and skepticism of the modern kind (very different from Pyrrhonism) becomes a recurring problem for and an integral part of modern philosophy.[15]

---

[12] Émile Durkheim, *Montesquieu and Rousseau: Forerunners of Sociology*, Ann Arbor: University of Michigan Press, 1970, 43.

[13] Charles Taylor, "Overcoming Epistemology," in Kenneth Baynes, James Bohman, and Thomas McCarthy (eds.), *After Philosophy: End or Transformation?*, Cambridge, MA: MIT Press, 1987, 466, 466–67. On the hylomorphic conception of knowledge see also Richard Rorty, *Philosophy and the Mirror of Nature*, Princeton, NJ: Princeton University Press, 1979, 45–46.

[14] As Rorty points out, Aristotle neither possessed, nor had any need for, a "theory of knowledge" (*Mirror of Nature*, 263).

[15] In Rorty's words, "'The seventeenth century gave skepticism a new lease on life. . . . Any theory which views knowledge as accuracy of representation, and which holds that certainty can only be rationally had about representations, will make scepticism inevitable." As a consequence, "Skepticism and the principal genre of modern philosophy have a symbiotic relationship. They live one another's death, and die one another's life" (*Mirror of Nature*, 113, 114). On the difference between Pyrrhonism and modern skepticism see Stephen Gaukroger, *The Collapse of Mechanism and the Rise of Sensibility*,

The intellectual transformation that produced modern Western knowledge was corrosive of certain long-standing forms and expressions of faith, but it was not "secular." Mechanical explanations of the natural world allowed for a divine creator, as captured in the widely used metaphor of physics as a clock, with a divine clockmaker. Many of the natural philosophers were deists, and many of the important thinkers of the Enlightenment were devout. Nonetheless, the new knowledge differed from the old in that God, the Devil, spirits, ghosts, dead ancestors, and the like could not be accorded a role in explaining natural or social phenomena. The knowledge producer could be religious, but the knowledge he or she produced did not count as such if God or gods were invoked in explanation.

By the nineteenth century, the intellectual transformation I have been painting in broad brushstrokes was largely victorious. A "knowledge settlement"—or if you prefer, a "knowledge culture," "tradition of reasoning," or even "social imaginary"—was in place that was very different from that which had preceded it. The knowledge formalized, disseminated, and produced in universities and schools was now one that presupposed that "nature" was an object radically distinct from society and the human. The former was the domain of impersonal processes and laws and required corresponding protocols, provided by the natural sciences, to produce knowledge of it. The latter was the preserve of the human sciences, which themselves often came to be internally divided between the humanities (attending to those objects and practices that were the productions of man and which could be decoded as expressions or objectifications of an individual, civilization, or culture) and the social sciences (assigned responsibility for those forces and processes that included but exceeded the will and purposes of men). All knowledge—whether of the natural or of the human—was a relation between a subject and an object and was achieved when the object was accurately or truly represented, in natural languages or in formalized ones. And while the knowledge producer could believe in the presence and agency of gods and spirits, such "belief" had a very limited place in knowledge production: knowledge was (for the most part) secular, even where the knower was not.

This knowledge settlement was of course marked by many ambiguities and internal tensions. Since humans were seen to be part of both nature and the world they had created, there have always been some who have argued that the human/social and nature distinction was of little consequence, for the doings and the productions of man were also, as with nature, explicable in naturalistic terms. Even among the majority who accept the division between the natural and the social or human sciences, there have always been those who have argued that the social world is also governed by lawlike regularities, and thus that producing knowledge of it is best done by adopting and adapting the methods and protocols of the natural sciences. Against this, there is a long tradition—often traced back to Vico, Herder, and Hamann—that readily concedes the distinct and special nature of the natural sciences, but only in order to demarcate the specificity of the *Geisteswissenschaften*.[16] Those insisting that the human sciences cannot adopt the procedures of the natural sciences point to the fact that in the study of man, the inquiring subject and the object coincide, and thus that the methods for producing knowledge must necessarily be different from those adopted for the study of nature; the human sciences, it has variously been proposed, are idiographic rather than nomothetic, search for meanings rather than (or as well as) causes, and seek to produce understanding rather than explanation. This has been the charter of many of the human sciences and especially of the humanities, where it has been further argued that the knowledge produced is self-knowledge rather than knowledge of an external object. Furthermore, in the human sciences, there continue to be debates as to how to find the balance between two presumptions that, while shared, are in tension with each other—that man is the source of all intentions and meanings, on the one hand, and that society determines or at least constrains man's freedom, delimiting what can be intended and meant, on the other. Many of the important and often recurring debates within modern knowledge have been related to these unresolved tensions, generating numerous debates: Should the human sciences aspire to the apodictic certainty that the natural sciences are thought to achieve? Are there "laws" of human development, or lawlike regularities in the world of men, as there are in nature? Is society best thought of as an organism or a mechanism? Does society (or the economy) "determine," or simply delimit, human actions?

New York: Oxford University Press, 2010, 441, and in greater detail, his "The Ten Modes of Aenesidemus and the Myth of Ancient Scepticism," *British Journal for the History of Philosophy* 3 (1995), 371–87.

[16] As Isabelle Stengers tartly notes, "There is nothing neutral about this gesture: to render unto Caesar what is Caesar's is also to claim for oneself everything that does not belong to him." *The Invention of Modern Science*, translated by David W. Smith, Minneapolis: University of Minnesota Press, 2000, 35.

These and other ambiguities, unresolved tensions, and outright contradictions indicate that to speak of a knowledge settlement is not to suggest that everything has been settled. It is rather to argue that even as the different positions staked out in these and other debates are genuinely different, they nonetheless occur upon a ground already laid, for they are enabled by the presuppositions previously sketched, in the absence of which such debates would be inconceivable. As Margaret Somers, who has proposed the concept of a "knowledge culture" puts it, such a culture provides a "spectrum of conceptual and practical possibilities,"[17] delimiting what the problems and issues are and how they should be pursued. The core presuppositions of the modern West's knowledge culture "carry within them frozen historical arguments"[18] that, however, have been forgotten and have hardened into axioms, such that we forget that these are the historically produced presuppositions of a particular way of thinking and not the presuppositions of thinking tout court. Where it is recognized that such presuppositions are not the requirement of thinking tout court, they are nonetheless treated as "truths" discovered by Western moderns, which must therefore form the premise and point of departure of the production of any and all knowledge.

A "Knowledge Settlement" Unsettled

The knowledge settlement whose principal features I have sketched is less settled than it once was; indeed, it is arguably in crisis. In recent years there have been sweeping "global" challenges to "Western metaphysics," the "modern episteme," and "Northern epistemologies"; and also and more significantly for our purposes, numerous "local," disciplinary problematizations and challenges that have arisen within the disciplines that were created by this knowledge and that are part of its architecture. These latter questionings have come from those who are practitioners of their disciplinary trades, not by "postmodern relativists," irrationalists, nativists, or other real or imagined soldiers in the culture wars. Below I show that the idea that there is a "nature," separate from "society," that can be "represented" with some certainty

[17] Margaret Somers, "Where Is Sociology after the Historic Turn? Knowledge Cultures, Narrativity, and Historical Epistemologies," in Terence J. McDonald (ed.), *The Historic Turn in the Human Sciences*, Ann Arbor: University of Michigan Press, 1996, 64. See also her *Genealogies of Citizenship: Markets, Statelessness, and the Right to Have Rights*, New York: Cambridge University Press, 2008, 254–68.
[18] Somers, "Where Is Sociology," 73–74.

through an activity named "science" has come under sustained challenge from within science studies itself. Likewise, the object "society" has been problematized in debates among social historians, as well as sociologists and social theorists. And social and cultural anthropology, which emerged at the confluence of nature and society, have become the sites of much critical reflection about their premises, in the course of which leading practitioners have argued that neither society nor nature are objects whose existence can simply be assumed.

"Nature" and Science Studies

The natural sciences have long been thought, by scholars and the wider public, to be the most secure and unchallengeable aspect of our knowledge, offering apodictic certainty and prediction. Studies of the development of science therefore have tended to be the most "whiggish" of all histories, and modern science has come to be held up as the privileged instance and decisive proof of why modern Western knowledge is superior to non-Western knowledges.[19] Indeed, the "philosophy of science" began as a discipline on the presumption that scientific knowledge was a special and privileged form of knowledge, and the philosophical investigation of it was directed at discovering and characterizing what made it so.

It is all the more significant, then, that the nature and status of science has been at the center of debates that call some of the core presumptions of modern Western knowledge into question. The prelude to these developments was Thomas Kuhn's immensely influential *The Structure of Scientific Revolutions*, which marked the beginnings of a profound transformation in how the history of science was studied and depicted.[20] Deploying an unfamiliar vocabulary (paradigm, normal science, puzzle-solving, anomaly, crisis, incommensurability, gestalt switch) to develop a novel argument, Kuhn argued that what distinguished science from other fields of intellectual endeavor was that some fields inquiring into nature developed a "paradigm"—a shared outlook on what entities the world was composed

[19] See Michael Adas, *Machines as the Measure of Men: Science, Technology, and Ideologies of Western Dominance*, new ed., Ithaca, NY: Cornell University Press, 2015.

[20] For an excellent discussion of earlier challenges to an ahistorical view of scientific knowledge, see Hans-Jorg Rheinberger, *On Historicizing Epistemology: An Essay*, translated by David Fernbach, Stanford, CA: Stanford University Press, 2010.

of, how they interacted with each other, what questions could and should be asked of nature, and what the appropriate protocols of inquiry, evidence, and the like were. Before such a paradigm developed, inquiry into nature was a more random process, and each practitioner could choose his or her own starting point, as was still the case in most of the human sciences. Once a paradigm did develop, however, "normal science" became possible—working within a shared outlook and with accepted notions of what questions were to be asked and what counted as an answer. This narrow but focused form of paradigm-guided inquiry applied itself to "puzzle-solving," and the ability to solve puzzles validated the paradigm. Inevitably, some problems would not yield answers, and answers to other questions created "anomalies," results that did not "fit" the paradigm. This did not derail paradigm-based research because as long as the paradigm continued to explain a good deal, it was assumed that the anomalies in question would eventually also be accounted for, by amending the paradigm if necessary.

However, an accumulation of anomalies—Kuhn's chief examples are the crisis in Ptolemaic astronomy, phlogiston theory, and the Newtonian conception of pure space—led to crisis, to a breakdown of normal, puzzle-solving activity. At this point, alternative paradigms arose or began to be taken seriously. However—and this is the crucial point—because all inquiry is theory dependent, and because what counts as evidence and proof is internal to each of the competing paradigms, paradigms are incommensurable (they are not comparing like with like), and "The competition between paradigms is not the sort of battle that can be resolved by proofs."[21] Kuhn described the paradigm changes or "revolutions" that were at the heart of his book as being like a "gestalt switch," or even more explosively—given that the advance of scientific knowledge has so often been staged as the victory of true knowledge over religion and superstition—as akin to a "conversion experience." The advance of scientific knowledge no longer appeared, in this account, as an incremental and progressive process whereby science got ever closer to understanding and representing a nature external to it. It was presented instead as a discontinuous process, in which one paradigm replaced another not because the new paradigm described the same objects and processes

[21] Thomas S. Kuhn, *The Structure of Scientific Revolutions*, 2nd ed., Chicago: University of Chicago Press, 1970, 148.

more accurately, but rather because the very objects to be explained themselves appeared differently.[22]

The Structure of Scientific Revolutions not only undermined a picture of natural science as a knowledge that incrementally moves closer to an accurate representation of its object; the manner in which it did so posed a challenge to the very idea of "true representation." Kuhn did not, despite the accusations of some of his outraged critics, declare that science was "irrational," but he did—reluctantly and as if borne by the force of his argument, and thus all the more tellingly—call into question the notion that science discovered truths about nature.[23] As Kuhn recognized, the view of science held by philosophers of science and laymen was precisely one in which "successive theories grow ever closer to, or approximate more and more closely to, the truth."[24] But while Kuhn declared that he had no doubt that Newton's views improved on Aristotle's, and Einstein's on Newton's, as means of "puzzle-solving," he doubted that there was any way of showing this improvement to be one where the improved theory was a better match with "what is 'really there.'"[25] The transformations in science that form the core of his book did not, Kuhn declared, bring science closer to the "truth" about nature, even adding that "if this position be relativism, I cannot see that the relativist loses anything needed to account for the nature and development of the sciences."[26]

About a decade later, the "strong program" in the sociology of scientific knowledge (SSK) further challenged the idea of science as a precise rendering of nature. But whereas Kuhn's argument had been largely an "internalist" account of the transformations in scientific knowledge, the SSK scholars were assertively "externalist," seeking to explain the production of scientific knowledge by searching for its social determinants. According to the dominant view scientific discoveries, as accurate representations of nature, did not require sociological explanation indeed, could not be sociologically

---

[22] As Kuhn describes a paradigm shift or a scientific revolution, "It is as if the professional community had been suddenly transported to another planet where familiar objects are seen in a different light and are joined by unfamiliar ones as well" (*Structure of Scientific Revolutions*, 111; see also 150).

[23] "We may . . . have to relinquish the notion . . . that changes of paradigm carry scientists and those who learn from them closer and closer to the truth" (*Structure of Scientific Revolutions*, 170).

[24] Kuhn, *Structure of Scientific Revolutions*, 206.

[25] Kuhn, *Structure of Scientific Revolutions*, 206.

[26] Kuhn, *Structure of Scientific Revolutions*, 207. Kuhn elaborates on the senses in which he is and is not a relativist in "Reflections on My Critics," in Imre Lakatos and Alan Musgrave (eds.), *Criticism and the Growth of Knowledge*, New York: Cambridge University Press, 1970, 264–65.

explained.[27] But once the image of scientific knowledge as a representation of the realities of nature had been decisively undermined by Kuhn, "once [scientific] beliefs are conceded not to derive completely from the constraints of reality," then, as Barry Barnes put it, "No further a priori argument can be made against their sociological investigation."[28] Such inquiry had to be "symmetrical" and hence "methodologically relativist"[29]; that is, it had to look for the sociological origins of both those scientific discoveries accepted as "true" and those deemed to be "false." But if *all* beliefs were explicable in terms of their social and cultural contexts, then it would appear that what counted as "truth" was inescapably context dependent. The major figures of SSK did not resile from this implication: Barnes concluded that skepticism and relativism were inescapable, for "no arguments will ever be available which would establish a particular epistemology or ontology as ultimately correct . . . belief systems cannot be objectively ranked in terms of their proximity to reality or their rationality."[30] David Bloor similarly concluded that there was no such thing as a context-independent Truth with a capital *T*, only conjectural, relative truths.[31]

Already by the 1970s, an earlier conception of science as the most developed and assured of our knowledges, one capable of representing the workings of nature (and serving either as a model for, or a point of contrast with, the human sciences) was coming undone. Kuhn and the SSK sociologists had problematized the *certainty* that could be accorded scientific knowledge, Kuhn by showing that its production always rested upon presumptions that were not derived from the study of nature but preceded its study, and the SSK theorists by showing that it was inescapably shaped by its social context. However, they did not doubt that there *was* an external object-world of nature, and that knowledge consisted of human subjects representing it. The SSK thinkers have rightly been described as "epistemologically relativist and ontologically realist," in that they did not doubt

---

[27] This was because, as David Bloor explained, "the rational aspects of science are held to be self-moving and self-explanatory. Empirical or sociological explanations are confined to the irrational." David Bloor, *Knowledge and Social Imagery*, 1976, 2nd ed., Chicago: University of Chicago Press, 1991, 10.

[28] Barry Barnes, *Scientific Knowledge and Sociological Theory*, London: Routledge and Kegan Paul, 1974, 12.

[29] Bloor, *Knowledge and Social Imagery*, 158.

[30] Barnes, *Scientific Knowledge*, 154.

[31] In his own words, "There need be no such thing as Truth, other than conjectural, relative truth, any more than there need be absolute moral standards rather than locally accepted ones. If we can live with moral relativism we can live with cognitive relativism" (Bloor, *Knowledge and Social Imagery*, 159).

that there was a single external nature, but questioned whether there were any grounds on which we could regard any representation of it as definitely true. Moreover, they treated the social determinants of knowledge as if *these* somehow escaped their relativist and perspectival strictures. Subsequent developments, in part enabled by these earlier ones, were to be even more radical in their arguments and implications.

As the image of natural science serenely and accurately representing nature was called into serious question, some scholars of science began to examine what it is that scientists *do*. A number of studies took an ethnographic approach to scientific knowledge, examining the process of the production of scientific knowledge, such as in the laboratory. The first and one of the most important of these was Bruno Latour and Steve Woolgar's *Laboratory Life: The Social Construction of Scientific Facts*, a work arising out of Latour's time spent as an ethnographer in one of the laboratories at the Salk Institute. Two years of closely watching and interacting with scientists led Latour and his coauthor to conclude that the conventional image of scientific knowledge—that of a nature that exists "out there," and which is then represented as a result of studies in the laboratory—was mistaken. Latour and Woolgar found that what was initially debated and disputed in the laboratory were statements and representations. However, once a degree of consensus emerged around a statement, more and more reality was attributed to the object of the statement, and "an inversion takes place: the object becomes the reason why the statement was formulated in the first place . . . the statement becomes the mirror image of the reality 'out there.' . . . It is small wonder that the statements appear to match external entities so exactly: they are the same thing."[32] The unsettling import of this argument was that scientific knowledge was not that which, after a period of investigation and dispute, finally discerned what reality really was, for "reality was the *consequence* of the settlement of a dispute rather than its *cause*."[33]

Kuhn and the SSK scholars had been concerned with the claim of scientific knowledge to be free of presuppositions and of social determination; but they had not doubted that the questions they asked and the doubts they raised were epistemological ones, and that ontology—the existence of an external natural world, independent of our statements about it—could be assumed. It is this that was now being called into question, not only by

---

[32] Bruno Latour and Steve Woolgar, *Laboratory Life: The Construction of Scientific Facts*, 1979, 2nd ed., Princeton, NJ: Princeton University Press, 1986, 177.

[33] Latour and Woolgar, *Laboratory Life*, 236.

Latour and Woolgar, but many others in science studies. Ian Hacking wrote that a great deal of philosophy of science "parallels seventeenth-century epistemology" in treating the question of knowledge as one of representation, so that the dominant issue is always one of "how we can ever escape from representations and hook-up with the world."[34] In fact, scientists have never just "represented," but also "intervened," helping to create the very phenomena that they explain; experiments, for instance, "create, produce, refine and stabilize phenomena."[35] Hacking concluded that the idea of science as the representation by a subject of an object wholly external to it was caught up in an intractable and anachronist metaphysics, and moreover one that never corresponded to what science really does.[36] Latour, Woolgar, and Hacking were not denying the *efficacy* of science, but they were calling into question the dominant understanding of science, one in which its efficacy derives from its accurate representation of the "facts of nature."

These and other works seemed to suggest that the objects that science produced knowledge of were not so much socially determined, as the SSK scholars had suggested, but rather that they were socially constructed; "social constructivism" now became a recognizable position or view in science studies. Some scholars embraced it, others denounced it,[37] and others still began to wonder if this swing of the pendulum—from regarding the "facts" of nature as imposing constraints on how it could be represented, to regarding nature as constructed by society—indicated that the terms of the debate needed to be rethought. A host of scholars began the search for new ways of thinking about scientific knowledge, often inventing neologisms along the way. Andrew Pickering proposed replacing a representational image of science with a "*performative* image of science,"[38] one that asked not whether "correspondence" obtained, but more productively sought to understand "how, in practice, connections between knowledge and the world are

---

[34] Ian Hacking, *Representing and Intervening*, New York: Cambridge University Press, 1983, 130.

[35] Hacking, *Representing and Intervening*, 230. Stengers, citing Hacking, suggests that this implication is already present in Kuhn: "The notion of a paradigm corresponds not to a new version of the 'impregnation' of facts by theories, but to the notion of *the invention of facts . . .* experimental facts are 'authorized' by the paradigm" (Stengers, *Invention of Modern Science*, 49).

[36] Hacking, *Representing and Intervening*, 146.

[37] For a judicious survey of the positions and the issues see Ian Hacking, *The Social Construction of What?*, Cambridge, MA: Harvard University Press, 1999, especially chap. 3 ("What about the Natural Sciences?").

[38] Andrew Pickering, *The Mangle of Practice: Time, Agency, and Science*, Chicago: University of Chicago Press, 1995, 7.

made."[39] Also rejecting the conception of scientific knowledge as a relation between knowing subjects and their objects of knowledge, Annemarie Mol argued that the objects of scientific inquiry were neither "entities waiting out there to be represented," nor "constructions shaped by the subject-knowers,"[40] but rather a thing or things *enacted*: not a once-and-for-all "construction," but an ongoing, precarious, and sometimes fragile process, one in which "maintaining the identity of objects requires a continuing effort."[41] *Mangle, enactment, chain, association, cyborg, network, assemblage, alignment, choreography*, and *entanglement* are some of the terms that the discipline of science studies has produced to suggest that the objects of science are neither merely "found" and represented nor simply "made up." What they collectively signify, differences between them notwithstanding, is that the idea of "nature" as something out there, mapped or represented by scientific knowledge but independent of it, is untenable.[42]

As our long-held idea of nature as independent of us and immune to our longings, desires, and projects (as "disenchanted," in short) increasingly came to be seen as a dubious inheritance, so too did the idea of "society" become problematic, for, as we have seen, the two were born together and each derived its identity from the other. It is telling that the second edition of *Laboratory Life* dropped the word "social" from its subtitle; in the postscript to this second edition, the authors explained that " 'social' was primarily a term of antagonism, one part of a binary opposition"; once "nature" was seen to be as much "produced, defined and stabilized" as found and represented, then the very distinction broke down, and "the social" became meaningless and redundant.[43]

Some of the implications of these debates came to be spelled out, with great elan, in a subsequent work by Bruno Latour, where he declared, "Nature and

---

[39] Pickering, *The Mangle of Practice*, 182. Attempts to theorize this turn to "practice" include Theodore Schatzki, Karin Knorr Cetina, and Eike von Savigny (eds.), *The Practice Turn in Contemporary Theory*, New York: Routledge, 2001.

[40] Annemarie Mol, *The Body Multiple: Ontology in Medical Practice*, Durham, NC: Duke University Press, 2002, 32.

[41] Mol, *The Body Multiple*, 43.

[42] See also Donna Haraway, *Simians, Cyborgs, and Women: The Reinvention of Nature*, New York: Routledge, 1991.

[43] Latour and Woolgar, *Laboratory Life*, 281. And in subsequent work Woolgar was to describe the concepts of "social" and "society" as "redundant." *Science: The Very Idea*, London: Ellis Horwood and Tavistock Publications, 1988, 13. For how the nature/culture distinction was made in modern philosophy, see among others Stephen Horigan, *Nature and Culture in Western Discourses*, London: Routledge, 1988, and Kate Soper, *What Is Nature? Culture, Politics and the Non-human*, Oxford: Blackwell, 1995.

Society are part of the problem, not part of the solution."[44] The knowledge settlement of which we are heirs was one that rigorously distinguished between nature and society, between the nonhuman and the human. That these are fundamentally different was treated as the discovery of a truth about the world, one that made our knowledge superior to all others, and which certified that we were "moderns," unlike all the premoderns who had not yet discovered, or accepted, this fundamental fact.[45] It was becoming inescapably evident, however, that this "discovery" was in fact an invention: the invention of nature was a peculiarity of our modern knowledge, one that distinguished it from all other knowledge cultures, but not one that warranted the extravagant claims made for it. As this becomes apparent—the discipline of science studies, according to Latour, occupies pride of place in bringing us to this realization—we are forced to recognize that nature and culture are not absolutely separate but always mixed, and that we are a nature-culture like all others: "If there is one thing we all do, it is surely that we construct both our human collectives and the nonhumans that surround them. In constituting their collectives, some mobilize ancestors, lions, fixed stars, and the coagulated blood of sacrifice; in constructing ours, we mobilize genetics, zoology, cosmology and haemotology."[46]

To conclude, the architecture of modern knowledge is organized around the fundamental difference that is thought to exist between nature, and man and the social. The natural sciences are tasked with producing accurate and predictive knowledge by representing the workings of nature. The social or human sciences have as their object humans, organized into societies. However the premises that underlie this architecture are under challenge, not only in science studies, but, as I shall go on to show, elsewhere as well. The fact that this reassessment has happened in science studies, indeed that this field has led the way, is especially significant, because natural science has long been assumed to be the most assured form of knowledge we

[44] Bruno Latour, *We Have Never Been Modern*, translated by Catherine Porter, New York: Harvester Wheatsheaf, 2003, 95.

[45] In Latour's description of how we moderns represent our "discovery" of the disenchantment of the world, "We are the only ones who differentiate absolutely between Nature and Culture, between Science and Society, whereas in our eyes all the others—whether they are Chinese or Amerindian, Azande or Barouya—cannot really separate what is knowledge from what is Society, what is sign from what is thing, what comes from Nature as it is from what their cultures require" (*Never Been Modern*, 99). See also Latour's *Politics of Nature: How to Bring the Sciences into Democracy*, translated by Catherine Porter, Cambridge, MA: Harvard University Press, 2004.

[46] Latour, *Never Been Modern*, 106.

moderns possess—and the one that most clearly demonstrates the superiority of modern knowledge to all others.

"Society": Social History

The discipline of history, as I will show in greater detail in chapter 3, begins with the presumption that the past it studies is the past of humans, not of gods and spirits or of nature. What aspect of human history is seen to be the most significant, and thus most likely to promote understanding of that past, has varied over the life of the modern discipline. The focus on political history, and the preoccupation with the character and actions of great men, that characterized the modern discipline in the nineteenth century later gave way to other concerns. In the postwar era, and especially from about the 1960s, social history—a form of historical inquiry that accorded central explanatory significance to "the social"—was increasingly prominent.[47] The intentions, desires, purposes, and actions of historical actors were here seen as linked to, and explicable in terms of, social relations or society, the material substrate that rendered meanings and actions intelligible and set limits on the possible. As Eric Hobsbawm, one of its leading practitioners, explained it, "One starts with the material and historical environment, goes on to the forces and techniques of production . . . the structure of the consequent economy—divisions of labour, exchange, accumulation, distribution of the surplus and so forth—and the social relations arising from these. . . . The practice is thus to work outwards and upwards from the process of social production in its specific setting . . . the tendency is to treat economic movements (in the broadest sense) as the backbone of such analysis."[48] Conceived thus, social history was not merely a subfield or specialized domain of history. The editor of the *American Journal of Social History* boldly stated its claims in the following terms: "Social history *is* history. . . . It is not a topic, like intellectual history, or even a set of topics. . . . The established topical fields of history—political, intellectual, even military . . . are all aspects

---

[47] There are a number of accounts of the rise of social history, including William H. Sewell Jr., *Logics of History: Social Theory and Social Transformation*, Chicago: University of Chicago Press, 2005, chap. 2; and Brian Lewis, "Social History: A New *Kind* of History," in Nancy Partner and Sarah Foot (eds.), *The Sage Handbook of Historical Theory*, London: Sage, 2013.

[48] Eric Hobsbawm, "From Social History to the History of Society" (1971), in his *On History*, London: Abacus, 1998, 108.

of social history."[49] The ambition of this claim lay not in the declaration that "everything is connected," but more specifically, in its assumption that everything is connected because in some sense it *derives* from the social and can therefore only be made fully intelligible and explicable by relating it "back" to the social realities (the economy or relations of production, class and, later, gender) that structure it.

By the 1970s social history was ascendant in the Western academy, especially in the United States, Britain, and France. However, in the course of the 1980s, as Geoff Eley was to observe, social history became "one site of a general epistemological uncertainty that characterizes large areas of academic-intellectual life in the humanities and social sciences."[50] Indeed, it began to unravel, and, unusually, it did so less because of criticism from "without" than because many leading social historians began to declare that the presumptions informing their work did not stand up to scrutiny. An early and influential expression of doubt came from Gareth Stedman Jones in a collection of his essays, dating from 1975 to 1982, on English working-class history. His aim in the earliest of the essays in this collection, Stedman Jones explained in his introduction, was to show how political history could be explained in social terms. However, as his work progressed, he became increasingly skeptical about the determining role of the social, and "increasingly critical of the prevalent treatment of the 'social' as something outside of, and logically—and often, though not necessarily, chronologically—prior to its articulation through language."[51] Thus in the later essays, Stedman Jones explained, "class" was treated as a discursive rather than an ontological reality, and these later essays sought to explain class from the nature of politics, rather than explain politics in terms of class.[52]

---

[49] Peter Stearns, "Coming of Age" (1976), quoted in Lewis, "Social History," 101. Or in the words of the editorial that introduced the first issue of the British-based journal *Social History*, "Social history is not simply another specialism . . . not a new *branch* of historical scholarship, but . . . a new kind of history" (quoted in Lewis, "Social History," 100).

[50] Geoff Eley, "Is All the World a Text? From Social History to the History of Society Two Decades Later," in Terence J. McDonald (ed.), *The Historic Turn in the Human Sciences*, Ann Arbor: University of Michigan Press, 1996, 194.

[51] Gareth Stedman Jones, *Languages of Class: Studies in English Working Class History, 1832–1982*, New York: Cambridge University Press, 1983, 7.

[52] Stedman-Jones, *Languages of Class*, 8. See also, among the many such works that began to question the premises of social history, William H. Sewell Jr., *Work and Revolution in France: The Language of Labor from the Old Regime to 1848*, New York: Cambridge University Press, 1980; Patrick Joyce, *Visions of the People: Industrial England and the Question of Class, 1848–1914*, New York: Cambridge University Press, 1991, and his subsequent *Democratic Subjects: The Self and the Social in Nineteenth Century England*, New York: Cambridge University Press, 1994.

Few followed Stedman Jones in concluding that class and the social could be explained by politics rather than, as previously assumed, the other way around,[53] but the suggestion that his intellectual trajectory might serve as "a case study of how the growing explanatory ambition of social history led to an increasing awareness of its limits as a self-sufficient form of historical interpretation"[54] proved to be prescient. For in the course of the 1980s and 1990s, increasing numbers of historians similarly found that society and the social did not have ontological solidity, and that social "causes" did not "determine," "shape," or even delimit other phenomena, because class (for instance) had to be perceived as such—mediated through language and/or culture—before it could have any salience or efficacy at all. Many social historians now announced that they had abandoned or modified social history by taking a cultural or linguistic "turn."[55] However, "culture" proved no more solid than "the social," and in any case was being deconstructed by anthropologists (from whom many of the historians taking the cultural turn were borrowing) around the very same time.[56] Thus the turn to culture had no sooner been announced than it was being problematized or surpassed, as indicated, for instance, by the fact that only one decade separated an influential edited collection propagating *The New Cultural History* (1989) from another (the eminent historian Lynn Hunt was editor of the first and coeditor of the second) seeking to go *Beyond the Cultural Turn* (1999).[57] A number of historians, including those who had begun as social historians, began to wonder whether the debate was caught in "a kind of vicious circle or perennial pendulum-like movement from which escape is impossible"[58] and to ask whether the terms of the debate themselves were the problem.

[53] Cogent criticisms of Jones's argument were offered in Joan W. Scott, "On Language, Gender, and Working-Class History," in Scott, *Gender and the Politics of History*, rev. ed., New York: Columbia University Press, 1999, 56–67.

[54] Stedman Jones, *Languages of Class*, 8.

[55] As in the influential collection of essays, Lynn Hunt (ed.), *The New Cultural History*, Berkeley: University of California Press, 1989. In the 2000s, some even wrote accounts of and reflections upon their transition, including Sewell, *Logics of History*; Geoff Eley and Keith Nield, *The Future of Class in History: What's Left of the Social?*, Ann Arbor: University of Michigan Press, 2007; and Geoff Eley, *A Crooked Line: From Cultural History to the History of Society*, Ann Arbor: University of Michigan Press, 2005.

[56] See, for instance, James Clifford, *The Predicament of Culture*, Cambridge, MA: Harvard University Press, 1988; and James Clifford and George Marcus (eds.), *Writing Culture: The Poetics and Politics of Ethnography*, Berkeley: University of California Press, 1986.

[57] Hunt, *The New Cultural History*; Victoria Bonnell and Lynn Hunt (eds.), *Beyond the Cultural Turn: New Directions in the Study of Society and Culture*, Berkeley: University of California Press, 1999.

[58] Miguel A. Cabrera, *Postsocial History: An Introduction*, translated by Marie McMahon, Lanham, MD: Lexington Books, 2004, 17.

Attempts to shift or dislodge the terms of the debate took two distinct, though often interrelated, forms. One was to recognize that the primacy accorded to the social in social history was part of a materialist paradigm according to which certain phenomena—especially economic ones—were regarded as "material" and thus as having greater causal power than the cultural, political, and ideological. This, former social historians such as William Sewell now came to argue, was an unsustainable position, for a great deal of what enabled economic activity and happened under what was termed "economic" life was "immaterial." Historians, Sewell concluded, needed to "deny as nonsensical . . . the opposition between ideal and material on which materialist common sense has been built."[59] This of course undermined the very enterprise of social history, which was premised precisely upon "materialist common sense."

The second and from our point of view more significant attempt to dislodge the terms of the debate took the form of historicizing "the social" itself, rather than treating it as natural and given. This entailed moving away "from the assumption of an objective "society" to the study of how the category of the 'social' was formed," thus treating the social and society not as a "global analytic category" but rather inquiring into "the historically located 'methods, techniques and practices' that allowed such a category to be constructed in the first place."[60] Keith Michael Baker suggested that society and the social were not something that had been there all along, the importance of which we moderns finally "discovered," but something that the Enlightenment "invented." As with others who sought to historicize the social, Baker was not claiming that human interdependence was an eighteenth-century invention, but rather drawing attention to that fact "that there are many possible ways in which this interdependence might be construed," and suggesting that "*society* is the conceptual construction of that interdependence we still owe to the Enlightenment."[61] A number of historians, including Baker, even suggested that from about this time "society" had come to replace God as the ultimate anchor and cause of all phenomena: in Sewell's

---

[59] William H. Sewell Jr., "Towards a Post-materialist Rhetoric for Labor History," in Leonard R. Berlanstein (ed.), *Rethinking Labor History*, Urbana: University of Illinois Press, 1993, 24.

[60] Nicholas Dirks, Geoff Eley, and Sherry Ortner, "Introduction," in Dirks, Eley, and Ortner, (eds.), *Culture/Power/History: A Reader in Contemporary Social Theory*, Princeton, NJ: Princeton University Press, 1994, 29.

[61] Keith Michael Baker, "Enlightenment and the Institution of Society: Notes for a Conceptual History," in William Melching and Wyger Velema (eds.), *Main Trends in Cultural History*, Amsterdam: Rodopi, 1994, 114.

words, "The concept of the social is vague and mysterious because it still carries a whiff of the divine."[62]

Many historians, including former social historians, now began to treat the social not as the ground of explanation and as the cause of other effects, but rather as itself a historical effect that needed to be explored and explained.[63] Anthropologists, sociologists, and social theorists were arriving at the same conclusion. The historically inclined anthropologist Eric Wolf argued that society is not a "thing," *pace* Durkheim, but "a claim advanced and enacted in order to construct a state of affairs that previously was not. The name is not the thing; and the thing had first to be built up in space and time,"[64] and concluded that the concept of "society" could not provide the ground of history because it itself had a history. The sociologist Alain Touraine announced "the disappearance of the idea of society"[65] and drew the logical conclusion, namely that this "obviously challenges the legitimacy of sociology itself, its existence as a coherent body of knowledge."[66]

In the 1960s and 1970s, social history was on the ascendant, and it seemed to many that the discipline of history would come to be synonymous with

[62] Sewell, *Logics of History*, 326. Baker similarly argues that in the course of the eighteenth century, "Society replaces religion as the ultimate ground of order, the ontological frame of human existence" ("Enlightenment," 107). See also Baker's "A Foucauldian French Revolution?," in Jan Goldstein (ed.), *Foucault and the Writing of History*, Oxford: Blackwell, 1994. See similarly Lynn Hunt, *Writing History in the Global Era*, New York: Norton, 2014, 80–88; Bruno Latour, "The Social as Association," in Nicholas Gane (ed.), *The Future of Social Theory*, New York: Continuum, 2004, especially 84. The claim that "the social" often has the same function in historical explanation as God once did is sometimes lent unwitting credence by those seeking to defend or rescue the enterprise of social history, as in the following passage by Christopher Lloyd: "Economic and social structures are mysterious formations—at once intangible, invisible, even somewhat incomprehensible, yet powerful and in many cases vast and very long-lived." *The Structures of History*, Oxford: Blackwell 1993, 5. One could easily substitute "God" for "economic and social structures" in this formulation.

[63] For a sample of the literature see Mary Poovey, *Making a Social Body: British Cultural Formation, 1830–1864*, 2nd ed., Chicago: University of Chicago Press, 1995; Nikolas Rose, "Towards a Critical Sociology of Freedom," in Patrick Joyce (ed.), *Class*, New York: Oxford University Press, 1995; Denise Riley, *"Am I That Name?" Feminism and the Category of "Women" in History*, London: Macmillan, 1988; Patrick Joyce, "The End of Social History?," *Social History* 20:1 (1995); Brian C. J. Singer, *Society, Theory and the French Revolution: Studies in the Revolutionary Imaginary*, New York: Palgrave Macmillan, 1986, and also his *Montesquieu and the Discovery of the Social*, New York: Palgrave Macmillan, 2013; Jean Terrier, *Visions of the Social: Society as a Political Project in France, 1750–1950*, Leiden: Brill, 2011; Peter Wagner, "An Entirely New Object of Consciousness, of Volition, of Thought," in Lorraine Daston (ed.), *Biographies of Scientific Objects*, Chicago: University of Chicago Press, 2000; Somers, *Genealogies of Citizenship*; Ernesto Laclau and Chantalle Mouffe, *Hegemony and Socialist Strategy: Towards a Radical Democratic Politics*, 2nd ed., London: Verso, 2001, chap. 3.

[64] Eric R. Wolf, "Inventing Society," *American Ethnologist* 15:4 (November 1988), 757.

[65] Alain Touraine, "Sociology without Society," *Current Sociology* 46:2 (1998), 128.

[66] Touraine, "Sociology without Society," 129. Though not necessarily for identical reasons, others also found that "society" and "the social" were in decline. See, for instance, Nikolas Rose, "Governing the Social," in Gane, *Future of Social Theory*, and Jean Baudrillard, *In the Shadow of the Silent Majorities, or The End of the Social*, translated by P. Fous, J. Johnston, and P. Patton, Los Angeles: Semiotext(e), 1983.

social history. However, just as the object "nature" came to be called into question in science studies, so similarly did "society" begin to unravel in the course of the very debates that presumed that "society" and the "social" had central explanatory significance for history. By the early twenty-first century this "uncertainty" had been resolved—inasmuch as the project of social history was concerned—with Geoff Eley delivering its obituary: "In the forms of the original project, 'social history' has ceased to exist. Its coherence derived from the sovereignty of social determinations within a self-confident materialist paradigm of social totality, grounded in the primacies of class. But since the early eighties, each part of that framework has succumbed to relentless and compelling critique."[67]

Nature, Culture. and Society: Anthropology

Whereas science has been principally concerned with nature, and social history with society and the social, the disciplines or subdisciplines of social and cultural anthropology have been concerned with the interaction between nature and society/culture. But some recent debates in social anthropology have followed a trajectory similar to debates in science studies and social history, in the course of which the very categories of nature and culture have come to be questioned.

Ever since its constitution as a discipline, anthropology has been concerned with understanding and explaining the differences that characterize human communities. The following sorts of statements, selected at random, are thus utterly commonplace in the literature. For the Waswanapi Cree peoples, a scholar tells us, "The animals, the winds and many other phenomena are thought of as being 'like persons' in that they act intelligently and have wills and idiosyncrasies."[68] Another informs us that the Amerindian Achuar "confer the attributes of social life upon plants and animals, regarding these as subjects rather than objects";[69] for them, "All of nature's beings have some

---

[67] Eley, *A Crooked Line*, 189.

[68] Feit, "The Ethnomethodology of the Waswanapi Cree: Or How Hunters Can Manage Their Resources," quoted in Tim Ingold, *The Perception of the Environment: Essays in Livelihood, Dwelling and Skill*, New York: Routledge, 2000, 48.

[69] Philippe Descola, *The Spears of Twilight: Life and Death in the Amazon Jungle*, translated by Janet Lloyd, New York: Free Press, 1996, 405–6.

features in common with mankind, and the laws they go by are more or less the same as those governing civil society."[70]

As anthropology came to be systematized and formalized as a discipline, "animism"—the primitive mind "projecting" spiritual and supernatural powers onto animals, spirits, and things—became the term of choice for characterizing such beliefs. Such (erroneous) beliefs and the rituals associated with them were often explained in evolutionary terms—confusing nature with culture, by ascribing to animals and natural objects the agency that in fact belonged only to humans, was diagnosed as a symptom and survival of an earlier stage in human evolution: a characteristic, according to Edward Burnett Tylor, of "tribes very low in the scale of humanity."[71] Rejecting such explanations, the founders of social and cultural anthropology argued that each culture produced its own ways of viewing and inhabiting the world, which had to be understood without recourse (for the most part) to evolutionary explanations. The native's rituals and beliefs were instead to be understood and explained in social terms. Social and cultural anthropology thus asked why

the people anthropologists studied should so often and in such varied ways get the world around them wrong (myths, rituals, magic, and all the other odd "beliefs" that went with them). Were these erroneous beliefs and practices perhaps useful to them in some way (functionalism)? Did they somehow help preserve the social structure of the group (structural functionalism)? Did they express the core values of its culture (cultural interpretivism)? Were they metaphors for basic social concerns (symbolism) or examples of people's false consciousness of them (Marxism)? Or were they in some deep sense expressions of how the human mind works in general (structuralism)?[72]

[70] Philippe Descola, *In the Society of Nature: A Native Ecology in Amazonia*, translated by Nora Scott, New York: Cambridge University Press, 1994, 93.

[71] Edward Burnett Tylor, *Religion in Primitive Culture*, Gloucester, MA: Peter Smith, 1970, 10. As Tylor's language indicates, for evolutionary anthropologists such peoples were "missing links in the evolutionary chain," their cultural forms studied "not for themselves, or in terms of the meaning they might have to the people who created them, but in order to cast light on the processes by which the ape had developed into the British gentleman." George W. Stocking Jr., *Victorian Anthropology*, New York: Free Press and London: Collier Macmillan, 1987, 185.

[72] Martin Holbraad, *Truth in Motion: The Recursive Anthropology of Cuban Divination*, Chicago: University of Chicago Press, 2012, 26.

"Culture" and "society" were now mobilized to explain why others behaved as they did and believed what they believed, including their beliefs about nature. Inasmuch as these beliefs were adjudged to be mistaken (whence the need for explanation), the native's knowledge was not on a par with that of the anthropologist. The categories of modern Western knowledge, including those mobilized in the discipline of anthropology, were regarded as superior, but the epistemological privilege accorded anthropology was no longer justified in naturalistic, evolutionary terms, but rather on the grounds that anthropological explanations of the rituals and beliefs of primitives or savages had an altogether different status from the native's own account of her beliefs and rituals: anthropological categories of explanation were "etic," whereas native categories were "emic."

But the knowledge culture of the anthropologist, once no longer tethered by the privilege accorded it by evolutionary doctrines, could and did start appearing, to some, as a culture like any other. To a growing number of anthropologists, the presumption that anthropological explanations were superior because they were scientific—of which the proof was the scientific character of anthropological explanations—began to seem question-begging, if not outrightly circular. Some important figures in the discipline began to wonder if anthropological knowledge was anything more than the folk knowledge of the West: David Schneider suggested that many of the organizing terms at the core of anthropology, such as kinship,[73] were the "ethnoepistemology" of Western culture, illegitimately generalized: "So much of what passes for science in the social sciences, including anthropology, derives directly and recognizably from the commonsense notions, the everyday premises of the culture in which and by which the scientist lives. These postulates of European culture are simply taken over . . . and served up as something special, sometimes even in Latin."[74] By the 1980s, anthropology was a lively and highly reflexive discipline, less inclined to explain the native's errors with reference to our scientific truths, and more likely to

---

[73] Described by Adam Kuper as "the technical core of social anthropology." *The Reinvention of Primitive Society: Transformations of a Myth*, New York: Routledge, 2005, 219.

[74] David M. Schneider, *A Critique of the Study of Kinship*, Ann Arbor: University of Michigan Press, 1984, 175. (That our taxonomies of nature are ordered in Latin rather than in a living speech, thus seemingly placed beyond the vagaries of folk cultures, has been noted by others. See, for instance, Marshall Sahlins, *How "Natives" Think: About Captain Cook, for Example*, Chicago: University of Chicago Press, 1995, 158–59). Schneider goes on to urge that anthropology, and the social sciences more generally, need to recognize that to adopt the "categories of one particular culture and use them directly as analytical tools with the assumption that they are somehow universally vital functions or kinds of activities just does not work" (184).

think of anthropology as an exercise in "translation" or "dialogue." Many anthropologists, like some of their counterparts in science studies, were in effect, if not always in name, social constructionists, for whom all statements and beliefs, including our own, were socially or culturally constructed.

In a trajectory not unlike that followed by science studies, once due allowance for the difference in subject matter is made, anthropology had gone from explanations that were naturalistic (evolutionary anthropology) or ones that were social (functionalism, symbolism), to ones that were social but "symmetrically" so (where anthropology and its categories were products and reflections of Western culture, including the very distinction between nature and culture). However, some noted that even a thoroughgoing social constructionism—that is, one that regarded Western beliefs about nature and society as socially and culturally constructed, and thus not necessarily as a privileged site from and by which to understand others—continued to operate within the terms of this distinction; and in doing so, could not escape privileging "our" culture and categories.[75] Philippe Descola was only one of those who pointed out that "if every culture is considered as a specific system of meanings arbitrarily coding an unproblematic natural world . . . then not only does the very cause of the nature-culture(s) division remain unquestioned, but declaration to the contrary notwithstanding, there can be no escape from the epistemological privilege granted to western culture, the only one whose definition of nature serves as the implicit measuring rod for all others."[76]

As was happening in science studies and social history, some anthropologists began to wonder whether the terms of the debate, where "one side reduces reality to representation (culturalism, relativism, textualism)," while "the other reduces representation to reality (cognitivism, sociobiology, evolutionary psychology),"[77] were the source of the problem.

[75] Including the very concept of "culture" itself—as Roy Wagner argued in an important book that prefigured and influenced subsequent debates, *The Invention of Culture*, Englewood Cliffs, NJ: Prentice Hall, 1975.

[76] Philippe Descola, "Constructing Natures: Symbolic Ecology and Social Practice," in Philippe Descola and Gisli Palsson (eds.), *Nature and Society: Anthropological Perspectives*, New York: Routledge, 1996, 84–85. Holbraad makes the same point about constructionism and its seeming relativism: "It is only by relying on the distinction between nature and culture—precisely the form of 'classifying the world' we are supposed not to project onto others—that we are able . . . to repudiate the 'ethnocentrism' of the distinction itself. We should not universalize the distinction between nature and culture, we say, because other cultures do not make it, and thus we reinscribe its universality in the very act of denying it" (*Truth in Motion*, 34–35).

[77] Eduardo Viveiros de Castro, "Supernature: Under the Gaze of the Other," in his *The Relative Native: Essays on Indigenous Conceptual Worlds*, Chicago: Hau Books, 2015, 294. Similarly Descola: "Either culture is fashioned by nature, whether this is composed of genes, instincts, and

Growing numbers of anthropologists now sought, in different and sometimes opposing ways, to escape the dualism of nature/culture by problematizing one or the other or both. Drawing upon the Heideggerian argument
that a subject confronting nature as an object to be known is a "derived" or
secondary mode of existence, one that arises "only when everyday practical
dealings in the environment have broken down,"[78] Tim Ingold, for example,
argued that "the world can only be 'nature' for a being that does not inhabit
it."[79] Hunter-gatherers, according to Ingold, do not regard or approach their
environment as an external world of "nature" that is "grasped" through the
conceptual and symbolic schemes their culture makes available to them; and
thus to seek a sociocultural answer to the question of why such peoples view
nature as they do is to ask the wrong question. The contrast between their
way and ours cannot be explained in terms of different cultures, worldviews,
social constructions, and the like, for it is not a matter of "two alternative
views of the world; it is rather between two ways of apprehending it, only
one of which (the Western) may be characterized as the construction of a
view. . . . As for the other, apprehending the world is not a matter of construction but of engagement . . . not of making a view *of* the world but of taking
up a view *in* it."[80] Drawing upon a structuralist rather than a Heideggerian
legacy, Descola similarly asked whether it was still plausible to treat the na-
ture/culture distinction as a human universal and to "scour the four corners
of the planet in order to discover how the most diverse of peoples may have
expressed such an opposition, meanwhile quite forgetting the altogether exceptional circumstances in which we ourselves belatedly forged it?"[81] His
answer was signaled in the title of the book from which this quotation is
drawn—*Beyond Culture and Nature.*

    In debates within anthropology, to question the category "nature" in-
evitably led to also problematizing "society," as was happening in science
studies. Marilyn Strathern's important and influential book, *The Gender of
the Gift*, challenged the presumption that anthropology's task is the study and
comparison of societies, as if "society" were an object that could be taken
for granted because it existed everywhere—a universal form imbued with

neuron networks or by geographical constraints, or else nature only takes on shape and relief as a
potential reservoir of signs and symbols on which culture can draw." *Beyond Nature and Culture*,
translated by Janet Lloyd, Chicago: University of Chicago Press, 2013, 79.
    [78] Charles B. Guignon, *Heidegger and the Problem of Knowledge*, Indianapolis: Hackett, 1983, 99.
    [79] Ingold, *Perception of the Environment*, 40.
    [80] Ingold, *Perception of the Environment*, 42.
    [81] Descola, *Beyond Nature and Culture*, 85.

different contents.[82] As with the debates in social history already discussed, Strathern was not denying the universality of human interdependence and sociality, but on the contrary suggesting that "as a concept 'society' has come to interfere too much with our apprehension of sociality."[83]

The work of Eduardo Viveiros de Castro has perhaps carried the questioning of the nature/culture dualism furthest. As long as we think in terms of epistemology and representation, we seem to have no alternative but to imagine a singular nature differentially represented. If we are to escape the horns of this dilemma, Castro has suggested, anthropology needs to recognize that what is at issue are different ontologies, not different epistemologies. Drawing upon his work among the Arawete people in Brazilian Amazonia (supplemented by other scholarship on the Amazonian region), he finds that the world they inhabit is, in fact, more than one. In a passage that has been frequently quoted in debates in anthropology, and which I therefore quote at length, he writes that, according to his Amerindian subjects,

> humans see humans as humans, animals as animals and spirits (if they see them) as spirits; however animals (predators) and spirits see humans as animals (as prey) to the same extent that animals (as prey) see humans as spirits or as animals (predators). By the same token, animals and spirits see themselves as humans: they perceive themselves as (or become) anthropomorphic beings when they are in their own houses or villages and they experience their own habits and characteristics in the form of culture—they see their food as human food (jaguars see blood as manioc beer, vultures see the maggots in rotting meat as grilled fish, etc), see their bodily attributes (fur, feathers, claws, beaks etc) as body decorations or cultural instruments, they see their social system as organized in the same way as human institutions are (with chiefs, shamans, ceremonies, exogamous moieties, etc).... In sum, animals are people, or see themselves as persons.[84]

[82] Her book begins with the following: "It may seem absurd for a social anthropologist to suggest that he or she could imagine people having no society. Yet the argument of this book is that however useful the concept of society may be to analysis, we are not going to justify its use by appealing to indigenous counterparts." Marilyn Strathern, *The Gender of the Gift*, Berkeley: University of California Press, 1988, 3.

[83] Marilyn Strathern, "1989 Debate: The Concept of Society Is Theoretically Obsolete," in Tim Ingold (ed.), *Key Debates in Anthropology*, New York: Routledge, 1996, 66.

[84] Eduardo Viveiros de Castro, "Cosmological Deixis and Amerindian Perspectivism," *Journal of the Royal Anthropological Institute* 4:3 (September 1998), 470.

Instead of treating this as a culturally determined epistemological outlook, which would lead to it being regarded either as an error ("projecting" human attributes and qualities onto nature) or as the Amazonian "worldview" (just as good, or as bad, as ours), Castro labels this "perspectivism," distinguishing it from representation. The notion of representation presupposes a mind, soul, or consciousness, whereas in Castro's account of Amerindian perspectivism, the point of view or perspective is located in the body. Since animals have souls like us humans, the reason they see different worlds—for example, see manioc beer where we see blood—is because of their bodies, not in any purely physiological sense, but in the sense that every species has dispositions or capacities that render the bodies characteristic of that species unique. Whereas the social anthropologist would see many different representations of the one world, for Amerindian perspectivism "all beings see ('represent') the world in the *same* way—what changes is the *world* that they see."[85] Thus Amerindian perspectivism posits or supposes a single epistemology and variable ontologies, the exact opposite of our metaphysics and cosmology. While we recognize different ways of seeing the same world, perspectivism recognizes the same way of seeing different worlds: "one culture, multiple natures—one epistemology, multiple ontologies."[86]

The originality—and the shock—of Castro's argument lies in taking seriously the possibility of many worlds, rather than many outlooks/descriptions of the same world. As we saw, Thomas Kuhn had shocked the world of science studies more than thirty years earlier by suggesting that when a paradigm switch or revolution occurred, scientists were "seeing" a different world. However, his was the epistemological point that our categories partly predetermine how we see the world: as he characterised his position, "I am a Kantian with moveable categories."[87] By contrast, Castro seeks to move anthropology, which he describes as the "most Kantian of all disciplines,"[88] away from its "boring dualism of representation versus reality" to ontology: "We need richer ontologies, and it is high time we put epistemological questions to rest."[89]

[85] Eduardo Viveiros de Castro, "Nature: The World as Affect and Perspective," in his *The Relative Native*, 251.

[86] Eduardo Viveiros de Castro, "Exchanging Perspectives: The Transformation of Objects into Subjects in Amerindian Ontologies," *Common Knowledge* 10:3 (Fall 2004), 474.

[87] "A Discussion with Thomas Kuhn," in his *The Road since Structure*, Chicago: University of Chicago Press, 2000, 264.

[88] Eduardo Viveiros de Castro, "Supernature," 293.

[89] Eduardo Viveiros de Castro, "Supernature," 294. Strathern similarly writes, "Social anthropology is not the only discipline that has at times turned an intellectual Euro-American obsession

It is not entirely clear whether Castro's somewhat ambiguous pronouncements are endorsing Amerindian perspectivism or using it to un-settle "our" picture of the world by showing that all ontologies rest upon a metaphysics, of which our modern, Western metaphysics is but one. Some of his writings seem to suggest that he regards the existence of multiple worlds not only as valid, but as tied to the political emancipation of indigenous peo-ples, as when he declares that anthropology should be guided by "one cardinal value: working to create the conditions for the conceptual, I mean ontolog-ical, self-determination of people."[90] But he also suggests—what is especially relevant for our purposes—that Amerindian perspectivism allows or even forces us to reconsider the status of anthropological knowledge and what it is "for." If our ontological partitions between nature and society, the human and the inhuman, cannot be taken as facts of the world, and if knowledge has ontological and not merely epistemological stakes, then anthropology as it has hitherto been conceived—whether evolutionary, functionalist, culturalist, or whatever—cannot continue as usual. The anthropologist's objective should no longer "be that of explaining, interpreting, contextual-izing, or rationalizing native thought," but of seeking instead to "deploy it, drawing out its consequences, and verifying the effects that it can produce on our own thinking."[91] The task of anthropology, consequently, should not be "to *explicate the worlds of others* but rather to *multiply our world*."[92] In a sim-ilar fashion, Strathern writes that her work is aimed not simply at showing that this or that Western concept—such as "society"—does not apply to the Hageners, but in so doing to disinter the deep assumptions, the "deeply rooted metaphysics," undergirding our knowledge; only then, she writes, will "we" be able to "displace them most effectively"[93] and thus open up a space in

with how we come to know and describe things into the issue of how we represent them . . . all the interesting questions [for this "Euro-American obsession"] seem to be about how we (subjects) know the world (object)—a simple minded ontology upholding a fantastic epistemological edifice." Marilyn Strathern, *Property, Substance and Effect: Anthropological Essays on Persons and Things*, London: Athlone Press, 1999, 251.

[90] Eduardo Viveiros de Castro, "AND," in his *The Relative Native*, 42.

[91] Eduardo Viveiros de Castro, "The Relative Native," in his *The Relative Native*, 24. For a debate among anthropologists and archaeologists on how the implications of the ontological turn may be construed, and what it might mean for their disciplines, see Benjamin Alberti, Severin Fowles, Martin Holbraad, Yvonne Marshall, and Christopher Witmore, "'Worlds Otherwise': Archaeology, Anthropology, and Ontological Difference," *Current Anthropology* 52:6 (December 2011), 896–912; and also Martin Holbraad and Morton Axel Pedersen, *The Ontological Turn: An Anthropological Exposition*, New York: Cambridge University Press, 2017.

[92] Eduardo Viveiros de Castro, "Zeno and the Art of Anthropology: Of Lies, Beliefs, Paradoxes and Other Truths," in his *The Relative Native*, 85.

[93] Strathern, *Gender of the Gift*, 12.

which to "glimpse what 'other' assumptions might look like."[94] But in either case, just as our assumption that there is a distinct "nature" has been called into question in science studies, and the object "society" has been called into question by historians who once took it as an ontological given, so too in anthropology society, nature, and the relation between the two have come to be rendered problematic.

A Crisis in Knowledge

This chapter has shown that the key elements of the "knowledge settlement" that produced modern Western knowledge have come under sustained questioning. In disciplines attending to nature, or society, or the interaction between them the certitudes that once informed knowledge production have been called into doubt. While there has been some exchange or traffic between the debates considered here, these conversations have been, for the most part, disciplinary affairs. Yet despite the differences between these disciplines and the objects they attend to, this questioning has followed a similar pattern and logic. In each discipline, the solidity of the very object (nature, and society) about which knowledge is sought has been called into question; the very terms in which inquiries and debates within a particular discipline have been framed and conducted have been put into doubt; and as a consequence, the conception of knowledge as a representation of an object external to and independent of it has given way to the suspicion that the object is, in part at least, produced by representation and knowledge, rather than preceding it.

Construing knowledge as a subject-object relation in which a subject correctly "represents" an external reality is a premise that had been challenged earlier, including in the works of Nietzsche, Heidegger, Wittgenstein, William James, Dewey, and Whitehead. In more recent times, the foregrounding of epistemology in the philosophical enterprise, which is the direct corollary of this conception of knowledge, has come under challenge, often inspired by a return to the insights of Heidegger and other earlier critics. Richard Rorty's *Philosophy and the Mirror of Nature*, which drew upon Heidegger, Wittgenstein, and Dewey to argue that "the notion of knowledge as accurate representation, made possible by special mental processes, and intelligible

---

[94] Strathern, *Gender of the Gift*, 4.

through a general theory of representation, needs to be abandoned"[95] was a landmark text; in Charles Taylor's assessment, it served "both to crystallize and to accelerate a trend towards the repudiation of the whole epistemological enterprise."[96] Since, there have been many other works that return to and retrieve earlier critics in order to explicate their insights and draw upon these insights to challenge the understanding of knowledge as a subject-object relation, and/or to develop other conceptions of knowledge.[97] What is especially significant however, as I have sought to show in this chapter, is that those who are not normally engaged in philosophical debates of this nature have nonetheless, in the course of their disciplinary investigations, found themselves calling into question this modern conception of knowledge as a subject-object relation. They have also, though to a lesser degree, grappled with the "secularity" of the human sciences, most commonly in those disciplines, such as anthropology and history, that study human subjects for whom gods and other nonhumans need to be accorded their due, for they are real and possessed of agency (not just things some people "believe" in). This latter point is one I will return to and expand upon when I discuss the discipline of history.

The debates examined in the previous pages are only one aspect of the disciplinary lives in question, and I am not suggesting that all anthropologists, historians, and scholars in science studies are engaged in epistemological and ontological self-questioning. They are not; the production of disciplinary knowledge, premised upon the presuppositions outlined earlier in this chapter, continues apace—though no longer unchallenged. For example, despite social historians questioning the category of "the social," taking account of "social" forces acting "behind the backs" of actors continues to be regarded as central to historical explanation in the discipline of history, as I shall show in chapters 3 and 4. Nevertheless, such problematizations are widespread enough to be a significant part of the contemporary intellectual landscape,

---

[95] Rorty, *Mirror of Nature*, 6.

[96] Taylor, "Overcoming Epistemology," 465.

[97] Works that I have found especially instructive include Guignon, *Heidegger*; Lee Braver, *A Thing of This World: A History of Continental Anti-realism*, Evanston, IL: Northwestern University Press, 2007, and his *Groundless Grounds: A Study of Wittgenstein and Heidegger*, Cambridge, MA: MIT Press, 2012; Isabelle Stengers, *Thinking with Whitehead: A Free and Wild Creation of Concepts*, translated by Michael Chase, Cambridge, MA: Harvard University Press, 2011; and Martin Savransky, *Around the Day in Eighty Worlds*, Durham, NC: Duke University Press, forthcoming. To this one would also have to add, of course, the works of Gilles Deleuze and also the works of the "new materialism"—see, for instance, Jane Bennett, *Vibrant Matter: A Political Ecology of Things*, Durham, NC: Duke University Press, 2010.

and they are too substantial to be characterized and dismissed as exemplifying irrationalism, postmodern relativism, or nihilism. Taken together, they indicate that modern Western knowledge, the superiority and universality of which was once taken for granted, now has to be defended. The chapter to follow evaluates these defenses, and with it this book takes an explicitly postcolonial turn by offering a postcolonial critique of contemporary defenses of Reason.

2

Defending Reason

A Postcolonial Critique

What I have been calling modern Western knowledge is dominant in the world, for it is widely accepted to be more accurate and "true" than its predecessors, or any other forms of contemporary knowledge. By the nineteenth century, the superiority of modern Western knowledge hardly seemed to need any argument. Modern societies, and the modern knowledge that was seen to be both an emblem and a precipitating cause of their modernity, were seen as marking a great historical advance. The evidence for this included greater prosperity, more effective and humane (and sometimes democratic) statecraft, technological and medical advances, the eradication or at least retreat of "superstition," and more generally, the intellectual, moral, and material superiority of modern societies compared with their predecessors or with contemporary "nonmoderns." The unrigorous nature of this claim for the superiority of modernity and of modern knowledge—indicated by the unsystematic and even grab-bag nature of the preceding list—has not prevented contemporary restatements of it.[1]

In recent times, however, there has been a chorus of criticism of the assumption that modern knowledge is true and therefore universal. These criticisms range from the disciplinary questionings and problematizations surveyed and assessed in the preceding chapter to more general arguments that modern knowledge, claims to the contrary notwithstanding, does not transcend its time and its place, or its imbrication in power relations; and that far from being universal, it is in fact, Western, or patriarchal, or heteronormative. These criticisms and questionings are sufficiently widespread, and some are intellectually serious enough, that the superiority and universality of modern Western Reason, which could previously be taken for granted, now has to be argued for and defended. Those who would still defend it, in the

---

[1] See, for example, Steven Pinker, *Enlightenment Now: The Case for Reason, Science, Humanism and Progress*, New York: Viking, 2018.

Beyond Reason. Sanjay Seth, Oxford University Press (2021). © Oxford University Press.
DOI: 10.1093/oso/9780197500583.003.0003

words of one of their number, have come to acknowledge "the intrinsic *im-purity* of what we call 'reason' "[2] and to recognize that "pure" reason has had to make fundamental and lasting concessions to the impurities of language and culture, temporality and history, practice and interest, body and desire."[3] That being so, the challenge they face, in the words of Jürgen Habermas, is to acknowledge that "there is no such thing as a context-transcending reason" while at the same time avoiding "the false conclusion that the criteria of reason themselves change with every new context."[4]

There is a historical-intellectual precedent to a refutation or overcoming of a different kind of skepticism; I am referring here, of course, to the philosophy of Kant. Kant responded to the skepticism of his time not by "dogmatically" asserting certain propositions to be true, nor by seeking to identify, on empirical grounds, a set of rational principles common to all men, but by asking instead what sort of conditions had to be satisfied for cognitions and perceptions to occur at all. In Henry Allison's description, Kant inquired into and sought to establish the "epistemic conditions" of any and all knowledge.[5] His answer deduced universal categories of Reason that were not derived from human experience (which was acknowledged to be varied) but were the ground for our having any experience in the first place. This "transcendental" move yielded a powerful argument for a Reason that was universal, because notwithstanding the immense variety of human experience, moralities, and notions of beauty, it was the precondition for humans having *any* sort of experience, morality, or conception of beauty in the first place. Modern knowledge, as elaborated and defended by Kant, could now stake a claim to having discovered and defined rational principles that had of necessity to be presupposed, and which were independent of social, cultural, and historical particularities. This argument was not without its problems, but it is testimony to the vitality of the line of argument initiated by Kant that many of the most sophisticated contemporary attempts to salvage or retrieve the

[2] Thomas McCarthy, "Part 1: Philosophy and Critical Theory: A Reprise," in David Couzens Hoy and Thomas McCarthy (eds.), *Critical Theory*, Oxford: Blackwell, 1994, 8.
[3] Thomas McCarthy, "Enlightenment and the Idea of Public Reason," in Richard Kearney and Mark Dooley (eds.), *Questioning Ethics: Contemporary Debates in Philosophy*, New York: Routledge, 1999, 168.
[4] Jürgen Habermas, *The Postnational Constellation: Political Essays*, edited and translated by Max Pensky, Cambridge, MA: Polity Press, 2001, 148–49. Here as elsewhere, Habermas attributes this "false conclusion" to "postmodernism." In fact, as seen in chapter 1, the challenge comes from much more diverse and variegated quarters than this vague reference to an ill-defined "postmodernism" recognizes.
[5] Henry Allison, *Kant's Transcendental Idealism: An Interpretation and Defense*, rev. ed., New Haven: Yale University Press, 2004.

idea of a singular and universal Reason, while acknowledging that Reason is of this world, do so by returning to Kant. It is usually a Kant stripped of much of the metaphysics, but some version or other of a transcendental argument has been the chief resource for contemporary defenders of Reason, including John Rawls, Karl-Otto Apel, Jürgen Habermas, Hilary Putnam, Axel Honneth, and Rainer Forst.

Just as Kant's revolution in philosophy was shaped by the prevailing intellectual climate, not least the threat posed to the very possibility of objective knowledge by Humean skepticism, so too are most of the contemporary defenses of Reason shaped by an intellectual climate in which the challenge is seen to issue from "postmodernism" and the "relativism" that is seen to be its inevitable corollary. As a consequence they seldom engage with the disciplinary problematizations discussed in the chapter 1, nor with postcolonial and decolonial critiques, which emphasize not merely the historical contingency that went into the making of our notion of truth, or the power relations inscribed therein that it reproduces, but also the Western origins, and the parochial nature, of a knowledge for which "universality" is claimed. Conversely, postcolonial and decolonial thinkers have seldom systematically engaged with these contemporary efforts to "save" modern Reason from its critics.[6] Thus two important elements in contemporary thought that are odds with one another have seldom seen the other as an interlocutor worth engaging with. A recent and important exception, Amy Allen's *The End of Progress: Decolonizing the Normative Foundations of Critical Theory*, tellingly begins with the author observing that "the gulf is so pronounced that the very project of this book might seem quixotic," for just as her critical theory interlocutors criticized her postcolonially inflected arguments for "flirting with relativism," so too her colleagues working with postcolonial theory were often "stunned" to find that anyone was still willing to seriously

[6] The works of Enrique Dussel are an important exception—see especially *Ethics of Liberation in the Age of Globalization and Exclusion*, translated by Eduardo Mendieta et al., Durham, NC: Duke University Press, 2013. Dussel's criticisms of the Frankfurt school of critical theory, especially of what he terms its "second generation," are relevant and trenchant. But his willingness to incorporate elements of Apel's and Habermas's discourse theory into his own project, and his affinities with the "first generation" of the Frankfurt school, which he describes as "a direct predecessor of [his own] . . . philosophy of liberation" (234), mean his critique of these defenders of Reason is an ambivalent one. For a short but useful assessment of Dussel's relation to the Frankfurt school tradition see Amy Allen, "The Ethics and Politics of Progress: Dussel and the Frankfurt School," in Allen and Eduardo Mendieta (eds.), *Decolonizing Ethics: The Critical Theory of Enrique Dussel*, University Park: Penn State University Press, forthcoming.

engage with "either ideas of historical progress and development or normative foundationalist projects."[7]

Defending Reason: Apel, Rawls, Habermas

A postcolonial project to parochialize the social sciences such as this one
must, perforce, engage with influential contemporary arguments that seek to
show that despite—or even because—of its origins in the modern West, these
social sciences transcend their particularities and have warrant to be considered as knowledge as such, rather than as a historically and culturally specific
form of it. In this chapter I outline and evaluate the arguments of three such
contemporary defenses of modern knowledge—briefly in the case of Karl-
Otto Apel and in greater detail for John Rawls and Jürgen Habermas.

Karl-Otto Apel's Discourse Ethics

Of these three defenders of an impure knowledge that still has warrant to
be considered "true" and thus universal, Karl-Otto Apel cleaves closest to
Kant. He describes his project as a "transcendental-pragmatic transformation of Kantian ethics," designed to take into account the historical and cultural "dependency" of all concrete forms of morality, but "without giving
up the moral universalism of Kantian provenance and falling a victim to
historical-relativism."[8]

Apel's project is thus conceived of and executed as the answer or solution
to a dilemma. Once we acknowledge—as Kant did not but as we must—"the
historical situatedness of ethics,"[9] two options seem to present themselves.
One is to conclude that all moralities are no more than the moralities of a time
and a place. This conclusion—an embrace of "historical relativism" that Apel
ascribes to Kuhn, MacIntyre, Walzer, Rorty, Lyotard, and the later Rawls[10]—is

---

[7] Amy Allen, *The End of Progress: Decolonizing the Normative Foundations of Critical Theory*,
New York: Columbia University Press, 2016, xv.

[8] Karl-Otto Apel, *The Response of Discourse Ethics*, Leuven: Peeters 2001, 50. Here as in subsequent quotations from Apel, I eliminate the frequent italicizations that occur in the original text.

[9] Apel, *Response of Discourse Ethics*, 74.

[10] Apel, *Response of Discourse Ethics*, 21. See also Apel, "Normatively Grounding 'Critical Theory'
through Recourse to the Lifeworld? A Transcendental-Pragmatic Attempt to Think with Habermas
against Habermas," in Axel Honneth et al. (eds.), *Philosophical Interventions in the Unfinished Project
of Enlightenment*, Cambridge, MA: MIT Press, 1992.

precisely the one Apel wishes to deny. Another option is to acknowledge that every morality is specific to a period and a people, but then to insert this into a historical teleology, a narrative of progress, where the modern "context" is itself found to be one that is "privileged" in that it produces a knowledge superior to all predecessor knowledges. This argument—subsequently I shall suggest that Habermas presents a sophisticated version of it—is also one that Apel rejects. Such a "metaphysical-dogmatic conception or tenet of the certainty of the progress of history"[11] makes our knowledge of morality dependent upon knowledge about the course of history; and because such knowledge of history is not secure (and indeed, being "metaphysical and dogmatic," cannot be secured), the inevitable failure of this argument would open the floodgates to the very relativism that Apel wishes to deny.

Rejecting both these possibilities, Apel argues that a return to Kant, but now stripped of insupportable metaphysical assumptions, and informed by the post-Kantian insights of hermeneutics and the linguistic turn in philosophy, provides a solution.[12] It is true that we always reason out of specific contexts and communities, and thus our reasoning is always grounded in the historical and cultural presuppositions of determinate lifeworlds. Nonetheless, all public argumentation, because it makes validity/truth/rightness claims for which acceptance is sought from others, also has a transcendental horizon in addition to its historical one; each "real" communication community presupposes an "ideal communication community." Any validity claim, irrespective of its historically and culturally specific content, also has a necessary "form," a form that is not historically contingent, because it is a transcendental feature of argument as such. The very performance of moral argumentation thus has certain necessary and inescapable presuppositions built into it, and these provide us with a context-independent standard by which to judge, not necessarily the specificities of the claims being made, but whether or not they contradict the necessary entailments of making *any* validity claim. The "undeniable presuppositions of arguing,"[13] as Apel describes them, are that any effort to argue and persuade cannot legitimately exercise coercion or make use of authority; that everyone has an equal right to participate in debate and present an argument; and that the consensus of

[11] Apel, *Response of Discourse Ethics*, 74.

[12] In Apel's words, "Transcendental pragmatics is indeed a transformation and renewal of classic transcendentalism under the conditions of the hermeneutic and linguistic turn" (*Response of Discourse Ethics*, 55).

[13] Apel, "Globalisation and the Need for Universal Ethics," *European Journal of Social Theory* 3:2 (2000), 145.

everyone who is potentially affected (and not only the active parties in a debate) must be sought. These are the "a priori" presuppositions that ground all public argument and disagreement, and they cannot be denied without "performative self-contradiction." Apel's discourse ethics thus arrives, in his words, at "an equivalent to Kant's universalization principle of the 'categorical imperative,'"[14] providing us with "an ideal yardstick of a possible examination of all rightness claims," including the rightness of existing institutions and conventions.[15] Through some additional steps (which need not detain us here, as they are dependent upon the persuasiveness of the initial steps in the argument), Apel thinks that discourse ethics can provide us with the tools by which to address pressing contemporary moral and political problems, including multiculturalism and globalization.[16]

At the heart of Apel's argument is the claim that we must recognize that what is moral is something that is always the subject of intersubjective argument and agreement, rather than (as in Kant's moral philosophy) a question consciousness poses to itself. This means that moral arguments are embedded in history and culture, but what seems to be a problem for universalist claims also provides the solution to that problem. For in arguing about what is moral, in inevitably particularistic ways, we also and inescapably invoke the transcendental presuppositions of any and *all* discourse. Reflection upon these allows us to see that whatever the merits or otherwise of the moral issue in question, there are certain parameters, part substantive and part procedural, that we simply cannot deny without "performative self-contradiction," the knockout phrase at the heart of his argument, and one that Apel repeats again and again. These inescapable and hence universal presuppositions of argument cannot be rationally denied because "the very attempt to do so brings them into play,"[17] thereby unwittingly affirming the universal presuppositions underlying argumentation in general.

This "transcendental-pragmatic" reformulation of Kant is ingenious, but the problems with it are also numerous. Habermas, who describes Apel as

---

[14] Apel, *Response of Discourse Ethics*, 59.

[15] Apel, *Response of Discourse Ethics*, 72. Or as he goes on to say, discourse ethics provides "an ultimate foundation of an [sic] universally valid, and thus far history-independent principle of ethics that allows us a critical stand with regards to the morally relevant facts of history, as eg institutions, conventions and habits of action" (74).

[16] See Apel, "Globalisation and the Need," 137–55, and "Discourse Ethics, Democracy, and International Law: Towards a Globalization of Practical Reason," in Steven V. Hicks and David E. Shannon (eds.), *The Challenges of Globalization: Rethinking Nature, Culture, and Freedom*, Oxford: Blackwell, 2007.

[17] Apel, "Normatively Grounding Critical Theory," 140.

his "philosophical mentor"[18] and was his collaborator in the early stages of the development of this "discourse theory," later came to argue that while this theory was invaluable inasmuch as it could ground the presuppositions of argument, it could not in and of itself thereby also ground common norms of action and behavior. As Habermas put it, "It is by no means self-evident that rules that are unavoidable *within* discourses can also claim to be valid for regulating actions *outside* of discourses . . . a separate justification is required to explain why the normative content discovered in the pragmatic presuppositions of *argumentation* should have the power to *regulate action*."[19]

The problems run much deeper than this, however. Apel seeks to preserve the force of Kant's transcendental argument while making it social and historical. But once (self-)consciousness is replaced by discourse—that is, once the point of departure is not an abstract consciousness but intersubjectivity—attempts at finding a "form" or "procedure" that is implicit in every context and is thus context independent will in fact always, wittingly or unwittingly, make presumptions that are not "merely" formal, procedural, or minimal. As Alasdair MacIntyre points out, Kant himself addressed a very specific reading public, "with its own stock of shared assumptions, expectations and focus of attention"; and as with Kant's public, so with others: "What is regarded as obvious or taken for granted, what is treated as problematic, which considerations have more weight and which less, which rhetorical modes are acceptable and which not, vary from reading public to reading public."[20] That is, what counts as an argument, who the legitimate participants in public argumentation are (everyone? only those over eighteen? only men? only community elders?), what form a valid argument must take, and so on, will vary according to context. The claim that truth or validity claims necessarily entail

---

[18] Habermas, "Reply to My Critics," in Craig Calhoun, Eduardo Mendieta, and Jonathan VanAntwerpen (eds.), *Habermas and Religion*, Cambridge: Polity Press, 2013, 377.

[19] Habermas, "Discourse Ethics: Notes on a Program of Philosophical Justification," in his *Moral Consciousness and Communicative Action*, translated by Christian Lenhardt and Shierry Weber Nicholsen, Cambridge: Polity Press, 1990, 85–86. On this see also "On the Architectonics of Discourse Differentiation: A Brief Response to a Major Controversy," in Habermas, *Between Naturalism and Religion: Philosophical Essays*, translated by Ciaran Cronin, Cambridge: Polity Press, 2008.

[20] Alasdair MacIntyre, "Some Enlightenment Projects Reconsidered," in Kearney and Dooley, *Questioning Ethics*, 248. And "Just as what Kant took to be the principles and presuppositions of natural science as such turned out to be the principles and presuppositions specific to Newtonian physics, so what Kant took to be the principles and presuppositions of morality as such turned out after all to be the principles and presuppositions of one highly specific morality, a secularized version of Protestantism that furnished modern liberal individualism with one of its founding charters." MacIntyre, "The Relationship of Philosophy to History: Postscript to the Second Edition of *After Virtue*," in Kenneth Baynes, James Bohman, and Thomas McCarthy (eds.), *After Philosophy: End or Transformation?*, Cambridge, MA: MIT Press, 1987, 413–14.

the free, equal, and uncoerced participation of all affected is the presupposition of discourse only in a modern, liberal community. As Michael Walzer
notes of theories that seek to abstract form from content, or procedure from
substance, "The procedural minimum turns out to be rather more than minimal. . . . The [procedural] rules of engagement constitute in fact a way of
life. How could they not? Men and women who acknowledge each other's
equality, claim the rights of free speech, and practice the virtues of tolerance
and mutual respect, don't leap from the philosopher's mind like Athena from
the head of Zeus. They are creatures of history."[21] Thus when philosophers (in
this case Apel) "abstract" a universal minimal morality from argument, "The
minimal morality prescribed by these theories is simply abstracted from, and
not very far from, contemporary democratic culture."[22]

The "knockdown" character and the polemical force of Apel's argument
derives from the claim that the presumptions underlying public argumentation cannot be denied without self-refutation; to dispute these presumptions
is unwittingly to affirm them. But ideas such as "inescapable universal presupposition" are neither universal nor inescapable. Barbara Herrnstein
Smith points out that "such concepts and their sense of inherent meanings
and deep interconnectedness are, rather, the products and effects of rigorous instruction and routine participation in a particular conceptual tradition and its related idiom," and instruction and participation "in some
other conceptual tradition, and familiarity with its idiom" would yield other
conceptions and descriptions of "what is presupposed by 'the very act of assertion.'"[23] It does not take too much imagination to think of communities
possessed of conceptual traditions and idioms in which the act of assertion
does not posit that all members are party to the debate, and in which the rules
by which debate is conducted and resolved are not those of a liberal democratic culture. Such communities exist—that is precisely why debates over
universalism occur, else they would be redundant. If the aim of such debates
is to persuade those who do not already reason out of "our" conceptual tradition, then smuggling in presuppositions that are necessarily those of historically particular communities, while claiming "unavoidable" or "inescapable"
status for them, is far from convincing. There is, in short, a circularity built

---

[21] Michael Walzer, *Thick and Thin: Moral Argument at Home and Abroad*, Notre Dame, IN: University of Notre Dame Press, 1994, 12.

[22] Walzer, *Thick and Thin*, 13.

[23] Barbara Herrnstein Smith, *Belief and Resistance: Dynamics of Contemporary Intellectual Controversy*, Cambridge, MA: Harvard University Press, 1997, 80.

into Apel's argument:[24] a transcendental argument "works," if at all, with a solitary, and hence dehistoricized, consciousness. Once made empirical and historical, transcendental arguments become circular, assuming what they are meant to "ground."

Rawls and the Liberal Public

John Rawls's *A Theory of Justice* draws upon Kant to seek to arrive at more or less universal principles of justice that could be affirmed by all. The "original position"—Rawls's ingenious thought experiment in which people deprived of knowledge of their particular circumstances are shown to "rationally" opt for the core principles of justice—is an attempt "to detach the structure of Kant's doctrine from its background in transcendental idealism and to give it a procedural interpretation";[25] and the principles of justice Rawls concludes would be chosen by those placed in the original position are "categorical imperatives in Kant's sense."[26] The universalist thrust of Rawls's theory is less assertive than Apel's (his magnum opus is presented as "a" rather than "the" theory of justice), but its Kantian ambition to arrive at a set of principles that would be accepted by any rational person, and which are thus of universal applicability, is unmistakable and is affirmed in its rousing last paragraph: "To see our place in society from the perspective of this [original] position is to see it *sub specie aeternitatis*: it is to regard the human situation *not only from all social but also from all temporal points of view*. The perspective of eternity is not a perspective from a certain place beyond the world, nor the point of view of a transcendent being; rather it is a certain form of thought and feeling that rational persons can adopt within the world . . . arrive[ing] together at regulative principles that can be affirmed by everyone as he lives by them, each from his own standpoint."[27]

Even in the midst of the first rapturous responses to *A Theory of Justice*, there were some who argued that what Rawls presented as principles of

[24] As Smith pithily puts it, the "re-grounding of transcendental rationalism centers on the demonstration of the inescapable necessity of (its conception of) reason as validated by the exposure of the inescapable performative contradiction of anyone denying it"; but as the argument depends "on the prior acceptance of just the system of ideas, claims and definitions at issue," "the supposed re-grounding is thoroughly circular" (*Belief and Resistance*, 118).

[25] Rawls, *Political Liberalism*, New York: Columbia University Press, 1996, 285 (hereafter cited as *PL*).

[26] Rawls, *A Theory of Justice*, New York: Oxford University Press, 1972, 253.

[27] Rawls, *A Theory of Justice*, 587; emphasis added.

justice that would be chosen sub specie aeternitatis would in fact be chosen only by those who were already members of a liberal society and who had internalized its individualism, its conception of rationality, and the absolute moral priority it assigned to autonomy.[28] Partly in response to these criticisms, in essays subsequent to *A Theory of Justice*, and culminating in *Political Liberalism*, Rawls reformulated his theory. His principles of justice remained unchanged, but the procedure for arriving at and justifying them changed very substantially. Rawls now proposed a "political" liberalism that explicitly renounced quasi-transcendental foundations, and which was presented as a theory fit specifically for liberal democracies. Previously I suggested, with reference to Apel, that Kant-influenced arguments smuggle in as presumptions what they purport to arrive at as conclusions. Part of the importance of Rawls's later work is that he recognized this to be so and reformulated his theory accordingly. Thus here what I offer is not a critique of Rawls, but rather an analysis of the logic that led him from Kantian universalism to a position that renounced claims to "truth" and recalibrated its claims such that they were limited to specific societies possessed of a particular history.

A Theory of Justice had been concerned, far more explicitly and consistently than Apel's discourse ethics, with a "public" Reason, and specifically with a conception of justice that could be shown to be in some sense rational and true, and that could be endorsed by a public composed of individuals with differing ideas of the good and pursuing diverse ends.[29] However, Rawls subsequently came to see that the project of finding or founding such a conception of justice was "unrealistic" or "impossible" because "a plurality of reasonable yet incompatible comprehensive doctrines is the normal result of the exercise of human reason."[30] The liberal values associated with Kant, Rousseau, and John Stuart Mill, Rawls now declared, are not values for which some independent verification can be found, such that they can be shown to be superior to, or to subsume, other comprehensive doctrines. They are "reasonable" but not "rational," where the latter means "true" and therefore (in Kantian fashion) compelling acceptance by all rational beings.[31] Religious

---

[28] Including Steven Lukes, "No Archimedean Point (a Review of John Rawls's *A Theory of Justice*)," in his *Essays in Social Theory*, London: Macmillan, 1977, and Robert Paul Wolff, *Understanding Rawls: A Reconstruction and Critique of "A Theory of Justice"*, Princeton, NJ: Princeton University Press, 1977.

[29] See *PL*, xviii and xlii.

[30] *PL*, xviii.

[31] On the distinction between "reasonable" and "rational" see *PL*, especially 48ff.

doctrines are also "reasonable," and thus to claim universality for liberal ideals—to claim that they are more true than, or subsume, other doctrines, including religious ones—is illegitimate, just as claiming that Catholicism must be the basis for a shared public life would be. "As comprehensive moral ideals, autonomy and individuality are unsuited for a political conception of justice. As found in Kant and J. S. Mill, these comprehensive ideals, despite their very great importance in liberal thought, are extended too far when presented as the only appropriate foundation for a constitutional regime. So understood," concludes Rawls, "liberalism becomes but another sectarian doctrine."[32]

Kantian projects to discover and elaborate a foundation that must undergird any political order are now declared to be fruitless projects: "Philosophy as the search for truth about an independent metaphysical and moral order cannot, I believe, provide a workable and shared basis for a political conception of justice in a democratic society."[33] And because there can be no compelling case for a comprehensive moral and political doctrine, any attempt to elevate one comprehensive doctrine above all others in public life—even the tradition of liberalism we associate with Kant and Mill—would be illiberal, and indeed would require the unacceptable and oppressive use of state power, as in the case—the startling analogy Rawls makes—of the Inquisition.[34]

The proceduralism of A Theory of Justice is, in short, now found wanting. Rawls acknowledges that attempts to abstract a "form" or "procedure" from content or substance can never be procedural enough: these always elevate one "substantive" (or in Rawls's language, "comprehensive") set of ideas or values over others. The "political" liberalism he elaborates and defends in later works seeks to be neutral in such matters, by elaborating principles of justice that can underpin a legitimate political order *without* favoring any one comprehensive doctrine over another. The strategy is to "bypass religion and philosophy's profoundest controversies."[35] "Rather than confronting religious and nonliberal doctrines with a comprehensive liberal philosophical

---

[32] Rawls, "Justice as Fairness: Political Not Metaphysical," *Philosophy and Public Affairs* 14:3 (Summer 1985), 245–46. "Kant's doctrine," writes Rawls, "is a comprehensive moral view in which the ideal of autonomy has a regulative role for all of life . . . as such it is not suitable to provide a public basis of justification" (*PL*, 99). Rawls writes that *A Theory of Justice* had mistakenly sought to defend and elaborate one such comprehensive doctrine above, or subsuming, others (see *PL*, xviii and xlii).

[33] Rawls, "Justice as Fairness: Political Not Metaphysical," 230. And thus, "Political liberalism must . . . reject Kant's constitutive autonomy" (*PL*, 100).

[34] *PL*, 37.

[35] *PL*, 152.

doctrine," Rawls writes, his aim "is to formulate a liberal political conception that these nonliberal doctrines may be able to endorse."[36]

Thus in Rawls's reworked version of justice as fairness, the project of affirming one set of principles or one doctrine as "true" or "rational" is abandoned. There is no transcendental warrant for fundamental liberal values such as autonomy and individualism, and to insist that these should be the public values underpinning the political order is as sectarian and unreasonable as the position of those who would insist (for example) that salvation is the highest good, that there is no salvation outside the church, and that the public order should be based upon these principles. To base a political order on any one comprehensive doctrine would require the oppressive use of state power and would be neither fair nor just nor liberal. We must simply accept that the citizenry will always consist of people and communities with diverse ethical commitments, and that there is no prospect of all citizens coming to agree upon one comprehensive doctrine.

However, this does not mean there is no prospect for a shared public life based around a shared conception of justice. Precisely because there are different comprehensive doctrines within the polity, it is in the interests of all to accept public values that accord the diverse members of the polity equal political and civic liberty, fair equality of opportunity, economic reciprocity, and mutual respect between citizens. These values or principles are not arrived at transcendentally (as true or right or inescapable), but nor are they, as in a Venn diagram, simply the area of overlap between different doctrines: they are instead "freestanding," that is, affirmed in their own right as normative and moral ideals. Political liberalism is "dualist": the political sphere and the sphere of comprehensive moral doctrines are separated out, so that a case may be made that the liberalism that is endorsed in the political sphere is not derived from the liberalism of Kant and Mill, but is rather what would be endorsed by the followers of all "reasonable" comprehensive doctrines, including nonliberal ones. This is reflected in Rawls's language—the contrast is not between "procedural" or formal principles that are abstracted out from substantive doctrines and then shown to be presupposed by all such doctrines, but rather between "comprehensive doctrines" on the one hand, and commonly affirmed principles that underpin public and political life on the other.

[36] *PL*, xlvii.

This dualism, Rawls explains, is not based upon the political and philosophical claim that politics and morality, or politics and religion, are two distinct spheres, for this claim is precisely one of the characteristics of "comprehensive" or "metaphysical" liberalism, and thus to affirm this as a truth about politics and morality would be to privilege one comprehensive doctrine over others. The dualism rather derives from a specific history. The religious wars following upon the Reformation culminated in the affirmation of religious toleration, first for pragmatic reasons, as the "only workable alternative to endless and destructive civil strife," but with this modus vivendi later developing into a consensus, actively affirmed.[37] That is, the parties to the religious wars that ravaged Europe came eventually to accept the principle of toleration, not because they resiled from their religious commitments, but because they recognized that the cost of seeking to impose them were too high. What was initially a modus vivendi eventually became part of political and public culture; an acceptance that "equal liberty of conscience and freedom of thought"[38] for all was the proper state of affairs, a value in its own right. This is the history that shaped the democratic constitutional states that subsequently emerged in Europe, and it provides the basis for an "overlapping consensus" affirming the principles of justice as fairness, and political liberalism, even from those who do not subscribe to the values of Kant, Hume, or Mill. This liberalism does not aim at being formal or procedural, but is unabashedly "substantive," "in the sense that it springs from and belongs to the tradition of liberal thought and the larger community of political culture of democratic societies."[39] It is "political" in that it is not based upon a public affirmation of any one doctrine, but rather on an agreement that in the *political* realm, equality and equality of opportunity, economic reciprocity, and civility in public life are affirmed by those who in other respects continue to cleave to other values and doctrines.

What is striking about Rawls's recast argument is that the historical source as well as the inspiration for political liberalism is found not in the Enlightenment search for principles of rational justification that could be shown to be independent of context, but rather in a very specific historical context of the Reformation: "The historical origin of political liberalism (and

---

[37] *PL*, 159.

[38] *PL*, xxviii.

[39] *PL*, 432. This passage comes from Rawls's "Reply to Habermas," included in *Political Liberalism*; here Rawls distances himself from the "formal," "universal," and "quasi-transcendental" arguments of Habermas.

of liberalism more generally)," Rawls writes, "is the Reformation and its aftermath, with the long controversies over religious toleration in the sixteenth and seventeenth centuries."[40] The principle of toleration provides both a model and the necessary historical precondition for political liberalism. The project of justice as fairness and political liberalism, he writes, "would complete and extend the movement of thought that began three centuries ago with the gradual acceptance of the principle of toleration. . . . To apply the principle of toleration to philosophy itself is to leave to citizens themselves to settle the questions of religion, philosophy and morals in accordance with views they freely affirm."[41]

The Kantian strategy that has influenced so much contemporary moral and political thinking was very much in evidence in *A Theory of Justice*, where Rawls sought to ground a certain version of liberalism by making a distinction between procedure and content, form and substance. He later came to recognize that this "proceduralism" in fact contained a great deal that was "substantive"; that it in fact presupposed and endorsed, in his chosen language, a "comprehensive doctrine." Instead of seeking to further "purify" this proceduralism, in his later work Rawls proposes instead a dualism—a distinction between a nonpolitical realm where different moralities legitimately coexist, and where there is no way of rationally affirming any one morality over others; and a political realm where notwithstanding differences between doctrines, common principles of public life are embraced. Whether *Political Liberalism* is persuasive or not is not my concern here;[42] what is of interest is that Rawls explicitly abandons the earlier attempt to deduce a moral universalism, and indeed declares this to be a mistaken and unachievable ambition. Further, his reformulated theory explicitly presupposes a specifically European history—the events of the Reformation and the subsequent religious wars, and later the slow rise of religious toleration—as the backdrop to the shared culture that he thinks will provide an overlapping consensus for the values of political liberalism. This immediately suggests that his argument is addressed to, and is relevant to, only those peoples and places that share this history, and is not generalizable, let alone universalizable. And indeed, in "The Law of Peoples," where Rawls extends the ideas of political

[40] *PL*, xxvi.

[41] *PL*, 154.

[42] In "Liberalism and the Politics of (Multi)culture: or, Plurality Is Not Difference," *Postcolonial Studies* 4:1 (2001), I argued that it is not persuasive, and that is still my view, though I now think that in this essay I failed to sufficiently recognize the dualist nature of Rawls's later arguments, misreading them instead as an attempt at a more "purified" proceduralism.

liberalism to the international domain, he does not argue that these principles should be embraced by all societies, but on the contrary that "not all regimes can reasonably be required to be liberal; otherwise the law of peoples itself would not express liberalism's own principle of toleration for other reasonable ways of ordering society."[43] Here Rawls argues that members of good standing in an international order must "respect the principles of peace and not be expansionist . . . meet the essentials of legitimacy in the eyes of its own people, and . . . honour human rights,"[44] but they may have an established religion (as long as they do not persecute the adherents of other religions), and they need not regard their members as free and equal citizens.[45]

Rawls is an instance of a philosopher—and a particularly distinguished and influential one—who sought to find and defend context-transcending principles of Reason, but who came to abandon that project. One of the reasons for doing so, as shown by the subsequent direction of his work, is a recognition that there is no effective formal or procedural defense of modern morality and of liberal politics. It is not surprising then that those committed to defending a context-independent and thus universal morality are dismayed by Rawls's later work and regard it as an ignominious retreat from his earlier ideas. In Apel's reading, having given up on a philosophical foundation for a universal conception of justice, Rawls "has recourse only to the historical genesis of the conditions of the modern democratic societies of the West,"[46] a "surrender" he describes as "disastrous."[47] Kukathas and Pettit, in an appreciative account of Rawls's *A Theory of Justice*, find that in his later work "Rawls comes to abandon Kant," offering instead "a particular (liberal democratic American) social conception of what is reasonable which *subordinates* considerations of rationality"; in their view, "Rawls has taken an unfortunate turn."[48] Brian Barry, who had similarly written a highly appreciative account

[43] Rawls, "The Law of Peoples," in Stephen Shute and S. Hurley (eds.), *On Human Rights: The Oxford Amnesty Lectures, 1993*, New York: Basic Books, 1993, 42–43.

[44] Rawls, "The Law of Peoples," 79.

[45] In his revised and expanded version of this argument—*The Law of Peoples*, Cambridge, MA: Harvard University Press, 1999—Rawls hypothesizes a state/peoples he calls "Kazanistan," in which Islam is the favored religion, religion and state are not separated, and only Muslims can occupy higher political and juridical offices. Since in this hypothetical country religious minorities are allowed to freely practise their religion, and their fundamental interests are taken into account in decision-making, Kazanistan passes Rawls's test and is deemed to be a nonliberal but "decent" society that merits being treated as a member of good standing in the international order (75–78).

[46] Apel, "The Problem of Justice in a Multicultural Society," in Kearney and Dooley, *Questioning Ethics*, 153–54.

[47] Apel, *Response of Discourse Ethics*, 108.

[48] Chandran Kukathas and Philip Pettit, *Rawls: "A Theory of Justice" and Its Critics*, Stanford, CA: Stanford University Press, 1990, 139, 129, and 148.

of *A Theory of Justice* soon after it was published,[49] subsequently and dismissively wrote, "Rawls has by now abandoned most of the ideas that made *A Theory of Justice* worthwhile. I have no interest in defending anything Rawls has written since about 1975."[50]

Habermas and "Occidental Rationalism"

Heir to the Frankfurt school of critical theory and thus to a tradition of thinking in which Kant, Hegel, Weber, and Marx loom large, Habermas seeks to show that post-Enlightenment knowledge marks an advance over all knowledges that preceded it, while denying that the dominance of instrumental rationality and a disastrous "dialectic of Enlightenment" is an inevitable correlate of Reason. In pursuit of this project, Habermas embraces the hermeneutical insight that social theory is not the same as natural science and hence cannot be modeled on it, while still seeking to find room for causal or quasi-causal explanations that are not necessarily available to the actors; and that thus afford a vantage point for criticism that is at once "etic" (not constrained by the actors' self-understandings) yet "immanent" (not an abstract and external vantage point from which critique is launched). Related to this, Habermas grants that there is no context-independent knowledge, while denying that this leads to the conclusion that all knowledges are creatures of their time and place. Habermas agrees that it is necessary to historicize and thus "detranscendentalize" Reason, but the question, as he poses it, is "whether the traces of a transcending reason vanish in the sands of historicism and contextualism or whether a reason embodied in historical contexts preserves the power of immanent transcendence."[51] As the rhetorical nature of the question indicates, Habermas thinks that Reason can be historicized and yet transcend its historical contexts, and provide an immanent basis for criticism and emancipation.

---

[49] Brian Barry, *The Liberal Theory of Justice: A Critical Examination of the Principal Doctrines in "A Theory of Justice" by John Rawls*, New York: Oxford University Press, 1973.

[50] Brian Barry, *Culture and Equality*, Cambridge: Polity Press, 2001, 331 n. 27. In a sympathetic engagement with Rawls's later work, Joseph Raz nonetheless argues that what he dubs Rawls's "epistemic abstinence"—the refusal to defend his theory of justice on the grounds that it is "true"—is a mistake. "There can be no justice," concludes Raz, "without truth." "Facing Diversity: The Case of Epistemic Abstinence," *Philosophy and Public Affairs* 19:1 (January 1990), 15.

[51] Habermas, "Communicative Action and the Detranscendentalized 'Use of Reason,'" in his *Between Naturalism and Religion*, 25.

Both these elements have remained integral parts of a project that has been pursued with remarkable consistency over many decades. However, in part because of changes in the intellectual environment—with positivist dominance receding, and "contextualist" challenges (often attributed by Habermas to a generic "postmodernism") coming to the fore[52]—the second has received special attention in Habermas's more recent work.

Habermas engages sympathetically with the work of Rawls, but he wants to show that principles of justice are legitimate not because they could be accepted by all, but rather that they should be accepted because they are legitimate, that is to say, are true.[53] Moreover, whereas Rawls's argument is confined to the moral/political domain, Habermas's ambitions are greater—he wishes to defend not only moral universality, but also claims to the truth and universality of the natural and human sciences. Habermas co-produced, with Apel, the claim that discourse necessarily and inescapably involves context-transcending presumptions that cannot be denied without self-contradiction, and he continues to advance this claim in subsequent works. However and as seen previously, he recognizes (or came to recognize) that it is not possible to extrapolate from discourse theory to "ground" or legitimate institutions and practices. He further acknowledges that since discourse is always embedded in institutions and practices, any Kantian defense of Reason must also be a defense of the modernity within which it is enmeshed. Thus as with Apel and Rawls, Habermas's project is indebted to Kant, but he also draws upon Hegel. In McCarthy's pithy characterization, Habermas wants to deploy "Kant's claim that there are universal and unavoidable presuppositions of theoretical and practical reason," but "he also wants, thinking now more with Hegel, to present a reconstructed conception of the *Bildungsprozesse*,

---

[52] And also, arguably, because Habermas's radical political ambitions have receded, and he has become a defender of social-democratic liberalism rather than one who seeks to surpass it.

[53] Habermas finds Rawls's strategy of avoiding moral controversies over substantive issues to not be feasible: "The concept of practical reason cannot be drained of moral substance and morality cannot be relegated to the black box of comprehensive doctrines. I cannot see any plausible alternative to the straightforward Kantian strategy." "'Reasonable' versus 'True,' or the Morality of Worldviews," in Habermas translated by Ciaran Cronin and Pablo De Grieff, *The Inclusion of the Other: Studies in Political Theory*, Cambridge, MA: MIT Press, 1998, 99. In the same essay Habermas suggests that Rawls needs to recognize that there are "requirements of practical reason that *constrain* rational comprehensive doctrines rather than merely *reflect* their felicitous overlapping" (78). As Finlayson characterizes Habermas's difference with Rawls, "Habermas objects that Rawls's political conception of justice sacrifices its cognitive status (its rational acceptability) to its functional or instrumental aim of ensuring social stability"; by contrast, for Habermas "Only those norms are justified that are rationally acceptable (that is, that *deserve* to be accepted by all) on the grounds that they demonstrably embody a universalizable interest." James Gordon Finlayson, *Habermas: A Very Short Introduction*, New York: Oxford University Press, 2005, 102; emphasis added.

the self-formative process of the individual and the species that have rational autonomy as their telos—a kind of systematic history of reason."[54] Habermas seeks a defense of modern knowledge that is also a defense of modernity, and one that very explicitly and unapologetically seeks, in his words, to connect "a claim to *universality* with our *Occidental understanding of the world.*"[55] Such an Occidental understanding is not merely one of many traditions of reasoning, as is suggested by "contextualists," who "maintain that the transition to post-metaphysical concepts of nature, to post-traditional ideas of law and morality [i.e., to what I have been calling modern, Western knowledge], only characterizes one tradition amongst others"; against this, Habermas declares in an interview, "I don't see how this thesis can be seriously defended. I think that Max Weber was right . . . [about] the general cultural significance of Western rationalism."[56] Whereas Apel's work and that of the early Rawls sought to show that modern knowledge was true and universal *even* though it had arisen in the West, Habermas argues that this knowledge is rational and universal *because*, not despite the fact, that it is modern and Western.

Why should we privilege modern Western knowledge? Habermas suggests that it is possible, even if somewhat speculatively, to "reconstruct the empirical succession of worldviews as a series of steps in learning," and that the history of worldviews of nonmodern and modern societies displays "an internally reconstructible growth of knowledge."[57] Habermas provides a speculative reconstruction of this growth, by means of a contrast between the mythical worldview of nonmoderns (specifically, the "savages" studied by anthropologists) and modern knowledge. Drawing upon a very narrow and selective reading of the anthropological literature available at the time, Habermas concludes that the most striking feature of savage, mythological thought is that it is "totalizing," relating everything to everything else; and

[54] Thomas McCarthy, "Rationality and Relativism: Habermas's 'Overcoming' of Hermeneutics," in John B. Thompson and David Held (eds.), *Habermas: Critical Debates*, London: Macmillan, 1982, 59.

[55] Jürgen Habermas, *The Theory of Communicative Action*, translated by Thomas McCarthy, vol. 1, Cambridge: Polity Press, 1984, 44 (hereafter cited as *TCA 1*). Habermas approvingly quotes Weber to the effect that any person who is a product of modern European civilization "is bound to ask himself, and rightly so, to what combination of circumstances the fact should be attributed that in Western civilization, and in Western civilization only, the cultural phenomena have appeared which (at least we like to think) lie on a line of development having *universal* significance and validity." But Habermas detects in the qualification "at least we like to think" an unfortunate concession to "relativism" and chides Weber for it!

[56] "Discourse, Ethics, Law and *Sittlichkeit*" (interview by T. Huiid Nielsen, January 1990), in Peter Dews (ed.), *Autonomy and Solidarity: Interviews with Jürgen Habermas*, rev. ed., London: Verso, 1992, 254.

[57] Habermas, *TCA 1*, 67, 66.

that as a consequence it is marked by a "confusion between nature and culture," and between "culture and internal nature or the subjective world."[58]
Because culture and nature have not been separated out from one another,
the mythological worldview is not even aware that it is a worldview, that, for
instance, animism and magic are superimpositons or projections of culture
onto nature.[59] For this reason, as well as the fact that intellectual traditions
are accepted on authority, savage thought is not open to questioning or to
revision.

With the transition from "archaic" to "developed civilizations"—in later
works Habermas will borrow Jasper's concept of an "Axial Age" to characterize this allegedly world-historical shift—mythological thought is replaced
by argument and reflection, though the first and highest principles, the
foundations of this worldview, "are themselves removed from argumentation and immunized against objections."[60] With the advent of modern
thought, even the highest principles or foundations of the modern worldview "lost their unquestionable character,"[61] and "a growing decentration
of interpretive systems . . . [led] to an ever-clearer categorical demarcation
of the subjectivity of internal nature from the objectivity of external nature,
as well as from the normativity of social reality and the intersubjectivity
of linguistic reality."[62] That is, modern thought came to recognize that the
objective, social, and subjective worlds fundamentally differ from one another, and that "propositional truth, normative rightness [and] subjective
truthfulness" belong to different domains and require different attitudes and
protocols of reasoning, namely the "objectivating, norm-conformative, and
expressive."[63] This allowed for development within each of these spheres—
for example, natural scientific inquiries were no longer constrained by religious requirements, and art become an exploration of subjectivity rather
than being subordinated to exiguous concerns. This "decentration" was
cause and effect of increasing reflexivity. Borrowing a distinction from Karl
Popper and Robin Horton, Habermas concludes that mythological and premodern worldviews are "closed," that is, are not capable of reflecting upon

---

[58] Habermas, *TCA 1*, 51.

[59] "Mythical worldviews are not understood by members as interpretive systems that are attached
to cultural traditions . . . and thus exposed to criticism and open to revision" (*TCA 1*, 52–53).

[60] Habermas, *Communication and the Evolution of Society*, translated by Thomas McCarthy,
London: Heinemann, 1979, 105.

[61] Habermas, *Evolution of Society*, 105.

[62] Habermas, *Evolution of Society*, 106.

[63] Habermas, *TCA 1*, 71.

and correcting their own presuppositions, whereas modern thought is re-flexive and "open."

So far, so-very-much a standard whiggish account of why we moderns are right whereas our historical predecessors were wrong, and why modern Western societies are reflexive whereas other, "savage" and "traditional," societies immunize their deepest beliefs from criticism. This account is more-over drawn from a highly selective reading of the anthropological literature of the 1960s and 1970s, containing presumptions and arguments that would, as we saw in chapter 1, be repudiated by many or most anthropologists today. What, in any case, are the *arguments* behind the reiteration of these by now rather shopworn and self-congratulatory Enlightenment distinctions?

One argument is that the development of worldviews parallels the cognitive and moral development of individual humans from childhood to adulthood: the ways in which peoples understand and engage with their world display "developmental-logical correlations with ontogenesis,"[64] because "the reproduction of society and the socialization of its members are two aspects of the same process," "dependent on the same structures."[65] Habermas is aware of, but nonetheless boldly undeterred by, the problems of drawing analogies between the development of an individual from childhood to adulthood and the development of worldviews or knowledges. He is simi-larly undeterred by the fact that such analogies have a long and unpleasant history, as justifications for the enslavement and colonization of irrational, childlike "races" by mature and rational ones. In *Theory of Communicative Action* and the earlier *Communication and the Evolution of Society* Habermas draws upon the work of Jean Piaget and Lawrence Kohlberg on the cognitive and moral development of children in order to establish homologies. At the center of a child's development is not this or that content of knowledge, but rather "the decentration of an egocentric understanding of the world."[66] A baby cannot distinguish between itself and the world; there are no bound-aries between its corporeal body and the world. Later the child learns to dif-ferentiate itself from nature, and from society, and then as a youth, learns that social principles and norms are humanly created, and thus criticizable and revisable. Later still, the "competent adult" now distinguishes between the ex-ternal world of nature, the social world, and his or her subjective world, and

---

[64] Habermas, *Evolution of Society*, 104.
[65] Habermas, *Evolution of Society*, 99.
[66] Habermas, *TCA 1*, 69.

recognizes that the statements or "validity claims" in each of these has its own protocols. All this, Habermas asserts—albeit with qualifications—roughly corresponds to the progression of mythical, axial, and modern worldviews. And just as once we are adult we cannot go "backward" to a child's point of view, so too with worldviews: "With the transition to a new stage the interpretations of the superseded stage are . . . *categorially devalued*. It is not this or that reason, but the *kind* of reason, which is no longer convincing. . . . These devaluative shifts appear to be connected with socio-evolutionary transitions to new levels of learning."[67]

Such a stadial ranking of knowledges and cultures has a long history, but it has been subjected to many criticisms on historical, political, and ethical grounds. The claim that history shows development and intellectual advance, and that modern cultures and knowledge are superior to "premodern" knowledges, is certainly a staple of post-Enlightenment worldviews, but it has always been a premise rather than an empirically arrived at conclusion.[68] The premise remained unaltered even as the grounds on which such distinctions were made changed, as claims to Western superiority shifted from its religion to its science.[69] For Habermas and those sympathetic to his project, the indubitable superiority of modern science is at the core of the claim for modern and Occidental superiority.[70] But even if we were to grant that the "scientific revolution" discovered a method that arrived at truths about "nature"—and we have seen in the previous chapter that many scholars of science would not grant this, because they suggest that the undoubted efficacy of science does not derive from its capacity to accurately "represent" the (invented object) "nature"—it does not thereby follow that the social sciences are also morally and aesthetically superior. Centuries of slavery and colonialism, two world wars, and a Holocaust surely call into question the presumption that the modern age has been marked by learning and progress in social, moral, and political matters. (If they do not, it is hard to imagine what would do so!). The claim is equally tenuous for art, unless one subscribes, as

[67] Habermas, *TCA 1*, 68.

[68] See Ronald Meek, *Social Science and the Ignoble Savage*, Cambridge: Cambridge University Press, 1976; Christopher Berry, *Social Theory of the Scottish Enlightenment*, Edinburgh: Edinburgh University Press, 1997; and especially, Gurminder Bhambra, *Rethinking Modernity: Postcolonialism and the Sociological Imagination*, New York: Palgrave Macmillan, 2007.

[69] See Stephen Gaukroger, *The Emergence of a Scientific Culture: Science and the Shaping of Modernity, 1210–1685*, Oxford: Clarendon Press, 2006, especially 11.

[70] Thus Thomas McCarthy writes, "It would be difficult—bordering-on-the-impossible to produce . . . a *warranted* denial that there has been a significant learning process underway in regard at least to our *technical* understanding of nature" ("Part 1," 48).

Habermas appears to, to a very modernist understanding of art, one in which the "autonomization" of art—the insistence that art is about inwardness and subjectivity, "purified of cognitive and moral admixtures"[71]—is taken to be the measure of progress in art. Even Habermas's admirers and fellow thinkers have doubted that it is possible to reconstruct a process of learning in the aesthetic domain.[72]

The attempt to anchor the claim for the superiority of modern knowledge through an analogy with ontogenesis does not, in short, make for a strong argument. There is no reason to believe that individual learning and growth can be correlated with social phenomena (or even what would count as empirical evidence for such a claim) and, indeed, every reason to believe that the analogy is a bad one, as are most attempts to map individual, semibiological processes onto social and historical ones. Here too, those sympathetic to and sharing in Habermas's project have been unwilling to fully endorse his argument,[73] and in later writings Habermas has ceased to invoke it,[74] although the claim that modern worldviews are the culmination of a "learning process" remains central to his theory.

Habermas wishes to show that differentiation of the cognitive, moral, and aesthetic spheres is a sign of progress, or as he puts it in a particularly Hegelian moment, stages in the development "of the spirit."[75] But he also sees these intellectual advances as being connected to material and sociological developments, "a historical result" that "arose . . . in the midst of a specific society that possessed corresponding features."[76] This "specific society" is a modern society, a form of social organization and collective life that comes about as result of capitalism and industrialization. This gives rise to his second argument, one where the emphasis is now placed on sociological factors. Here the distinctions between the external world (the domain of theoretical reason), the moral and political world (the domain of

[71] Habermas, "Questions and Counterquestions," in Richard Bernstein (ed.), *Habermas and Modernity*, Cambridge: Polity Press, 1985, 207.
[72] See, for instance, McCarthy, "Reflections on Rationalization in *The Theory of Communicative Action*," in Bernstein, *Habermas and Modernity*.
[73] See McCarthy, "Rationality and Relativism," 69ff, and the revised version of this essay, "Reason and Rationalization: Habermas's 'Overcoming' of Hermeneutics," in McCarthy, *Ideals and Illusions: On Reconstruction and Deconstruction in Contemporary Critical Theory*, Cambridge, MA: MIT Press, 1991.
[74] Though see "Lawrence Kohlberg and Neo-Aristotelianism," in Habermas, *Justice and Application: Remarks on Discourse Ethics*, translated by Ciaran Cronin, Cambridge: Polity Press, 1993.
[75] Habermas, *Evolution of Society*, 123.
[76] Habermas, "Morality and Ethical Life: Does Hegel's Critique of Kant Apply to Discourse Ethics?," in *Moral Consciousness*, 208.

morality, law and politics), and subjective inwardness (the domain of the arts) only become possible in their fully developed form with modernity, when each of these becomes systemically separated from the others, as distinct "subsystems" of the modern lifeworld: it is thus modernity that "*objectively* affords contemporaries a privileged access to the general structures of the lifeworld."[77] In premodern societies these distinctions are not institutionalized and cannot be; modernity lies at the end of a long process of historical development, one that makes it possible to now see that making such distinctions represents a cognitive advance, that it marks the culmination (if still one-sided and imperfect) of a process of the rationalization of worldviews.[78]

In this argument, the superiority of modern Western knowledge is connected to the superiority of modernity as a social phenomenon. Modernity is moreover a product of Occidental history, which is why Habermas concurs with Weber on "the general cultural significance of Western rationalism." Since Habermas does not, like some, sing paeans of praise to "the European miracle,"[79] one could charitably read him as saying that the Occident merely "happened" to be the historical site and bearer of a historical process of social advance and rationalization. Nonetheless, once this historical process has occurred, it must constitute the "horizon" for all thinking; no one is exempt, and there is no "going back." Non-Western societies may continue to be different in some cultural ways, but the social and institutional changes that characterize modernity, and the modern Western knowledge that accompanies it—with its divisions between science, law and morality, and aesthetics—are inescapable and, furthermore, mark progress. Or as Habermas puts it, in the form of a rhetorical question to which he provides an answer,

> Are or are not the structures of scientific thought, posttraditional legal and moral representations, and autonomous art, as they have developed in the framework of Western culture, the possession of that "community of civilized men" that is present as a regulative idea? The universalist position does

[77] Habermas, *Theory of Communicative Action*, vol. 2, translated by Thomas McCarthy, Cambridge: Polity Press, 1987, 403.

[78] Habermas describes this as the "ineliminable Hegelian element" in Weber's theory of rationalization (*TCA 1*, 220).

[79] Unlike, for instance, Eric Jones, *The European Miracle*, 3rd ed., New York: Cambridge University Press, 2003; and David Landes, *The Unbound Prometheus*, Cambridge: Cambridge University Press, 1969.

not have to deny the pluralism and the incompatibility of historical versions of "civilized humanity"; but it regards this multiplicity of forms of life as limited to *cultural contents*, and it asserts that every culture must share certain *formal properties* of the modern understanding of the world. . . . Thus the universalist assumption refers to a few necessary structural properties of modern life forms as such.[80]

This second argument, one where the emphasis is now on historical-social changes rather than on cognitive advances, is subject to the same objection as the first, namely that it assumes what needs to be shown, this time in the context of social evolution rather than "learning." Even a sympathetic interlocutor like Apel wonders whether seeking to ground the claims for Reason in such an empirical and historical manner runs the risk of "giving the impression of a dogmatically posited teleological philosophy of history."[81] Habermas's project is underpinned, as Amy Allen has argued, by a notion of "progress" that is asserted rather than convincingly argued, and one that is highly contestable.[82] And indeed, it *has* been contested, by legions of anticolonial and indigenous thinkers and activists, and by the many scholars who have drawn attention to the ways in which "modernity" was not something that developed autochthonously in the West, but was from the beginning a global process, and one that was heavily dependent on the conquest, colonization, and exploitation of the non-Western world. As Allen puts it, parsing the arguments of scores of anticolonial thinkers, past and present, "The notion of historical progress as a 'fact' is bound up with complex relations of domination, exclusion and silencing of colonized and racialized subjects,"[83] and there is every reason to doubt the claim that there has been progress in history. It is striking that a scholar of Habermas's stature should be so unaware of these anticolonial, decolonial, and postcolonial arguments or, at any rate, should consistently fail to engage with them, instead assuming that the main challenge to his defense of progress and modernity comes from "postmodernism."[84]

Habermas's two arguments—namely, that modern knowledge represents a cognitive advance, and that modernity represents historical evolution and

---

[80] Habermas, *TCA 1*, 180.
[81] Apel, "Normatively Grounding Critical Theory," 147.
[82] Allen, *The End of Progress*, especially chap. 2.
[83] Allen, *The End of Progress*, 19.
[84] See especially *The Philosophical Discourse of Modernity*, translated by Frederick Lawrence, Cambridge: Polity Press, 1987.

progress—are clearly meant to reinforce each other. The division of reason into three autonomous spheres (corresponding exactly, we may note, with Kant's three critiques) marks an advance and therefore also shows that modernity, the historical "stage" in which these divisions become possible and then institutionalized, is a more advanced sociohistorical form. Conversely, modernity is a historically advanced form of social organization, and since it is characterized by a division of knowledge into three spheres, such an organization of knowledge must also be seen as an advance, and as a marker of progress. The two arguments certainly imply each other, but they do not ground each other: rather, each presupposes the validity of the other. The entire edifice of his argument, as others have also noted, is circular.[85]

In more recent works, Habermas has acknowledged that "the suspicion that mechanisms of exclusion are often embedded within the hidden presumptions of universalistic discourses is well-founded—up to a point."[86] He has even conceded that this well-founded suspicion means that the West "must be only one voice amongst many, in the hermeneutical conversation between cultures."[87] The Olympian insouciance with which the superiority of modern Western knowledge was previously affirmed has come to be supplemented, though not replaced, by the (very different) claim that as modernity has come to encompass the entire world, so that no premodern societies are left, the knowledges and institutions that accompany and characterize modernity are *unavoidable*.[88] But even in the "conversation between cultures" to which Habermas passingly refers, it is clear that modern Western knowledge will be a privileged interlocutor. Since one of the greatest cultural achievements of "Occidental rationalism" lies in "the capacity for decentring one's own perspectives, self-reflection, and a self-critical distancing from one's own traditions," even "overcoming Eurocentrism demands that the West make proper use of its own cognitive resources."[89] Moreover, adds

---

[85] See Allen, *The End of Progress*, especially 66 and 78; also Georgia Warnke, *Gadamer: Hermeneutics, Tradition and Reason*, Cambridge: Polity Press, 1987, 133–34.

[86] Habermas, "Conceptions of Modernity: A Look Back at Two Traditions," in *The Postnational Constellation: Political Essays*, translated by Max Pensky, Cambridge: Polity Press, 2001, 147.

[87] Habermas, "A Conversation about God and the World: Interview with Eduardo Mendieta," in *Religion and Rationality*, Cambridge: Polity Press, 2002, 154.

[88] See "Remarks on Legitimation through Human Rights," in *The Postnational Constellation*.

[89] Habermas, "Conversation about God," 154. Quoting this passage, Amy Allen observes—with great understatement—that "there's a certain irony involved in saying that the way to avoid Eurocentrism is for the West to celebrate its own cultural achievements, to be even more like itself: even more reflexive and self-critical than it already is." "Having One's Cake and Eating It Too: Habermas's Genealogy of Postsecular Reason," in Calhoun, Mendieta, and VanAntwerpen, *Habermas and Religion*, 152.

Habermas—without the slightest sense of irony—the critics of Occidental rationalism inadvertently confirm this, for the distance from their own tradition that is the condition of their critique is "one of the advantages of occidental rationalism"![90]

Habermas's minor "concessions" to critics do not mark any substantial departure from his argumentative strategy, which remains unchanged in essentials—and remains unpersuasive. A Kantian strategy supplemented by a Hegelian account of the progress of Reason does not overcome the problems of the first, but rather opens itself to a new set of objections. Claims to truth and universality, whether on the grounds of a cognitive learning process or on the grounds that modernity enabled progress in knowledge, presuppose what they are meant to establish; and in concert they are circular, rather than mutually validating. The ambitious attempt to show that our knowledge is universal because, rather than despite it being Western and modern, does not succeed in showing that "Occidental rationalism" is truly rational and is thus superior to any and all other forms of knowledge.

Parochializing Reason

Apel and the early Rawls draw upon Kant to show that while knowledge is always shaped by its historical and cultural contexts, modern Western knowledge nonetheless "rises above" the circumstances of its production and has warrant to be considered as knowledge tout court, rather than simply the knowledge of the modern West. Arguments of this sort are among the most important and influential reasons for regarding post-Enlightenment knowledge not simply as one among many historical and contemporary knowledges, but as different from and superior to all others. I have sought to show that this, however, presupposes what it seeks to prove, or to make the same point in a different language, that its conclusions are built into its premises. The significance of the later work of John Rawls, I have suggested, is that partly in recognition of this, he comes to the conclusion that knowledges are true or false only with reference to the particular histories with which they are intertwined. Thus Rawls's later "political liberalism" is proposed as a political system fit and proper only for that part of the world that underwent a Reformation and wars of religion and then saw the rise of "tolerance."

---

[90] Habermas, "Remarks on Legitimation," 119.

Recognizing some of the insufficiencies and problems of Kantian arguments, Habermas additionally draws upon Hegel, the prime source, along with Kant, for the valorization of modern Reason. Working with the tradition begun by Kant, Hegel's strategy for overcoming Kant's aporia was, paradoxically, to acknowledge the inescapable historicity of all categories. There is no knockdown transcendental argument that will establish the truth of certain categories once and for all, only categories through which historical communities know their world and organize their place in it. However, though the standards of modern morality are specific to modernity, modernity is itself an expression, and a higher working out, of a rationality immanent in social institutions, the most basic content of which is autonomy and free self-determination. Collective life always rests upon shared conceptions of what constitutes and legitimates the institutions of society. These shared conceptions—demonstrations that social life is the product of (collective) human thought—invariably, however, present themselves as "givens," as norms and conceptions that are a limit upon, rather than products of, human making. Social institutions and ways of life break down because these conceptions come into contradiction with the social forms with which they are associated, and the resolution of this crisis advances to the next logical/historical stage. There is teleology or progress in all this, inasmuch as each breakdown and reconstitution progresses to a "higher" level, one where the autonomy of subjectivity/spirit is more fully (if still only partially) recognized, and comes to underlie social institutions and practices. Modernity most fully "realizes" or lives out and instantiates the autonomy that is presupposed by all collective life, and modernity's self-understanding is the self-consciousness of this fact, and this is what makes it superior to other forms of knowledge. This argument treats modernity as a privileged historical moment and a privileged site, one where the facts and processes that have always governed human history finally became discernable and reveal what has always been true but could not be fully grasped till now. Reason and its discovery are here historicized, and Reason, though universal, only becomes available with the advent of the modern.

This account is in fact of wider provenance than Hegel and those directly influenced by him, and indeed has been at the heart of modern understandings of modernity and its knowledge. When in the early nineteenth century Jacob Burckhardt wrote that the "veil" that made man "conscious of himself only as a member of a race, people, party, family or corporation" finally lifted in Renaissance Italy, enabling man to recognize himself as a "spiritual individual," he was contributing to this narrative.[91] When early in the twentieth century Weber wrote that disenchantment was what allowed men to recognize the melancholy fact that the world had never been imbued with purpose and with meaning, but that all meanings and purposes "out there" were what we had "put" there, he too was making the point that it was only at a certain point in the history of humankind that certain truths could finally be discerned—truths that, however, had retrospective validity.[92] And Marx was making the same claim when he wrote that "bourgeois society is the most developed and the most complex historic organization of production. The categories which express its relations, the comprehension of its structure, thereby also allows insights into the structure and the relations of production of all the vanished social formations. . . . Human anatomy thus contains the key to the anatomy of the ape."[93]

Hegel's was the first and most important version of an argument/narrative that, in all its recensions, privileges modernity and thereby accords epistemological privilege to modern knowledge, the self-consciousness of modernity. In all versions of this narrative, premodern or "traditional" cultures, including those of the West, are presented as being in thrall to enchantments and cosmologies, whereas we moderns are regarded as having grasped (or having been forced to grasp) the bedrock truths that underpinned these misperceptions all along. This is the narrative, as Charles Taylor characterizes it, according to which "modernity involves our 'coming to see' certain kernel truths about the human condition."[94] In all versions of this narrative—Weberian, Hegelian, Marxist, Habermasian, and others—the core presumptions of modern knowledge are not yet another set of parochial assumptions claiming universal validity, like a proselytizing religion, but rather embedded in an account that purports to explain both why we humans were once bound to get things wrong, and how it became possible to get them right. This is what I have elsewhere called the "once was blind, but now can see" narrative.[95]

---

[91] Jacob Burckhardt, *The Civilization of the Renaissance in Italy*, translated by Samuel G. C. Middlemore, New York: Mentor, 1960, 121.

[92] Max Weber, "Objectivity in Social Science and Social Policy," in Edward Shils and Henry Finch (eds.), *Methodology of the Social Sciences: Max Weber*, New York: Free Press, 1949.

[93] Karl Marx, *Grundrisse*, translated by Martin Nicolaus, New York: Penguin, 1973, 105.

[94] Charles Taylor, "Two Theories of Modernity," *Public Culture* 11:1 (1999), 170.

[95] In "'Once Was Blind but Now Can See': Modernity and the Social Sciences," *International Political Sociology* 7:2 (June 2013). The preceding paragraphs are drawn from this essay.

Once knowledges are acknowledged to be historical, as they are in the preceding narratives—that is, once the transcendental argument is not the sole or chief argument—assertions of the superiority of modern knowledge rest upon the claim that transitions between worldviews mark some sort of progress. Such privileging of the modern and of modern knowledge—and thus of the modern West, which until recently was regarded as the site and source of modernity and its self-knowledge—may have once seemed self-evident, but it has ceased to be so. A chorus of criticism—ranging from specific and disciplinary problematizations encountered in the last chapter, to feminist, postmodern, postcolonial, decolonial, and other critiques—signal a changed intellectual, ethical, and political scene. These criticisms are not always consonant with one another and sometimes even contradict each other. In drawing attention to the power-knowledge nexus, some critics suggest that truth is always a matter of how "effects of truth" are produced and defined *within* epistemes and discourses; modern knowledge corresponds to a specific "regime of truth," a regime that is itself neither more true nor more false than others. Other critics have questioned the homology between modern knowledge and modernity, arguing that modernity is not only compatible with, but in fact characterized by, a variety of knowledges and social relations. Others have simply questioned our valorization of the modern, given that the proclamation of liberty, equality, fraternity, and rights coincided with conquest, genocide, the slave trade, and the growing despoliation of the environment and the very conditions of human life.

It is precisely in this new context of growing criticism and challenges that defenses of modern knowledge, and of its universality, became necessary. I have argued that these defenses, whether indebted to Kant or to Hegel, are not persuasive. Moreover, once we acknowledge the Hegelian-historicist point that the presuppositions of thought are fundamentally related to time and culture, but can no longer plausibly claim that there is a teleology at work in transitions between worldviews, then "the legacy of Hegel's historical radicalisation of Kantian modernism"[96] can only be a recognition of the historical specificity of *all* forms of reasoning, including "Occidental rationalism." And this, I suggest, best characterizes the contemporary intellectual scene: we are possessed of an acute consciousness of the historicity of our

---

[96] Robert Pippin, *Idealism as Modernism: Hegelian Variations*, New York: Cambridge University Press, 1996, 172.

knowledge, but without any compelling argument for its superiority to other knowledges.

Parochial, yet Global

This chapter has argued that modern Western knowledge cannot be regarded as true and universal, and that even the most sophisticated arguments to this effect are unpersuasive. Nonetheless, by the nineteenth century modern Western knowledge was dominant. It traveled to new domains in the wake of gunboats, conquest, and trade. That they were the conquerors and colonizers, rather than the conquered and colonized, provided proof to many Europeans that "European modes of thought and social organization corresponded much more closely to the underlying realities of the universe than did those of any other people or society, past or present."[97] The superiority of Western intellectual traditions to modes of reasoning encountered elsewhere increasingly came to be assumed, or blithely asserted. Asking themselves why European military organization, technology, and statecraft was superior to their own, non-Western elites also frequently concluded that this derived from a knowledge that underpinned and enabled sophisticated technology and effective military organization. Reformers and nationalists began to urge that the knowledge of the foreigner be adopted and disseminated among their own peoples, in order that they may avoid being colonized, or to emancipate themselves from colonial rule and join the ranks of sovereign, powerful, and prosperous nations.

These non-Western elites neither accepted European claims to superiority in all areas, nor did they seek to become mirror images of their rulers. Indeed, as Partha Chatterjee has powerfully and influentially argued, the anticolonial nationalist project was one to become modern yet different,[98] and "culture" became an increasingly common term for thinking and designating the difference that was to be "preserved" even as it was being constituted and defined.[99] Thus in nineteenth-century China, reformers urging

---

[97] Michael Adas, *Machines as the Measure of Men*, Ithaca, NY: Cornell University Press 1989, 7.

[98] See Partha Chatterjee, *Nationalist Thought and the Colonial World: A Derivative Discourse?*, Delhi: Oxford University Press, 1986; and also *The Nation and Its Fragments: Colonial and Postcolonial Histories*, Princeton, NJ: Princeton University Press, 1993.

[99] See, for instance, Andrew Sartori, *Bengal in Global Concept History: Culturalism in the Age of Capital*, Chicago: University of Chicago Press, 2008. On how the national/cultural essences that were to be "preserved" were also being created—often with "woman" as their site and guardian—see

changes that would allow China to resist Western depredations made a distinction between "essence" and "utility" (*ti-yong*); Chinese essence was to be preserved, while "useful" knowledges and practices from the West needed to be learned and freely borrowed. The elites who led the Meiji Restoration and implemented a state agenda to "modernize" Japan in order that it could avoid the fate of India or China adopted the slogan of *wakan yôsai* (Japanese spirit, Western technique), a similar endeavor to acquire Western knowledges and techniques precisely as a means to preserve that which was deemed to be at the very heart of Japanese identity. In colonial India most nationalists embraced Western knowledge and schooling, while urging that this education be a "national" education, delivered in the vernaculars. The nationalist and educationalist Lajpat Rai spoke for many when he declared that while there were things to admire in the indigenous system(s) of education, "any widespread revival of the ancient or medieval systems of education is unthinkable,"[100] for it would mark national regress rather than progress. Progress required acquiring modern Western knowledge as a necessary means to becoming modern and sovereign, whilst preserving "Indianness" required an education disseminated in Indian languages rather than principally in English, and one that preserved and inculcated Indian culture and patriotism: for as Lajpat Rai put it, "We do not want to be English or German or American or Japanese . . . we want to be Indians, but modern, up-to-date, progressive Indians."[101]

The inherent tension between imitation and appropriation on the one hand, and the assertion of national/cultural difference on the other, was usually navigated by treating the knowledge in question as Western and modern in origin, but at the same time as "unmarked." Thus it was acknowledged that modern knowledge first developed in the West, but this was declared to be a matter of historical contingency, for this knowledge was not intrinsically or essentially Western. Indeed, in proportion as the colonizer sometimes asserted that his knowledge was intimately tied to uniquely Occidental cultural traits and was thus intrinsically and not accidentally European, colonized elites insisted all the more stridently that the human and natural sciences belonged to no one and thus to everyone and could be appropriated

Sanjay Seth, "Nationalism, Modernity and the 'Woman Question' in India and China," *Journal of Asian Studies* 72:2 (May 2013).

[100] Lajpat Rai, *The Problem of National Education in India*, London: Allen and Unwin, 1920, 55.

[101] Rai, *Problem of National Education*, 75. On the debates surrounding modern knowledge in colonial India, see Sanjay Seth, *Subject Lessons: The Western Education of Colonial India*, Durham, NC: Duke University Press, 2007.

without cultural and other entailments. Having embraced and championed these sciences during the period of colonial rule, following decolonization the leaders of postcolonial states sought, with varying degrees of success, to disseminate this knowledge among their peoples through schools and universities, and to utilize it to govern their peoples. The globalization of modern Western knowledge was thus the joint outcome of the actions of the colonizer, of nationalist elites, and of postcolonial nation-building.

In the first part of this book I have suggested that the social sciences are global, but not universal—that is, they do not and cannot transcend the particularity of their origins. In the second part, I reverse the emphasis—for even though they are not universal, the social sciences *are* now global and are accepted, utilized, produced, and disseminated far beyond their European origins. To challenge their claims and deflate their pretensions is important, but inasmuch as they are a force in the world, it is also necessary to examine how a knowledge founded upon core presumptions that are not true and universal "works": to anatomize these presumptions and to inquire into what effects these have, into what they make visible and what they occlude. Since, as argued in the introduction to this work, a defining feature of modern knowledge is that it is divided into disciplines, in the second part of this book I seek to so inquire with reference to the disciplines of history and politics.

PART II
POSTCOLONIALISM AND SOCIAL SCIENCE

3

The Code of History

The first part of this book has explored some of the presuppositions that undergird what I have been calling modern, Western knowledge. This knowledge, once an insurgent challenger to the forms of knowledge that preceded it in Europe, has in the course of the last two centuries become hegemonic and global. As it became so, positions that were once novel and had to be argued for became routinized and naturalized and came to be seen as the "discovery" or the "unveiling" of truths that, although they were discovered in a time and a place, were true for all times and places. Thus it is difficult to conceive of knowledge as anything other than a relation between a subject and an object, with true knowledge consisting of the former accurately "representing" the object. It is more or less an axiom that the world is divided into the human, the sphere of meanings and purposes, on the one hand; and of nature, devoid of meanings and purposes, on the other. This distinction provides the architecture of modern knowledge, a knowledge divided between the natural sciences and the human sciences (the latter itself often subdivided into the humanities and the social sciences). And this knowledge is resolutely secular—its producers may "believe" in God or gods in their private capacity, but gods, spirits, and the like have no role in explanation in the natural or human sciences.

These very general presumptions underpin our knowledge in general. When pressed into service in the various disciplines that constitute the social sciences, they are supplemented by further presumptions, ones that are thought to be consonant with, and required by, the object of inquiry of these disciplines. In this and the following chapters I anatomize the disciplines of history and politics. In chapter 1 we saw that in the discipline of history the presumption that "society" is an ontological, transhistorical given, determining or shaping human actions, has been questioned and challenged by some. But these challenges notwithstanding, in history—and even more so in the discipline of political science—the presuppositions that define and enable disciplinary practice have remained relatively secure; unwarrantedly

Beyond Reason. Sanjay Seth, Oxford University Press (2021). © Oxford University Press.
DOI: 10.1093/oso/9780197500583.003.0004

so, as I seek to demonstrate in the second part of this book. This chapter and the next are concerned with modern history writing and its object, "the past."

History as a Code (or Technology or Genre)

In the standard, textbook account of the history of the discipline, the ancient Greeks are usually credited with having begun history writing, the Romans with adding the genre of historical biography to it, and the Renaissance with rediscovering the model of the ancients and developing it into a more general "sense of the past," including a sense of anachronism, an awareness of evidence, and an interest in causation.[1] The emergence of this historical sense is subsequently manifested in, and furthered by, the works of great historians like Gibbon, Michelet, and Macaulay, as well as by an almost unquenchable thirst for historical novels, such as those of Walter Scott.[2]

In fact, historical writings of the eighteenth century, and some of the nineteenth century, still owed as much or more to the discipline of rhetoric as they did to the discipline of history as we have come to understand and practice it.[3] History was required to be truthful, but "truth" was the antonym of "lying" and did not preclude the use of literary devices, and nor was it seen to require footnotes and references.[4] It is in the nineteenth century that history finally "comes into its own," and Leopold von Ranke figures large in the textbook accounts I am parsing. Rejecting all philosophies of history and more generally any search for a meaning and teleology in the historical process, eschewing "positivism" if by that is meant a search for overarching laws of which the particulars of history are instantiations, Ranke practiced history

---

[1] The classical statement of this is Peter Burke, *The Renaissance Sense of the Past*, London: Edward Arnold, 1969.

[2] On the extraordinary popularity of Scott's Waverly novels—not only in Britain but on the continent and in North America—see James Chandler, *England in 1819*, Chicago: University of Chicago Press, 1998, 12–13.

[3] In the Renaissance and in eighteenth-century manuals of rhetoric, "History writing was viewed as art of presentation and argument rather than a scientific inquiry, and its problems belonged therefore to rhetoric rather than to epistemology." Lionel Gossman, *Between History and Literature*, Cambridge, MA: Harvard University Press, 1990, 228. See also Hayden White, "The Fictions of Factual Representation," in his *Tropics of Discourse: Essays in Cultural Criticism*, Baltimore: Johns Hopkins University Press, 1978, and *Metahistory*, Baltimore: Johns Hopkins University Press, 1973.

[4] Replying to critics of his *Rise and Fall* in 1776, Gibbon boasted—a mark of how unusual this was—that he had "carefully distinguished the *books*, the *chapters*, the *sections*, the *pages* of the authors to whom I referred, with a degree of accuracy and attention . . . as has seldom been so regularly practiced by any historical writers." Quoted in Stephen Bann, *The Clothing of Clio*, New York: Cambridge University Press, 1984, 35.

writing as an empirical discipline, one that sought to represent the past, as his now-famous phrase goes, "as it really was." This required painstaking archival research, making a strong distinction between primary and secondary sources, and an aspiration to complete objectivity. In the course of this century history writing increasingly became professionalized, something to be practiced by properly accredited people who had mastered its ethos and its methods; and archives and archival bibliographies, essential to the practice of this method, were assembled and produced. As it became introduced as a separate discipline in universities—at different rates in different European locations[5]—university training and employment at a university increasingly became the most widely accepted sign of one's authorization to write history. The relations between the historian and his (at this point, the accredited historian was almost always male) readers began to change; the historian now wrote above all for other specialists, who were best placed to assess the truth of his account and to appreciate, judge, and confirm the protocols (the long hours in the archive, the properly critical evaluation of documents) that had produced it.

This standard genealogy is enabled by the presumption, in Hayden White's words, that "historical consciousness, historical thought, and historical writing share some essential trait or attribute that appears at a certain time and place, undergoes certain vicissitudes, but continues to develop, enters upon a phase of realization or comes into its own at a specific time, and finally achieves a kind of consummation in our own age and place."[6] But it is precisely this presumption—that the past is a constant (it is always already just "there"), while the forms of representing that past are variable and changing (and have improved)—that has come under sustained criticism for some decades now. Figures as diverse as Louis Althusser, Michael Oakeshott, Paul Veyne, Claude Lévi-Strauss, and Constantine Fasolt have argued, in their different ways, that history as discipline does not simply "find" and apply itself to "the past," as if the past were available like stones and apples,

---

[5] See, inter alia, Joseph M. Levine, *Humanism and History: Origins of Modern English Historiography*, Ithaca, NY: Cornell University Press, 1989; Stephen Bann, *The Inventions of History: Essays on the Representation of the Past*, Manchester: Manchester University Press, 1990; Doris Goldstein, "History at Oxford and Cambridge," in Georg Iggers and James Powell (eds.), *Leopold von Ranke and the Shaping of the Historical Discipline*, Syracuse, NY: Syracuse University Press, 1990; William R. Keylor, *Academy and Community: The Foundations of the French Historical Profession*, Cambridge, MA: Harvard University Press, 1975; and Peter Novick, *That Noble Dream: The "Objectivity Question" and the American Historical Profession*, Cambridge: Cambridge University Press, 1988.

[6] Hayden White, "The Westernization of World History," in Jörn Rüsen (ed.), *Western Historical Thinking*, New York: Berghahn Books, 2002, 117.

but that it constitutes the object that it then investigates and represents.[7] It is not the object, "the past," that "generates" a knowledge adequate to it, but rather the knowledge that constitutes its object, defining what "the past" is taken to be. They thus describe history as a "code" (Lévi-Strauss), a "technology" (Fasolt), a "genre" (Veyne), or an "idiom" (Oakeshott), one that rests upon certain presuppositions and operations that constitute an object that is then available and amenable to historical investigation.

If this is so, the claim that the discipline has a genealogy stretching back to the ancient Greeks begins to look very suspect. And indeed, this genealogy, once widely accepted, is increasingly being called into question, not least by historians of the ancient world.[8] This retrospective genealogy, Hayden White suggests, is designed to give historical depth to what are in fact choices and inventions: the purported similarities between Greek and Roman historiography and post-Renaissance historiography, he concludes, "are not genetic. . . . They are, rather, a consequence of a retrospective choice by cultural groups and their representatives to treat themselves as descendants and heirs of earlier ones . . . what passes for professionally respectable historiographical practice today in the West bears no resemblance whatsoever to its putative Greek and Roman prototypes."[9]

If Lévi-Strauss, Veyne, and others are right to argue that history as a discipline constitutes the past as a particular sort of object subject to investigation and representation through its code—as I believe they are—then a number of questions present themselves, questions that would not (and did not) appear on the horizon as long as history was conceived of as the unproblematic representation of the past through the documents and other sources that it bequeathed to us. We are, first, in a position to ask what the presuppositions

---

[7] See Louis Althusser, "The Errors of Classical Economics: Outline of a Concept of Historical Time," in Althusser and Etienne Balibar, *Reading Capital*, translated by Ben Brewster, London: Verso, 2009; Michael Oakeshott, "The Activity of Being an Historian," in his *Rationalism in Politics and Other Essays*, London: Methuen, 1977, and his *On History and Other Essays*, Indianapolis: Liberty Fund, 1999; Paul Veyne, *Writing History*, translated by M. Moore-Rinvolucri, Middletown, CT: Wesleyan University Press, 1984; Claude Lévi-Strauss, *The Savage Mind*, London: Weidenfeld and Nicolson, 1972, chap. 9 ("History and Dialectic"); and Constantine Fasolt, *The Limits of History*, Chicago: University of Chicago Press, 2004.

[8] According to Paul Veyne, "History then [at the time of the Greeks] and history now are alike in name only"; and he compares the "historical" writings of the Greeks to contemporary reportage, that is, journalism. *Did the Greeks Believe in Their Myths?*, translated by Paula Wissing, Chicago: University of Chicago Press, 1988, 5, 11. And Moses Finley expresses incredulity at the idea that there is a more or less direct line of continuity between Thucydides and Ranke: "I find it a remarkable act of faith that so many intelligent and knowledgeable students of history have believed that for so long." *Ancient History: Evidence and Models*, London: Chatto and Windus, 1985, 48. See also Finley's "Myth, Memory, and History," *History and Theory* 4:3 (1965).

[9] White, "Westernization of World History," 114.

of history are—to inquire into the elements of this code. And if it is a code, a particular way of constituting the past, then we can ask what it is that the code *does*, a question that does not normally arise if history is assumed to be the accurate and truthful representation of the past, for truth is not normally thought to require explanation. And further, if history is a code, other modes of historicity should perhaps also be regarded as "codes" or "technologies" or "genres" of historicity—as some of the many ways that humans have related to and represented their pasts. In which case, we also need to inquire into what it means to represent the past of others through the genre of modern history, where these others have or had their own genres of presenting, and relating, to their past.

In short, once history writing is denaturalized or defamiliarized—once it is seen as an elaborate theory and operation rather than the disinterested investigation of the past guided by rigorous methodological protocols—an array of fresh questions present themselves. The remainder of this chapter and the next are devoted to these questions, beginning with an inquiry into the nature of the historical code. I will pursue these questions with reference to the writings and reflections of historians—not because I aim to provide a survey of the discipline, but because the workings of the code are best illustrated by reference to those who deploy it. And I will pay special attention to those forms of history that are in some way at odds with, or at the margins of, the discipline, such as art, music, and science history: it is my wager that the presumptions and protocols of the discipline are most clearly visible in those parts of it that do not fully comply with, or transgress, these protocols.

Elements of the Code: The Past Is Dead

Every student of history is familiar with the oft-cited passage from Ranke's preface to his *Histories of the Latin and Germanic Peoples from 1494 to 1514*: "History has been attributed the office to judge the past and instruct the present to make its future useful. . . at such high functions this present attempt does not aim–it merely wants to show how things really were [*wie es eigentlich gewesen*]."[10] This has usually been quoted as an instance of modern history writing's aspiration to "objectivity" and has been lauded as the charter

---

[10] Quoted in George Nadel, "Philosophy of History before Historicism," *History and Theory* 3:6 (1964), 315.

of the modern discipline by some, and condemned by others as an impossible and therefore self-deceiving aspiration. But what is surely just as striking about this passage is the explicit distinction it draws between judging and instructing on the one hand, and knowing and truthfully representing on the other. History here is being conceived of as a relation to the past that is solely *cognitive*; the measure of good history is not, or is no longer to be, its capacity to instruct, or to please or delight, but solely its capacity to accurately represent. History is now defined as a discourse of Truth, and as such it requires, not facility in rhetoric or moral or theological reasoning, but a *method* that is conducive to the discovery and representation of the truth about the past. And history is a cognitive enterprise because it assumes—and this is the first element of the code of history I wish to draw attention to—that the past is dead. It was not always so: as David Lowenthal observes, "During most of history men scarcely differentiated past from present, referring even to remote events . . . as though they were then occurring."[11]

By contrast, modern historiography, Michel de Certeau writes, "bear[s] witness to another relation with time or, in what amounts to the same thing, another relation with death . . . an odd procedure that posits death . . . and that yet denies loss by appropriating to the present the privilege of recapitulating the past as a form of knowledge. A labor of death and a labor against death."[12] Gabrielle Spiegel elaborates the point by means of a contrast with what she calls "tradition," ways of relating to the past that, while immensely varied, when contrasted to historiography have in common the fact that they treat the past as something still alive, and thus as a resource that may provide ethical and political guidance on how to live in the present and face the future: "Historians must draw a line between what is dead (past) and what is not, and therefore they posit death as a total social fact, in contrast to tradition, which figures a lived body of traditional knowledge . . . borne by living societies. . . . The chief aim of modern historiography has become that of representing—rather than, as formerly, resurrecting—the past."[13]

[11] David Lowenthal, *The Past Is a Foreign Country*, Cambridge: Cambridge University Press, 1985, xvi. See also Zachary Sayre Schiffman, "Historicizing History/Contextualizing Context," *New Literary History* 42:3 (Summer 2011) and his *The Birth of the Past*, Baltimore: Johns Hopkins University Press, 2011.

[12] Michel de Certeau, *The Writing of History*, translated by Tom Conley, New York: Columbia University Press, 1988, 5. Elsewhere Certeau describes historiography as "the operation that creates a space of signs proportionate to an absence . . . in the form of *a discourse structured by a missing presence*" "History and Mysticism" (1972), in Jacques Revel and Lynn Hunt (eds.), *Histories: French Constructions of the Past*, New York: New Press, 1995, 440.

[13] Gabrielle M. Spiegel, "Memory and History: Liturgical Time and Historical Time," *History and Theory* 41 (May 2002), 161.

Before modern historiography became the dominant way in which the past is remembered and represented, alternative ways of remembering the past were usually subject to denunciation: for their anachronisms, for presuming that the past blended into the present, for confusing history with myth, and so on. It is only in recent times, when modern history has become hegemonic, that a space has opened for (some) historians to recognize that these other ways of relating to and representing the past were not failed versions of our mode of historicity, but alternative modes of historicity; and even to compose elegies to their decline.

In *Zakhor: Jewish History and Jewish Memory*, Yosef Yerushalmi writes out of "an acute awareness that there have been a number of alternative ways, each viable and with its own integrity, in which human beings have perceived and organized their collective pasts. Modern historiography is the most recent, but still only one of these."[14] The Jews, he writes, are a people for whom memory of the past was a central aspect of their collective experience and identity; but the rabbinic literature that was one of the primary means of remembering and transmitting the past was far from being historiography. It is not merely that the Talmud and Midrash do not record significant events or are unreliable sources. More fundamentally, they often ignore our conception of time, placing "all the ages . . . in an ever-fluid dialogue with one another";[15] and they are often unaware of, or freely practice, anachronism. This was, in short, a way of remembering and relating to the past that sought "not the historicity of the past, but its eternal contemporaneity."[16]

This mode of recording and relating to the past was central to the transmission of tradition and the preservation of Jewish identity. When a modern historiography of the Jews emerged in the nineteenth century, it was not a deepening of or improvement upon this mode of remembering and transmitting a collective past and a tradition, but a caesura, a "chasm that separates modern Jewish historiography from all the ways in which Jews once concerned themselves with their past";[17] for modern historiography "repudiate[s] premises that were basic to all Jewish conceptions of history in the past . . . the belief that divine providence is not only an ultimate but an active causal factor in Jewish history, and the related belief in the uniqueness of

---

[14] Yosef Hayim Yerushalmi, *Zakhor: Jewish History and Jewish Memory*, 2nd ed., Seattle: University of Washington Press, 1996, "Prologue to the Original Edition," xxxv.

[15] Yerushalmi, *Zakhor*, 17.

[16] Yerushalmi, *Zakhor*, 96.

[17] Yerushalmi, *Zakhor*, 101.

Jewish history itself."[18] As a historian, Yerushalmi thus produces history with "the ironic awareness that the very mode in which I delve into the Jewish past represents a decisive break with that past."[19]

Pierre Nora's introduction to the massive *Lieux de Memoire* project similarly counterposed a declining culture of "memory" to the rise of historiography, drawing a series of contrasts between the two:

> Memory is life, borne by living societies founded in its name . . . open to the dialectic of remembering and forgetting . . . vulnerable to manipulation and appropriation. . . . Memory is a perpetually actual phenomena, a bond tying us to the eternal present; history is a representation of the past. Memory, insofar as it is affective and magical, only accommodates those facts that suit it. . . . History, because it is an intellectual and secular production, calls for analysis and criticism. . . . Memory is blind to all but the group it binds. . . . History, on the other hand, belongs to everyone and to no one, whence its claim to universal authority.[20]

Collectively, these contrasts add up to a decisive difference, namely that memory establishes continuities and assumes that the past can be retrieved, while with the triumph of history, the past appears "as radically other . . . a world apart."[21]

Both Yerushalmi and Nora draw inspiration from Maurice Halbwachs' earlier and important work on "collective memory," and as a consequence their works have sometimes been read as contributions to a burgeoning debate that counterposes memory to history. I suggest that because Yerushalmi and Nora discuss remembrances of the past that are written, and not simply unrecorded generational experiences, they are in fact drawing attention to modes of historicity rather than memory—to ways of representing and relating to the past that are different from that of modern historiography.[22]

---

[18] Yerushalmi, *Zakhor*, 89.

[19] Yerushalmi, *Zakhor*, 81.

[20] Pierre Nora, "Between Memory and History: *Le Lieux de Memoire*," *Representations* 26 (Spring 1989), 8–9.

[21] Nora, "Between Memory and History," 17.

[22] For Halbwachs collective memory designated a shared, usually generational experience, which ceased to be memory if written or recorded (see Maurice Halbwachs, *The Collective Memory*, translated by F. J. Ditter and V. Y. Ditter, New York: Harper Colophon, 1980, especially 78). By contrast, Yerushalmi discusses a tradition stretching over more than two millennia, embodied in and transmitted through liturgy *and* written texts; and Nora's declining "memory-history" includes the work of most French historians, including Augustin Thierry and Michelet. Yerushalmi is aware of this major difference and cautions that his work is indebted to Halbwachs "in spirit if not always in substance" ("Prologue to the Original Edition," xxxiv).

It is precisely this aspect of their work that makes it so important, for these are works by historians who recognize that in the course of human history, there have been many ways of representing and relating to the past. When contrasted with modern historiography, these earlier modes have many features in common: they are highly selective in what is preserved and transmitted, they need not be secular, and they are often untroubled by anachronism. These forms of historicity attend to a past that is not dead but is in a real sense a part of the present and future; these are modes of "resurrecting" the past, of seeking its "eternal contemporaneity." What is novel and distinctive about historiography, and a central and defining element of its code, is that the past is treated as dead; it cannot be resurrected, only represented.

That the past is dead is not, however, a presumption governing *all* of modern history writing. There are practices of modern historiography that do not treat their objects as belonging solely to the past. We need to attend to these "exceptions" to my claim that modern historiography treats the past as dead, because exceptions need to be explained and accounted for; but also because what characterizes and licenses these exceptions will, in the next chapter, become germane to my argument that historiography cannot adequately represent non-Western pasts.

Exceptions to the Code: Histories of Beauty and Truth

History takes humankind as its subject, but actual histories are always more specific, taking a period, country/region, or practice as their subject matter, with historians specializing in (say) eighteenth-century Germany, or in military history, and so on. Such divisions are usually a consequence of pragmatic factors—for no one can be a historian of everything. There are, however, subfields of history—the three that I shall consider here are the history of art, music, and science—which are demarcated not for reasons of practicality, but because their object is thought to be distinctive in that it is at once of the past (and hence historicizable) and yet not "dead." It is unfortunate that discussions of historiography usually do not engage with these marginal or outlying cases,[23] for modes of historicizing that insist that their object cannot

---

[23] An important exception is Siegfried Kracauer, *History: The Last Things before the Last*, Oxford: Oxford University Press, 1969, chap. 7.

be treated in the same way as "general history" cast light on what it is that marks and defines this general history.

For art and music historians, the distinctiveness of their object lies in the fact that art and music from the past are also part of the present. This does not just mean that they still exist in the present—so, after all, does the document that a historian of eighteenth-century Germany consults—but that, unlike this document, the artwork or music work can be a *living* part of the present. Whereas the historicity of a document of eighteenth-century German diplomatic history—what it tells us about the past from which it issues—exhausts its being, the same is not true for art and music. For the artwork and the work of music are thought to be "autonomous"—that is, they cannot be "reduced" to simply being a "sign" or "trace" of the past in which they were made or composed.[24] As Eduard Hanslick, a leading German music critic of the nineteenth century, magisterially put it, "Aesthetic inquiry knows nothing—and is content to know nothing—of . . . the historical circumstances of a composer."[25] Henslick did not deny that music had a history or that musical works were influenced by the historical circumstances of their production; he was making the claim that as aesthetic objects, musical works transcended, or had a life beyond and wholly independent of, these historical circumstances. A distinguished contemporary scholar of music history makes much the same point: "Music of the past belongs to the present as music, not as documentary evidence. . . . Music historiography . . . differs from its political counterpart in that the essential relics that it investigates from the past—the musical works—are primarily aesthetic objects and as such also represent an element of the present; only secondarily do they cast light on events and circumstances of the past."[26] And the same distinction has been central to the history of the "fine arts": Hans Belting writes, "In the practice of art historiography . . . autonomy has been the very precondition for distinguishing art history from social history or cultural history of a general type."[27]

This has at once been a premise of art and music history and also the dilemma that has defined and plagued it. Since art and music are presumed to

[24] This is rendered in the legend that when asked what the "Moonlight Sonata" meant or was about, Beethoven went to the piano and played it again. See Leonard B. Meyer, *The Spheres of Music: A Gathering of Essays* (Chicago: University of Chicago Press, 2000), 21.

[25] "Vom Musikalisch-Schonen," in Bojan Bujic (ed.), *Music in European Thought, 1851–1912*, Cambridge: Cambridge University Press, 1988, 28.

[26] Carl Dahlhaus, *Foundations of Music History*, translated by J. B. Robinson, Cambridge: Cambridge University Press, 1983, 4.

[27] Hans Belting, *Art History after Modernism*, translated by C. Saltzwedel and M. Cohen, Chicago: University of Chicago Press, 2003, 117.

THE CODE OF HISTORY 97

be historicizable and yet also in some sense beyond the pale of history, histories of objects and practices that belong to the aesthetic have been characterized by a struggle to steer between Scylla and Charybdis. As Lydia Goehr describes it, "One of the most basic problems of music history" is how to "reconcile the desire to treat musical works as purely musical entities with value and significance on their own, on the one hand, with the desire, on the other, to acknowledge that such works are tainted, influenced, shaped, and conditioned by their contexts—historical cultural, social, political, economic, religious, and psychological. . . . This opposition has been formulated in many ways, most commonly as the aesthetic versus the historical or as the musical versus the extra-musical."[28] The same problem shadows any history of art: as Michael Podro characterizes it, "Either the context-bound quality or the irreducibility of art may be elevated at the expense of the other. If a writer diminishes the sense of context in his concern for the irreducibility or autonomy of art, he moves toward formalism. If he diminishes the sense of irreducibility in order to keep a firm hand on extra-artistic facts, he runs the risk of treating art as if it were the trace or symptom of these other facts."[29]

The history of science is in important ways different from the history of music and art (which in turn are different from each other, in ways overlooked here), for it is a history of Truth, and truth is assumed to always be there, awaiting discovery, whereas art and music are created.[30] Indeed, why truthful beliefs about the natural world came to be embraced was usually thought to need no explanation; as David Bloor observes, in the history of science it is usually error that needs to be accounted for, whereas "logic, rationality and truth appear to be their own explanation."[31] Given this, the very idea of a history of science, as one commentator notes, seems an oxymoron, like "jumbo shrimp" or "deafening silence."[32] But even if *why* truthful beliefs about the natural world came to be embraced needed no explanation, *when* and how these came to be embraced, and with what consequences, could

[28] Lydia Goehr, "Writing Music History," *History and Theory* 31:2 (May 1992), 185.

[29] Michael Podro, *The Critical Historians of Art*, New Haven: Yale University Press, 1982, xx. Podro goes on to argue that the great art historians of the nineteenth and early twentieth centuries "oscillated uneasily" between the two possibilities (216).

[30] Without endorsing the distinction, Isabelle Stengers pithily sums up it up: if Beethoven had died at birth, his symphonies would not have been performed, while if Newton had died when young, someone else would have taken his place. *The Invention of Modern Science*, translated by Daniel W. Smith, Minneapolis: University of Minnesota Press, 2000, 39.

[31] David Bloor, *Knowledge and Social Imagery*, 2nd ed., Chicago: University of Chicago Press, 1991, 9.

[32] Ken Alder, "The History of Science as Oxymoron: From Scientific Explanations to Episcience," *Isis* 104:1 (March 2013), 89.

and did form the subject matter of historical narratives: many histories of science were accounts of the historical circumstances in which ahistorical truths were discovered, of the heroes who discovered them, and of the ways in which the human place in the cosmos changed as we discovered more about it. As Lorraine Daston describes it, "The history of science was written as if . . . Nature was eternal and universal; hence the sciences of nature were assumed to be as well. . . . The role of science's past became to make science's present inevitable."[33]

Here too, as in art and music history, navigating the boundary between historicity and the extrahistorical while doing justice to both proved difficult. Expressed as a tension between formalism and historicity in art history and music history, in the history of science this appeared, as seen in chapter 1, as a debate between "internalists" and "externalists": between those who investigated change and progress in the natural sciences principally with reference to their internal intellectual development, and those who accorded explanatory importance to factors "external" to science, such as social factors, the "spirit of the age," and so on.

The histories of art, music, and science are thus exceptions to my claim that an important and defining element of the code of history is that the past is dead. But they are exceptions that confirm the rule. That there are specialized domains of history that are thought to be special or different because their object is historical and yet not so, that it is of the past and yet also of the present, only serves to underline the fact that the unmarked category of "general" history—history tout court, as it were—constitutes its object as belonging wholly to the past, that which can be historicized without remainder, because it is well and truly dead.

Exceptions No More?

Once unleashed however, the practice of historicizing has a corrosive effect on all claims to autonomy from history, including those of art, music, and science history. This has been especially apparent in the history of science. The premises that inform it—that science is truth uncovered; that truth is by definition that which is timeless and contextless; and thus that any

---

[33] Lorraine Daston, "The History of Science as European Self-Portraiture," *European Review* 14:4 (October 2006), 529.

history of it can only historicize the discovery of truth and the consequences thereof, but not truth itself—have been subjected to sustained challenge and indeed have been progressively undermined. As briefly discussed in chapter 1, David Bloor and his colleagues in the "strong program" in the sociology of science rejected the assumption that "the rational aspects of science are . . . self-moving and self-explanatory,"[34] and thus that historical and sociological explanations were required only for unreason and error, enjoining sociologists instead to treat "both true and false beliefs alike for the purposes of explanation."[35] The study of science was not to be undertaken on the assumption that science was special, but rather from the position that "there is no essential difference between science and other forms of knowledge production; that there is nothing intrinsically special about 'the scientific method.'"[36] A host of studies painted a picture of emergent scientific practices that were decisively interlinked with, and shaped by, prevailing cultural and intellectual settings. And the more science was historicized, "the more context historians unearthed, the less unitary, formal, valid, and in short, rational science looked."[37]

Historicizing science, scholars in the field have increasingly realized, has had an unexpected effect: "Although the name of the discipline embeds within it an assumption that a singular thing called science is the object of its attention, that object has become harder to pin down as historical and other studies have gone in search of it. . . . The historicization of the category of science has ended up fragmenting the entity in question."[38] From being a history of a constant that undergoes development and unfolding, the history of science increasingly is becoming a history of the *emergence* of the category "science" in the nineteenth century,[39] a category that cannot be applied to earlier times and to other places without anachronism. Surveying recent developments in the history of science, Lorraine Daston observes that "historians of premodern science grew increasingly skittish about

[34] Bloor, *Knowledge and Social Imagery*, 10.

[35] Bloor, *Knowledge and Social Imagery*, 37.

[36] Steve Woolgar, *Science: The Very Idea*, London: Ellis Howard and Tavistock Publications, 1998, 12.

[37] Lorraine Daston, "The Historicity of Science," in Glenn W. Most (ed.), *Historicization-Historisierung*, Gottingen: Vandenhoeck and Ruprecht, 2001, 215.

[38] Jan Golinski, "Is It Time to Forget Science? Reflections on Singular Science and Its History," *Osiris* 27:1 (2012), 19.

[39] See, for instance, Peter Dear's "What Is History of Science the History Of? Early Modern Roots of the Ideology of Modern Science," *Isis* 96:3 (September 2005), "Science is Dead: Long Live Science," *Osiris* 27:1 (2012) and *The Intelligibility of Nature*, Chicago: University of Chicago Press, 2006.

calling what they study science at all, and the word *scientist* when applied to Archimedes and Galileo put their teeth on edge."[40] Increasingly, science appears not as the premise, but rather as the outcome, of the history that is plumbed by historians of science; and as it does so, history of science ceases to be different in any fundamental way from history tout court.[41]

Though less marked, something similar has happened in the fields of art and music history; the claim that these are a special domain of history, because their object resists being completely historicized, has come under challenge. In part this has been due to developments in practice, for art and music history are closely linked to the worlds of art and music production. As artists have questioned and challenged the ontological distinctiveness of art, and (though less so) musicians have done so with music—Warhol's Brillo boxes and John Cage's *4′33″* may be taken as emblematic—this has inevitably had an effect on art and music historians. For once the ontological distinctiveness of art and music is challenged, the premise authorizing the treatment of art and music history as specialized forms of history—namely, that their object is distinctive because it is autonomous—is undermined.

However, and this is what most interests me here, this undermining has also been a consequence of the very process of historicizing art and music. Writing the history of music has led some historians to conclude that "the aesthetic premises that might sustain the writing of music history are themselves historical."[42] It has been argued, for instance—most influentially by Lydia Goehr in *The Imaginary Museum of Musical Works*—that the idea of music as a "work," existing in and for itself rather than subordinate to religious, pedagogical, or other concerns, was a late eighteenth-century development, which went hand in hand with the elevation of the composer and the score, the emergence of the professional orchestra and the concert hall, and copyright over music.[43] This became a "regulative ideal" that then governed the production and performance of musical works. In the repertoire of

---

[40] Lorraine Daston, "Science Studies and the History of Science," *Critical Inquiry* 35 (Summer 2009), 806.

[41] As is argued in Daston, "Science Studies."

[42] Dahlhaus, *Foundations of Music History*, 20.

[43] Before this, argues Goehr, the question "'what is music?' asked for specification of music's *extra-musical* function and significance. Music was predominantly understood as regulated by, and thus defined according to, what we would now think of as extra-musical ideals. . . . Those who sought to describe the nature of music looked mostly at music's ritualistic and pedagogical value. How could music successfully acquire an acceptable moral, political, or religious status that would render its production a valuable contribution to the good life?" Lydia Goehr, *The Imaginary Museum of Musical Works: An Essay in the Philosophy of Music*, new ed., New York: Oxford University Press, 2007, 122.

classical music that solidified in the nineteenth century, it was retrospectively and anachronistically projected backward onto music that had not been governed by the work-concept; and this same anachronism has underpinned music history, which has treated music from the eighteenth century and before as if these too were "works" that can and should be treated as autonomous aesthetic objects.

The example of Bach is much cited in this context. In his own time, Bach neither composed "works" nor was considered a great composer. Yet in the nineteenth century, he became central to the repertoire of great classical music and is treated as such in music histories. Carl Dahlhaus writes, "Bach's works, in their original form, were relegated to an existence on the sidelines of history; it was not until they were reinterpreted as autonomous music in the nineteenth century that they unfolded into works of an historical significance that was denied to them in the eighteenth.... The fact that Bach's works could become the paradigm of a concept of art that they did not originally partake of is an historiologically baffling, almost monstrous occurrence."[44] This "baffling" move became possible when, around 1800, we moderns "began to reconstruct musical history to make it look as if musicians had always thought about their activities in modern terms. Even if it was not believed that early musicians had thought explicitly in these terms, the assumption was that they would have, had circumstances allowed them to do so."[45] The anachronism becomes more pronounced the further back in time we go; Leo Treitler writes, "Medieval music culture, in which we locate the roots of our Western tradition, lacked all the conditions that have been for us the premises for the possibility of a history of music: a transmission founded on a written score, a work concept, the idea of musical structure, the idea that the musical work is autonomous."[46] And if "the "work" concept [itself] has a history," then, concludes Treitler, "it cannot sensibly be taken as a premise for that history."[47]

Something similar has happened in the history of art. Art historians have of course long been aware that for much of Western history art objects were not regarded as autonomous, but as bearers of religious messages, as items of prestige, and so on; and that their producers were not accorded the exalted

---

[44] Dahlhaus, *Foundations of Music History*, 157.

[45] Goehr, *Imaginary Museum*, 245.

[46] Leo Treitler, "History and Music," in Ralph Cohen and Michael S. Roth (eds.), *History and Histories within the Human Sciences*, Charlottesville: University Press of Virginia, 1995, 217.

[47] Leo Treitler, *Music and the Historical Imagination*, Cambridge, MA: Harvard University Press, 1989, 171.

status that (some) artists came to have from the nineteenth century, but were usually on a par with craftsmen and often organized in guilds. But because the artwork (unlike the musical "work"), had a material existence as an object—it could, for instance, be wrenched out of its context and displayed in a gallery or museum—it could be and usually was assumed that "art" was a universal, that there was some ontological essence to art that distinguished it from nonart, and thus that there was a constant-in-change that was the object of art history. However, such assumptions have been widely questioned in recent times. Hans Belting, for instance, has distinguished between "image" and "art," arguing that the "era of images" in the West gave way to the "era of art" following the Reformation, when reformed churches banished images from their bare walls, which now ended up in picture cabinets in private houses and eventually in galleries: "Images, which had lost their function in the church, took on a new role in representing art."[48] In this account "art" is a product of history, not the object that underpins (art) history; and it is therefore anachronistic to retrospectively label earlier objects as "art" when, in Arthur Danto's words, "their being art did not figure in their production, since the concept of art had not as yet really emerged in general consciousness, and such image-icons . . . played a quite different role in the lives of people than works of art came to play when the concept at last emerged and something like aesthetic considerations began to govern our relationships to them."[49]

As this understanding has gained currency, some scholars have emphasized that the ways in which art is "seen" is itself the product of changing and historically specific forms of visualizing.[50] Others have abandoned, or at least scaled down, claims to the distinctiveness of the art object by replacing art history with "visual culture," which, according to one expositor, does not presume the autonomy of the art object but rather treats this as an open question and thus "offers the possibility of maintaining an analytic balance

[48] Hans Belting, *Likeness and Presence: A History of the Image before the Era of Art*, translated by Edmund Jephcott, Chicago: University of Chicago Press, 1994, 458. In a similar vein, Jacques Rancière suggests that "art is a historical configuration that has existed in the Western world since the end of the eighteenth century." "Rethinking Modernity," *Diacritics* 42:3 (2014), 7.

[49] Arthur C. Danto, *After the End of Art: Contemporary Art and the Pale of History*, Princeton, NJ: Princeton University Press, 1997, 3. According to Danto, with the decline of modernism and the advent of what he terms "post-historical" art, we are in a situation similar to the earlier era: "I would like to suggest that our situation at the end of art history resembles the situation before the beginning of art history" (114).

[50] Two important such works are Svetlana Alpers, *The Art of Describing: Dutch Art in the Seventeenth Century*, Chicago: University of Chicago Press, 1983; and Michael Baxandall, *The Limewood Sculptors of Renaissance Germany*, New Haven: Yale University Press, 1980.

between the primacy of social 'man' and that of material 'art,' examining the constant and productive tension . . . between these two underlying governing conceits."[51] Others still, like Hans Belting, urge that we recognize that "art, as we understand it today, was a phenomenon not present at all times and in all places,"[52] and thus that rather than write art history on the assumption that art is a transhistorical object that changes over time, art historians could more profitably address themselves to inquiring into "how art entered certain periods and societies and in which sense it was able to become accepted."[53]

Not many art historians have followed the path suggested by Belting. It would require rethinking and even abandoning the premises that have informed the discipline. Moreover, art and music history *are* different from science history, in that even after they have been historicized, art objects and music performances have a living presence in the present, constantly raising questions about the relation of their present to the past from which they issue. In the next chapter I shall return to this, examining a debate among musicians and music historians on how historical knowledge of "early music" shapes, or should shape, contemporary performances of that music. My point for now is that the history of art and music have been premised on the claim that the domain of beauty or aesthetics is in some sense autonomous. But as the historicization of art and music has raised the possibility that making this claim entails reading a feature of the present into the past, we are left, to put it schematically, with two possibilities. Either art and music are "in fact" autonomous and always have been, even if this was not discovered until the eighteenth and nineteenth centuries;[54] or the autonomy of art and music is itself a historical artifact. Either the line from Baumgarten through Kant to Hegel to Habermas was a *discovery* of the aesthetic domain, hitherto "mingled" and unfortunately subordinated to exiguous concerns; or the existence of an aesthetic domain, and the implications drawn from this, is a historical *creation* and does not have universal validity.[55] The questions that

[51] James D. Herbert, "Visual Culture/Visual Studies," in Robert S. Nelson and Richard Shiff (eds.), *Critical Terms for Art History*, 2nd ed., Chicago: University of Chicago Press, 2003, 455.

[52] Belting, *Art History after Modernism*, 165.

[53] Belting, *Art History after Modernism*, 165.

[54] In 1837 Heinrich Rotscher, a pupil of Hegel, could observe that whereas in the eighteenth century it was common to require that art have a moral or edifying effect, or that it imitate nature, by his century it was "recognized" that art was autonomous, and that artworks were to be judged by criteria immanent to themselves. See Stephen Bungay, *Beauty and Truth: A Study of Hegel's Aesthetics*, Oxford: Oxford University Press, 1984, 188.

[55] Which is the conclusion drawn, for instance, by Terry Eagleton: "The emergence of the aesthetic as a theoretical category is closely bound up with the material processes by which cultural production, at an early stage of bourgeois society, became "autonomous"—autonomous, that is, of

animate this book—whether modern Western knowledge is the discovery of truths or a historically and culturally particular way of constituting the objects that it then seeks knowledge of—reappear in the "regional" domain of historiography and present themselves especially acutely in its margins, in science, music, and art history.

Elements of the Code: Anthropology/Humanism and Social Determination

Proposing that history does not simply find the past lying around in the traces it has left behind, but is rather a code that constructs its object, I have suggested that one important element of the code of history is that the past is dead. I have argued that exceptions to this, including the histories of art, music, and science, only serve to confirm that this is part of the code of "general history": the condition for being exempt from the code is to establish that the object being historicized is of a different and special kind because it is a living part of the present. I have further suggested that the exceptional status of these histories has been undermined as a result of historicization and allusively suggested that this has broader implications, an allusiveness I hope to redeem in the next chapter. But for now, I return to the question of "code" to explore other elements of the code of history.

What is history the history of—that is, what is its subject? The answer is so self-evident—history is the history of humanity—that the question seems redundant. It is worth reminding ourselves, however, that the ways in which peoples have remembered their pasts have not always been ones in which humans have been the sole subjects. Reinhart Koselleck reminds us that this conception of history is in fact no older than the late eighteenth century; it was only with and after the Enlightenment that what Koselleck terms a "collective singular," namely man, became the subject whose changes history narrated.[56] This required the expulsion not only of God, but also of nature, as

the various social functions which it has traditionally served. Once artefacts become commodities in the marketplace, they exist for nothing and nobody in particular, and consequently can be rationalized, ideologically speaking, as existing entirely and gloriously for themselves. It is this notion of autonomy or self-referentiality which the new discourse of aesthetics is centrally concerned to elaborate." *The Ideology of the Aesthetic*, Oxford: Basil Blackwell, 1990, 8–9.

[56] Reinhart Koselleck, *Futures Past*, translated by Keith Tribe, New York: Columbia University Press, 2004, 194.

in the same period *historia naturalis* came to be classified as part of physics rather than history.[57] To equate the past solely with the human past is thus itself a historical event, one that then becomes a presupposition or element in the code of history. Following both its proponents and some of its critics, we could, in shorthand form, call this element of the code of history "anthropology," the study of humans.

This anthropology is almost always also a humanism, meaning not only that the subject of history is man and only man, but also that this subject is a Subject, that is, a meaning- and purpose-endowing being who objectifies himself in the world through texts, artworks, institutions, buildings, and activities. "The transcendental presupposition of every cultural science," as Max Weber put it, is that "we are cultural beings, endowed with the capacity and the will to take a deliberate attitude toward the world and to lend it significance."[58] The genealogy of this presupposition is usually traced back to Giambattista Vico and Herder,[59] and is often seen as the charter of the humanities, as the "discovery" that allowed the humanities to be differentiated from the natural sciences. Eric Auerbach, Wilhelm von Humboldt, Paul Ricoeur, Johann Gustav Droysen, Clifford Geertz, and numerous others affirm that in the human sciences human beings study their own products, that this "original, antecedent congruity between subject and object"[60] means that the knowledge acquired is self-knowledge, and that this knowledge can only be gained through protocols very different from those of the natural sciences.

I refer to these luminaries, writing in different domains, including philosophy, literature, and history, to demonstrate that these "anthropological" and humanist presumptions underlie all of the humanist disciplines and

[57] As in Voltaire's article "Historie" in the *Encyclopedie* (see Koselleck, *Futures Past*, 37).
[58] Max Weber, "Objectivity in Social Science and Social Policy," in Edward Shils and Henry Finch (eds.), *The Methodology of the Social Sciences: Max Weber*, New York: Free Press, 1949, 81.
[59] See, for instance, Eric Auerbach, "Vico and Aesthetic Historism," in *Scenes from the Drama of European Literature*, Manchester: Manchester University Press, 1984; Ernst Cassirer, *The Problem of Knowledge*, translated by W. H. Woglam and C. W. Hendel, New Haven: Yale University Press, 1950, especially 218; and Isaiah Berlin, *Vico and Herder*, London: Hogarth Press, 1976.
[60] Wilhelm von Humboldt, "On the Historian's Task," *History and Theory* 6:1 (1967), 65. Similarly Droysen: "The possibility of this [historical] understanding arises from the kinship of our nature with that of the utterances lying before us as historical material." Droysen, "History and the Historical Method," in Kurt Mueller-Vollmer (ed.), *The Hermeneutics Reader*, New York: Continuum, 1997, 121. And according to Paul Ricoeur, the historian "is part of history not only in the trite sense that the past is the past of his present, but also in the sense that the men of the past are part of the same humanity; it is a sector of the communication of minds which is divided by the methodological stage of traces and documents; therefore it is distinct from the dialogue wherein the other answers, but is not a sector wholly cut off from full intersubjectivity." *History and Truth*, Evanston. IL: Northwestern University Press, 1965, 29.

many of the social science disciplines too. In the case of history writing, they take the specific form of presuming that the remnants or traces of the past are the objectified meanings and purposes of persons like us, from which we can piece together the meanings and purposes with which these people endowed their world, what sort of people these were, and what sort of world they inhabited. As the great historian Marc Bloch put it, "Behind the features of the landscape, behind tools or machinery, behind what appear to be the most formalized written documents, and behind institutions . . . there are men, and it is men that history seeks to grasp."[61]

Alongside this, however, is another presupposition, one that delimits the humanist presumption. In chapter 1 I suggested that modern knowledge divided the world into nature and the human, and with regard to the latter, posited both freedom and constraint—man as the self-determining maker of meanings and history, and yet also always constrained and shaped by "society." The same dualism or tension, I suggested, runs through most of the human sciences, to different degrees and in different ways. In the case of history, if the humanist/anthropological presumption defines it—as both the champions and the critics of it aver—then so too does the presumption that the actions and meanings of human beings are shaped or determined, often in ways unbeknownst to them, "behind their backs," as it were. And if there are forces or constraints that shape and frustrate human desires and meanings, then recreating the meanings that men and women gave their world may be irrelevant to representing and understanding that world, or at least may be the first, rather than the last word, in historical explanation. We may take as an example the work of the Annales historians, not because they were unique in embracing this presumption—for I am suggesting that this is embedded in almost all history writing—but rather because they theorized it and turned it into a program for the writing of history.

The Annales' well-known critique of narrowly political or "events" history derived from their insistence that there were different "time spans" and that the history of events only attended to one, and not the most important one at that.[62] The *longue durée*—the "time of societies . . . for whom, sometimes, a

---

[61] Marc Bloch, *The Historian's Craft*, translated by P. Putnam, Manchester: Manchester University Press, 1979, 26.

[62] "Social time does not flow at an even rate, but goes at a thousand different paces, swift or slow, which bear almost no relation to the day-to-day rhythm of a chronicle or of traditional history." Fernand Braudel, "The Situation of History in 1950," inaugural lecture at Collège de France, December 1, 1950, in *On History*, translated by Sarah Matthews, Chicago: University of Chicago Press, 1980, 12.

whole century lasts but a moment"—was one "which to a great extent escapes the awareness of the actors, whether victors or victims: they make history, but history bears them along."[63] This "time of societies" included all those things that shaped people's lives without being intended, willed, or "meant," including price movements, long-term changes in diet, demographic changes, and so on. The innovation here was not merely "scalar," but lay above all in the insistence that history "to a great extent escapes the awareness of the actors." For it was this that led to a different approach to historical sources, which were no longer valued for what they could reveal of what people thought, desired, willed, and did, but rather needed to be "worked upon" in order to extract information that they were *not* designed to yield up. History writing as practiced by the Annales historians, as Paul Veyne astutely observed, required "a struggle against the optics imposed by the sources";[64] it aimed not simply at using traces left behind to reconstruct the past as it had been experienced by those whose present it had been, but at *constructing* a past they could not have experienced or known. The importance of assembling quantitative series thus lay not simply in quantifying, but in the fact that the historian was arranging and producing her sources to answer the questions she asked of them. By contrast, treating the sources as "testimony" was epistemologically naive: it succumbed to the danger of simply reproducing the bias of the archives, most of which had been institutionalized in the nineteenth century as "the memory of nations,"[65] and which prioritized political events and processes. The work of Annales instead sought to "rearrange" sources, in order that they could provide information and answer questions they were

---

[63] Fernand Braudel, "History and Sociology" in *On History*, 67.

[64] Veyne, *Writing History*, 222. Michel Foucault's appreciative comments about the Annales historians were also prompted by a recognition of this. Whereas the "old" history, Foucault wrote, had treated the document as "inert material through which it tries to reconstitute what men have done or said," the new history by contrast sought "the interplay of material determinations, rules of practice, unconscious systems, rigorous but unreflected relations, correlations that elude all lived experience." In order to unearth these, "History is now trying to define within the documentary material itself unities, totalities, series, relations"; it "deploys a mass of elements that have to be grouped, made relevant, placed in relation to one another to form totalities." History, concluded Foucault, was undergoing an "epistemological mutation," one that began with Marx but had been and was still being resisted, because its opponents recognized that what were at stake were the "twin figures of anthropology and humanism." *The Archaeology of Knowledge*, translated by A. M. Sheridan Smith, New York: Harper Colophon Books, 1976, 6–14. See also "On the Ways of Writing History" and "Return to History," both in James Faubion (ed.), *Michel Foucault: Aesthetics, Method, and Epistemology*, translated by Robert Hurley and others, London: Penguin, 1998.

[65] Francois Furet, "Quantitative Methods In History," in Jacques Le Goff and Pierre Nora (eds.), *Constructing the Past: Essays in Historical Methodology*, Cambridge: Cambridge University Press, 1985, 16.

not formulated to answer, questions those who had left behind these traces or sources often could not even have asked.

It is not that the Annales project was opposed to approaching sources as "expressions" of meanings and purposes. Even Fernand Braudel warned against "the dangers of forgetting, in contemplation of the deep currents in the lives of men, each separate man grappling with his own life and his own destiny"; it was necessary, Braudel went on to add, "to remain sensitive to both [social history and individual or event history] at one and the same time and, fired with enthusiasm for one, not to lose sight of the other."[66] Annales historiography produced not only Braudel's monumental multivolume study of the Mediterranean world from ancient times to the sixteenth century, but also Le Roy Ladurie's study of carnival in the town of Romans in 1579–1580, and his ethnographic study of the French town of Montaillou. Many of the next "generation" of Annales, without renouncing the emphasis accorded to statistical series and to the *longue durée*, immersed themselves in recreations of the "mentalities" of social groups, the social imaginary underpinning feudal society, and other themes that were very much concerned with meanings and purposes.

My point is that both these elements—humanism/anthropology and the premise that there were unseen and unknown forces that shaped and constrained historical actors—are among the enabling presuppositions of the code of history. To be sure, they do not mesh seamlessly; indeed, there is a tension between them. But most history writing includes elements of both or at least acknowledges that both are a necessary part of what it means to write history. Hence many historians, Marxist or not, are fond of quoting Marx: "Men make their own history, but not of their own free will; not under circumstances they themselves have chosen but under the given and inherited circumstances with which they are directly confronted."[67]

In any given historical work the accent may fall more on one than on the other, but both are implicitly or explicitly present, and the "ideal" work of history is often thought to be that which gives the impression of seamlessly combining both. In the discipline taken as a whole, the emphasis has been placed more on one than the other at different times. Very roughly, one could say that from the 1960s through to the 1970s, in European and Anglo-American historical scholarship, the accent was on social history, on that

---

[66] Fernand Braudel, "The Situation of History in 1950," in *On History*, 20.

[67] Karl Marx, "The Eighteenth Brumaire of Louis Bonaparte," in Marx, *Surveys from Exile*, London: Verso, 2010, 146.

which eluded or transcended meanings and purposes. Beginning around the 1980s, there has been a general shift in a number of disciplines toward—in the words of Clifford Geertz, whose works have played a significant role in bringing about the shift he summarizes—"connecting action to its sense rather than behavior to its determinants."[68] In the discipline of history, as shown in chapter 1, this contributed to a crisis of social history. That such alternations occur reveals that the code of history presumes *both* that history is the recreation and representation of the meanings that men and women in the past endowed their world with, *and* that these meanings were determined or shaped or constrained (and a great deal of ink has been spilt on which of these is pertinent) by external factors, unknown and often unknowable to historical actors, most commonly those designated as "social."

Once again, there is an exception to my claim. Recently practitioners and protagonists of what they call "deep" or "big" history have in fact dispensed with, or outrightly rejected, the humanist presumption that history is the history of man, conceived as a meaning-producing and purposeful being. And as I did with art, music, and science history, I will suggest that examining exceptions or challenges to the code of history leads to a heightened understanding of the code.

'Deep" or "Big" History

Deep history begins by challenging the division between prehistory, which attends to the vast span of the human past, and history, which covers only the last few millennia—and for the most part, only the last few hundred years. According to deep historians, none of the reasons offered for this division between prehistory and history "proper"—for instance, that history cannot be recounted in the absence of written sources; or that sometime around 4000 BC, there was a profound rupture which saw human beings surpass their purely biological being to become cultural beings, capable of "making"

---

[68] Geertz, "Blurred Genres: The Refiguration of Social Thought," in his *Local Knowledge*, London: Fontana Press, 1993, 34. Geertz adds that this does not entail a rejection of social constraint or determination, but rather an insistence that these can only be apprehended through interpretation of meanings. William Sewell similarly writes, "Unless we can represent to ourselves and our readers the *form* of life in in one historical moment or era, unless we can describe systematically the interlocking meanings and practices that give it a particular character, how are we to explain its transformation—or, for that matter, even to recognize when and how it has been transformed?" "Geertz, Cultural Systems, and History: From Synchrony to Transformation," in Sherry B. Ortner (ed.), *The Fate of "Culture": Geertz and Beyond*, Berkeley: University of California Press, 1999, 42.

history—stand up to scrutiny. History should therefore include the whole human past, stretching back to the Paleolithic era and even before, rather than be divided into two unequal parts, one belonging to prehistory and the other to history.

Breaching the divide between prehistory and history is not, however, just a change of temporal scale; it entails a fundamental rethinking of the presumptions and protocols of history writing. Thus it entails recognizing that textual sources are only one type of evidence, unduly fetishized by the discipline: in Daniel Smail's words, "Lumps of rock, fossils, mitochondrial DNA, isotopes, behavioral patterns, potsherds, phonemes: all these things encode information about the past."[69] That some of these forms of evidence—DNA is an example—are "not the product of anyone's intention"[70] is of no matter—the notion that history is "about" human desires, meanings, and purposes is an unwarranted prejudice.[71]

In fact, it turns out that history is not even exclusively about man. David Christian writes that Paleolithic man cannot be understood without going back to the beginnings of life on earth, which in turn requires understanding the conditions under which life first became possible, and so on, in an endless regress that terminates—and where history must therefore begin—with the Big Bang and the emergence of the universe.[72] Daniel Smail refers to a natural history of horses on display at the American Museum of Natural History in New York, which shows the changing body sizes of equine species, and concludes, "By any measure, there is history in this display. The difference is that horses do not make their own history."[73] But the difference is of no consequence, for the insistence that human beings make history—even if under circumstances not chosen by them—is unwarranted: "History is something that *happens* to people, things, and organisms, and is not *made* by them."[74]

[69] Daniel Lord Smail, *On Deep History and the Brain*, Berkeley: University of California Press, 2008, 48.

[70] Smail, *On Deep History*, 49.

[71] The deep historians sometimes draw an analogy with social history, which, in their reading of it, also came to recognize that what transpired in the past was a result of impersonal forces and of the unintended outcomes of human actions, and thus that intention, meaning, and purpose—what I have called the humanist presumption of the code of history—are not in fact of great consequence. See Smail, *On Deep History*, 71–72, and also Andrew Shryock and Daniel Lord Smail, "Introduction," in Andrew Shryock and Daniel Lord Smail, *Deep History: The Architecture of Past and Present*, Berkeley: University of California Press, 2011, 13. Smail at one point even suggests that his rejection of the relevance of intentions is "the logical extension of a line of inquiry introduced by Michel Foucault" (*On Deep History*, 63).

[72] David Christian, "The Case of 'Big History,'" *Journal of World History* 2:2 (1991), 224–25; see also his *Maps of Time: An Introduction to Big History*, Berkeley: University of California Press, 2004.

[73] Smail, *On Deep History*, 69–70.

[74] Smail, *On Deep History*, 57.

Deep history thus rejects what I have called the anthropological and humanist presumption that is part of the code of history. One consequence is that the discipline of history, as a discipline specifically authorized to investigate the past, loses its remit. Deep historians reject the distinction, made, for example, in an authoritative and much-republished textbook on prehistory, that "the scholar who studies Neanderthal man's bones is a natural scientist while he who studies Neanderthal man's artifacts is a historian";[75] for deep history, "The archaeologists, anthropologists, molecular biologists, and neuroscientists who study the deep past are also historians, regardless of the archive they consult."[76] "The past," in the form of the many and diverse traces it leaves behind, is an object of investigation by any and all disciplines equipped to decipher these traces.

The practitioners of deep history urge that we abandon the preconceptions and prejudices that have hitherto kept history "shallow": such as the idea that history writing necessarily requires retrieving meanings and intentions, that men and women make history, and even that history is necessarily the history of humanity. There are certain similarities between the Annales project and deep history, including the emphasis on long periods of time, on all that which escapes human intentions and yet shapes human lives, and on the inherently interdisciplinary requirements of representing the past. But deep history in fact goes very much "further." In rejecting the humanist/anthropological presupposition, in rejecting the idea that men make history and are not just made by it, and in suggesting that there is no fundamental difference between a history of horses and the history of men, deep history marks a break with the code of history.

The deep historians present what they advocate and practice as a better way of doing history: not a break, but an improvement. They suggest that once we have stripped away the prejudices that govern "what academics call history"[77] but which occlude a clear view of the past, we may be left with a clear and unobstructed view of it; that once we strip away the anthropological/humanist presumption, we can confront "the past" without any disabling preconceptions.[78] However, to reject humanist presuppositions is not

---

[75] Glyn Daniel and Colin Renfrew, *The Idea of Prehistory*, 1962, rev. ed., Edinburgh: Edinburgh University Press, 1988, 119.

[76] Smail, *On Deep History*, 11.

[77] Andrew Shryock, Thomas R. Trautmann and Clive Gamble, "Imagining the Human in Deep Time," in Shryock and Smail, *Deep History*, 42.

[78] As a video recorder—in Smail's revealing image—would do: "To write a natural history of the earth is to imagine that all the events of the past four and a half billion years could have been captured by a video recorder capable of tracking events in all their minutiae. The film, alas, has now been

to make the past finally available in transparent form. I have been insisting in this chapter that "the past" does not exist other than as constituted by us humans as an object of inquiry. Deep history breaks with the modern code of history, but it breaks with it not by offering us an unobstructed view of the past, but by constructing a different code. Whether this different code is "better" cannot be adjudicated by the criteria of faithful representation or Truth, but rather in terms of what we want of history, of what different codes "do." It may be that one day a seamless "pastness" stretching back to Paleolithic times, or even the Big Bang, where the natural and the human are intertwined and inseparable, will become the dominant code through which we conceive and represent the past; and history will have dispensed with the search for human purposes and meanings. The case has already been persuasively made that the distinction between "nature" and the human or social or cultural was an artificial one that is coming undone, and in particular, that the advent of the Anthropocene erodes or collapses this distinction.[79] It may be that in the future, the code of modern history that I have been anatomizing may come to seem as quaint, or misleading, as myth and epic now seem to us. But if such a change happens, it will not be because deep history represents the past more accurately, objectively, or truthfully than modern history, but because some of the "deep" presuppositions of our thought and our culture will have changed.

---

lost. . . . Happily, however, the passage of events remains embedded in various traces that were left on earth. . . . To take the stance of the video recorder is to hold that history is a narrative of the things that have happened in the past (Smail, *On Deep History*, 70).

[79] Most notably in the writings of Bruno Latour, including *We Have Never Been Modern*, translated by Carolyn Porter, New York: Harvester Wheatsheaf, 1993, and *Politics of Nature*, translated by Carolyn Porter, Cambridge, MA: Harvard University Press, 2004. It has also been persuasively argued that the advent of the "Anthropocene" poses challenges to how we think of history. Dipesh Chakrabarty, "The Climate of History: Four Theses," *Critical Inquiry* 35 (Winter 2009), 197–222.

4

The Anachronism of History

In the preceding chapter I argued that it is not the availability of the past that gives rise to the discipline of history, but rather that history writing is a code or technology, a specific way of producing "the past" as an object. I further specified the most important elements of this code. If, then, history is a specific way of constituting, representing, and relating to the past, rather than simply the truthful and objective representation of it, at least two further questions arise. First, what sort of knowledge is being produced when we write history in the modern mode, and what does it do? And second, what is the status of the knowledge produced when we apply the code of history to times and places that had their own, different modes of historicity? This chapter pursues these two issues, beginning with the first.

History and Humanity

Whereas many other forms of historicity (what historians sometimes call "tradition") treat the past as a living resource, a storehouse of examples that bleed into the present and provide a guide on how to act in it, a key element of modern history, as seen in the previous chapter, is that the past is dead. By the end of the nineteenth century, Langlois and Seignobos's widely used *Introduction to the Study of History* could note with satisfaction, "It is within the last fifty years that the scientific forms of historical exposition have been evolved and settled, in accordance with the general principle that the aim of history is not to please, nor to give practical maxims of conduct, nor to arouse the emotions, but knowledge pure and simple."[1] However, even as "knowledge pure and simple," Langlois and Seignobos affirmed, history had

---

[1] Charles-Victor Langlois and Charles Seignobos, *Introduction to the Study of History*, translated by G. G. Berry, 1898, London: Frank Cass, 1966, 303. On how a new generation of French historians—Langlois and Seignobos among them—transformed history into a scholarly discipline, "severing the umbilical cord that had tied history to its two parent disciplines, literature and philosophy," see William R. Keylor, *Academy and Community: The Foundation of the French Historical Profession*, Cambridge, MA: Harvard University Press, 1975, 2.

Beyond Reason. Sanjay Seth, Oxford University Press (2021). © Oxford University Press.
DOI: 10.1093/oso/9780197500583.003.0005

its uses, for it was "an indispensable branch of instruction in a democratic society," rendering "the pupil fitter for public life."[2] This is one among a class of "pragmatic" answers to the question of what history is "for"—others (commonly heard at university Open Days) include, "You have to know the past to avoid repeating its mistakes," and "You have to know where you came from to know where you are going." These are "pragmatic" in the sense that once history has turned into a purely cognitive matter—once it has been denied any propaedeutic role—to ask what it is "for" becomes a question the answer to which must perforce be framed in terms of social utility.

Another class of answers begins by observing that the code of history is modern, and then seeks connections between history writing and other features of modernity. Constantine Fasolt argues that a modern sense of history and the autonomous individual both emerged in the Renaissance, and that this was no coincidence, for this new way of representing the past promised "enhanced control . . . to human beings over the world of self and society. That promise is why it was accepted in early modern times and why it spread."[3] According to Sande Cohen, modern history is closely connected to bourgeois modernity and serves to secure the "cultural reproduction" of "advanced societies," by neutralizing their contradictions.[4] In these two examples, as in others like them, history is functional for, or an instrument of, whatever is seen as the defining feature of the modern—be it bourgeois society or the autonomous individual.

These and other answers indicate that there is no consensus on what history is "for" or what it "does." This should not puzzle us: like any long-standing practice, especially one that is ubiquitous, modern history-writing performs a multitude of functions, and no doubt has effects that are unrelated or tangential to or even at odds with each other. The forms of public life to which a knowledge of the historical past is said to conduce vary considerably, as do the social and economic settings in which history writing is practiced, which is why it is not persuasive to see history as necessary to democracy, capitalism, the ruling class, or the autonomous individual. However, what the code of history does in all cases—and this is given by the very nature and structure of the code, rather than being dependent on the circumstances in which it is practiced—is to connect past and present. In Michel de Certeau's

[2] Langlois and Seignobos, *Study of History*, 332.

[3] Constantine Fasolt, *The Limits of History*, Chicago: University of Chicago Press, 2004, xiv.

[4] Sande Cohen, *Historical Culture: On the Recoding of an Academic Discipline*, Berkeley: University of California Press, 1986, 16–17.

words, history "constantly mends the rents in the fabric that joins the past and present. It assures a 'meaning' which surmounts the violence and division of time. It creates a theater of references and common values . . . reunite[ing] all sorts of separated things and people into a semblance of unity."[5] Hayden White similarly observes that even as the transformation of history into a pure knowledge or science entailed surrendering its authority to serve as a propaedeutic to life, "history still served communities by providing a genealogical account of the formation of group identities. . . . This is the social or political or . . . ideological function of 'the historical past.' "[6] The most general and therefore the most convincing answer to the question of what modern history is for or what it does, I suggest, is that it does what other forms of historicity do: it establishes continuities and ensures identity. Like the other forms of historicity that it is an alternative to, and which it threatens to supersede, modern history establishes continuities with the past; but it does so not by treating the past as available, as present, but precisely by the opposite means, insisting that the past is dead, and thus establishing different *kinds* of continuities. The code of history introduces division and rupture in order to then bridge the gap between the then and the now, between identity and difference.

Two elements in the code I drew attention to in the previous chapter—the anthropological/humanist and the determinist elements—are the means by which this is done. The humanist presumption specifies that the subject of history is man and that man is a subject, a meaning-creating being. Men and women of the past were different from us, and in recreating their thoughts, actions, and their times through the traces they have left behind, we must avoid the cardinal sin of anachronism, of seeing them through our contemporary lenses and thereby making them "like us." But when we historicize, subject and object coincide—these figures from the past humanized the world they inhabited just as we do, endowing it with purpose and meaning, even if these purposes and meanings were different from ours—and this offers a guarantee that while we are different from those we study, we are also alike. This, as seen in the previous chapter, is the presumption underlying history writing that is outlined and celebrated by figures like Erich Auerbach, Wilhelm von Humboldt, and Paul Ricoeur and often traced back to a

[5] Michel de Certeau, *Heterologies: Discourse on the Other*, translated by Brian Massumi, Manchester: Manchester University Press, 1986, 205.
[6] Hayden White, *The Practical Past*, Evanston, IL: Northwestern University Press, 2014, 98.

"discovery" made by Vico and Herder; and it is this same presumption that is characterized and criticized by Lévi-Strauss, Foucault, Derrida, and other "antihumanists" as "transcendental humanism" or "transcendental narcissism." In putting this presumption to work—in performing it, as it were—the gap between then and now, them and us, is acknowledged, but only because we have an a priori guarantee that this gap can be bridged and that history writing will do it for us.

The "determinist" element of the code also effects an operation that establishes identity and difference. The past is dead and cannot be resurrected, only represented; and yet we are still connected to the past through all the ways in which it has shaped or determined the present. Here origin/genesis and causality establish continuity; our "now" is very different from past humanity's "then," but our now is in some sense—a sense to be determined by historical writing—a product of their then. The role of the determinist element of the code of history is to locate and identify those changes and ruptures that mark a difference and a division, and yet in the very act of doing so establish a (causal, or genetic) connection and continuity.

These two elements, as I observed earlier, certainly do not logically imply each other, but when they are brought together to work in tandem, as they are when the code of history is employed to represent the past, they establish the Sameness and Otherness, and Identity and Difference, of past and present. But unlike "tradition," they do so by insisting upon, rather than blurring or effacing, the distinction between past and present.[7]

Furthermore, the subject/object of the code of history is also different from that of tradition. Tradition is always the "history of" some specific group, practice, or region. The transition from "a plurality of specific histories to a general and singular history"[8] in modern times was made possible, Reinhart Koselleck argues, by the emergence of a new subject, a "collective singular": man or humanity. Capitalism, conquest, and colonialism were among the conditions of possibility of the emergence of this collective singular, for hitherto "differential temporalities and histories" now came, in

---

[7] As Andre Burguiere puts it, "Revealing through its remoteness from the present the variability of the characteristics of a humanity one would be tempted to believe eternal: and by offering itself to be read as an archaeology of the present," history assures us of the continuity between past and present, and the constancy (in the midst of change) of its subject. *The Annales School: An Intellectual History*, translated by Jane Marie Todd, Ithaca, NY: Cornell University Press, 2009, 25–26.

[8] Reinhart Koselleck, *Futures Past: On the Semantics of Historical Time*, translated by Keith Tribe, New York: Columbia University Press, 2004, 195.

Stuart Hall's words, to be "irrevocably and violently yoked together."[9] It is thus in the sixteenth century that the long-established genre of "universal history" comes to be joined by histories of the world, that is, "secular" histories that take many regions and peoples as their subject matter.[10] Specific historical works continued to be "of" something more particular—most commonly, for a very long period, the nation—but for the first time, these numerous histories were now all, in principle, subsets of "history in general," of the historicity of humankind. By the end of the twentieth century, this was being thematized in the form of "world history" and "global history," with its proponents declaring that with globalization, "'humanity' has become a pragmatic reality with a common destiny."[11] Indeed, according to one of the founding figures in the subfield of world history, now that this was a "palpable reality,"[12] "cultivating a sense of individual identification with the triumphs and tribulations of humanity as a whole" was "the moral duty of the historical profession in our time."[13]

Thus unlike many other forms of representing the past, modern historiography is about all humanity and does not belong to any specific peoples or epoch. It appears or presents itself as "a kind of transcendental category," in Koselleck's description;[14] or in Pierre Nora's, as that which "belongs to everyone and to no one, whence its claim to universal authority."[15] This is part of the reason why modern history threatens to replace other forms of historicity—not only because Western domination has globalized this form of constituting and representing the past, but because it *can* be generalized, since it claims all humankind as its object. The "transcendental humanism" affirmed by so many, and more recently criticized by Foucault and others, is thus central to historiography.

[9] Stuart Hall, "When Was 'the Post-colonial'? Thinking at the Limit," in Iain Chambers and Lidia Curti (eds.), *The Post-colonial Question*, New York: Routledge, 1996, 252.

[10] These begin to be produced not only in Europe, but also in parts of the non-Western world—see Sanjay Subrahmanyam, "On World Historians in the Sixteenth Century," *Representations* 91:1 (Summer 2005), 26–57. On eighteenth-century efforts to narrate a "global" history see Jennifer Pitts, "The Global in Enlightenment Historical Thought," in Prasenjit Duara, Viren Murthy, and Andrew Sartori (eds.), *A Companion to Global Historical Thought*, Malden, MA: John Wiley and Sons, 2014.

[11] Michael Geyer and Charles Bright, "World History in a Global Age," in Bruce Mazlish and Akira Iriye (eds.), *The Global History Reader*, New York: Routledge, 2005, 29.

[12] William H. McNeill, "The Changing Shape of World History," *History and Theory* 34:2 (May 1995), 23.

[13] William H. McNeill, "Mythohistory, or Truth, Myth, History, and Historians," *American Historical Review* 91:1 (February 1986), 7.

[14] Koselleck, *Futures Past*, 195.

[15] Pierre Nora, "Between Memory and History: Le Lieux de Memoire," *Representations* 26 (Spring 1989), 9.

However, this also creates a tension, even a paradox, in the practice of history. For even if it is the case that humanity is now (or has for some time been) a "palpable" or "pragmatic" reality, it has not always been so, and yet modern history takes humanity as its object for *all* historical periods, not just the period when different temporalities came to be "yoked together" and world history became conceivable. Jürgen Habermas points to the resulting contradiction, noting that if it is only in recent centuries that "particular histories have coalesced into the history of *one* world," this "cannot then retrospectively be made to cover history as a whole; the fact that global unity has only come to be historically contradicts an approach that makes the totality of history from the very beginning its premise."[16]

There is another aspect of this paradox: it is not just that the object "humanity" only becomes available at a particular point in time, but that the code that takes the past of this humanity as its object is itself the product not of humanity, but of a subset of it. This point can be illustrated with the help of an example, one drawn from Jean-François Lyotard's *The Differend: Phrases in Dispute*.[17] Lyotard contrasts the *miyoi* (myths or legends about past events) of the Cashinahua peoples with modern historiography. To be authorized to narrate *miyoi* one must have a Cashinahua name, and the story is addressed to Cashinahua listeners: "In repeating it, the community assures itself of the permanence and legitimacy of its world of names by way of the recurrence of this world in its stories." This community is an "exclusive" community, distinct from all others, and thus the narrative reinforces an identity that is solely "Cashinahua." Lyotard contrasts Cashinahua *miyoi* with history, which is "cosmopolitical," in that the narrator need only be human (not specifically Cashinahua) to be authorized to tell it, and the story is that of humanity. Cashinahua *miyoi* exclude "humanity," to the degree that they are even aware of it; by contrast modern history is about all humans, including, in principle, the Cashinahua. But when Cashinahua pasts are included in modern history, "The savage . . . suffers a wrong on account of the fact that he or she is 'cognized' [i.e., included in our historical account] . . . according to criteria and in an idiom which are neither those which he or she obeys nor their 'result.'"

---

[16] Jürgen Habermas, *Theory and Practice*, translated by John Viertel, Heinemann, 1974, 251. Marx also elliptically notes, in the *Grundrisse*, that "World history has not always existed"—translated by Martin Nicolaus, New York: Penguin and New Left Review, 1973, 109.

[17] Translated by Georges van den Abbeele, Minneapolis: University of Minnesota Press, 1989. All quotations and paraphrases are from pp. 153–57. Cashinahua narratives are also discussed in Lyotard and Jean-Loup Thebaud, *Just Gaming*, translated by Wlad Godzich, Minneapolis: University of Minnesota Press, 1985, 32–35.

As I read him, Lyotard is making two related points here. One is that a history that includes the Cashinahua will not be a history written in terms of their categories and self-understandings; in the language that I have been using, the "code" of history will be at odds with their own sense of historicity. But—and this is the second point—that difficulty need not, perhaps, concern us too much if we can see "humanity" and the code that then narrates "its" past as emerging out of Cashinahua pasts. In Lyotard's words, "In order for the history of humanity to be recounted, a universal 'human' narrator and corresponding narratee would have to be able to be engendered from 'savage' ('national') narrators and narratees in their particularity and multiplicity." But this cannot plausibly be done; the Cashinahua may now be part of a globalized modernity where humanity has become a "palpable reality" whose past modern history retells, but they are not producers of that globalization, and modern historiography does not issue from their *miyoi*.

Below I argue that the resulting situation can be characterized as follows: the code of history is in part defined by its rejection of anachronism, and yet anachronism lies at its very heart.

The Anachronism of History

In the discipline of history, anachronism is counted as one of the gravest sins, for to recognize the otherness of the past is a defining feature of the code of history; the great historian Lucien Febvre was moved to condemn anachronism as "absurd," "puerile," and "utter madness."[18] And yet the practice of history requires pressing this modern and Western code into service to understand those who do not share it. This is something that historians encounter all the time, perhaps most obviously when the historian writes about those who attributed a real existence and agency to gods and spirits, an agency that the secular code of history disallows. In such cases, Michel de Certeau writes, "Historians spontaneously take their task to be the need to determine what a field delineated as 'religious' can teach them about a society"; here, "'society' is . . . the axis of reference, the obvious model of all possible intelligibility," and so "'comprehending' religious phenomena is tantamount to repeatedly asking something else of them than what they meant to say . . . taking as

[18] Lucien Febvre, *The Problem of Unbelief in the Sixteenth Century: The Religion of Rabelais*, translated by Beatrice Gottllieb, Cambridge, MA: Harvard University Press, 1982, 460.

a *representation* of society what, from *their* point of view, *founded* that so-ciety."[19] Or as Dipesh Chakrabarty explains, "Historians will grant the super-natural a place in somebody's belief system or ritual practices, but to ascribe it any real agency in historical events will be to go against the rules of evi-dence that gives historical discourse procedures for settling disputes about the past."[20] Thus when confronted by a source in which a subject attributes agency to God or her own agency to God's will, such a statement "has to be anthropologized (that is, converted into somebody's belief or made into an object of anthropological analysis) before it finds a place in the historian's narrative."[21] Certeau characterizes this operation, one where the source of agency is reversed, through a metaphor drawn from chess: "Between their time and ours, the signifier and the signified have castled. We postulate a coding which inverts that of the time we are studying." He adds, "We have to wonder what may be the meaning of an enterprise that consists of 'un-derstanding' a time organized as a function of a standard of comprehension other than ours."[22] What, for instance, is the "understanding" achieved—to return to an example discussed in the previous chapter—in writing a modern history of the Jews, an undertaking standing in opposition to its own subject matter, given that historiography "cannot credit God's will as the active cause behind Jewish events, and it cannot regard Jewish history as being unique"?[23]

Disallowing agency to gods is only one (especially dramatic) instance of what Certeau calls "castling," and what I am (provocatively) calling anachro-nism. Such instances—where the presuppositions defining the code of his-tory (including that the world is disenchanted; that the past is dead; that only humans are the producers of meanings and purposes, and that this is what history disinters and represents; and that "society" provides the context for, and shapes, human actions) are applied to those who do not share the code, and yet whose past that code seeks to illuminate and explain—arise all the time in the course of writing history. One might expect that this would lead historians to ask what sort of knowledge is being produced when this code is applied to pasts where its presumptions are not widely shared; but in fact, the

[19] Certeau, *The Writing of History*, translated by Tom Conley, New York: Columbia University Press, 1998, 138.
[20] Dipesh Chakrabarty, *Provincializing Europe*, Princeton, NJ: Princeton University Press, 2000, 104. See also Robert A. Orsi, *History and Presence*, Cambridge, MA: Belknap Press of Harvard University Press, 2016.
[21] Chakrabarty, *Provincializing Europe*, 105.
[22] Certeau, *The Writing of History*, 138.
[23] Harold Bloom, "Foreword" to Yosef Hayim Yerushalmi, *Zakhor: Jewish History and Jewish Memory*, 2nd ed., Seattle: University of Washington Press, 1996, xix.

reflective questions asked by a Chakrabarty or a Certeau are rare, rather than being central to debates in the discipline.

Drawing upon some recent works of history and historiography, in what follows I seek to show that the anachronism I am suggesting is an inescapable feature of history writing can nonetheless be "redeemed," that is, can be put to productive use—in some circumstances. These circumstances are not available, I will go on to suggest, where non-Western pasts are being represented.

Redeeming Anachronism

In *The Limits of History*, Constantine Fasolt seeks to show that history is a technology that was invented by Renaissance humanists, who placed this technology at the service of European rulers who were seeking to establish that their political authority did not derive from that of the pope and emperor. He develops his argument, in part, through a close reading of Hermann Conring's (1608–1681) *Discoursus novus de imperatore Romano Germanico* (*New Discourse of the Roman-German Emperor*—1642),[24] in which Conring sought to refute claims that the Roman Empire still existed, that the king of Germany was the Roman emperor, and that he derived his title from the church and ultimately from God. One of those whom he singled out as upholding these unjustifiable claims was Bartolus of Sassoferrato (1313/14–1357), the great medieval jurist. Surveying this debate, Fasolt concludes that Conring and Bartolus were arguing at cross-purposes:

> Bartolus focused on law; Conring focused on politics . . . Bartolus looked to eternity; Conring looked to history. For Bartolus the universe was integrated into one hierarchy; for Conring it was divided into an infinity of separate self-subsisting parts. Bartolus maintained that politics and law were fundamentally the same, Conring that they were essentially distinct. Bartolus thought the nature of things consisted of relationships; Conring, that it consisted of an invariant essence. And so on.[25]

[24] This book was published under Conring's name, possibly by one of his students (it is the text of a "dissertation" submitted by one of Conring's students to the University of Helmstedt, in 1841), a practice not unusual at the time; Conring disowned the work, but Fasolt suggests that the ideas in it are those of Conring, for they are a reprise of a work he had written earlier.

[25] Fasolt, *The Limits of History*, 199.

These multiple differences had a common root: for Bartolus the source of all overlordship and of the unity of the world was God, the "efficient cause" of the empire and the church; while Conring's argument was historical in a way that Bartolus's was not and, in Fasolt's reading, could not be: "could not be" because this mode of understanding was new; the Renaissance humanists had invented it, and Conring was drawing upon and developing their legacy, of which we too are heirs. That is why, in revisiting this debate, we cannot but find ourselves in sympathy with Conring, and why, according to Fasolt, even when we exercise historical charity and seek to place Bartolus "in his own context," this historicizing maneuver only aligns us all the more securely on the side of Conring and history: "To seek a historical understanding of the relationship between Bartolus and Conring is . . . an oxymoron: either the understanding will be historical, and then it will confirm the wall of historical consciousness that Conring built to separate himself from Bartolus. Or it will break that wall: but then it cannot be historical."[26]

Fasolt seeks to show that the reason why Conrad and Bartolus were arguing at cross-purposes was because their intellectual worlds were "hermetically sealed off from each other, not in all respects (there are connections, echoes, overtones, traditions connecting them), but in a fashion so elementary that the thought of one cannot be translated into the thought of the other."[27] But despite this suggestion of incommensurability, Fasolt himself provides evidence suggesting that this gulf was bridged by a shared set of references and vocabulary (a common, inherited language of *ius*, *lex*, *dominium*—and thus "connections, echoes, overtones, traditions connecting them"), which is surely an important qualification to his claim that their worlds were "hermetically sealed off." Thus even as Fasolt seeks to show that history is an invention of the Renaissance humanists, and therefore that the code of history is anachronistic when applied to the medieval world, he also sheds light on how the struggle to refute and replace earlier ways of understanding shaped the mode of understanding to which we are now heirs. The anachronism is "redeemed" insofar as it illuminates the continuities and breaks in a tradition where, to put it too simply, once God explained the world, and later history came to do so. A recognition of this anachronism serves to connect us, who live in an age of history, with our intellectual forbears, who did not.

---

[26] Fasolt, *The Limits of History*, 218.
[27] Fasolt, *The Limits of History*, 213.

The question of anachronism also came to be sharply posed in one of the most "worked upon" areas of historiography, the French Revolution. Alfred Cobban's *The Social Interpretation of the French Revolution* was a major revisionist work of its time, contesting what was then the dominant historical interpretation of the Revolution: one that characterized it as a social revolution that overthrew feudalism and ushered in bourgeois society. Cobban argued that far from overturning feudalism and facilitating unfettered capitalist development, the Revolution was a triumph for the conservative, propertied, landowning classes, a revolution against, rather than for, "the penetration of an embryo capitalism into French society."[28] That this was so completely misread by the dominant historical interpretation was a consequence, according to Cobban, of the fact this interpretation employed anachronistic categories of analysis. Indeed, there was a double anachronism at work. First, the dominant interpretation failed to recognize that sociological terms used in the eighteenth century had often changed meaning by the nineteenth and twentieth centuries. In the eighteenth century a *laboureur* was a fairly substantial peasant proprietor, and a *manufacturier* was someone who manufactured products with his hands—not the social roles and classes that these terms designated by the nineteenth century. The dominant interpretation thus superimposed a nineteenth-century sociology (of which Marxism was an especially influential variant) upon an eighteenth-century social reality. But worse still, the analytic categories deployed by revolutionary actors, such as "feudalism" and "bourgeoisie," were already "out-of-date" even at the time; for instance, the "feudalism" that was a main target of the revolutionaries had long ago ceased to be "feudal" in any meaningful sense, just as the idea that there were three clearly demarcated estates or orders had "long before 1789 ceased to bear any close relation to social realities."[29]

In Jacques Rancière's summary of Cobban's argument, "For Cobban, Marxist interpretation sticks words and notions from later times onto the past event. But it can do this because it takes for granted the words of the actors, contemporaries, and chroniclers of the Revolution. Now, these words were themselves anachronistic. . . . They referred to a situation that in fact no longer existed in their epoch."[30] The logic of this argument would

---

[28] Alfred Cobban, *The Social Interpretation of the French Revolution*, first delivered as the Wiles Lectures in 1961, Cambridge: Cambridge University Press, 1968, 172.

[29] Cobban, *Social Interpretation*, 21.

[30] Jacques Rancière, *The Names of History*, translated by Hassan Melehy, Minneapolis: University of Minnesota Press, 1994, 33.

seem to lead to the conclusion that the revolutionaries, and most subsequent interpreters of the Revolution, were neither good historians nor good sociologists, because they were guilty of anachronism; to avoid such anachronism we must (again in Rancière's summary of Cobban's position) "abandon the terminology of the Revolution—that of the actors, contemporaries, and interpreters—in order to examine the social facts as would a sociologist who was contemporary with the Revolution."[31]

This is not, however, the conclusion that Rancière draws. For according to Rancière, "There is nothing accidental about this misfortune [that the Revolution did not produce a sociology adequate to itself]. It is because there was a French Revolution that sociology is born."[32] If this is so, any attempt to explain the French Revolution in terms of "underlying" social realities is to seek to explain it through a paradigm and vocabulary that is itself an invention of modern times. The important point Rancière is making is that irrespective of whether or not Cobban is right in arguing that the Marxist historical interpretation of the Revolution has been mistaken, to seek to make sense of the Revolution through social categories of analysis like worker, bourgeois, and so on is something that *only comes into being* with the Revolution; and is thus itself anachronistic.[33]

What I think this debate allows us to see is that the problem with the Marxist interpretation of the Revolution is not merely (in the words of François Furet) that it "fails to take any distance from the revolutionary consciousness whose illusions and values it shares" (which is Cobban's point), but also (and this now applies to Cobban as well) that it fails to see the most radically new aspect of the Revolution, namely that it invented a new political culture, one that has shaped successive generations and to which we all, including the interpreters of the Revolution, are heirs.[34] And so while Cobban may see himself as a scourge of anachronism, his equation/reduction of history to a historical sociology is itself anachronistic, or always prey

---

[31] Rancière, *The Names of History*, 35.

[32] Rancière, *The Names of History*, 36.

[33] We encountered a very similar argument in chapter 1, in the form of the claim by Keith Michael Baker and others that the Enlightenment "invented," rather than discovered, "the social," and thus that society, and the sociological terms in which we understand it, emerged coterminously.

[34] As Furet puts it, "Not only did the Revolution found the political culture that makes 'contemporary' France intelligible, but it also bequeathed to France conflicts between legitimacies and a virtually inexhaustible stock of political debates"; it is "Mother of the political culture into which all of us are born." *Interpreting the French Revolution*, translated by Elborg Foster, Cambridge: Cambridge University Press, 1981, 6, 10. See also his "The French Revolution Revisited," in Gary Kates (ed.), *The French Revolution: Recent Debates and New Controversies*, 2nd ed., New York: Routledge, 2006.

to becoming so when applied to "pre-sociological" pasts. But even if it is the case that to deploy sociological categories to study pre-revolutionary France is anachronistic, there is a dividend for this anachronism. It allows us to mark an origin for our modern age; to mark discontinuity and difference. This is not a point zero, because it has its origins in what preceded it: the intelligibility of the difference it marks, and of the newness it brings into the world, is provided by that which preceded and produced it—feudalism according to the Marxists, and the political culture of the ancien régime, according to Furet and others.

For my third example I return to Certeau, who, as we saw earlier, "wonders" at the status of a knowledge that translates religious explanations into secular terms. When historians write about historical subjects of the seventeenth century, they cannot give explanatory credence to subjects' explanations where these explanations attribute agency to God. Instead, historians explain such ascriptions with reference to social conditions, to alienation, to self-estrangement, and so on. This anachronism is inescapable, because our mode of historicity is premised upon the claim that history is about men and women and is made by them and only by them. However, our historical practice is not an ex nihilo creation but arises out of previous debates. Certeau writes, "When they refer to their own practices . . . historians discover constraints originating well before their own present, dating back to former organizations of which their work is a symptom, not a cause."[35] "Our" historical discourse is a product of those debates and processes that, beginning some centuries ago, rendered religion into a phenomenon susceptible to sociological explanation, rather than regarding the human world as one to be understood in terms of divine instigation. "Just as the 'model' of religious sociology implies, among other things, the new status of practice or of knowledge in the seventeenth century, so do current methods—erased as events and transformed into codes or problematic areas of research—bear evidence of former structurings and forgotten histories. Thus founded on the rupture between a past that is its object and a present that is the place of its practice, history endlessly finds the present in its object and the past in its practice."[36] Thus while anachronism is unavoidable, it can nonetheless yield insight: in this case, a better understanding of our relation to a tradition in which God once bestrode the world and made it in his image, but which later

---

[35] Certeau, *The Writing of History*, 36.
[36] Certeau, *The Writing of History*, 36.

gave way to a "secular" view in which God had his historical agency with-drawn from him.

I have been presenting these examples to suggest that using secular and his-toricist categories to discuss the late medieval world or seventeenth-century France, and socioeconomic categories to understand France before and at the time of the French Revolution, is anachronistic. But I am also claiming that even where anachronism cannot be avoided, history writing can lead us to critically examine the continuities and breaks between the past under ex-amination and our present. In some cases, such as in the preceding examples, we may, in Gadamerian fashion, conclude that there is a bridge connecting "us" to "them," assuring us that just as we are born of them, so our categories are also born of theirs; that the transformations and ruptures that make our present different from their past also arise out of that past, rather than being wholly external to it. The application of the code to the past may illuminate the emergence of the code; the "former structurings and forgotten histories" that have brought us to our present historical situation can be disinterred and re-examined, so that historical inquiry yields a better understanding of the tradition that produced us and through which we speak.

This is only so, however, where we conceive of the past in question not as the past of a collective singular—everyman's past—but a specific past, or that which I have been calling "tradition." A debate on the history of music serves to illustrate this point well.

Everyman's Past versus Someone's Tradition

The early music movement, which became increasingly prominent (and commercially successful) from the 1950s, sought to promote baroque, Renaissance, and medieval music that would be played "authentically," that is, as intended by the composer, using instruments of the period, and as it would have been heard by audiences of the time.[37] Part of what propelled this movement was an investment in historicity, manifested both in the de-sire to retrieve "past" music and in the determination to avoid anachronism in the playing of that music. The idea of authenticity, however, soon came

[37] For an account of this movement see Harry Haskell, *The Early Music Revival: A History*, New York: Dover Publications, 1996. The more academic debate about "authenticity" and the perfor-mance of early music is surveyed in John Butt, *Playing with History: Historical Approaches to Musical Performance*, New York: Cambridge University Press, 2002, chap. 1.

under challenge on multiple grounds. It was pointed out that the evidence that would allow us to recreate how earlier music was performed was simply not available;[38] and that even if such knowledge were available to us and this music were played as it would have been "in its own context," contemporary performances of it could not possibly be authentic, given that they usually occurred "in the most anachronistic of all settings, the concert hall."[39] And even if "sonic authenticity" could be achieved, this was not the same as "sensible authenticity," that is, reproducing how music was heard when performed in its time: for "when we—that is to say, present-day audiences—hear music, we hear it in its history. . . . Each time a listener hears an 'anticipation,' he or she hears a musical property that could not have been heard by audiences contemporary with the work."[40] To hear music "historically," Peter Kivy pointed out, is, paradoxically, to hear it "inauthentically," for it is to hear and experience the music as no audience contemporaneous with it could have heard it.[41]

This chorus of criticisms led to claims to "authenticity" being moderated, and some champions of the movement came to speak instead of "historically informed" performance. But the controversy did not abate. The debate increasingly turned, not simply on whether authenticity could be achieved, but rather on whether it was even desirable; that is, on the relation between knowledge of the history of music and its contemporary performance. One of the most critical and effective voices was that of Richard Taruskin, a musicologist who was himself an accomplished conductor of early music. Historically informed performances of early music, Taruskin averred, all too often sought "mere freedom from error or anachronism,"[42] wrongly assuming that avoiding anachronism was a guarantee of aesthetic value. In the opinion of Taruskin and some others, many early music performances had confused

[38] Thus according to Daniel Leech-Wilkinson, "We still don't know how medieval music was typically performed. . . . We don't know how it was composed . . . nor how carefully it was listened to, nor how it was understood as musical process." *The Modern Invention of Medieval Music*, New York: Cambridge University Press, 2002, 260.

[39] Richard Taruskin, *Text and Act: Essays on Music and Performance*, New York: Oxford University Press, 1995, 93.

[40] Peter Kivy, *Authenticities: Philosophical Reflections on Musical Performance*, Ithaca, NY: Cornell University Press, 1995, 55.

[41] Kivy, *Authenticities*, 71–72.

[42] Richard Taruskin, "The Authenticity Movement Can Become a Positivistic Purgatory, Literalistic and Dehumanizing," *Early Music* 12:1 (February 1984), 6.

historical accuracy or "authenticity" with good performance, and even worse, "appeals to authenticity" were "used to defend bad performances."[43]

If historical accuracy did not guarantee good performance, then what was the proper relation between historical knowledge and performance, if any? According to Taruskin, when it came to performance, historical knowledge was a means to an end, not an end in itself. For instance, using old instruments had the effect of "open[ing] the mind and ear to new experiences," thereby enabling the performer "to transcend his habitual, and therefore unconsidered, ways of hearing and thinking about the music."[44] It was important to be attentive to history, "But the object is not to duplicate the sounds of the past, for if that were our aim we would never know whether we had succeeded. What we are aiming at, rather, is the startling shock of new-ness, of immediacy."[45] Historically informed performances could not, and moreover should not, seek to recapture the musical past "as it really was": "At their best and most successful historical reconstructionist performances are in no sense recreations of the past. They are quintessentially modern performances, modernist performances in fact, the product of an aesthetic wholly of our own era, no less time-bound than the performance styles they would supplant."[46]

But in that case, in what sense were they "historical" at all? The answer to this, according to Taruskin, was that "the past" at issue was not the past in general, not the historical past that (in Nora's description) "belongs to everyone and to no one," but rather *tradition*, something that belonged to *someone*. The Western art-musical tradition had been passed on and developed by successive generations, but it could no longer be unreflectively inherited and continued in contemporary times; invoking T. S. Eliot, Taruskin argued that because this tradition "cannot be inherited," those who wished to continue it

---

[43] John Kerman, *Contemplating Music: Challenges to Musicology*, Cambridge, MA: Harvard University Press, 1985, 192.

[44] Taruskin, "Authenticity Movement," 11.

[45] Taruskin, "Authenticity Movement," 11. See similarly Laurence Dreyfus, "Early Music Defended against Its Devotees: A Theory of Historical Performance in the Twentieth Century," *Musical Quarterly* 69:3 (Summer 1983), and Butt, *Playing with History*, 8. Taruskin's trenchant interventions over some two decades were regarded by some as an attack on "authentic" or "historically informed" music, but his argument, in his later words, "was that the 'mainstream' or 'modern' performers, whose hegemony the 'authenticists' were challenging, were the ones who were mimicking obsolete historical styles (the ones in which they had been trained), and that those who *claimed* to be mimicking obsolete historical styles were in fact creating something new and vital." Taruskin, *The Danger of Music and Other Anti-Utopian Essays*, Berkeley: University of California Press, 2009, 448.

[46] Richard Taruskin, "On Letting the Music Speak for Itself: Some Reflections on Musicology and Performance," *Journal of Musicology* 1:3 (July 1982), 346.

"must obtain it by great labour."[47] Historically informed music performance could be part of this "great labour," a powerful means by which past music and the tradition that produced it were made a living part of our present. But according to this analysis, the early music movement had not grasped its own implications and possibilities, namely that what was at issue was not how to accurately represent and reproduce a general past—"everyman's past" as we might call it—but rather how to relate to and continue "our" tradition. Historically informed music performance could contribute to this, but only if it was recognized that the purpose of such performances was not historical accuracy and the avoidance of anachronism, but rather an effort at making anachronism "work" for us, by allowing us to encounter the musical tradition(s) that produced us with fresh ears, and to appropriate them according to our aesthetic: "Early Music is . . . to be this generation's way of claiming Beethoven for its (our) own . . . it shocks us out of our comfortable genetic fallacies . . . [and] can play a major role in the endless process of renewal that keeps our cherished repertoire alive. *That* is tradition."[48]

Operating from similar premises—that what was at issue was appropriating tradition and keeping it alive, rather than avoiding anachronism—Robert Morgan drew the opposite conclusion. In his view, the early music movement's desire to play works of the past in something approximating their original form was a symptom of the decline and even death of a shared and once vibrant musical tradition. This tradition had once been characterized by an untroubled sense of continuity with the past. For instance—and this returns us to an example raised in the previous chapter—performances of Bach in the nineteenth century were made to conform to the musical traditions of that century. From a historical point of view "such liberties may strike us as unforgivable perversions," but from a musical point of view they indicated that "Bach's music persisted as part of a flourishing tradition . . . renewing itself through new ideas and developments."[49] Such a healthy relationship with past music was untroubled by the sin of anachronism: "Within this framework one is not inclined to think about the past in a conscious way at all; one does not think of it primarily as the *past*, but as part of a living—and thus constantly changing—musical culture."[50] By contrast,

---

[47] Taruskin, *Text and Act*, 79.
[48] Taruskin, *Text and Act*, 234.
[49] Robert P. Morgan, "Tradition, Anxiety and the Musical Scene," in Nicholas Kenyon (ed.), *Authenticity and Early Music*, Oxford: Oxford University Press, 1988, 68.
[50] Morgan, "Tradition, Anxiety," 59.

the early music movement's desire for historical authenticity, its desire to "reconstruct as faithfully as possible,"[51] was a symptom of the decline of a living musical tradition, and thus constituted "what might be described as a cultural identity crisis."[52] In Morgan's analysis of it, early music signified the death and "museumification" of a once living and vibrant musical tradition; by contrast for Taruskin, early music, if performed in the right way, could be a way of inheriting and renewing that tradition.

What Taruskin, Morgan, and some other participants in this debate came to see is that the injunction to avoid anachronism may be at odds with maintaining a living connection with a "tradition." As we saw in the last chapter, Pierre Nora and Yosef Yerushalmi also recognize that to historicize in the manner that the code of history requires may be at odds with its subject matter and may sever links with a living tradition. However, while they can recognize this and draw attention to it, unlike Taruskin and Morgan, as *historians* it is not possible for them to press for a knowledge of the past that is untroubled by the prospect of anachronism. The specific, ontological character of music (or the performing arts more generally), which includes an inescapable gap between past/original text and present performance, is what makes it possible for Taruskin and Morgan to embrace anachronism. By contrast historians, even where they are alert to and troubled by the anachronism that is inherent in pressing modern categories into service to represent nonmodern pasts, can only hope that they will find "the present in its object and the past in its practice." That is, they can only hope that this anachronism can be redeemed, that the code of history can itself plausibly be shown to be connected to, and to emerge out of, the past that is being narrated.

But this is precisely what cannot be done for Indian, and more generally for non-Western, pasts, for here the advent of modern historical writing marks a break with their own modes of historicity.

Historiography and Non-Western Pasts

Just as modern history writing does not emerge out of Cashinahua *miyoi*, so too the modern mode of history writing did not emerge out of the many indigenous traditions of historicity in the Indian subcontinent, whether it be

---

[51] Morgan, "Tradition, Anxiety," 78.
[52] Morgan, "Tradition, Anxiety," 78.

the "high" *itihasa-purana* tradition, or regional practices of historicity such as *bakhars, buranjis, puwada, lavani, bats, khyats, kulagranthas,* and others.[53] It did not emerge through engaging with and displacing these modes of historicity, but came instead with the colonizer, and its victory was cheaply won, as a result of colonial administrative fiat. Although the presumptions that characterized it were historically and culturally specific ones, it was presented by the colonizer not as a British or European way of representing the past, but as the right and true way of doing so, in contrast to what were denounced as the fictional and "superstitious" indigenous modes of representing it— what Macaulay in his Minute on Education of 1835 dismissed as histories "abounding with kings thirty feet high and reigns thirty thousand years long."[54]

Nonetheless, like the English language, history writing has become native to India. From the moment that the British became territorial rulers of Bengal, down to the moment they were forced to relinquish their Indian possessions, they wrote histories of India of the modern type.[55] Indians too

---

[53] Since the rise of Indian nationalism, it has been claimed that India *was* in fact possessed of a tradition of history writing. That claim continues to be made today, in scholarly works that have no difficulty in showing that there are texts from the subcontinent that pay some attention to chronology, are sometimes attentive to evidence, and, more generally, possess at least some of the attributes that we take to distinguish history from myth and epic (see, for example, Velcheru Narayana Rao, David Shulman and Sanjay Subrahmanyam, *Textures of Time: Writing History in South India, 1600–1800,* New Delhi: Permanent Black, 2001; and Kumkum Chatterjee, *The Culture of History in Early Modern India: Persianization and Mughal Culture in Bengal,* New Delhi: Oxford University Press, 2009). But the claim for the existence of historical writing in India prior to colonialism rests, I suggest, upon a misunderstanding: it mistakes or conflates evidence for the existence of modes of *historicity* for evidence of *historiography.* For instance, Kumkum Chatterjee surveys Mughal writings in India and concludes that these display similarities with modern historical writing, because "both comprise the process of engaging in a self-conscious commemoration of various aspects of the past" (47). Just so—but this common ground is a shared historicity, as is possessed by all peoples, *not* a shared way or mode of representing that historicity. The sense of history Kumkum Chatterjee refers to—what Dipesh Chakrabarty characterizes as "history as a developmental story, as an explanation of how things came to be the way they were in the present, history as a story of human action devoid altogether of divine intervention, history as a process of change both illustrating and subject to sociological laws"—was, as Chakrabarty rightly insists, new, "and came to India as a result of British rule." "Globalisation, Democratisation and the Evacuation of History?," in J. Assayag and V. Benei (eds.), *At Home in Diaspora,* New Delhi: Permanent Black, 2003, 129.

[54] Minute recorded by Thomas Babington Macaulay, law member of the Governor-General's Council, February 2, 1835, reprinted in Lynn Zastoupil and Martin Moir (eds.), *The Great Indian Education Debate: Documents Relating to the Orientalist-Anglicist Controversy, 1781–1843,* Richmond: Curzon, 1999, 166.

[55] These included Alexander Dow's *The History of Hindostan* in the latter eighteenth century; Mark Wilks's *Historical Sketches of the South of India,* John Malcolm's *Sketch of the Political History of India,* James Mill's *The History of British India,* Duff's *History of the Mahrattas,* Mountstuart Elphinstone's *The History of India,* and W. W. Hunter's *A Brief History of the Indian Peoples* in the nineteenth century; and V. A. Smith's *Oxford History of India* and the multiauthor and multivolume *Cambridge History of India* in the twentieth century.

began to write history in the same vein: the demand that Indians write their own history was raised by Bankimchandra Chatterjee in the nineteenth century, and this demand was met in subsequent decades. Indian nationalism was one of the main vehicles for this—it succeeded both in producing a nation and in producing histories of that nation. The practice of writing history in the modern mode has thus been going on for almost two centuries now in the subcontinent. My argument that it is a modern and Western code does not therefore lead me to the polemical conclusion that historiography is a form of epistemic violence or foreign imposition, but rather to a question: namely, what sort of knowledge do we produce when we apply the code of history to South Asian and, more generally, non-Western pasts?

The discussion of music, art and science history from the previous chapter can provide us with some guidance. It will be recalled that these histories were premised upon the claim that there was an object/practice (art, music, or science) that was constant across time, even as the forms it took were variable; and that this object or practice was at once historicizable and yet not fully so, because these practices were autonomous, at once part of the past and yet a living part of the present. In recent times, as I showed, historians of these practices are less inclined to claim that their objects/practices have some sort of transhistorical, ontological solidity, and more likely to regard the histories of these practices as histories of their *emergence* (usually in what historians periodize as the early modern or modern period). I submit that analogously, in applying the code of history to subcontinental pasts, what we are doing is tracing and narrating the emergence of a disenchanted, secular world, and of subjects who come to see themselves as the producers of meaning against a backdrop of a nature devoid of meaning and purpose. In short, to write the history of India in the modern mode is to narrate the conditions that mark the emergence of that code and make it possible and intelligible.

When the code of history is also applied to pasts that precede these processes—as happens when the code is applied to any premodern past—the historian of the non-Western world cannot presume that the code was engendered by the past to which she applies it. The resulting, *unredeemable* anachronism should lead us to recognize that here the application of the historical code *translates* the lifeworld and the self-understandings of historical subjects into our intellectual and conceptual language.

The metaphor of translation, long in use by anthropologists, has in recent decades been subjected to a critical reworking, at the heart of which is the claim that anthropological "translation" of the practices of a different society or culture should not be directed at revealing their "real meanings"— regardless of whether or not these would be acknowledged (or even understood) by those who are the subjects of study.[56] Where anthropology does so, on the presumption that it is an "etic" knowledge that understands the native better than she can understand herself, it becomes nothing more, in David Schneider's description (cited in chapter 1), than "the ethnoepistemology of European culture."[57] According to Eduardo Viveiros de Castro, "Anthropology compares *so as to translate*, and not to explain, justify, generalize, interpret."[58] There is no reason why this insight should be confined to anthropology. I suggest it applies wherever the object of representation cannot be presumed to inhabit the same knowledge culture as the producer of that knowledge. Let me illustrate what I mean through some examples.

The use of the cadaster to measure land in colonial Egypt, Timothy Mitchell argues, was not a leap in the precision with which land is mapped: it was not a superior way of measuring the same object, land, but rather a change in how land was conceived and could thereby be measured. "The twentieth century's new regime of calculation," Mitchell writes, "did not produce, necessarily, a more accurate knowledge of the world, despite its claims, nor even any overall increase in the quantity of knowledge. Its achievements were to redistribute forms of knowledge, increasing it in some places and decreasing it in others."[59] The cadastral survey and associated forms of mapping, and of statistics, did not represent the same object as the indigenous knowledges they displaced—except now more accurately—but rather produced "a reformatted knowledge, information that has been translated."[60] In Thailand, Thongchai Winichakul shows, modern forms of mapping the nation did not do a better job of representing the space of Siam than the indigenous conceptions of sacred and political space they supplanted: "The

[56] See Talal Asad, "The Concept of Cultural Translation in British Social Anthropology," in James Clifford and George Marcus (eds.), *Writing Culture: The Poetics and Politics of Anthropology*, Berkeley: University of California Press, 1986. On the "folly" of using "an analytical concept or category indifferently anywhere as if that which makes sense in one place must necessary obtain elsewhere," see Lydia H. Liu, *Translingual Practice: Literature, National Culture, and Translated Modernity—China, 1900–1937*, Stanford, CA: Stanford University Press, 1995, 6.

[57] David Schneider, *A Critique of the Study of Kinship*, Ann Arbor: University of Michigan Press, 1984, 175.

[58] Eduardo Viveiros de Castro, "Prespectival Anthropology and the Method of Controlled Equivocation," in his *The Relative Native: Essays on Indigenous Conceptual Worlds*, Chicago: Hau Books, 2015, 57.

[59] Timothy Mitchell, *Rule of Experts: Egypt, Techno-Politics, Modernity*, Berkeley: University of California Press, 2002, 92.

[60] Mitchell, *Rule of Experts*, 115.

emergence of the geo-body of Siam was not a gradual evolution from the in-digenous political space to a modern one," but instead "a replacement of the former by the latter."[61] Modern mapping did not simply spatially represent Siam more accurately, it helped to produce the object it was mapping, Siam.

The colonial census, similarly, did not produce more accurate informa-tion about Indian society than had previously been available. Rather, with an imaginary of "the social" and of "population" built into its optic, it translated (or reformatted) indigenous understandings of sociality into new terms, thereby also, as a growing literature demonstrates, serving to give "the so-cial" a life and a significance that it did not previously have.[62] The categories of the colonial censuses undertaken in Southeast Asia in the latter nine-teenth century, Benedict Anderson shows, were frequently more revealing of the sociological imaginary of colonial officials than of the sociality of those being enumerated: nonetheless, the new demographic topography informed by the census "put down deep social and institutional roots as the colonial state multiplied its size and functions. Guided by its imagined map it organ-ized the new educational, juridical, public-health and police and immigra-tion bureaucracies. . . . The flow of subject populations through the mesh of differential schools, courts, clinics, police stations and immigration offices created 'traffic habits' which in time gave real social life to the state's earlier fantasies."[63]

Mitchell, Anderson, Winichakul, and others have shown that modern knowledges and practices such as the cadaster, census, map, and museum did not simply describe or represent what had already and always been there; they sometimes served to bring it into being. They were not more truthful or more accurate representations of reality than the indigenous knowledge

[61] Thongchai Winichakul, *Siam Mapped: A History of the Geo-Body of a Nation*, Honolulu: University of Hawai'i Press, 1994, 131.

[62] A large literature includes N. Gerald Barrier (ed.), *The Census in British India: New Perspectives*, New Delhi: Manohar, 1981; Bernard Cohn, "Notes on the History of the Study of Indian Society and Culture" and "The Census, Social Structure and Objectification in South Asia," both reprinted in his *An Anthropologist among the Historians and Other Essays*, New Delhi: Oxford University Press, 1987; Richard S. Smith, "Rule-by-Records and Rule-by-Reports: Complementary Aspects of the British Imperial Rule of Law," *Contributions to Indian Sociology* 19:1 (new series), 1985; Rashmi Pant, "The Cognitive Status of Caste in Colonial Ethnography: A Review of Some Literature on the North West Provinces and Oudh," *Indian Economic and Social History Review* 24:2 (1987); Nicholas Dirks, *Castes of Mind*, Princeton, NJ: Princeton University Press, 2001; Sanjay Nigam, "Disciplining and Policing the "Criminals by Birth,'" Parts 1 and 2, *Indian Economic and Social History Review* 27:2 and 27:3 (1990); and Sanjay Seth, *Subject Lessons: The Western Education of Colonial India*, Durham, NC: Duke University Press, 2007, chap. 4.

[63] Benedict Anderson, *Imagined Communities*, rev. ed., London: Verso, 1991, 169.

THE ANACHRONISM OF HISTORY   135

forms they sought to replace, but rather anticipations of the reality that they were helping to produce.

The same, I submit, is true of history writing. History as a modern intellectual technology became central to how India and its people were governed by their colonial masters. James Mill's *History of British India* was a required reading for generations of colonial officials, and the ways in which the history of India was narrated shaped policy on land settlements and revenue collection, on the dispensation of justice, and a great deal more. From the late nineteenth century, history writing became a terrain of conflict, as nationalists began to write histories that set out "to claim for the nation a past that was not distorted by foreign interpreters,"[64] and these histories helped to shape how this nation was imagined, and what form it took after Independence in 1947. Just as it is impossible to imagine life in contemporary India without the census and the modern map, so it is impossible to imagine it without history writing in the modern mode. We need such history because it is enmeshed in the functioning of modern institutions, has become one of the languages through which struggles for social justice are waged, and has become part of the self-understandings of some—but as we shall see, by no means all—of the citizens of India. The conclusion I draw from the arguments of these two chapters is thus not that we should denounce history and cease to write it, or that we should seek to retrieve indigenous traditions of historicity. It is rather that history is practiced best when accompanied by a self-conscious recognition that it is narrating and diagnosing the conditions of its emergence and intelligibility. And when it is applied to pasts that precede these conditions and thus precede the emergence of this code as the authoritative way of representing the past, it should be written with the recognition that it is a form of translation.

Such translation is eminently justified, provided it meets two conditions. The first I have already discussed: as with any translation, we should not assume that the translation is superior to the original. It is not that history writing is the "right" way of representing precolonial Indian pasts, superior to the forms of representing and relating to the past that it replaces, but rather that it has become our way of translating and rendering those pasts in and for a world that is disenchanted, where the past is dead, where gods lack agency, and where texts and artifacts are all the congealed repositories

---

[64] Partha Chatterjee, *The Nation and its Fragments: Colonial and Postcolonial Histories*, Delhi: Oxford University Press, 1995, 76.

of human meanings and purposes. Second, and related to the first, in translating thus we must recognize that there will be much that escapes, or gets lost, in translation. Having defined anthropology as a form of translation, Castro goes further to suggest that a good translation "is one that betrays the destination language, not the source language. A good translation is one that allows the alien concepts to deform and subvert the translator's conceptual toolbox."[65] Similarly, a superior historical practice is one that, in translating the past of those who were not rational and disenchanted moderns into the code of history, "conduct[s] these translations," in Chakrabarty's words, "in such a manner as to make visible all the problems of translating diverse and enchanted worlds into the universal and disenchanted language of sociology."[66]

The Politics of the Code of History

Many will object that to argue thus is to open the floodgates to Holocaust deniers, nationalist mythmakers, and other abusers of history. Unless we accord epistemic authority to history writing, how can we make the necessary distinctions between an objective recounting of the past and mythical distortions and abuses of it? The accusations of "postmodern relativism," "irrationalism," and the like, often leveled at those who call the epistemological certitudes of the discipline into question, are a sign that some of our deepest convictions are informed by, even anchored in, historical accounts; and thus that any questioning of the epistemological privilege accorded the discipline threatens to untether these convictions.

Those who make this objection wittingly or unwittingly draw our attention to the fact that the status we accord history—how we understand it and how we practice it—is not simply an epistemological question, but a pressing political question, in a manner that is not true of all disciplines. While politicians and members of the public may have strong opinions on, say, whether stem-cell research should be conducted and what uses it can legitimately be put to, it is—with exceptions—rare for nonscientists to have strong opinions on the "science" itself. In part because history is not highly

[65] Castro, The Relative Native, 57–58. Benjamin makes a similar point about the translation of texts. See "The Task of the Translator," in his Illuminations, translated by Harry Zohn, edited by Hannah Arendt, London: Pimlico, 1999, especially 81.
[66] Chakrabarty, Provincializing Europe, 89.

technical and thus continues to be written in ordinary language, it is by contrast something on which nonhistorians have opinions, and how the past is to be recounted is sometimes a matter for public debate and disputation. The discipline of history thus exists on two levels or operates through two registers. It has a "cloistered" life, one lived through journals, reviews, specialized conferences, university departments, professional associations, and so on, which may and sometimes does include vigorous contestation, but within the terms of the code of history, and subject to its protocols. It also has a public life, where what happened in the past and how that is to be understood can sometimes be the subject of heated political contestation, *not* always within the terms of the code or conforming to its protocols.[67]

The form of relation between these two registers varies. In its public life in Western Europe and North America, history writing contends with other forms of historicity, including novels, plays, films, and other mediatized forms of representing the past. But because the code of history has accrued considerable prestige in the two centuries or more of its existence, the coexistence of these forms of historicity with the code of history does not, usually, lead to conflict. Certain distinctions have become widely accepted, allowing different forms of historicity to exist in their separate domains. The most significant and sweeping of these is the distinction between fact and fiction, which usually maps onto the distinction between truth and entertainment, between the "found" and the "invented/created." Works that deal with the past but do not aspire to being "history proper" are deemed to be, and usually deem themselves to be, fiction or entertainment, in contradistinction to history. That this "deeming" happens institutionally rather than as a result of intentions—in a context where the "slots" of "academic" and "popular," fiction and nonfiction, fact and imagination are already available to sort and organize all productions and texts—only goes to show how much these distinctions are embedded in practices, institutions, and markets. Where representations of the past that do not conform to disciplinary history aspire nonetheless to some sort of historical verisimilitude, by claiming to be more than "merely" fiction, they usually do so by paying obeisance to the code of history, such as by advertising that they are based upon "research," or (as with some historical television dramas and films) by hiring and crediting professional historians as "advisors": indicating that the code has a near monopoly

---

[67] I borrow this distinction from Chakrabarty, *The Calling of History: Sir Jadunath Sarkar and His Empire of Truth*, Chicago: University of Chicago Press, 2015, 7.

on verisimilitude, and that it has a certain regulatory function, serving as the "horizon" of other forms of representing the past.

The same is not so in India, where, as I have discussed, the code of history did not emerge out of engagements with other modes of historicity, but came from outside, with British rule. As a result, it also came late, was initially confined to small circles, and even as it spread beyond these limited confines, neither wholly displaced other forms of historicity nor came to serve a regulatory function in relation to these other forms of historicity. There has thus always been a gap between "history" as it is understood and practiced by the professional historian, and history as it has been debated, contested, and written in Indian public life. Historians fully accredited and acculturated into the code have often found themselves denouncing inauthentic applications of it, policing the boundary between real history and corruptions of it. In the concluding section of these chapters on the discipline of history, I will consider the relation between the public and political life of history and its "cloistered" and epistemological life. I will do so with reference to an Indian example, where the problematic relation between these two aspects of the discipline became the subject of sustained reflection among historians of India.

History and Politics

In 1992, a mob numbering some thousands gathered in the north Indian town of Ayodhya and violently destroyed the Babri Masjid (mosque), sending shockwaves through the nation. The organized Hindu Right had been campaigning to build a temple to the god Rama in the town believed to be his birthplace, a temple that it claimed had existed since antiquity, until in the sixteenth century the Mughal emperor Babur ordered its destruction and had a mosque built in its place. The movement, part of a crusade by the sinister organizations that collectively comprise the Sangh Parivar, staked many of its claims on historical and archaeological grounds. They claimed that the town of Ayodhya had for centuries been regarded by Hindus as the birthplace of Rama; that a temple consecrating this fact had existed for a millennium; that its destruction at the order of Babur was an established historical fact; and that some of the pillars of non-Islamic design in the mosque complex had originally been part of the destroyed temple, proving that a temple had preexisted the mosque. Some of these claims were even attested to by a handful of historians and archaeologists, of mainly minor or ill repute, but including the former director of the Archaeological Survey (in contradiction to the findings he had submitted to this body more than a decade earlier).

More interesting than the historical claims made by obscure historians-for-hire were the popular pamphlets that were cheaply sold (or sometimes freely distributed) in large numbers in Ayodhya and in Hindu pilgrimage sites, and which provided a justification for the temple movement in the form of a "history" of Ayodhya. These, as one study of them observed, "made claims to be history—in a way that popular Hindu tradition . . . would never have bothered to do."[68] They provided precise dates, were arranged chronologically, cited archaeological evidence, and quoted historical records (although, sometimes, invented ones). And yet they began with the birth of the god Rama and were "characterized by a timeless epic quality," including "an easy . . . intervention of the divine."[69] "These narratives," another study of them concluded, "seek the sanction of myths and belief on the one hand, and 'history' on the other."[70] The past constructed and appealed to by the Sangh Parivar was thus not a continuation of the *itihasa purana* tradition, nor of the many local and popular forms of historicity that characterized the subcontinent. Nor was it consistent with the protocols of historiography. It rather cloaked itself in the garb of history, in the way that creation science mimics, and seeks to capitalize upon, the prestige of science.

The veracity of these communal (or sectarian) histories was challenged by many professional historians, including some of the most distinguished historians of India, who sought to show that this was a tattered cloak, full of holes that had been filled in by other materials. Those properly trained and accredited to practice history had little difficulty in showing that the historical claims of the Hindu Right dissolved once filtered through the prism of history.[71] They cast overwhelming doubt on the claim that the modern town

[68] Gyanendra Pandey, "Modes of History Writing: New Hindu History of India," *Economic and Political Weekly* 29:25 (June 18, 1994), 1523.

[69] Pandey, "Modes of History Writing," 1527, 1526. See also Neeladri Bhattacharya, "Predicament of Secular Histories," *Public Culture* 20:1 (Winter 2008).

[70] Neeladri Bhattacharya, "Myth, History and the Politics of Ramjanmabhumi," in S. Gopal (ed.), *Anatomy of Confrontation: The Babri Masjid–Ram Janmabhumi Issue*, New York: Penguin, 1991, 124–25. Tapati Guha-Thakurta makes the same point, that these popular narratives "share with the historical discipline the core claim to the real and comprehensive truth; yet at the same time, they remain essentially ahistorical in the way the verities of fact are bolstered by the certainties of belief, in the way legends are reproduced through the scientific apparatus of dates, statistics, and geographical details." *Monuments, Objects, Histories: Institutions of Art in Colonial and Postcolonial India*, New York: Columbia University Press, 2004, 279.

[71] See the statement authored by twenty scholars associated with the Centre for Historical Studies at Jawaharlal Nehru University. Sarvapelli Gopal, Romila Thapar, et al., "The Political Abuse of

of Ayodhya was, or had even long been regarded by Hindus, as the birthplace of Rama; they showed that there was no evidence to suggest that a temple had existed there for many centuries, and that the emperor Babur ordered the destruction of any such temple; and so on. In the cloistered life of the discipline, the debate was easily won.

In the public domain, this made no difference. On December 6, 1992, thousands of Hindu "volunteers," a great many convinced that they were righting a historic wrong, tore down the mosque, and it became shockingly and violently apparent that the code of history was not the only, and not even the most potent, mode of historicity in the public sphere of the Indian republic. Sumit Sarkar, one of the foremost historians of modern India, summed up the implications of these events for historians thus:

> Secular historians refuted, with ample data and unimpeachable logic, the justifications put forward by the Hindu Right, for its eventually successful campaign to demolish a four-hundred-year-old masjid at Ayodhya. . . . Yet for a decisive year or two the views of the leading historians of India . . . had less impact than pamphlets of the order of *Ramjanmabhumiki Rakta-ranjita Itihas* (Bloody History of the Birthplace of Ram). This, however, was very far from being a simple triumph of age-old popular faith over the alienated rationalism of secular intellectuals. Vishwa Hindu Parishad (VHP) pamphlets, and audio and visual cassettes, systematically combined an ultimate appeal to faith with a battery of their own kind of historical facts: quotations from (real or spurious) documents, a certain amount of evidence fielded by archaeologists of some stature, a parade of alleged facts and dates about precisely seventy-six battles fought by Hindus to liberate the birthplace of Ram. . . . What this VHP quest for historical facticity revealed was that history of one kind or another has come to occupy a position of exceptional importance in a variety of Indian discourses, but in the moulding of many such histories the best scholars often have a very limited role.

"Historical consciousness," Sarkar ruefully concluded, "evidently cannot be equated with the thinking of professional historians alone."[72]

History: Babri Masjid–Rama Janmabhumi Dispute," reprinted in *South Asia Bulletin* 9:2 (1989), 65. See also K. N. Panikkar, "A Historical Overview," in Gopal, *Anatomy of Confrontation*.
[72] Sumit Sarkar, "The Many Worlds of Indian History," in *Writing Social History*, New Delhi: Oxford University Press, 1997, 2.

This disconcerting proof that "historical truth," as determined by the code of history, had limited efficacy in Indian public life sparked reflection among many historians of India. How historians ought to react to this unsettling fact generated different responses. For some, perhaps the majority, the victory of "myth" and "faith" over history made it all the more important that historians continue to press the distinction between the two. A few years after the destruction of Babri Masjid, when a Bharatiya Janata Party government was busily rewriting school history textbooks, the most eminent historian of ancient India, Romila Thapar, insisted that "what is really at stake in the current row over history textbooks is the right of the professional historian to assert the pre-eminence of history over myth and fantasy."[73]

A diametrically opposed response came from Ashis Nandy, according to whom the cataclysmic events of December 1992 derived from an excess of historical consciousness, rather than an insufficiency of it. Modern historical consciousness came to India from without, and although modern India, like most "nonhistorical" societies, had embraced this newcomer, it had never completely sidelined myths. According to Nandy their continued salience was not a matter for regret, but rather a source of hope, for societies where myths were the predominant mode of representing and relating to the past were societies capable of acting on the "principle of principled forgetfulness"; because they did not treat history as "dead," they refused to separate the past from its ethical meaning in the present, recognizing that "it is often important not to remember the past, objectively, clearly, or in its entirety."[74] Myth was on the side of ethics, for in a civilization "where there are many pasts, encompassing many bitter memories and animosities, to absolutize them with the help of the European concept of history is to attack the organizing principles of the civilization."[75]

Nandy was not endorsing the claims of the Hindutva ideologues, whom he consistently and vehemently opposed: he rather disputed the claim of "secular" historians that what was at stake was myth versus history. The catastrophe at Ayodhya arose, he argued, not because myth triumphed over history, but because historical consciousness was triumphing over other modes of historicity, and "The domination of that consciousness has now become, as the confrontation at Ayodhya shows, a cultural and political liability."[76]

[73] Quoted in Vinay Lal, *The History of History: Politics and Scholarship in Modern India*, New Delhi: Oxford University Press, 2003, 18.
[74] Ashis Nandy, "History's Forgotten Doubles," *History and Theory* 34:2 (May 1995), 47.
[75] Nandy, "History's Forgotten Doubles," 65.
[76] Nandy, "History's Forgotten Doubles," 65.

This was a minority position, but the intellectual force of Nandy's argument resonated for some. Endorsing and expanding upon Nandy's claim, Vinay Lal wrote, "While secular historians view the debacle at Ayodhya as arising partly from attempts at the 'mythification of history,' we should perhaps wonder if it is not the historicization of myths which has contributed to the increasing communalization of Indian politics."[77]

In part no doubt due to the febrile atmosphere of the time, some intellectuals reacted to such arguments with great force, suggesting that "postmodernism" and fashionable critiques of Enlightenment (the *Subaltern Studies* group of historians were seen as the principal bearers of such pernicious ideas on the Indian intellectual scene) had licensed irrationalism, and that the destruction of Babri Masjid was in part enabled by this intellectual cast of mind. But the identification of Reason—here in the form of the code of history—with liberal or leftist politics was surely a mistake. A disregard for the protocols of modern historiography is not confined to the Hindu Right, but is also sometimes to be found among movements that Indian liberals and leftists sympathize with and often support.[78] Dalit-Bahujan leaders and intellectuals have also sometimes rejected the conventions of the code of history as mere masks for the production of "upper caste" history, defiantly declaring that "there is no question of their seeking validation from the historian's history or even being amenable to the usual method of historical verification";[79] and Dalit social and political movements have recreated pasts by blending history, myth, legend, and religion.[80]

Disregarding the code of history is thus not solely the prerogative of reactionaries, and the code itself is not intrinsically allied with social justice. Liberal and leftist historians cannot have their cake and eat it too, by assuming that to defend historiography is somehow also, ipso facto, to defend or promote "progressive" politics. There is cause to doubt that the emergence of historiography in Europe complemented and promoted liberal or radical politics; in any case, in the different conditions of twentieth- and

[77] Lal, *The History of History*, 124.

[78] As is noted and discussed by Prathama Banerjee, "Histories of History in South Asia," in Prasenjit Duara, Viren Murthy, and Andrew Sartori (eds.), *A Companion to Global Historical Thought*, Malden, MA: John Wiley and Sons, 2014, especially 300.

[79] Dipesh Chakrabarty, "The Public Life of History: An Argument out of India," *Public Culture* 20:1 (Winter 2008), 160. An example is the essay by the Dalit-Bahujan intellectual Kancha Ilaiah, "Productive Labour, Consciousness and History: The Dalitbahujan Alternative," in Shahid Amin and Dipesh Chakrabarty (eds.), *Subaltern Studies IX*, Delhi: Oxford University Press, 1996.

[80] For an illuminating study see Badri Narayan, *Women Heroes and Dalit Assertion in North India: Culture, Identity and Politics*, Thousand Oaks, CA: Sage, 2006.

twenty-first-century India, no such intrinsic complementarity can be assumed.

Perhaps recognizing this, some historians began to wonder, in Partha Chatterjee's words, whether "there was something wrong with the grounds on which disciplinary autonomy was being defended; may be in the social-institutional conditions of the present, it was useless, and perhaps even un-warranted, to demand that history not seek its legitimation from the domain of the popular; consequently, what was perhaps required was a redefinition of the grounds of the discipline—not, as before, by excluding popular practices of memory from its list of approved practices, but rather by incorporating within itself an appropriate analytic of the popular."[81] A number of studies have appeared in the last two decades that engage indigenous traditions of historicity in India and moreover do not treat these traditions as merely mis-taken, or mine them for anticipations and premonitions of a proper histor-ical consciousness and historiography.[82] Interesting and important as these are, what they do not do is incorporate into the discipline an "analytic of the popular." It is difficult to see how they could do so: like any code, history is subject to change and amendment, but it cannot be changed beyond a certain point without becoming an altogether different code.

The debate over the historical past that was part of lead-up to, and after-math of, the destruction of Babri Masjid demonstrated that the discipline of history is sufficiently important in Indian public life that the reactionary champions of Hindutva invoked it for their own purposes, howsoever se-lectively. But it also demonstrated that history as the historian conceives and practices it is far from being hegemonic in Indian public life. The many responses of historians to these events, some of which have been detailed and discussed here, can schematically be divided into two broad positions on the relation between the epistemological and the political, the private and the public, life of history.

---

[81] Partha Chatterjee, "Introduction: History and the Present," in P. Chatterjee and Anjan Ghosh (eds.), *History and the Present*, New Delhi: Permanent Black, 2002, 19. See also Chatterjee, "History and the domain of the popular," *Seminar* 522 (February 2003), themed issue, "Rewriting History: A Symposium on Ways of Regarding Our Shared Past."

[82] These include Ajay Skaria, *Hybrid Histories: Forests, Frontiers and Wildness in Western India*, New Delhi: Oxford University Press, 1999; Shail Mayaram, M. S. S. Pandian, and Ajay Skaria (eds.), *Subaltern Studies XII*, Delhi: Permanent Black, 2005; Yasmin Saikia, *Assam and India: Fragmented Memories, Cultural Identity, and the Tai-Ahom Struggle*, New Delhi: Permanent Black, 2005; Prachi Deshpande, *Creative Pasts: Historical Memory and Identity in Western India, 1700–1960*, New York: Columbia University Press, 2007; and Shail Mayaram, *Against History, against State: Counterperspectives from the Margins*, New York: Columbia University Press, 2003.

One is to insist that historical truth is the best defense against irrationalisms, self-interested inventions, and the substitution of faith for historical Reason; and that such truth can be obtained, or at least approximated, only through historiography. The alternative is to accept the argument advanced in these two chapters, namely that historiography is but one mode of historicity, rather than the correct and true way of representing the past. Each position comes with entailments and costs. Since many Indians fail to recognize that only history gives us objective and truthful access to the past, it means that those holding to this position are obliged to regard many of their fellow citizens as cognitively backward; and to cleave to the hope that the gap between proper history and false modes of historicity will be bridged as literacy and education do their work in advancing the march of Reason in Indian life, as is presumed to have happened in Europe. The role of the champions of historical Reason is then to assist this process by playing the role of pedagogue to their peoples/pupils.

Conversely, to see historiography as a mode of historicity rather than the correct way of representing the past comes with the uncomfortable corollary that history cannot validate, "ground," or anchor our political and ethical choices, but is rather one of the things in contention in making such choices. Like many others, I would very much like my political convictions to be anchored in "truth"; and the relation between forms of knowledges, and political commitments, is an issue I will address in the epilogue. But if there is one thing that the tragic events of December 1992 clearly showed, it is that what was at issue was not historical truth, but whether India was to be a polity where people of all religions and no religion were equal citizens, or whether it was to be one where a Muslim minority was relegated to second-class citizenship, living at the will and behest of the leaders of Hindutva. What was at stake, in other words, was not the truth about the past, which could then serve to underwrite our political convictions in the present, but rather what sort of nation India was to be and, accordingly, how its past was to be understood.

5

International Relations

Empire and Amnesia

"Political science," "politics," or "government" did not begin to be institution-alized as a university discipline until the latter nineteenth century, and when it did so it displayed little unity beyond a concern with the nature and activi-ties of the state. The topics taught in the earliest political science programs in the United States at that time, such as at Columbia, Michigan, and Harvard Universities, were a grab bag including political and constitutional history, jurisprudence, the government of cities, the poor and almshouses, eth-nology, sanitary science, the best methods of supplying pure water and air, and the like.[1] The founding of the American Political Science Association in 1903 gave the discipline a professional association, but it remained "less a dis-tinct discipline than a holding company for a variety of endeavors that were in various ways related, but no longer easily resided in other disciplines."[2] On the other side of the Atlantic, the picture was not very different—what was taught at Cambridge under the rubric of politics did almost everything, in the judgment of Collini, Winch, and Burrow, except study politics, for it identified neither a distinct object of inquiry nor a method for such inquiry.[3] Things did not improve as the twentieth century proceeded, and in the 1950s Hans Morgenthau complained that "contemporary political science has no unity of method, outlook and purpose."[4] In that same decade the "behavioral revolution," an attempt to give the discipline a clearly defined object and a

---

[1] Hans Morgenthau, "Reflections on the State of Political Science," *Review of Politics* 17:4 (October 1955), 437–38.

[2] John Gunnell, "Political Theory: The Evolution of a Sub-field," in Ada W. Finifter (ed.), *Political Science: The State of the Discipline*, New York: APSA, 1983, 6.

[3] Stefan Collini, Donald Winch, and John Burrow, *That Noble Science of Politics: A Study in Nineteenth-Century Intellectual History*, Cambridge: Cambridge University Press, 1983, 360.

[4] Morgenthau, "Reflections on the State of Political Science," 439. The same absence of discipli-nary unity was on display in Britain—see Brian Barry, "The Study of Politics as a Vocation," in Jack Hayward, Brian Barry, and Archie Brown (eds.), *The British Study of Politics in the Twentieth Century*, New York: Oxford University Press, 1999. See also Rodney Barker, "A Tale of Three Cities: The Early Years of Political Science in Oxford, London and Manchester," in Christopher Hood, Desmond King, and Gillian Peele (eds.), *Forging a Discipline*, New York: Oxford University Press, 2014.

Beyond Reason. Sanjay Seth, Oxford University Press (2021). © Oxford University Press.
DOI: 10.1093/oso/9780197500583.003.0006

method by which to investigate it, came to be ascendant in the United States, and some hoped that the "dream of finding a core"[5] around which the discipline could unite was within sight. But the value-free scientific aspirations of behaviorism foundered on the shoals of America's war in Vietnam, according to its leading exponent,[6] and two decades later another leading behaviorist, Gabriel Almond, was to complain that "the various schools and sects of political science now sit at separate tables, each with its own conception of political science."[7]

Assessments of the "state of the discipline," of the kind commissioned by professional associations, are repeatedly obliged to concede that while there is a well-established *profession*, the existence of a *discipline* is less certain. In 1975 such a review commissioned by the American Political Science Association characterized the discipline as "ill-defined, amorphous, and heterogenous."[8] A successor volume in 2002 began by observing that reviewing the state of the discipline "implies a discipline, but yet even this much about political science cannot be taken for granted."[9] Such judgments are confirmed by surveys that find that those located in the discipline displayed no agreement on "the men [sic] who have made contributions to political science."[10] Political science has thus always been, in the words of the editor of

[5] John Gunnell in Kristen Monroe et al., "The Nature of Contemporary Political Science: A Roundtable Discussion," *PS: Political Science and Politics* 23:1 (March 1990), 37.

[6] David Easton, "The New Revolution in Political Science," *American Political Science Review* 72:4 (December 1969).

[7] Gabriel A. Almond, "Separate Tables: Schools and Sects in Political Science," *PS: Political Science and Politics* 21:4 (Autumn 1988), 829. See similarly David Easton, who a few years before Almond observed that "there are now so many approaches to political research that political science seems to have lost its purpose." "Political Science in the United States: Past and Present" (1984), in James Farr and Ronald Seidelman (eds.), *Discipline and History: Political Science in the United States*, Ann Arbor: University of Michigan Press, 1993, 299–300.

[8] Fred Greenstein and Nelson Polsby, "Introduction," in *Political Science: Scope and Method*, vol. 1 of *Handbook of Political Science*, quoted in Rogers M. Smith, "Still Blowing in the Wind: The American Quest for a Democratic, Scientific Political Science," *Daedalus* 126:1 (Winter 1997), 253.

[9] Ira Katznelson and Helen Milner, "American Political Science: The Discipline's State and the State of the Discipline," in Katznelson and Milner (eds.), *Political Science: State of the Discipline*, New York: Norton and APSA, 2002, 1. There are of course exceptions to this judgment, ones that find integrative tendencies at work across the subdisciplines that constitute political science—see, for example, Robert Goodin and H. D. Klingemann, "Political Science: The Discipline," in Goodin and Klingemann (eds.), *A New Handbook of Political Science*, New York: Oxford University Press, 1996.

[10] Albert Somit and Joseph Tanehaus, *American Political Science: A Profile of a Discipline*, New York: Atherton Press, 1964, 67. Conducted in 1963 (at the high point of the behavioral tendency, when consensus might have been most expected) this survey sent out 832 questionnaires and received a response rate of over 50%. A similar survey undertaken some forty-five years later, in the wake of Almond's article (see note 7) and the ensuing discussion, found—though on the basis of a negligible 1% return rate on a questionnaire sent to 8,500 faculty, mostly located in the United States, United Kingdom, continental Europe, Australia, and Canada—that when asked to list three works that helped define "political science," there was virtually no overlap in the works listed: "The absence of coincidence for the submitted lists is dramatic, not just across the subfields of the discipline but

the *American Political Science Review* on the occasion of its centenary, less a field than "a federation of loosely connected subfields."[11] In short, there is no discipline of political science, but rather an archipelago of subdisciplines, upon which an almost purely administrative unity has been conferred in the form of the university department that houses these diverse undertakings.[12] An inquiry into the fundamental presuppositions of the discipline, of the type undertaken in the previous two chapters for the discipline of history, is therefore not possible for the discipline of politics. This chapter and the next will instead examine the governing assumptions of two of its subdisciplines, international relations and political theory: the first closer to the social sciences, the second to the humanities; the former concerned with the "outside" of political communities, and the latter principally with the "inside."

Inventing International Relations

Most disciplines emerge as such when they are able to locate a distinct object of study, demarcating it from adjacent and overlapping objects. "The international" is an impossibly large field, for what transcends the borders of political communities can be studied in any manner of ways, through legal relations, economic transactions, cultural flows, diplomatic relations, and so on. Before the emergence and consolidation of the discipline of international relations, economists, scholars of international law, diplomats and diplomatic historians, military historians, those writing on "colonial affairs," and numerous others were among those engaged in producing knowledge about some aspect or other of "the international." Immediately after World War II, despite an increase in student interest in courses on international relations, and the creation of centers for the study of international matters (frequently funded by the Rockefeller Foundation), a discussion among American scholars made it clear that a discipline of international relations did not yet exist.[13] The participants all expressed doubt about whether "international

---

within them as well." Ronald King and Cosmin Gabriel Marian, "Defining Political Science: A Cross-National Survey," *European Political Science* 7 (2008), 215.

[11] Lee Sigelman, "Introduction to the Centennial Issue," *American Political Science Review* 100:4 (November 2006), x.

[12] In Almond's trenchant description, a political science department is "a loose aggregation of special interests, held together by shared avarice in maintaining or increasing the departmental share of resources." Monroe et al., "The Nature of Contemporary Political Science: A Roundtable Discussion," 35.

[13] *World Politics*, which commenced publication in 1948, was one of the main forums for this.

relations" had a clearly defined subject matter, let alone a shared method of investigation. It was pointed out that the study of international relations overlapped with and drew upon numerous other disciplines and fields,[14] and that one of the difficulties of teaching it as a university course was that it was unreasonable to expect students to draw upon, let alone master, these diverse fields.[15] It was a common complaint that much of what was taught as international relations was either current affairs, diplomatic history, or the study of international organizations such as the League of Nations and the newly established United Nations.[16] The participants all agreed that international relations was, as yet, far from being a discipline: according to Frederick Dunn, international relations was in its infancy, and "much of what is talked about under that label scarcely deserves recognition as a legitimate subject of academic concern."[17] Kenneth Thompson, who through his membership in the Division of Social Sciences of the Rockefeller Foundation was energetically engaged in trying to put the study of the international on a properly disciplinary footing, declared in 1952 that, for now, "no serious student would presume to claim that the study of international relations had arrived at the stage of an independent academic discipline."[18]

The account of its origins that was subsequently to be widely retold—once international relations had become established as an academic discipline—is thus a fiction in almost every regard. The prehistory of the discipline does not go back to the mists of time, beginning with Thucydides and proceeding

[14] Those mentioned were geography, economics, international law, history, diplomatic history, anthropology, demography, social psychology, and comparative government. See Waldemar Gurian, "On the Study of International Relations," *Review of Politics* 8:3 (July 1946), 277; and also Frederick S. Dunn, "The Present Course of International Relations Research," *World Politics* 2:1 (October 1949), 86.

[15] See Klaus Knorr, "Economics and International Relations: A Problem in Teaching," *Political Science Quarterly* 62:4 (December 1947), 533.

[16] See, for example, Russell H. Fifield, "The Introductory Course in International Relations," *American Political Science Review* 42:6 (December 1948), 1190–91.

[17] Frederick S. Dunn, "The Scope of International Relations," *World Politics* 1:1 (October 1948), 143. On the other side of the Atlantic, the Montague Burton Professor of International Relations at Oxford University confessed that since the study of international relations presupposed a knowledge of law, economics, and history, "the main problem of a professor of international relations must be the delimitation of his own field of research and teaching." E. L. Woodward, *The Study of International Relations at a University, an Inaugural Lecture at Oxford on 17 February 1945*, Oxford: Clarendon Press, 1945, 12.

[18] Kenneth W. Thompson, "The Study of International Politics: A Survey of Trends and Developments," *Review of Politics* 14:4 (1952), 433. On the role of the Rockefeller Foundation in promoting the emergence of the discipline, see Nicolas Guilhot, "The Realist Gambit: Postwar American Political Science and the Birth of IR Theory," *International Political Sociology* 2:4 (December 2008), and also his "Introduction: One Discipline, Many Histories," in Guilhot (ed.), *The Invention of IR Theory: Realism, the Rockefeller Foundation, and the 1954 Conference on Theory*, New York: Columbia University Press, 2011.

through Machiavelli, Hobbes, and Kant; such comically anachronistic and selective retrieval of canonical thinkers is the telltale sign of a recently created and intellectually insecure discipline manufacturing a lineage in order to endow itself with intellectual dignity. The "great debate" between idealists and realists that is supposed to have set the discipline on its feet is a fiction, as recent scholarship decisively shows, and a fiction that serves to ratify realism's claims to being synonymous with the discipline itself.[19] The second and third "great debates" that often form part of the history of international relations, as retold by the discipline, are additional ballast, serving to disguise the shallowness of the discipline with claims to intellectual heft.[20] And the discipline did not begin in 1919, when the first chair in international relations (specifically, for the study of the League of Nations) was established at Aberystwyth, for endowing a chair does not thereby a discipline create.

A discipline emerges when it defines and demarcates an object and when presuppositions for the proper inquiry into that object come to be widely accepted. International relations, I will argue, emerged and consolidated itself as a discipline in the years after World War II, constituting its object through the essentially empirical claim that "anarchy"—the existence of multiple sovereign territorial states without any overarching state or body with legitimate authority over them all—is the defining characteristic of the international domain. The "discovery" that this is what distinguishes the international, was, I will subsequently show, accompanied by a "forgetting"—a forgetting of the centrality of colonialism and imperialism to the making of the world order.

---

[19] See Peter Wilson, "The Myth of the 'First Great Debate,'" *Review of International Studies* 24:5 (1998); Lucian Ashworth, "Did the Realist-Idealist Great Debate Really Happen? A Revisionist History of International Relations," *International Relations* 16:1 (2002); Cameron Thies, "Progress, History and Identity in International Relations Theory: The Case of the Idealist-Realist Debate," *European Journal of International Relations* 8:2 (2002). See also B. de Carvalho, H. Leira, and J. H. Hobson, "The Big Bangs of IR: The Myths That Your Teachers Still Tell You about 1648 and 1919," *Millennium* 39:3 (2011); and Joel Quirk and Darshan Vigneswaran, "The Construction of an Edifice: The Story of a First Great Debate," *Review of International Studies* 31 (2005).

[20] The oddity of telling the history of a discipline through great debates is noted by Miles Kahler, "Inventing International Relations: International Relations Theory after 1945," in Michael W. Doyle and John Ikenberry (eds.), *New Thinking in International Relations Theory*, Boulder, CO: Westview Press, 1998, 21. Ole Waever notes, "Ask an IR scholar to present the discipline in fifteen minutes, and most likely you will get the story of three great debates. There is no other established means of telling the history of the discipline." "The Sociology of a Not So International Discipline: American and European Developments in International Relations," *International Organization* 52:4 (Autumn 1998), 715. As if to prove the point, elsewhere Waever himself reproduces the "great debates" narrative: "The Rise and Fall of the Inter-paradigm Debate," in Steve Smith, Ken Booth, and Marisyn Zolewski (eds.), *International Theory: Positivism and Beyond*, Cambridge: Cambridge University Press, 1996, especially 150.

Anarchy, Sovereignty, Territoriality, and State

That the object of international relations is characterized by an "anarchy" that differentiates it from what happens "inside" states or political communities is a claim made by most of the influential figures in the discipline, and one cutting across the differences between the "schools" that otherwise characterize the contemporary discipline. Seeking what is distinctive about world politics, Raymond Aron finds it in the fact that the international realm, unlike the domestic, is in a "state of nature" characterized by "the absence of an entity that holds a monopoly of legitimate violence."[21] Stanley Hoffman, similarly searching for what makes international relations "a largely autonomous field," finds this in the "decentralized international milieu" that sharply differentiates the international from the "integrated *Rechstaat*."[22] According to Hedley Bull, thinking about international relations presupposes a recognition of "the limits of the domestic analogy": "Whereas men within each state are subject to a common government, sovereign states in their mutual relations are not. This anarchy it is possible to regard as the central fact of international life and the starting-point of theorizing about it."[23] Kenneth Waltz, whose *The Theory of International Politics* has proved to be one of the most influential texts in the discipline, founded neorealism as a "systemic" theory, one in which the workings of the international system were to be found not at the level of human nature and motivations nor at the level of state interests, but in the nature of the international system. But for Waltz too, it is the difference between "domestic" and "international" systems that makes international politics unique: "Domestic systems are centralized and hierarchic. . . . International systems are decentralized and anarchic."[24] As a consequence, "To achieve their objectives and maintain their security, units in a condition of anarchy . . . must rely on the means they can generate and the arrangements they can make for themselves. Self-help is necessarily the principle of action

[21] Raymond Aron, "What Is a Theory of International Relations?," *Journal of International Affairs* 21:2 (1967), 192. He adds that this definition "coincides with actual experience; statesmen, jurists, moralists, philosophers, and military men throughout the ages have perceived the essence of international to be just what I see as the starting point for a theory" (196–97).

[22] Stanley H. Hoffman, "International Relations: The Long Road to Theory," *World Politics* 11:3 (April 1959), 346, 347.

[23] Hedley Bull, "Society and Anarchy in International Relations," in Herbert Butterfield and Martin Wight (eds.), *Diplomatic Investigations*, Cambridge, MA: Harvard University Press, 1968, 35. On the rejection of the "domestic analogy" by "English School" figures, Bull included, see Andrew Linklater and Hidemi Suganami, *The English School of International Relations: A Contemporary Reassessment*, New York: Cambridge University Press, 2006, 44–47.

[24] Kenneth Waltz, *The Theory of International Politics*, Long Grove, IL: Waveland Press, 1979, 88.

in an anarchic order."[25] And reasoning thus from the starting point of "anarchy," Waltz arrives, albeit via a different "systemic" route, at realpolitik conclusions that are similar to the "classical" realists: "National politics is the realm of authority, of administration, and of law. International politics is the realm of power, of struggle, and of accommodation."[26]

Anarchy, then, is what makes the international political realm distinct, which in turn is why a separate discipline is needed to uncover and explain its workings. The unique nature of this object, as we have seen, is usually specified by means of a contrast with politics within a state—hence the warnings about the unhelpfulness of the "domestic analogy," which loses sight of the crucial difference between the national and the international. Sometimes, the distinction is more specifically made by contrasting political theory, concerned with questions of the legitimacy and authority of the reigning power, with theorizing the international domain, where altogether different questions are thought to arise. As Martin Wight, for example, put it, "Political theory and law are maps of experience within the realm of normal relationships. . . . They are the theory of the good life. International theory is the theory of survival."[27] But while this inside/outside distinction is central to the constitution of the discipline, we should not leap to the conclusion that international relations is only concerned with the "outside" whereas political theory in concerned with the "inside." Political theory for the most part does disregard what lies outside the bounds of political communities, for it has been preoccupied with the political arrangements of such communities and the principles that legitimate (or fail to legitimate) their political order. By contrast, international relations does not disregard the domestic, but rather *presumes* it: it presumes it in the form of the sovereign, territorial state.

This does not logically follow from the presumption of anarchy, for the absence of an overarching international or global authority does not, as Richard Ashley points out, entail that this unregulated global sphere "would be populated by a number of states, each an identical subject that is able and

[25] Waltz, *Theory of International Politics*, 111.
[26] Waltz, *Theory of International Politics*, 113.
[27] Martin Wight, "Why Is There No International Theory?," in Butterfield and Wight, *Diplomatic Investigations*, 33. Such reiterated insistence on the fundamental differences between inside and outside leads R. B. J. Walker to the conclusion that "modern accounts of the political occur as twin, though mutually contemptuous, discourses: as a properly political theory, or sociology, of life within, and a more wretched theory of relations between territorial states," with the latter "largely constructed as a negation of assumptions about political life within the authentic statist community." "International Relations and the Concept of the Political," in Ken Booth and Steve Smith (eds.), *International Relations Theory Today*, Cambridge: Polity Press, 1995, 306, 308.

disposed to make choices, that has its own identifiable sets of interests, and that controls some significant set of social resources, including means of violence. . . . It would not even mean that the [international] domain would be populated by similar units."[28] In other words, to construe the object of the discipline as anarchy *additionally* requires assuming that the international domain lacking a sovereign authority is composed of smaller sovereign units, each with a monopoly of legitimate violence within its own territorial sphere.

For some strands within the discipline, such as neorealism, the sovereign state, or something very like it, is an ontological given. Thus according to Waltz, while the international system explains the relations of its units, this does not mean that the parts have no existence other than their function in the whole. Sovereign states are presupposed, just as the economist presupposes the existence of the very firms whose behaviors and interactions are, however, then constrained by the logic of the market. The analogy with the market is, for Waltz, an exact one, for states are to the international system what firms are to the market: "International political systems, like economic markets, are formed by the coaction of self-regarding units. International structures . . . emerge from the coexistence of states. . . . International-political systems, like economic markets, are individual in origin, spontaneously generated, and unintentional."[29]

This presumption—that the state is simply part of the furniture of the world, to be found wherever an international system exists—is not an induction from the historical record, but rather a consequence of the formal requirements of Waltz's theory. Neoliberal institutionalists differ in regarding anarchy as coexisting with norms and patterns of interaction that mitigate that anarchy (and relatedly, lead to self-regarding state behavior in which the "self" is less sharply defined against others); but the sovereign state is nonetheless, for them as for neorealists, the given and basic unit of the international order. The more philosophically inclined "constructivists" insist that state identities are not given and do not precede interaction with other states; identities and interests are thus not to be assumed (an independent variable),

[28] Richard Ashley, "Untying the Sovereign State: A Double Reading of the Anarchy Problematique," *Millennium* 17:2 (1988), 239.

[29] Waltz, *Theory of International Politics*, 91. Waltz recognizes that the units constituting an international order have varied greatly, from the city-states of ancient Greece to the empires and absolutist states of the early modern and modern periods, and the nation-states of his own time. But what is of significance, for the purposes of his theory, is the anarchy that results from the absence of any overarching authority; as a consequence of this, the changing nature of the "units" that constitute international politics notwithstanding, we witness "the striking sameness in the quality of international life through the millennia" (66).

but are intersubjectively co-constituted (and thus a dependent variable).[30] The sovereign state is seen as a historical product, and moreover as "an on-going accomplishment of practice, not a once-and-for-all creation."[31] While this avoids eternalizing the state—as constructivists accuse neorealism and liberal institutionalism of doing—for most constructivists the sovereign state has been the defining feature of international life for a long period, and is likely to continue being so for the foreseeable future, so that it is reasonable to treat it as a point of departure for theorizing about international politics. For constructivism, neorealist presumptions about the sovereign state as the foundation of international politics are warranted, as long as we do "not let this legitimate analytical stance become a de facto ontological stance."[32]

For the more historically minded, including the so-called English School, the sovereign state is a modern invention, developing hand in hand with the anarchic international "society" of which it is a part. The sovereign state and international system are thus a product of history; but this is a very long history, beginning in 1648 with the Peace of Westphalia.[33] An acknowledgment of the historicity of the sovereign state is thus not a disavowal of the premises of the discipline, but simply a historical delimitation of its object: Westphalia is the "big bang"[34] that brings the modern international domain into being, and later sees the emergence of an intellectual discipline devoted to producing knowledge of this domain.[35]

All the major strands of the discipline thus constitute its object as an international system without a central authority ("anarchy"), inhabited by political entities that exercise control over their own territory (sovereign states), a control that is recognized (though not always respected) by formally similar

---

[30] I am parsing the argument and deploying the language of Alexander Wendt, in whose characterization constructivism supplies the discipline with "a systematic communitarian ontology in which intersubjective knowledge constitutes identities and interests." "Anarchy Is What States Make of It: The Social Construction of Power Politics," *International Politics* 46:2 (Spring 1992), 425.

[31] Wendt, "Anarchy," 413.

[32] Wendt, "Anarchy," 423. And since Wendt accepts, as realists do, that "in the medium run sovereign states will remain the dominant political actors in the international system," "to that extent," he announces, "I am a statist and a realist" (424).

[33] The British Committee on the Theory of International Politics came to accept the premise, in the words of one of its members, that "the European system since Westphalia—that is, during most of its existence—has theoretically been a society of independent states which all recognise each other as such." Adam Watson, "Systems of States," *Review of International Studies* 16 (1990), 103.

[34] I borrow this helpful description of the role that "1648" plays in the discipline from de Carvalho, Leira, and Hobson, "Big Bangs of IR."

[35] In the case of Bull and Wight in particular, the story of the emergence of the modern international system is told principally by a return to those seventeenth- and eighteenth-century thinkers who are portrayed as seeking to make sense of, and thereby sometimes shaping, the new international order that was emerging in their time.

units.[36] A great deal of the debate in the discipline is about how specifically to understand the functioning of this structure and to discern its future trajectory: Does the self-interested character of the units mean that anarchy will always prevail, or do economic ties and/or the effects of shared norms mitigate that anarchy? Does the increased importance of supranational bodies signify a dilution of sovereignty, or does the multiplication of states since the events of 1989 indicate the continued centrality of the nation-state form? Given that states are only formally equal but substantively unequal, should the discipline emphasize hierarchy as much or more than equality in explaining world politics, and modify its understanding and account of anarchy accordingly? And so on.

The presumptions of the discipline that underlie the debates I have mentioned are themselves sometimes subjected to critical examination by its practitioners. It has been repeatedly pointed out that the Peace of Westphalia (comprising the treaties of Osnabrück and of Münster) did not enshrine the principle of a state's sovereignty over its people, nor was it the point zero where sovereignty came to be identified with territory.[37] In fact, the Peace of Westphalia continued to follow the earlier practice of specifying "estates" as its constituents elements, some of which were territorially based, others not;[38] and even in the eighteenth century, "Most negotiated settlements—as well as actual divisions—between European polities more closely resembled medieval lists of places and rights than they did modern linear boundaries."[39]

[36] Stephen Krasner describes the sovereign state as an "ontological given" for neorealists, an "analytic assumption" for neoliberal institutionalists, and a "constitutive norm" for constructivists. "Rethinking the Sovereign State Model," *Review of International Studies* 27 (2001), 21–22. For the "English school" it is "understood as a behavioral regularity based on shared understandings." Krasner, "Compromising Westphalia," *International Security* 20:3 (Winter 1995–96), 122.

[37] See Derek Croxton, "The Peace of Westphalia of 1648 and the Origins of Sovereignty," *International History Review* 21:3 (1999); Stephane Beaulac, "The Westphalian Legal Orthodoxy—Myth or Reality?," *Journal of the History of International Law* 2 (2000), and also her *The Power of Language in the Making of International Law*, Dordrecht: Martinus Nijhoff 2004, chap. 5; Andreas Osiander, "Sovereignty, International Relations, and the Westphalian Myth," *International Organization* 55:2 (2001); and Benno Tesche, *The Myth of 1648: Class, Geopolitics and the Making of Modern International Relations*, London: Verso, 2003.

[38] My thanks to Ian Hunter for clarifications on the Peace of Westphalia.

[39] Jordan Branch, *The Cartographic State: Maps, Territory, and the Origins of Sovereignty*, New York: Cambridge University Press, 2014, 5. See also John Agnew, "The Territoriality Trap: The Geographical Assumptions of International Relations Theory," *Review of International Political Economy* 1:1 (Spring 1994). John Ruggie seeks to provide a historical account of this conjunction or isomorphism between territory and rule (one that he finds to be peculiarly modern and "unique in human history") in "Territoriality and Beyond: Problematizing Modernity in International Relations," *International Organization* 47:1 (Winter 1993), 151; as does Alexander Murphy, "The Sovereign State System as Political Territorial Ideal: Historical and Contemporary Considerations," in Thomas J. Biersteker and Cynthia Weber (eds.), *State Sovereignty as Social Construct*, Cambridge: Cambridge University Press, 1996. R. B. J. Walker's *Inside/Outside: Political Theory as*

It was not until after the eighteenth century that the sovereign territorial state became something like a "norm" even in Europe, and, then and since, there continue to be numerous exceptions to and abrogations of sovereignty.[40] Enumerating a large number of these, Stephen Krasner argues that "the characteristics that are associated with sovereignty—territory, autonomy, recognition and control—do not provide an accurate description of the actual practices that have characterized many entities that have been conventionally viewed as sovereign states,"[41] and he concludes that the principles associated with Westphalian and international legal sovereignty are "best understood as examples of organized hypocrisy."[42] Like any intellectually serious discipline, international relations exhibits self-reflexivity and allows for critical examination of some of its governing premises. What the discipline does not examine, however, or even acknowledge, is that for most of the history of the modern international system it was characterized not by sovereign territorial states in a condition of anarchy vis-à-vis each other, but rather by empires.

Sovereignty and Empire

Until very recently, formally equal sovereign territorial states did not cover the earth's surface. The larger part of the world and its people were ruled, directly or indirectly, by others. Until well into the twentieth century white settler colonies such as Australia, South Africa, Canada, and New Zealand were "dominions," self-governing over internal matters, but governed in foreign affairs and war by the British Empire, of which they were part.[43] Much larger swaths of territory and larger numbers of people were simply colonial

---

International Relations, Cambridge: Cambridge University Press, 1992, is an excellent exploration of how time and space came to be reconfigured to produce both the international system and the discipline that is an expression of the unresolved tensions of this system.

[40] For a discussion of some of these anomalies see the essays in Douglas Howland and Luise S. White (eds.), *The State of Sovereignty: Territories, Laws, Populations*, Bloomington: Indiana University Press, 2009.

[41] Stephen D. Krasner, *Sovereignty: Organized Hypocrisy*, Princeton, NJ: Princeton University Press, 1999, 237.

[42] Krasner, *Sovereignty*, 24.

[43] In the closing decades of Queen Victoria's reign, some even imagined a "Greater Britain" that would incorporate the "Anglo-Saxon" dominions into a single political unit. See Duncan Bell, *The Idea of Greater Britain: Empire and the Future of World Order, 1860–1900*, Princeton, NJ: Princeton University Press, 2007.

possessions. If the sovereign territorial state of international relations is taken as the norm, exceptions far outnumber this putative norm.

In recent decades scholars of international relations have been much concerned with whether it is "still" accurate to regard states as the main elements and actors in the international or global domain. What they do not usually recognize is that the very "expansion" of Europe beyond the European continent was in part enabled by nonstate actors. Perhaps the most important of these, though by no means the only one, was the East India Company, which exercised political power, established fortifications, made law and created courts, issued punishments, coined money, and engaged in diplomacy and in war. The East India Company was far from being an oddity, as Philip Stern reminds us in his study of it, for early modern empires "more often than not were pioneered and governed not by states alone but in cooperation and competition with a medley of companies and corporations, *conquistadores*, explorers, privateers, proprietors, and itinerant merchant, family and religious networks."[44]

Colonized peoples and territories were not always governed by their distant sovereign masters: the British Empire, for instance, was not always governed by or from England, but was rather a hybrid affair, constantly negotiated among "a multiplicity of royal agencies, local governors, councils, assemblies, courts, and corporate and legal communities."[45] For over a century, almost a quarter of the people of Britain's most important colony, and over a third of its territory, was nominally governed by its princes and rajas.[46] The institution of "paramountcy" preserved the fiction, and sometimes a measure of substance, of princely sovereignty. What resulted was a sort of "quasi" or divided sovereignty, a situation in which "rather than signifying a quality that a state either possessed or failed to retain, sovereignty could be held by degrees."[47] "Protectorates" were another form of quasi sovereignty,

---

[44] Philip J. Stern, *The Company-State: Corporate Sovereignty and the Early Modern Foundations of the British Empire in India*, New York: Oxford University Press, 2011, 10. As Stern observes, in later times the functions and powers exercised by the East India Company would be interpreted as anomalous and even aberrant; but this is because we anachronistically projected the dominance of the modern territorial state into the past, such that "our thinking about the nature of political communities outside the state" came to be shaped by "the general assumptions at the core of that state's own expectations and ideologies"—at the cost of an almost willed amnesia about "the specific historical processes by which the British empire itself was made in India and around the globe" (212).

[45] Stern, *The Company-State*, 10.

[46] The princely states varied enormously in size and importance, with some (Hyderabad, for instance) larger than many European states, and others barely larger than hamlets. At the time of independence in 1947 there were over five hundred princely states.

[47] Lauren Benton, *A Search for Sovereignty: Law and Geography in European Empires, 1400–1900*, New York: Cambridge University Press, 2010, 245. As Benton notes, "By defining native states'

stretching from West Africa and the Middle East to Asia and the Pacific, and involving a number of European countries. Indeed, much of Britain's West African empire was ruled in this indirect fashion, one that allowed the imperial power complete control over the external affairs of the "protected" territory, while allowing the non-European state some sovereignty over internal matters.[48] Internal sovereignty, however, could be and was abrogated in the name of "good government." The institution of "protection" thus provided a flexible form of political control: competing European powers were excluded from it, and the "protector" was spared the costs and dangers of governance yet could intervene when it was considered desirable or necessary, thus retaining the power to "regulate the degree of sovereignty of a local ruler,"[49] all the while claiming that sovereignty was located in or with the native ruler.[50]

After World War I, the former colonies of the defeated powers were transformed into "mandates" under the newly created League of Nations, "vast territories . . . not under the sovereignty of any state but in a status new to international law,"[51] with the exact nature of this status being the subject of extensive disagreement.[52] The mandates were divided into three classes,

sovereignty, the British government diminished it; by articulating a right to contain warfare, the British had removed interstate relations from the realm of international relations" (249).

[48] For a study of this form of indirect rule—as well as its consequences for contemporary Africa—see Mahmood Mamdani, *Citizen and Subject: Contemporary Africa and the Legacy of Late Colonialism*, Princeton, NJ: Princeton University Press, 1996.

[49] Antony Anghie, *Imperialism, Sovereignty and the Making of International Law*, New York: Cambridge University Press, 2004, 89. See also Siba Grovogui, *Sovereigns, Quasi Sovereigns, and Africans: Race and Self-Determination in International Law*, Minneapolis: University of Minnesota Press, 1996; and Lauren Benton, "From International Law to Imperial Constitutions: The Problem of Quasi-Sovereignty, 1870–1900," *Law and History Review* 26:3 (Fall 2008). On the jurisdictional problems this created, given the uncertainty of territorial boundaries, see Inge van Hulle, "British Protection, Extraterritoriality and the Protectorates in West Africa," in Lauren Benton, Adam Clulow, and Bain Atwood (eds.), *Protection and Empire: A Global History*, New York: Cambridge University Press, 2018.

[50] Such "quasi-sovereign" arrangements usually rested upon treaties, giving rise to a curious paradox, which Anghie characterizes as "the ambivalent status of the non-European entity, outside the scope of law and yet within it, lacking in international personality and yet necessarily possessing it if any sense was to be made of the many treaties which European states relied on"; this was a paradox, he adds, that "was never satisfactorily resolved" (*Imperialism, Sovereignty*, 81).

[51] Quincy Wright, *Mandates under the League of Nations*, Chicago: University of Chicago Press, 1930, vii. On the discussions and negotiations that resulted in the mandate system being established, see Wright, 24–63. For a detailed account of how the British assiduously planned for such an outcome at the Paris Peace Conference and "left the conference gorged with almost all its colonial desiderata," see Eric Goldstein, *Winning the Peace: British Diplomatic Strategy, Peace Planning, and the Paris Peace Conference, 1916–1920*, Oxford: Clarendon Press, 1991, chapter 5 (quotation from 190).

[52] The conflicting views of jurists and others are summed up as follows by Wright: "Joint and sometimes divided sovereignty has been attributed to the Principal Powers and the League, to the mandatories and the mandated communities, to the League and the mandated communities, to the League and the mandatories, or even to the League, the mandatories, and the mandates communities" (*Mandates*, 319). To which list we can add the of interpretation of Arthur Balfour, according to whom a mandate was "a self-imposed limitation on by the conquerors on the sovereignty which

of which one consisted of colonies being transferred from the vanquished to the victorious colonial powers.[53] The class of territories that were meant to be shepherded to independent sovereign status presented a clear anomaly, for while the League was a product of and subordinate to the will of sovereign states—in line with the presuppositions of the discipline—here this relationship was in effect reversed, for "international institutions, rather than being the product of sovereign states, were given the task of creating sovereignty out of the backward peoples and territories brought under the mandate regime."[54]

Those non-Western territories and peoples who escaped the direct or indirect control of the colonial powers did not thereby retain full sovereignty as it is understood in international relations. The practice and institution of "extraterritoriality," whereby powerful states claimed legal jurisdiction over their own citizens (and their commercial interests), was one imposed upon many "independent" states. This was not a minor anomaly, for extraterritoriality was institutionalized and practiced over a period of a hundred years. The Ottoman Empire, Japan, and China were all subjected to this intrusion in a sustained and systematic fashion, but so too were a host of others, including Tunisia, Madagascar, Samoa, Korea, Thailand, and Morocco. The states claiming extraterritorial jurisdiction included not only the "great powers" of Britain, France, and the United States, but also Portugal, Italy, the Netherlands, Belgium, Greece, Denmark, Sweden, Norway, Spain, Switzerland, and later Japan, which went from suffering extraterritoriality to claiming it in China and in occupied Korea. In some cases, claims to extraterritoriality were a prelude to full colonial rule and the loss of all sovereignty; in others, and most notably in China, the Ottoman Empire, and Japan, this was one of the important mechanisms by which European powers and the United States exercised partial control over otherwise "sovereign" countries, producing what has often been characterized, particularly in the case of China, as "semicolonialism." In 1926, there were more than 120

---

they exercised over conquered territory." Quoted in Leonard V. Smith, *Sovereignty at the Paris Peace Conference of 1919*, New York: Oxford University Press, 2018, 250.

[53] The "C" mandatory powers (South Africa, Australia, and New Zealand) "held their mandated territories as colonies in all but name." Wm. Roger Louis, "The Era of the Mandates System and the Non-European World," in Hedley Bull and Adam Watson (eds.), *The Expansion of International Society*, Oxford: Clarendon Press, 1984, 212. In fact all the mandatory powers seem to have harbored a desire to transform their mandates into colonies; as Wright observed in 1930, "They prefer mandates to nothing but doubtless would prefer colonies to mandates" (*Mandates*, 97).

[54] Anghie, *Imperialism, Sovereignty*, 133.

consular courts operating in China.[55] British consular courts had their own legal codes and were organised in a hierarchy, with appellate courts reaching all the way to the Privy Council, the final court of appeal for the British extraterritorial courts.[56] This was, in short, a highly developed and intricate system of exercising legal and political control, not an ad hoc and temporary measure; it sits ill with the notion that sovereign states have uncontested legal jurisdiction over their own territory and do not seek such jurisdiction over other territories.

It is commonly assumed to be a characteristic of state sovereignty that it entails control of migration across state borders and, indeed, that "such control is a defining, definitive, unchanging, and unchangeable element of (state) sovereignty."[57] It is similarly assumed that war is fought by the armies of sovereign territorial states and that state, army, and society are isomorphic. But until very recent times, these were far from being the norm. At the end of World War II the French nation and the French state were two distinct if overlapping entities. Those living in "overseas France" were part of the French state, but usually not of the French nation-state. Some of these were French nationals but not citizens; a majority were neither nationals nor citizens, but subjects who were part of the French imperial state,[58] and France sought to keep these subjects "in" this empire rather than, as now, seeking to keep them "out."[59] In the wake of the abolition of slavery in 1833, the British Empire played an active role in facilitating the movement of its Indian subjects into its ex-slave plantation colonies as much-needed indentured labor, and developed an elaborate governmental machinery to do so; by contrast, the movement of peoples other than indentured laborers within the British Empire was largely unregulated and not constrained by a passport system. It was the white dominions of the empire, as Radhika Mongia has shown, that sought to restrict and regulate the entry of nonwhite imperial

[55] Turan Kayaoglu, *Legal Imperialism: Sovereignty and Extraterritoriality in Japan, the Ottoman Empire, and China*, New York: Cambridge University Press, 2010, 151.

[56] Kayaoglu, *Legal Imperialism*, 6. For a brief account of the development of British extraterritoriality in China see Paul Ch'en, "The Treaty System and European Law in China: A Study of the Exercise of British Jurisdiction in Late Imperial China," in W. J. Mommsen and J. A De Moor (eds.), *European Expansion and Law*, New York: Berg, 1992.

[57] Radhika Mongia, *Indian Migration and Empire: A Colonial Genealogy of the Modern State*, Durham, NC: Duke University Press, 2018, 7.

[58] See Frederick Cooper, "Alternatives to Empire: France and Africa after World War II," in Douglas Howland and Luise White (eds.), *The State of Sovereignty: Territories, Laws, Populations*, Bloomington: Indiana University Press, 2009.

[59] As observed in Frederick Cooper, *Colonialism in Question: Theory, Knowledge, History*, Berkeley: University of California Press, 2005, 115.

subjects, finally achieving their aim following the *Komagata Maru* incident in 1914.[60] It was only after this that the freedom of British subjects to move from one part of the empire to another was abandoned, and a passport system allowing race-based restriction introduced. Far from being a defining feature of sovereignty, the control of immigration within empires occurred late and helped to *produce* state sovereignty: as Mongia concludes, "Control over mobility does not occur *after* the formation of the nation-state . . . the very development of the nation-state occurred, in part, to control mobility across the axis of the nation/race."[61]

National armies are assumed in common sense, as in the discipline, to be a characteristic feature of the state system. But as Tarak Barkawi observes, "the model of the sovereign state" in fact "turns out to be a poor guide to the organization of military power for much of world politics."[62] The armies that fought in most of the colonial campaigns of the colonizer countries, and in World War I and World War II, were imperial armies, most notably in the cases of France and Britain. The British Indian army numbered some five hundred thousand men during World War I, and 10% of the soldiers who fought for the British Empire in the war were in the British Indian army;[63] in World War II the Indian army comprised some two million troops and operated across three continents.[64] The nation-state ontology reified by the discipline is in significant measure an *outcome* of World War II, rather than being the basis of it and the mode in which it was fought; it was only well after that war that national armies and sovereign states became congruent.[65]

An international order composed of states exercising a monopoly of legitimate violence and legal jurisdiction within their own territory

---

[60] In 1914 the ship *Komagata Maru* arrived at the coast of Vancouver with 376 Indian passengers on board, seeking entry to Canada as British subjects; protests by the Canadian government led to the end of such free movement. For a detailed account and analysis, see Mongia, *Indian Migration and Empire*, chap. 4.

[61] Mongia, *Indian Migration and Empire*, 139.

[62] Tarak Barkawi, "Empire and Order in International Relations and Security Studies," in *Oxford Research Encyclopedia of International Studies*, New York: Oxford University Press, 2010, 13.

[63] Tarak Barkawi, *Soldiers of Empire: Indian and British Armies in World War II*, New York: Cambridge University Press, 2017, 7 and 84.

[64] Barkawi, *Soldiers of Empire*, 51. When Singapore fell to the Japanese in 1942, some forty thousand Indian soldiers were among those who surrendered, some of who would subsequently join the "Indian National Army" and fight against the British.

[65] As Tarak Barkawi colorfully expresses it, this war "consumed one world order and spat out another." "War, Armed Forces and Society in Postcolonial Perspective," in Sanjay Seth (ed.), *Postcolonial Theory and International Relations: A Critical Introduction*, New York: Routledge, 2013, 92.

has *not*—the assumptions of the discipline of international relations notwithstanding—been the norm historically. And the "anomalies" I have enumerated—including colonial rule, quasi sovereignty, mandates, and extraterritoriality—were not in fact anomalies or mere exceptions to the norm, for they encompassed the larger part of the world's people and were an important and defining feature of "the international" until very recently. The conclusion, in David Armitage's words, is inescapable: "Perhaps the most momentous but least widely understood development in modern history is the long transition from a world of empires to a world of states. Until at least the late nineteenth century, and in many places for decades after, most of the world's population lived in the territorially expansive, internally diverse, hierarchically organised political communities called empires."[66]

As even the preceding brief discussion of the legal and political complexities of colonialism and empire illustrates, these empires were not simply "superstates," sovereign states writ large. In this regard, the nineteenth- and twentieth-century maps in which the various European empires were portrayed as territorial entities—the largest, the British Empire, usually in red or pink—are profoundly misleading representations of the political and legal order of the time. The map of empire with its neatly shaded territories did not, Lauren Benton shows, correspond to the exercise of political power or the functioning of law, one of the modalities of that power: "Empires did not cover space evenly but composed a fabric that was full of holes, stitched together out of pieces, a tangle of strings. Even in the most paradigmatic cases, an empire's spaces were politically fragmented; legally differentiated; and encased in irregular, porous and sometimes undefined borders," including "areas of partial or shared sovereignty," all this producing "political geographies that were uneven, disaggregated, and oddly shaped—not at all consistent with the image produced by the monochrome shading of imperial maps."[67]

---

[66] David Armitage, *Foundations of Modern International Thought*, New York: Cambridge University Press, 2013, 191.

[67] Benton, *A Search for Sovereignty*, 2. "A graphic representation of imperial power more accurate than the standard, multicoloured maps," Benton writes, "would show tangled and interrupted European-claimed spaces and would represent, perhaps in colours of varying intensity, the changing and locally differentiated qualities of rule within geographic zones" (3). See also her *Law and Colonial Culture: Legal Regimes in World History, 1400–1900*, New York: Cambridge University Press, 2009. Ann Laura Stoler similarly argues that "the legal and political fuzziness of dependencies, trusteeships, protectorates and unincorporated territories" was not anomalous, but "part of the deep grammar of . . . the nineteenth- and twentieth-century imperial world." "Degrees of Imperial Sovereignty," *Public Culture* 18:1 (2006), 137. See also Stern, *The Company-State*. As Jeremy Adelman sums up the implications of this expanding historical literature, "Sovereignty did not only have one

The presumptions of international relations notwithstanding, for most of the last few centuries, territory and sovereignty have not coincided; sovereignty has not been indivisible but often divided, overlapping or even indeterminate; and legal jurisdictions and legal regimes have not been isomorphous with clearly marked territories, nor have the boundaries at which their writ ceases been clearly distinguishable.

The "Expansion of European Society": First the West, Then the Rest

How then, is it, that the discipline of international relations manages to ignore or elide all this and treat the sovereign state in a condition of anarchy as the empirical given that is presupposed in all inquiries into international politics? This is achieved by subsuming the preceding facts (where they are acknowledged at all) in a teleology, one according to which all historical events lead to the normalization of the contemporary world system, and all evidences to the contrary are treated as merely residual anomalies, destined to be swept away. The most influential such account, that of the expansion of international society from its original European home until it encompassed the globe, is offered by scholars of the retrospectively invented "English School" of international relations. It is the local, international relations version of the "first the West, then the Rest" narrative that has dominated the social sciences.

Hedley Bull and Adam Watson acknowledge that the European states that pioneered an international order of formally equal sovereign states "at the same time established a number of empires which, while they were rival and competing, taken together amounted to a European hegemony over the rest of the world."[68] This recognition leads them not, however, to an inquiry into the character of a world order in which colonialism and empire loomed so large, but rather to an account of how this initially European system of states, based upon absolute and undivided sovereignty and juridical equality, spread outward

layer to it, radiating outward to territorial boundaries with concentric circles of authority; it had many layers, which rearranged according to shifting structures and circumstance." "An Age of Imperial Revolutions," *American Historical Review* (April 2008), 330.

[68] Hedley Bull and Adam Watson, "Introduction," in Bull and Watson, *Expansion of International Society*, 6.

beyond its European homeland. In their account this sovereign state system, once established, "applied logically to any new members of the society, and so proved eminently exportable."[69] Thus in the course of the eighteenth and nineteenth centuries the United States and the newly independent countries of Latin America became sovereign states and part of this system. The polities of Asia, Africa, and elsewhere had not been forged in the same culture and were not able to honor their international obligations, whether unwritten or arising from treaties. These were thus subjected to the "standard of civilization" test, a test arising out of "a need for reciprocity in dealings between European and non-European powers, which the latter in many cases were either not able or not willing to meet."[70] When they had reformed and modernized sufficiently, as Japan and the Ottoman Empire were the first to do, they were "admitted" to international society. Later, under the impact of Western ideas and the homogenizing effects of the "culture of modernity,"[71] other subject polities were also to reform themselves and be admitted to, or force their way into, the club of sovereign states. In Bull and Watson's account, decolonization and the emergence of scores of new states appear as the culmination of an international system born in Europe some centuries earlier. All that contradicts or complicates this picture—Bull himself mentions, if only in passing, "spheres of influence, protected states, protectorates, subjection to imperial paramountcy"—is treated as "the survival, alongside the concept of a society of equally sovereign states, of the older and historically much more ubiquitous concept of international relations as the relations between suzerains and vassals."[72] There is, in short, a direct line from Westphalia to the present world order.[73]

---

[69] Adam Watson, "European International Society and Its Expansion," in Bull and Watson, *Expansion of International Society*, 24.

[70] Hedley Bull, "Preface," in Gerrit W. Gong, *The Standard of "Civilization" in International Society*, Oxford: Clarendon Press, 1984, viii. For a critical evaluation of this very sanguine account of imperialist expansion see William A. Callahan, "Nationalising International Theory: Race, Class and the English School," *Global Society* 18:4 (2004). As Callahan observes, "Although the link between empire and International Society is seemingly obvious . . . the celebrated historical method of the English School skirts over this historical fact: although decolonisation is discussed, colonisation rarely is" (310). Shogo Suzuki provides a useful counterpoint to the sanitized accounts offered by Bull, Watson, and others, in his *Civilization and Empire: China and Japan's Encounter with European International Society*, New York: Routledge, 2009.

[71] The expression used by Hedley Bull, who qualifies that this "so-called" culture of modernity is, in fact, the culture of the West. *The Anarchical Society: A Study of Order in World Politics*, New York: Columbia University Press, 2002, 37.

[72] Bull, "European States and African Political Communities," in Bull and Watson, *Expansion of International Society*, 126.

[73] As Adam Watson puts it, "What Westphalia legitimized for the princes and cities of the Holy Roman Empire, admission to the United Nations legitimizes today for newly independent states." *The Evolution of International Society*, London: Routledge, 1992, 317.

In *International Systems and World History*, Buzan and Little provide an updated version of the English School account "by setting it on firmer historical and theoretical foundations."[74] Their account differs in specifics, but not in its general argument, from that which had earlier been offered by Bull and by Watson. Buzan and Little offer analyses of earlier international systems in which states were not the prime units, and anarchy did not prevail. But in their narrative as in Bull and Watson's, the modern international system of sovereign territorial states first emerges in Europe and is subsequently spread throughout the world. Like Bull and Watson, Buzan and Little acknowledge that until after World War II, "empires with modern states at their core were the dominant unit."[75] However, here too the logic or imperative unleashed by the emergence of the sovereign state form in Europe is seen to be inexorable; the European empires proved to be not an independent political form, but rather "the nursery, or mechanism, by which the political form of the modern state was transposed onto the rest of the world."[76]

This teleology that overrides an inconvenient history, subsuming all evidence to the contrary as "survivals," is not a peculiarity of the English School alone, but is rather central to the discipline—or at least, those segments of it that recognize that state sovereignty is not a given, but has a history. Daniel Philpott argues that it took two "revolutions," not one, to globalize the sovereign state and produce the international system presumed and analyzed by international relations: one was the Peace of Westphalia, the other the process of decolonization. Unlike the scholars of the English School, in *Revolutions in Sovereignty* Philpott devotes considerable space to colonialism and empire. He is aware that these two revolutions are separated by three centuries, and during these centuries much of the globe and its people "was less than sovereign: partitioned, divided spheres of influence, colonized, or otherwise restricted in authority."[77] But "The exceptions, the violations, the contestation . . . do not annul . . . the collective movement of the two revolutions, the movement by which the sovereign state system took over the globe."[78] Thus while Philpott complicates the narrative of a straight line from Westphalia to

---

[74] Barry Buzan and Richard Little, *International Systems and World History: Remaking the Study of International Relations*, New York: Oxford University Press, 2000, 408.

[75] Buzan and Little, *International Systems*, 264.

[76] Buzan and Little, *International Systems*, 264.

[77] Philpott, *Revolutions in Sovereignty: How Ideas Shaped Modern International Relations*, Princeton, NJ: Princeton University Press, 2001, 153. See also Philpott, "Westphalia, Authority, and International Society," *Political Studies* 47 (1999).

[78] Philpott, *Revolutions in Sovereignty*, 255–56.

the current global order by introducing or recognizing a second "revolution," this only modifies the narrative without derailing its teleology: "Westphalia began and colonial independence completed an unprecedented feat—the extension of the sovereign state to the entire land surface of the globe. . . . The two revolutions in sovereignty, as diverse as they may be, form a common story, a single movement."[79]

Empire and Amnesia

With rare exceptions, the centuries of colonialism and empire are barely registered in the discipline of international relations.[80] Where they are registered, the fact that the sheer weight and historical duration of empire challenges the assumptions of the discipline is conjured away by a teleology that treats the complications it introduces as mere "survivals" or "anomalies," destined to be swept away: empire appears as a way station to, or a nursery for, the sovereign state system that is its final destination.

One of the exceptions to this rule, Edward Keene's *Beyond the Anarchical Society*, recognizes that beginning with the emergence of state sovereignty in Europe and then tracing its "expansion" prevents us from acknowledging and taking seriously other forms of international order, such as imperial systems. If we fix our gaze beyond Europe, he argues, we can see that something very different was unfolding there: "The range of actors was more diverse, including the absolutist monarchs from the orthodox narrative, but also chartered corporations engaged in trade and colonization, noble proprietors, individual settlers, colonial administrators, and, of course, indigenous rulers and peoples."[81] Once this is brought into the frame, Keene writes, it becomes apparent that "the orthodox way of thinking about order in modern world politics in terms of the Westphalian system and the society of states is so misleading that it obscures their real nature."[82] Instead of seeing a European system "expanding" to include what lay beyond its boundaries, we are

[79] Philpott, *Revolutions in Sovereignty*, 255.

[80] It will be noted that my alternative account of the international sphere in the preceding pages draws mostly on scholarship that is not produced from those working within international relations. An earlier exception, if a partial one, is Michael Doyle's *Empires*, Ithaca, NY: Cornell University Press, 1986.

[81] Edward Keene, *Beyond the Anarchical Society: Grotius, Colonialism and Order in World Politics*, New York: Cambridge University Press, 2002, 118.

[82] Keene, *Beyond the Anarchical Society*, 10.

compelled to recognize that "the world was clearly divided into two for the purposes of international political and legal order": one a world centered in Europe, where a system of sovereign states provided the mechanisms, through mutual recognition, nonintervention, and the like, to respect differences; and a very different political and legal order beyond Europe, based upon the assumed inferiority of non-Western peoples, and organized on the basis that "the central purpose of international order was to promote the civilization of decadent, backward, savage or barbaric peoples."[83] In Keene's important analysis, the global order that emerges after World War II, when this distinction ceases to be tenable, is an unhappy mix of the divergent principles underlying these two orders.

Even here, however, the language of "two worlds" militates against full recognition of what Keene is otherwise well aware of, namely that these worlds were closely connected, were in fact a single world of colonial domination and empire. In recent times it is scholars outside of international relations—most notably historians and scholars of international law—who have begun the task of understanding, in David Armitage's words quoted earlier, the "most momentous but least widely understood development in modern history," namely "the long transition from a world of empires to a world of states." The prerequisite to this, of course, is to treat empire as an analytical category, not as a way station or interregnum. Thus Lauren Benton, for example, in drawing attention to the many "anomalies" that present themselves if one assumes that preceding centuries were but a march toward sovereign, territorial states, cautions against yielding to the temptation to regard these as "merely temporary formations." She seeks instead to show that "layered" and divisible sovereignty, legal differentiation and "anomalous legal zones," the absence of a neat isomorphism between sovereignty and territory, and porous and sometimes undefined borders were not the "result of persisting, older irregularities," that is, survivals of an earlier world, but were rather continually being created or produced as "a function of the routine operations of empire."[84] In short, far from being a "nursery" for the cultivation and spread of the sovereign territorial state, empire was a political system or form possessed of its own logic(s); and these logics neither required nor consistently reproduced and spread an indivisible, undiluted sovereignty exercised over a clearly demarcated territory. Moreover, empire was a defining feature of the

---

[83] Keene, *Beyond the Anarchical Society*, 7.
[84] Benton, *A Search for Sovereignty*, 4.

world until quite recently—more recently than is commonly remembered or registered. The end of World War I saw the end of some *empires*, but not of empire as a political form; indeed, as seen, under the mandate system the colonies of the vanquished were redistributed to other empires and would-be empires. As World War II was drawing to an end and discussions began on the postwar world order at Dumbarton Oaks and San Francisco, dismantling empire was not on the agenda: Jan Smuts was entrusted with drafting the preamble to the UN Charter, and "Mandates were turned into trusteeships, and colonies became dependent territories, but little seemed to change apart from words."[85] Today it is seen as an embodiment and thus an illustration of the world as imagined by the discipline—a world composed of numerous territorial, sovereign, and formally equal states—but the United Nations, as Mark Mazower reminds those with short memories, was "a product of empire and indeed, at least at the outset, was regarded by those with colonies to keep as a more than adequate mechanism for its defense."[86] It was not until the creation of many new states in the process of decolonization that the UN began to resemble and represent the world as it is conceived by the discipline of international relations.

The object of the discipline and the discipline itself thus emerged coterminously in the years immediately after World War II, and the discipline has anachronistically projected its object back into the past. Barkawi summarizes the resulting paradox: "IR was founded amidst empire, but discovered instead only a world of sovereign states."[87] At its origins and since, the discipline has mistaken the world as it began to appear to observers and statesmen after World War II and decolonization, for the world as such.

Since it is not plausible that sophisticated practitioners should be so innocent of history and capable of so egregious an error, I suggest that we should interpret this as an *active* forgetting of empire, a *willed* amnesia.[88] This conclusion is made more plausible by the fact that the same amnesia is at work in

---

[85] Mark Mazowar, *No Enchanted Palace: The End of Empire and the Ideological Origins of the United Nations*, Princeton, NJ: Princeton University Press, 2009, 63.

[86] Mazower, *No Enchanted Palace*, 17.

[87] Barkawi, "Empire and Order in International Relations and Security Studies," 2. As a consequence, "IR's central categories of sovereignty and the states-system generate a systematic occlusion of the imperial and global character of world politics, past and present." Barkawi and Mark Laffey, "Retrieving the Imperial: Empire and International Relations," *Millennium* 31:1 (2002), 110.

[88] I borrow this term from Sankaran Krishna, who powerfully argues that the discipline "was and is predicated on a systematic politics of forgetting, a wilful amnesia, on the question of race." "Race, Amnesia, and the Education of International Relations," in Branwen Gruffydd Jones (ed.), *Decolonizing International Relations*, Lanham, MD: Rowman and Littlefield, 2006, 89.

the discipline's remembering, and retelling, of its own origins. Earlier in this chapter I suggested that the discipline's account of its origins is almost wholly fictional: but it is not just that it invents a fictional history for itself, but that it leaves out a central aspect of it *actual* (pre)history, namely its engagement with questions of colonialism, race, and empire. For recent scholarship shows that in the early years of the twentieth century, "the study of colonial administration within political science comprised a considerable share of the discourse about international politics,"[89] and further, that "imperialism and internationalism oriented much of the interwar discussions of international relations."[90] *Foreign Affairs*, founded in 1922 and today a very influential journal in the field, began its life as the *Journal of Race Development*.[91] The "idealists" or liberals of the so-called interwar debate were less than "idealist" when it came to the right to self-determination of colonized peoples, for they assumed that these people, being lower on the civilizational "scale," were destined to be ruled by the great powers. The issue of the colonies and the "subject races" loomed large in their thinking, so much so that Jeanne Morefield has influentially argued that the internationalism of liberal idealists such as Gilbert Murray and Alfred Zimmern is best read "as an attempt to reconcile an older system of world politics governed by the competing claims of empires with the newly emerging rationale of international cooperation organized around sovereign nation states."[92] But just as the discipline forgets empire, so in the standard accounts of the history of its own emergence international relations also represses its earlier recognition of the significance of empire. It would seem that a discipline that misdescribes the history of its object must perforce misrepresent or forget the history of its own engagement with that object.

---

[89] Brian C. Schmidt, *The Political Discourse of Anarchy: A Disciplinary History of IR*, Albany: State University of New York Press, 1997, 125.

[90] Long and Schmidt, "Introduction," in David Long and Brian C. Schmidt (eds.), *Imperialism and Internationalism in the Discipline of International Relations*, Albany: State University of New York Press, 2005, 10. Robert Vitalis goes further, suggesting that "the 'birth of the discipline' of international relations is . . . a story about empire." "The Noble American Science of Imperial Relations and Its Laws of Race Development," *Comparative Studies in Society and History* 52:4 (October 2010), 910. See also Errol A. Henderson, "Hidden in Plain Sight: Racism in International Relations Theory," *Cambridge Review of International Affairs* 26:1 (2013). For a sustained argument that the discipline of international relations does not so much "explain" international politics as function "to parochially celebrate and defend or promote the West," see John M. Hobson, *The Eurocentric Conception of World Politics: Western International Theory, 1760–2010*, New York: Cambridge University Press, 2012, 1.

[91] See Robert Vitalis, "Birth of a Discipline," in Long and Schmidt, *Imperialism and Internationalism*.

[92] Jeanne Morefield, *Covenants without Swords: Idealist Liberalism and the Spirit of Empire*, Princeton, NJ: Princeton University Press, 2005, 220.

International Relations Today and Tomorrow

The world as it has been portrayed, studied, and normalized by the discipline of international relations—one of sovereign states in a condition of anarchy vis-à-vis one another—only fully emerged as a result of decolonization, a process that transformed a world of (mostly) European states possessed of colonies into a world of sovereign states. With this transformation, "state" and "nation" now came to be sutured together in a way that had not been so before. The "first truly global international society that the world had known," as James Mayall observes, is a consequence of "the doctrine of national self-determination."[93]

Why should decolonization have resulted in the globalization of the sovereign nation-state? That this would prove to be the outcome of the revolt against colonial rule would not have been obvious in the mid-nineteenth century, at the time of the Indian "mutiny," or at the beginning of the twentieth century, which was ushered in by the Boxer Rebellion: neither of these massive anticolonial uprisings aimed at establishing a sovereign nation-state.[94] As these and numerous other millenarian uprisings and peasant jacqueries attest, anticolonial nationalism was by no means the only form that resistance to colonial rule took. Nonetheless, anticolonial nationalism proved by far to be the most historically consequential, for in the course of the twentieth century, it seemed to become "obvious" and "natural" to many that emancipation from colonial domination must necessarily take the form of founding an independent nation-state. Why was this so, especially given that the nation-state was a product of European histories, rather than emerging from the histories and traditions of the colonized?

The answer, in summary form, is that the nation-state came to appear, to those fighting against colonial rule, as an institution that could transcend the parochialism of its origins. For nationalists, the "form" of the state was not tied to any particular content, but could be used to express any (national) content. The *nation*-state, in this understanding of it, would express

---

[93] James Mayall, *Nationalism and International Society*, Cambridge: Cambridge University Press, 1990, 35, 33.

[94] Pan-African, pan-Asian, pan-Islamic, and pan-Arab movements are also evidence that "imaginations of race, religion, and civilization . . . represent a significant force in modern world history, even if they have often been overshadowed by the emphasis on nationalism." Cemil Aydin, *The Politics of Anti-Westernism in Asia: Visions of World Order in Pan-Islamic and Pan-Asian Thought*, New York: Columbia University Press, 2007, 3. See also Prasenjit Duara, "The Discourse of Civilization and Pan-Asianism," *Journal of World History* 12:1 (2001).

and embody the specificity, that is, the cultural and other particularities of a non-Western people; by constituting themselves as independent and sovereign nations, non-European peoples could claim their place under the sun, and do so *without* surrendering and losing the national particularities that underwrote their desire for independence in the first place.[95] Shaped by and embodying this understanding of the relation between state as "form" and national culture as "content," anticolonial nationalism remade the world; in the two decades after World War II, a world of empires and colonies gave way to a world of nation-states.

This being so, even if international relations' account of its object displays a profound amnesia about the centrality of empire to international political arrangements in the past, could we nonetheless conclude that it is a useful guide to the international realm in the present and future? I will end this chapter by advancing three reasons why it seems to me that even this consolation is not available to the discipline.

The generalization of the nation-state form marked the end of empire, but the legacies of empire continue to shape the international order. A host of contemporary phenomena attest to this, including the US wars in Afghanistan, Iraq, and elsewhere (which display uncanny continuities with earlier colonial and imperial interventions), and the recrudescence of white nationalism and other racisms (which have deep roots in the imperial past). The ubiquity of "human rights" talk on the international scene, as Samuel Moyn has powerfully argued, is in its own perverse way a legacy of empire, in this case as a concerted project to forget and bury the aspirations once embodied by the revolutionary anticolonial nationalisms that contested empire.[96] There exists a large body of political writings and of academic scholarship that is keenly attentive to the numerous ways in which the ideas, practices, and power relations that characterized empire have taken new forms rather than disappeared, but the discipline of international relations has not been a significant contributor to this literature. The reasons for this lie in what has been explored in the preceding pages—a discipline that systematically forgets the centrality of empire in the making of the world is in no position to attend to

---

[95] This point is elaborated in Sanjay Seth, "A Postcolonial World?," in Greg Fry and Jacinta O'Hagan (eds.), *Contending Images of World Politics*, New York: Macmillan, 2000.

[96] Samuel Moyn, *The Last Utopia: Human Rights in History*, Cambridge, MA: Belknap Press of Harvard University Press, 2010.

and explain the continuing salience of the legacies of empire in the contemporary world system.

Second, the "international" is today characterized by great heterogeneity, for it is a domain with multiple actors—not only sovereign states but also international bodies such as the United Nations, transnational corporations, nongovernmental agencies, and many others. International relations is cognizant of this array, and indeed a great deal of the energy of its practitioners is taken up with describing and seeking to make sense of it, including by reconsidering the centrality customarily accorded by the discipline to the sovereign state. But it is hamstrung in its efforts to do so, inasmuch as it fails to recognize that this heterogeneity is not a novel development but rather, as seen in the preceding pages, has characterized the modern international system for most of the past few centuries. The present heterogeneity of the world order is of course not a mere repetition of the complexities of the earlier imperial world order; but a recognition of the political and legal heterogeneity characteristic of empire, and a corresponding acknowledgment that the dominance of the sovereign state as the principal actor in the international arena is the historical oddity in need of explanation, are, I suggest, the sine qua non for a discipline that seeks to produce knowledge about the international. The amnesia regarding empire that marks and mars the discipline renders it ill-equipped to understand the continuing shadows of empire on the contemporary international scene, or to explain the heterogenous nature of the contemporary international scene.

The third reason why I suggest that international relations is a poor guide to the contemporary international is a speculative one. I suggested earlier that the nation-state was embraced by many anticolonial thinkers and activists because it afforded the promise of combining imitation of the state form with an embrace of national difference. This was, however, always a fraught enterprise, and anticolonial nationalism was marked by a paradox or tension—a tension between anticolonial nationalism's imitative or derivative project of founding a modern sovereign state, and its claims to do so in the name of cultural/national uniqueness and difference. If we saw in anticolonial nationalisms only a political movement for state sovereignty, it would appear that Asian and African nationalisms are modeled upon European precedents and therefore wholly imitative: the independent postcolonial states of Asia and Africa very much resemble their European and American counterparts in claiming territorial and jurisdictional exclusivity and are equipped with all the customary panoply of flags, anthems, national armies, and the like. But this would be to overlook the dualism at the heart of anticolonial nationalism; because anticolonial nationalism also posited and elaborated a distinctive national culture and new forms of community, it was not and could not be mere mimicry of Europe. Partha Chatterjee, who has written about this tension with great sensitivity and insight, argues that "the most creative results of the nationalist imagination in Asia and Africa are posited not on an identity but rather on a *difference* with the 'modular' forms of the national society propagated by the modern West."[97] In other words, the new states of the global South that emerged in the course of decolonization neither were born of the "expansion of European international society," and nor were they mere replicas of their European counterparts. They sought instead to "fit" non-Western lifeworlds and indigenous forms of community into the container or "form" provided by the nation-state.

They have not always succeeded in doing so. Reflecting upon a lifetime of the anthropological study of culture, social change, and nationalism in Indonesia and Morocco, Clifford Geertz, like Chatterjee, also contests the presumption that postcolonial states were a mimicry of "Euronationalism," one that affirmed a natural homology between people/culture, sovereignty, and territory. In one of his last essays, Geertz wrote,

> The diffusionist notion that the modern world was made in northern and western Europe and then seeped out like an oil slick to cover the rest of the world has obscured the fact . . . that rather than converging toward a single pattern those entities called countries were ordering themselves in novel ways, ways that put European conceptions, not all that secure in any case, of what a country is, and what its basis is, under increasing pressure. The genuinely radical implications of the decolonization process are only just now coming to be recognized. For better or worse, the dynamics of Western nation building are not replicated. Something else is going on.[98]

That "something else," Geertz suggested, was that the isomorphism between culture/people, territory, and "country," presumed and reproduced "by the pictorial conventions of our political atlases, polygon cutouts in a fitted

---

[97] Partha Chatterjee, *The Nation and Its Fragment: Colonial and Postcolonial Histories*, Delhi: Oxford University Press, 1993, 5. See also his *Nationalist Thought and the Colonial World: A Derivative Discourse?*, Oxford: Oxford University Press, 1986.

[98] Clifford Geertz, "The World in Pieces: Culture and Politics at the End of the Century," in his *Available Light: Anthropological Reflections on Philosophical Topics*, Princeton, NJ: Princeton University Press, 2000, 230–31.

jigsaw," was an illusion, as was increasingly becoming apparent.[99] The new forms of community that had been imagined and given flesh in the course of the struggle against colonialism were not, as nationalists had hoped and striven for, a content that could easily be poured into the container of the nation-state. For the nation-state was not and is not an empty container into which anything can be poured; it already has a content, and it presupposes and serves to create specific connections between authority and the people, and between custom and law, and it presupposes certain forms of selfhood and community. The much-commented-upon failure of postcolonial nation-states to live up to their promise and to the expectations of their people has been, in part, a consequence of this tension or contradiction between the forms of community they imagined and mobilized, and the constraints imposed upon these by the form of the modern state; as Chatterjee puts it, "Autonomous forms of imagination of the community were, and continue to be, overwhelmed and swamped by the history of the postcolonial state. Here lies the root of our postcolonial misery: not in our inability to think out new forms of community, but in our surrender to old forms of the modern state."[100]

The absence of any "natural" congruence of culture, territory, and political sovereignty reveals, to return to Geertz, a more general truth about *all* nation-states, not only those born of anticolonial nationalism. It is a truth most clearly apparent in the case of the new states that emerged with decolonization, simply because "like Bismarck's sausages, we have seen them made. . . . The contingencies that produced them, and that virtually everywhere contrive to maintain them, are . . . evident"[101]; but the unstable and contingent nature of this conjunction is apparent everywhere, and not just in the global South. And so rather than presume (as the discipline of international relations does), that Western countries demonstrate the more or less normal isomorphism of culture, territory, and polity, and so embody the future of those currently troubled countries that have not yet attained to the norm, Geertz wonders whether "We may come in time to see Asia's and Africa's political reconstruction as contributing more to transforming Euro-America's view of social selfhood than vice versa."[102]

---

[99] Geertz, "The World in Pieces," 229.
[100] Chatterjee, *Nation and Its Fragments*, 11.
[101] Geertz, "The World in Pieces," 252.
[102] Geertz, "The World in Pieces," 251.

This is highly speculative, no doubt. But it is a speculation founded on something that is incontestably true, namely that culture, territory, and statehood do not neatly map onto each other, and that where they have done so, this has been a fragile and unstable achievement. If the longer-term and "genuinely radical implications of the decolonization process" prove to be a demonstration of this, rather than an affirmation of the inescapability of the nation-state, then the presumptions underpinning international relations and the inquiries undertaken in its name will prove to be of as little value as are its accounts of the historical emergence and consolidation of the global political system. The discipline will continue to be a symptom of the historical moment that saw the sovereign territorial nation-state become a global political norm, rather than an optic into the complex forces, conjunctures, and desires that made it so and might yet unmake it.

6

Political Theory and the Bourgeois Public Sphere

Political theory came to be institutionalized as a subdiscipline within political science in the course of the twentieth century, as a study of and engagement with a form of reflection purportedly stretching back more than two millennia, beginning in ancient Greece. Embodied in a series of canonical texts, this was taken to be a more or less continuous historical tradition, though one that had high points of great vitality and periods when it was in relative decline. Such identity and unity across long spans of time was thought to be a consequence of the fact that there were "abiding" or "enduring" questions of politics, and political theory was that form of reflection that identified and addressed these questions.[1] As George H. Sabine explained in "What Is a Political Theory" in 1939, "Because a political theory refers to the historical occasion from which it originated, it need not be applicable to that alone. Political problems and situations are more or less alike from time to time and from place to place.... The greatest political theorizing is that which excels ... in analysis of a present situation and in suggestiveness for other situations."[2] Or as the Chichele Professor for Social and Political Theory at Oxford put it, the great works of political theory, those that repaid close study, were "more original, more profound" than lesser ones, one important index of which was that they were "products of their age but are also ageless."[3] As with the histories of art, music, and science encountered in chapter 3, political theory supposed that the texts that provided its subject

---

[1] "Preface to the First Edition" (1963), in Leo Strauss and Joseph Cropsey (eds.), *History of Political Philosophy*, Chicago: University of Chicago Press, 1987, 1.

[2] George H. Sabine, "What Is a Political Theory?," *Journal of Politics* 1:1 (February 1939), 4.

[3] John Plamenatz, *Man and Society*, vol. 3: *Hegel, Marx and Engels, and the Idea of Progress*, 2nd ed., London: Longman, 1992, xix and xxix. Plamenatz follows through the logical implication of this initial claim—lesser works are so in part because they are not ageless, and "Our approach in discussing their doctrines must therefore be more historical than may be the case with regard to the pre-eminent thinkers" (xviii).

Beyond Reason. Sanjay Seth, Oxford University Press (2021). © Oxford University Press.
DOI: 10.1093/oso/9780197500583.003.0007

matter were historical and yet were not tethered to the time and context in which they were produced.

This provided an important criterion for discerning/constructing a canon of the most important works in political theory: these were works that transcended the historical circumstances of their production because they were addressed to the perennial questions of politics and thus spoke to (or could be made to speak to) the present. Sabine had constructed such a canon, one spanning twenty-five hundred years, in his monumental *A History of Political Theory* (1937). This work and Leo Strauss and Joseph Cropsey's edited *History of Political Philosophy* (1963) were translated into multiple languages and reissued in successive editions, becoming a staple resource for generations of teachers and students of political theory. Whereas a historian studied the past and an anthropologist studied other cultures, the political theorist studied the texts produced by other political theorists, resuscitating what the canonical texts had to say about the perennial questions of politics, and/or using these as scaffolding for developing his own thoughts about justice, equality, political obligation, and the like. In either case, "The academic political theorist saw himself if not quite as the heir, at least as the executor of a great inheritance. He moved among the 'classics' of the great tradition almost as if they were contemporaneous with each other and with him. He argued with them; he elicited arguments between them; he judged their merits."[4]

However, a form of intellectual inquiry and practice that was thought to have continued unbroken for more than two thousand years was suddenly found, in the 1950s and 1960s, to be in decline, under threat of extinction, or already dead. In 1956 Peter Laslett declared that—for now at least—political philosophy was dead.[5] One might have thought that the publication of Sheldon Wolin's major work of political theory, *Politics and Vision* (1960) put the lie to Laslett's pronouncement; but Wolin's was an embattled book, prefaced by the observation that "in many intellectual circles today there exists a marked hostility towards, and even contempt for, political philosophy in its traditional form," and Wolin expressed the mournful hope that if the tradition of political philosophy was coming to an end, his book might "at least

---

[4] Conal Condren, "The Death of Political Theory: The Importance of Historiographical Myth," *Politics* 11:2 (1974), 146.

[5] Peter Laslett, "Introduction" to Laslett (ed.), *Philosophy, Politics and Society*, 1st series, Oxford: Oxford University Press, 1956, vii.

succeed in making clear what it is we have discarded."[6] In 1962 Isaiah Berlin offered a rousing defense of political theory, but his defense was necessitated precisely because many scholars were now suggesting, in Berlin's words, that "political philosophy, whatever it might have been in the past, is to-day dead or dying";[7] his talk, tellingly, was entitled "Does Political Theory Still Exist?"

But no sooner was political theory dying or dead than it was resurrected. From the 1970s, formerly embattled political philosophers and political theorists—I will be treating the terms interchangeably—began to cautiously comment on the unexpected flourishing of their subdiscipline. Surveying "The Condition of Political Theory" in 1977, George Kateb observed with satisfaction that there was "great vitality" in the field.[8] Brian Barry, who in 1961 had joined those glumly wondering, in the words of his title, "Has Political Philosophy a Future?," returned to the topic in 1980 to write, "Who would have imagined in 1961 that one would so soon have the luxury of being able to complain about a glut of political philosophy?"[9] The earlier pronouncements of the last rites of the discipline were now replaced by fulsome self-congratulation over its rebirth.[10]

The discipline that was "resurrected," however, was not the same as the discipline that "died." Below I trace how and why it was that political theory, conceived as an ongoing tradition focused on the abiding or perennial questions of politics, became untenable in the face of multiple and compelling criticisms. I then suggest that the key to understanding the discipline that was born—rather than reborn—in the 1970s is to recognize that political theory, unlike history and international relations, does not have an

[6] Sheldon Wolin, *Politics and Vision*, Boston: Little, Brown, 1960, v. Looking back some forty years later, William Connolly writes, "To study political theory in 1960 was to participate in an enterprise widely thought to be moribund. The air was thick with funeral orations." "Politics and Vision," in Aryeh Botwinick and William E. Connolly (eds.), *Democracy and Vision: Sheldon Wolin and the Vicissitudes of the Political*, Princeton, NJ: Princeton University Press, 2001, 3.

[7] Berlin, "Does Political Theory Still Exist?," in Peter Laslett and David Runciman (eds.), *Politics, Philosophy and Society*, 2nd series, Oxford: Oxford University Press, 1962, 1.

[8] George Kateb, "The Condition of Political Theory," *American Behavioral Scientist* 21:1 (September–October 1977), 135.

[9] Brian Barry, "The Strange Death of Political Philosophy," *Government and Opposition* 15:3–4 (July 1980), 284. Barry refers to his unpublished paper of 1961 in this article.

[10] See, for instance, Michael Freeman and David Robertson, "Introduction: The Rebirth of a Discipline," in Freeman and Robertson (eds.), *The Frontiers of Political Theory*, New York: Harvester Press, 1980; David Miller, "The Resurgence of Political Theory," *Political Studies* 38 (1990); Terence Ball, *Reappraising Political Theory*, Oxford: Clarendon Press, 1994. The establishment of the journal *Political Theory* in 1972 (its first issue appeared in 1973, and the first issue of *Philosophy and Public Affairs* in 1971) is usually seen as both consequence and cause of the rebirth of political theory. See, for instance, Stephen White, "Introduction: Pluralism, Platitudes, and Paradoxes: Fifty Years of Western Political Thought," *Political Theory* 30:4 (August 2002), 472.

object it seeks to produce knowledge "of"; it is instead a knowledge "for," a performance rather a representation. As such, it is oriented toward its audience in a manner that is very different from most other disciplines; political theory at once presumes and is directed toward the bourgeois public sphere, imagined as a domain where individuals possessed of their own values, but sharing political and moral space, engage in rational debate about what principles will govern that common space. The social imaginary that conceives of the public sphere as an aggregation of value-bearing or value-holding individuals engaged in critical-rational dialogue is a historically particular, and specifically liberal, imaginary; and I argue that its orientation toward the bourgeois public sphere renders political theory an inescapably liberal and Western form of knowledge production.

Death and Resurrection

The first of what was to become a chorus of criticisms of political theory took the form of the complaint that it had become little more than an unilluminating history of political thought, disengaged from any serious effort to explain political phenomena. Hans Morgenthau, for instance, thundered that "political theory as an academic discipline has been intellectually sterile," because "it has hardly been more than an account of what writers of the past, traditionally regarded as 'great,' have thought about the traditional problems of politics." If it remained part of the academic curriculum, this was not because of its vitality or its importance to the discipline of political science, "but rather because of a vague conviction that there was something venerable and respectable in this otherwise useless exercise."[11] The most concerted and influential attack along these lines came from the behaviorist "movement" in American political science. The young Turks of behaviorism, led by David Easton, offered a sweeping indictment of the discipline of political science, which they declared had applied diverse and unsystematic methods to the study of an object that had itself remained ill-defined. The proper object of political science, Easton declared, was the "political system," an aspect

---

[11] Morgenthau, "Reflections on the State of Political Science," *Review of Politics* 17:4 (October 1955), 444. A similar (if less polemical) critique was offered by Alfred Cobban, "The Decline of Political Theory," *Political Science Quarterly* 68:3 (September 1953), 321–37.

or subset of the social system, but "a separable dimension of human activity,"[12] allowing or requiring political scientists to "distinguish our interests from those of economists, anthropologists, sociologists, and other social scientists."[13] This object was best studied by examining political behavior, which in turn required, as Gabriel Almond put it, studying "what goes on inside the black box of the political system."[14]

As with any attempt to put a discipline on a new footing, the behavioral "revolution" was deeply critical of what political science had hitherto been, and the subdiscipline of political theory was singled out for criticism. Lamenting the poverty of political theory over the preceding fifty years, Easton ascribed this poverty to its focus upon an "unrewarding historical study" of past texts, which had served "to divert the attention and energies of political theorists from building systematic theory about political behavior and the operation of political institutions."[15] According to Easton, while the great political theorists of the past had sought to develop an analytic and normative theory of politics, since about 1900 the ambition to be "a truly theoretical organ for political science"[16] had been replaced by mere historical excavations. The proper task of "political theory," in the understanding of Easton and many other behaviorist critics, was "conceptualizing the basic areas for empirical research in political science,"[17] that is, providing a paradigm that would define the discipline's object, identify the relevant questions, and provide the criteria for what is to be counted as evidence—as "theory" was thought to do in disciplines such as economics, chemistry and physics.[18] This task political theory was signally failing to do; as another critic put it, "All types of inquiry involve the construction of *theory*, implicit or explicit,

[12] David Easton, "The Idea of a Political System and the Orientation of Political Research," extracts from *The Political System*, in James Farr and Ronald Seidelman (eds.), *Discipline and History: Political Science in the United States*, Ann Arbor: University of Michigan Press, 1993, 231.

[13] Easton, "Political Science in the United States: Past and Present," in Farr and Seidelman, *Discipline and History*, 291.

[14] Gabriel A. Almond, "Political Theory and Political Science," *American Political Science Review* 60:4 (December 1966), 871.

[15] Easton, "The Decline of Modern Political Theory," *Journal of Politics* 13:1 (February 1951), 58, 37. "As everyone knows," he added, "little theory, if any, finds its way into this field" (51).

[16] Easton, "Decline of Modern Political Theory," 51. See similarly William A. Glaser, "The Types and Uses of Political Theory," *Social Research* 22:1 (1955), 275.

[17] Easton, "Decline of Modern Political Theory," 57. This was to be done, Easton went on to say, "first, by synthesizing and codifying the limited generalizations we have in various fields of political science . . . and second, by attempting the more massive task of elaborating a usable conceptual framework for the whole body of political science" (57–58).

[18] Easton, "Political Science in the United States," 294. After the publication of Kuhn's *Structure* in 1962, some of the behavioralists were to press the idea of "paradigm" into service, albeit not always in ways consonant with Kuhn's use of the term.

and . . . the title 'political theory' has been unjustifiably appropriated by the historians of political thought."[19]

The "scientism," "positivism," embrace of "value free" social science, and a consequent hostility to "normative" speculation of which the behaviorists have been accused were certainly elements in their hostility to political theory. However, their criticisms for the most part evinced not a hostility to "theory" per se—many of the leading behaviorists had completed their PhDs in political theory[20]—but rather a very different conception of "theory." In this understanding, "political theory" was what the behaviorists were striving to do, and what the subdiscipline of political theory had signally failed to do; at the height of the behavioral revolution, Almond was to equate "contemporary political theory" with the concept of the "political system."[21] Political theory as it was in fact practiced was judged to be deficient because it misunderstood the nature and task of theory; it had been failing in this task since 1900, according to Easton, and from the latter nineteenth century, according to some other critics.

A second line of criticism came from an altogether different quarter, that of intellectual historians who shared no sympathy with the behaviorists. From the latter 1960s J.G.A. Pocock, John Dunn, and especially Quentin Skinner offered a wide-ranging critique of the pretensions of the history of political thought as it was being practiced.[22] Skinner's coruscating "Meaning and Understanding in the History of Ideas" exposed many of the fallacies underlying political theory, with unsparing illustrations taken from the works of distinguished historians of political thought, all to devastating effect. Skinner showed that there were in fact no transhistorical "perennial questions" that were a focus of concern for the thinkers and the texts assembled in the canon of political theory, but rather "a sequence of episodes in which the questions as well the answers have frequently changed."[23] The fiction of perennial

[19] Harry Eckstein, "Political Theory and the Study of Politics: A Report of a Conference," *American Political Science Review* 50:2 (June 1956), 476.

[20] Including Easton, Dahl, Deutsch, and Eulau. See John Gunnell, "Political Theory: The Evolution of a Sub-field," in Ada W. Finifter (ed.), *Political Science: The State of the Discipline*, New York: APSA, 1983, 13.

13. Easton, in particular, insisted that any investigative endeavor has presuppositions built into it that are partly normative and that need to be excavated and critically examined.

[21] See Almond, "Political Theory and Political Science," especially 876.

[22] See Dunn, "The Identity of the History of Ideas," *Philosophy* 43 (1968); and Pocock, *Politics, Language and Time: Essays on Political Thought and History*, Chicago: University of Chicago Press, 1989. Here I overlook the differences in the intellectual positions of Dunn, Pocock, and Skinner.

[23] Skinner, "A Reply to My Critics," in James Tully (ed.), *Meaning and Context: Quentin Skinner and His Critics*, Cambridge: Polity Press, 1988, 234. The implication was fully drawn out, namely that "there is in consequence simply no hope of seeking the point of studying the history of ideas in the

questions had led to an anachronistic treatment of political thought, and to the imposition of a false coherence on thoughts and texts, resulting in "a history of thoughts which no one ever actually succeeded in thinking, at a level of coherence which no one ever actually attained."[24] A properly historical study of political thought would not necessarily discover similarity but would often uncover difference; not the "relevance" of past thoughts and texts to current political concerns, but the changing languages of politics. The intellectual and even moral value of such inquiries, Skinner concluded, lay precisely in showing "the extent to which those features of our own arrangements that we may be disposed to accept as traditional or even 'timeless truths' may in fact be the merest contingencies of our peculiar history and social structure."[25]

The third and chronologically last challenge to the self-conception and practice of political theory was focused upon disciplinary history. Historical inquiry into the subdiscipline of political theory revealed that the earliest works that assembled a tradition and a canon were no older than the second half of the nineteenth century, and that it was well into the twentieth century before the idea that there was a "tradition" of political theory stretching from ancient Greece to the present became sufficiently entrenched in the United States for political theory to become a "standard subject of college textbooks and academic research."[26] The constitution of the subdiscipline as the study of the canonical texts summarized in these textbooks was mirrored in Britain, where histories of political thought were written primarily to serve university courses.[27] The subdiscipline assumed that the canonical names and texts assembled in these textbooks were "the residue of a historically specifiable activity characterized by relatively persistent and stable concerns, and . . . these works may be fruitfully understood . . . as a continuing dialogue regarding the great perennial issues of political life."[28] However, this conception of a tradition of political theory as an age-old activity that much later came to be studied and practiced in universities was a reversal of the actual historical

---

attempt to learn directly from the classic authors by focusing on their attempted answers to supposedly timeless questions." "Meaning and Understanding in the History of Ideas," *History and Theory* 8 (1969), 50.

[24] Skinner, "Meaning and Understanding," 18.

[25] Skinner, "Meaning and Understanding," 53.

[26] John Gunnell, *Political Theory: Tradition and Interpretation*, Cambridge, MA: Winthrop Publishers, 1979, 18.

[27] P. J. Kelly, "Contextual and Non-Contextual Histories of Political Thought," in Jack Hayward, Brian Barry, and Archie Brown (eds.), *The British Study of Politics in the Twentieth Century*, New York: Oxford University Press, 1999, 46–47.

[28] Gunnell, *Political Theory*, 69.

sequence: "The enterprise known as the 'history of political thought' initially came into being and derived its identity from an educational practice . . . it was not the case that some previously existing activity called the 'history of political thought' was . . . taken into universities; rather, that notion . . . is the *creation* of these disciplinary practices."[29] A growing number of scholars described, and sometimes denounced, the "tradition" of political theory as "invention," "myth," "reification," or "fabrication posing as fact."[30]

These three distinct lines of criticism pulled in different directions. The behaviorist critique of political theory began by accepting that there was a long-standing and valuable "tradition" of political theory, but argued that it had been in decline—since about 1900 according to Easton, and from around the latter nineteenth century, according to some other critics. For the behaviorists, a revivified political theory would take the form of a paradigm for the systematic study of political behavior, rather than a subdiscipline of political science concerned with historical texts. In the event, it was behaviorism, which had taken the discipline by storm, especially in the United States, that declined, whereas political theory survived or was born again, albeit in a very different form. Drawing attention to the anachronisms characterizing the practice of political theory, Skinner, Pocock, and Dunn demonstrated that the "perennial issues" understanding of the subdiscipline was unhistorical nonsense, and brought the hitherto dominant form of the subdiscipline into crisis. Once the claim to extrahistorical status was punctured, the study of political texts ceased to plausibly belong to a distinct subdiscipline of political theory and instead became—as in the distinguished works of the aforementioned scholars—a species of intellectual history. There is a clear and striking parallel here with the history of aesthetics and science, where, as we saw in chapter 3, historicizing the object of study had corrosive effects on claims that it was possessed of an extrahistorical dimension that licensed special protocols for the study of it. The very important difference, however, is that art, music, and science are practices that long predate their academic study, whereas Gunnell and others showed that "political theory"

---

[29] Stefan Collini, "Postscript: Disciplines, Canons and Publicness: The History of the 'History of Political Thought' in Comparative Perspective," in Dario Castiglione and Iain Hampsher-Monk (eds.), *The History of Political Thought in National Context*, New York: Cambridge University Press, 2001, 283. Gunnell similarly concluded, "What is presented as a historical tradition is in fact basically a retrospective analytical construction which constitutes a rationalized version of the past" (*Political Theory*, 70).

[30] Timothy Kaufman-Osborn, "Political Theory as Profession and as Subfield?," *Political Research Quarterly* 63:3 (2010), 658.

was an academic invention, a reified "tradition" posited to enable a purely *academic* practice. Moreover, this was invented in the course of the latter nineteenth century and not institutionalized until well into the twentieth century, so that the widely told story of its decline or death was more or less coterminous with the history of its very emergence!

The combined effect of these criticisms was that while the earlier "perennial issues" version of political theory continues to be taught in university classrooms, and textbooks designed for these classrooms continue to be churned out, there are very few serious scholars who would defend it. The political theory that has been dominant in scholarship from the 1970s was not so much reborn as newly born, for the discontinuities between the born-again form of political theory, and its predecessor that had been the subject of so much criticism, are more striking than the continuities. The new political theory, as has commonly been noted, has flourished less as a secure part of the discipline of political science than at a tangent to it or sometimes even in active hostility to it. It is also, as a survey of it notes, "an unapologetically mongrel sub-discipline, with no dominant methodology or approach," and "seem[s] to lack a core identity."[31] This diffuseness of themes and methods makes it exceedingly difficult to generalize about the subdiscipline. The survey of the it quoted above goes on to note, however, that notwithstanding this diffuseness, political theory is characterized by "an irreducibly normative component"[32]; and this provides a useful starting point for a characterization of what is specific about the discipline and distinguishes it from other disciplines.

Political Theory and the Bourgeois Public Sphere

To characterize political theory as a normative endeavor certainly captures something important about it, but I suggest that a better way of framing its distinctiveness is to recognize that political theory does not have a referent: it is not knowledge "of" but rather knowledge "for," performance rather than representation. Unlike disciplines such as history or international relations, examined in previous chapters, political theory does not represent, map,

---

[31] John S. Dryzek, Bonnie Honig, and Anne Phillips, "Introduction," in Dryzek, Honig, and Phillips (eds.), *The Oxford Handbook of Political Theory*, New York: Oxford University Press, 2006, 5.
[32] Dryzek, Honig and Phillips, "Introduction," 5.

or explain an object or process external to itself. History seeks to produce knowledge about the past, and international relations about international politics; by contrast, justice and political obligation are not objects that can be represented, requiring specialist knowledge to do so, but are rather on-going matters of common concern. One immediate consequence of this is that the relation of political theory to its audience is different from that of most other disciplines. The scholar who writes as a political theorist is presumed to have thought more deeply about issues such as justice, equality, liberty, and the like than those she addresses, but these are issues of collective concern and debate, and she is thus positioned as a partner in a dialogue or conversation; less a specialist who produces knowledge of an object or process than someone who draws upon a common stock of concerns and concepts in order to clarify and persuade. This is what leads Sheldon Wolin to describe political theory as "primarily a civic and secondarily an academic activity."[33] This does *not* mean that political theory has a mass audience or is engaged in a dialogue with "ordinary people"—like other academic disciplines, its audience is mostly limited to other scholars. Nonetheless, this important and insufficiently noted aspect of the subdiscipline has far-reaching implications and allows us to identify a further feature that underlies political theory and shapes the performance of it. Political theory does not simply, like all disciplines, have a readership or an audience, but is more specifically oriented toward what I shall call, following Habermas, the bourgeois public sphere. This is reflexively built into its practice and performance and thus shapes the very nature of the subdiscipline.

Habermas's *The Structural Transformation of the Bourgeois Public Sphere* influentially argued that while the very terms, and the normative force, of the concepts of "civil society" and of "publicness" derived from classical precedents, the public sphere of his title was "a category of bourgeois society," enabled by the emergence in modern Europe of generalized commodity production, social labor, and an impersonal state authority. The Greek distinction between the *oikos* as the domain of necessity and the *polis* as the domain of freedom gave way in modern times to a tripartite division between the private, intimate sphere of the conjugal family; civil society, where the (male) heads of households who were forged in this private sphere engaged

---

[33] Sheldon Wolin, *Presence of the Past*, Baltimore: Johns Hopkins University Press, 1989, 1.

in commercial relations; and the bourgeois public sphere that emerged out of the salons and coffeehouses of modern Europe, and coalesced around the "the bourgeois reading public of the eighteenth century."[34] This public sphere was not simply the sum of the opinions of individuals but presupposed, in Charles Taylor's words, a recognition of "something we hold in common."[35] The significance of this was recognized by many and was championed by Kant. In "What Is Enlightenment?," Kant conceded that a civil/public official was obliged to discharge his office in his "private" capacity; a military officer could not argue with a superior's command, or a clergyman preach contrary to the authorized views of his church. However, their "public" use of reason, when they spoke not in their capacity as officials but "*as a scholar before the entire public of the reading world*,"[36] could not be restricted, for here complete freedom was the foundation of enlightenment. As Habermas writes, summarizing Kant, "Anyone who understood how to use his reason in public qualified for it. . . . The public sphere was realized not in the republic of scholars alone but in the public use of reason by all who were adept at it."[37]

It is in this historically unprecedented feature of the public sphere that Habermas finds its normative potential. Habermas is well aware that the public sphere was confined to the propertied and educated—that it was not only a category of bourgeois, that is, modern, society, but was in fact limited to the bourgeoisie (also that it was limited almost exclusively to men, though this figures less prominently in Habermas's analysis).[38] Nonetheless, the idea/claim that all members of a society could legitimately exercise their reason on matters of common concern, including by commenting critically on political authority, marked a historical advance. Not only were political matters subject to public comment and deliberation, the principle upon which this was based mandated, in theory at least, that the public was composed of all those

[34] Habermas, *The Structural Transformation of the Bourgeois Public Sphere*, translated by Thomas Burger and Frederick Lawrence, Cambridge: Polity Press, 1989, 85.

[35] Charles Taylor, "Modes of Civil Society," *Public Culture* 3:1 (Fall 1990), 109. See also Taylor's "Liberal Politics and the Public Sphere," in his *Philosophical Arguments*, Cambridge, MA: Harvard University Press, 1995.

[36] Immanuel Kant, "An Answer to the Question 'What is Enlightenment?'," in James Schmidt (ed.), *What Is Enlightenment? Eighteenth-Century Answers and Twentieth-Century Questions*, Berkeley: University of California Press, 1996, 60.

[37] Habermas, *Structural Transformation*, 105.

[38] This has given rise to a number of works that revise or challenge Habermas's conception of the public sphere, specifically with an eye to how women were—or were not—configured in it. These include Joan Landes, *Women and the Public Sphere in the Age of the French Revolution* (Ithaca, NY: Cornell University Press, 1988); and Nancy Fraser, "What's Critical about Critical Theory? The Case of Habermas and Gender," in Fraser, *Unruly Practices: Power, Discourse, and Gender in Contemporary Social Theory*, Minneapolis: University of Minnesota Press, 1989.

capable of rational-critical deliberation, without regard to authority or status. As Calhoun glosses Habermas, "However often the norm was breached, the idea that the best rational argument and not the identity of the speaker was supposed to carry the day was institutionalized as an available claim."[39]

It will immediately be apparent that political theory presupposes, and functions as if it were addressed to, a public sphere of individuals possessed of "values," who inhabit a common world and perforce engage in rational, critical debate about that which they "hold in common." Political theory, in other words, has a conception of the public sphere built into its imaginary and its functioning. Other disciplines, of course, also have a relation to the public sphere. History, for example, presupposes public records and archives for the historian to do her work and for readers to verify her claims. The historian must subject her findings and narratives to a public that is not limited to other historians, and the public to which the historian's investigations and narratives are presented is free to question and to disagree. However, the historian's investigations have a referent—some aspect or slice of "the past"—and to count as reasonable, any criticism must also display some knowledge of that referent. By contrast, the political theorist engages in rational-critical debate over matters of common concern to collective life with others who, in principle, are positioned as equals in that dialogue, and indeed whose moral intuitions and forms of collective life the political theorist frequently seeks to explicate and elucidate. Political theory is thus imagined as a conversation or discussion in a way that the historian's practice is not; as Michael Warner observes, "In the dominant tradition of the public sphere, address to a public is ideologized as rational-critical dialogue . . . consistently imagined, both in folk theory and sophisticated political philosophy, as dialogue or discussion."[40] Political theory is, par excellence, an instantiation and enactment of the bourgeois public sphere—one in which the political theorist does not simply, as Kant advised, act "as if" he were a scholar addressing the public, but actually *is* a professional scholar addressing the public. Since, as observed

[39] Craig Calhoun, "Introduction: Habermas and the Public Sphere," in Calhoun (ed.), *Habermas and the Public Sphere*, Cambridge, MA: MIT Press, 1992, 13. Or as Cohen and Arato summarize Habermas's view, "The public sphere was an ideology, but because it contained a utopian promise, it was more than an ideology." Jean L. Cohen and Andrew Arato, *Civil Society and Political Theory*, Cambridge, MA: MIT Press 1992, 227. The second half of *Structural Transformation of the Bourgeois Public Sphere* is an analysis of, and a lament on, how the possibilities inherent in this have largely been lost.

[40] Michael Warner, *Publics and Counterpublics*, New York: Zone Books, 2002, 114–15.

earlier, political theory does not in fact have a public audience, it is an enactment, in miniature, of the public sphere.

Performing Liberalism

It is often noted (and sometimes bemoaned) that the subdiscipline that was reborn in the 1970s is deep-seatedly liberal in its presumptions and its prescriptions.[41] Why should this be so?

In part it is because, as a dialogue or debate, rather than a representation of an object or process, political theory is always addressed to a specific body of people at a specific time, and thus appeals to the values and intuitions of this body of people As Stefan Collini notes, "Political arguments, and their attempted systematization as bodies of theory, must, if they are to have any persuasiveness, deploy, re-work, or otherwise make use of the shared evaluative language of those to whom they are addressed, and hence must appeal to the ideals and aspirations which that language represents. In this sense, political theories are parasitic upon the less explicit habits of response and evaluation that are deeply embedded in the culture."[42] There is, in other words, always a strong sense of a "we" built into political theory and its modes of address; as one political theorist describes the discipline, "Political theory is a continuing conversation or argument over what precisely *we* value in *our* social and political lives and why, how to understand the internal structures of *our* values, what the rival interpretations of these values are, which of these is better and why, and finally, what social and political institutions should be designed to realize these values."[43] The "we" in question, given the circumstances of the discipline—a latter twentieth-century practice largely confined to Western Europe and North America—is an unacknowledged liberal "we," and thus what is to be valued and articulated is, by definition, liberalism. It is not any particular liberal sect—Kantian or utilitarian, rights based or communitarian—but rather liberalism in its broadest and deepest sense: the presupposing and naturalizing of the idea that the world is

---

[41] Dryzek, Honig, and Phillips for instance, observe that "in many areas of political theory, liberalism has become the dominant position," "swallowing up . . . critical alternatives" ("Introduction," 17, 21).

[42] Collini, *Public Moralists: Political Thought and Intellectual Life in Britain, 1850–1930*, Oxford: Clarendon Press, 1991, 4–5.

[43] Rajeev Bhargava, "Why Do We Need Political Theory?," in his *What Is Political Theory and Why Do We Need It?*, New Delhi: Oxford University Press, 2010, 46; emphasis added.

composed of individuals who can and should be abstracted from their particularities, who embrace certain "values," who hold something in common with each other, and who seek through rational-critical debate to reconcile their individual values with this "something in common."

Liberalism is also often an explicit part of the self-understanding of the subdiscipline, as can be seen, for instance, in Isaiah Berlin's elaboration and defense of political theory in 1962, when it had been declared to be dead or dying. In this essay Berlin observes that while most of the basic questions that human beings have asked have proved to be ones that can be answered in empirical or formal terms, some questions had not proved amenable to empirical or formal formulation and answer, for they belonged to a class of problems "that in their very essence involve value judgements."[44] Having made this very Kantian distinction between pure and practical reason, Berlin proceeds to ask the Kantian question, "In what kind of world is political philosophy ... in principle possible?"[45]

It will be recalled that posing a similar question, Kant famously arrived at an answer, albeit a very abstract and formal one, in the shape of the categorical imperative. For Berlin—now departing from Kant—the condition of possibility of political theory is that there is not and cannot be a single answer to that question: "The only society in which political philosophy ... is possible, is a society in which there in no total acceptance of any single end," in other words, "a pluralist, or potentially pluralist, society."[46] According to Berlin, this is not a description of one world among many, but rather a description of the world as such. "Totalitarian" societies such as the (then) USSR are not ones where one value/end has secured general acceptance, but rather societies that have suppressed other, competing values and ends. They illustrate, not other possible worlds, but the denial, through coercive and despotic means, of the world as it really is. This, it is important to remember, is not a moral position, but rather a factual claim— Berlin's well-known and eloquent championing of moral pluralism follows from this claim that different and sometimes irreconcilable values are an inexpungable feature of human existence. Any society or historical epoch is characterized by a diversity of moral and political outlooks, reflecting the categories through

[44] Berlin, "Does Political Theory Still Exist," 6.
[45] Berlin, "Does Political Theory Still Exist," 8.
[46] Berlin, "Does Political Theory Still Exist," 9. Later Berlin was, if only in passing, to make his disagreement with Kant explicit—see "In Conversation with Steven Lukes," *Salmagundi* 120 (Fall 1998), 119.

which men perceive and relate to the world, and their place and function in it. People have frequently believed that there is a single, objective human end, which overrides all others or else can incorporate and subsume them, and which should therefore be recognized and embraced by all. "Monist" doctrines, as Berlin calls them (he names Platonism and Aristotelianism, Stoicism, Thomism, positivism, and Marxism), have abounded, but the very plethora of these puts the lie to the dream of a single value or constellation of values, accepted and embraced by all. Thus while political theories may be monist, political theory as an enterprise or discipline exists because a multiplicity of political theories—or in Rawls's formulation, "a plurality of reasonable yet incompatible comprehensive doctrines"[47]—is part of the human condition. Political theory arises from this condition and is also an expression or performance of it—liberals and communitarians, Christians and atheists, utilitarians and Kantians, monists and pluralists contend with each other in public academic debate, such that the very practice or performance of political theory is an exemplification of liberal pluralism. The condition for existence of political theory is thus a liberal society; conversely, the very existence and performance of political theory is an affirmation that liberal presumptions about the plurality of "values" are well founded. It is the very way in which political theory as a subdiscipline is conceived and practiced that makes liberalism so hard to escape—even for those who seek to do so.

In short, it is not because political theorists are liberal that so much of political theory is liberal; it is rather because political theory is inherently a liberal enterprise that so much political theory produced is liberal. Or if you prefer, the two are mutually reinforcing. As Bruce Ackerman puts it, "There is a perfect parallelism, then, between the role of political conversation *within* a liberal state, and the role of conversation *in defense of* a liberal state."[48] What Ackerman regards as a happy "parallelism" is given a more jaundiced, and I think more apt, description by Alasdair MacIntyre. According to MacIntyre "the culture of liberalism" treats moral and political viewpoints as "values" or preferences; philosophical debate reveals that these often cannot be reconciled, or subsumed within some larger rationality, but "liberalism requires for its social embodiment continuous philosophical and quasi-philosophical debate about the principles of justice, debate which . . . is

---

[47] John Rawls, *Political Liberalism*, New York: Columbia University Press, 1996, xviii.
[48] Bruce Ackerman, *Social Justice in the Liberal State*, New Haven: Yale University Press, 1980, 359.

perpetually inconclusive but nonetheless socially effective."[49] This, I suggest, is a very good description of political theory as it has been practiced since its "rebirth" in the 1970s, with the debates over how to articulate and defend and develop "our" values revolving around different ways of conceiving and defending liberalism—deontological, communitarian, utilitarian, and so on.

This is not to say that such defenses of liberalism are intellectually effective. Berlin himself, of course, thought that his value pluralism entailed an embrace of liberalism. If the monist (sometimes he labels this "rationalist") conviction that all important values must be compatible with each other and perhaps even entail each other was grievously mistaken, and the necessity of choosing between values that do not necessarily harmonize but sometimes come into conflict is "an inescapable characteristic of the human condition,"[50] then for Berlin it followed that a liberal polity in which negative liberty is given priority is vindicated as the best of all possible worlds. But the rationale driving Berlin's argument, when pushed to its logical conclusion, renders liberalism itself as one of many "values," rather than as the "solution" to value pluralism. This can be seen, for example, in the intellectual trajectory of John Gray, his "renegade disciple."[51] Author of an intellectual biography of Berlin, heir to his pluralism, and a champion of liberalism, Gray later came to the conclusion that if value pluralism was an inexpungable feature of the world, then "This truth subverts liberal moralities which accord a unique primacy to some good such as negative liberty or personal autonomy."[52] For a period Gray continued to seek a union of value pluralism and liberalism in the form of an "agonistic liberalism," but he found that pluralism, once acknowledged, was corrosive of any and all forms of liberalism. As he describes his intellectual itinerary, "Agonistic liberal theory . . . seeks to show that the liberal form of life has a superior claim on reason arising from its supposed tolerance of value-pluralism. This was the view I myself held, and termed post-liberal."[53] He subsequently came to see, however, that the pluralism that Berlin had rightly embraced inexorably led to the conclusion that *all*

---

[49] Alasdair MacIntyre, *Whose Justice? Which Rationality?*, Notre Dame, IN: University of Notre Dame Press 1988, 343–44.

[50] Berlin, "Two Concepts of Liberty," in *Four Essays on Liberty*, Oxford: Oxford University Press, 1969, 169.

[51] The description is that of Bernard Yack, "The Significance of Isaiah Berlin's Counter-Enlightenment," *European Journal of Political Theory* 12:1 (2013), 50.

[52] John Gray, "Where Pluralists and Liberal Part Company," *International Journal of Philosophical Studies* 6:1 (1998), 19. See also "From Post Liberalism to Pluralism," in his *Enlightenment's Wake: Politics and Culture at the Close of the Modern Age*, New York: Routledge, 2007, 142.

[53] "From Post Liberalism to Pluralism," 143.

moralities and politics were based upon historically contingent and culturally specific values, including liberalism, and thus that "liberal forms of life enjoy no special privileges of any kind."[54]

Traveling different routes, others have arrived at similar conclusions. As we saw in chapter 2, in his later work John Rawls came to argue that since "a plurality of reasonable yet incompatible comprehensive doctrines" was the inevitable result of the exercise of reason, even the core values of liberalism, such as autonomy and individuality, could not be accorded any privilege, for to do so was to convert liberalism into yet another "sectarian doctrine." Rawls continued to defend and elaborate "political liberalism," but it was now defended as suitable for those societies that had been shaped by the Reformation and the subsequent embrace of religious toleration, and not as a universal that had a transcendental grounding, or a teleological warrant.[55] As with Gray and Rawls, Richard Rorty also finds that there is no transcendental "grounding" to be found for liberalism and the practices and moralities associated with it; these are, he concedes, "parochial . . . local and culture-bound."[56] Rorty still urges their embrace, but now on the pragmatic and frankly ethnocentric grounds that "we" postmodernist bourgeois liberals of the rich North Atlantic democracies have "come up with a way of bringing people into some degree of comity, and of increasing human happiness."[57] If a large part of the discipline is taken up defending and elaborating versions of liberalism in happy ignorance of the non-Western world, the remainder consists of those who acknowledge that the liberal values being articulated are those of the West or the rich North Atlantic democracies. Some, like Rawls, conclude that these need not apply to the rest of the world; Rorty urges that these admittedly parochial values nonetheless be embraced by others; and Gray concludes that liberalism is but one possibility among many, and not necessarily best suited to places and peoples possessed of different histories.

No wonder, then, that the discipline of political theory has not flourished, indeed, barely exists, outside the West. Many parts of the non-Western world are characterized by impassioned political arguments about collective

---

[54] "From Post Liberalism to Pluralism," 143. See also 175.

[55] See chapter 2, 60–67.

[56] Rorty, "On Ethnocentrism: A Reply to Clifford Geertz," in his *Objectivity, Relativism and Truth*, Cambridge: Cambridge University Press, 1991, 208.

[57] Rorty, "Afterword: Pragmatism, Pluralism and Postmodernism," in his *Philosophy and Social Hope*, New York: Penguin, 1999, 273. See also "Postmodernist Bourgeois Liberalism," in his *Objectivity, Relativism and Truth*.

concerns, including social justice, rights, and equality; but it is striking that
the subdiscipline of political theory not only makes no contribution to
these debates (something that is arguably also the case in North America
and Europe), but that it barely has any existence even in universities. Non-
Western political theorists—a few do exist—have recognized and lamented
this parochialism. Rajeev Bhargava complains that "existing, mainly western
political theory is excessively ethnocentric,"[58] and Bhikhu Parekh similarly
observes that "Western political theory is ethnocentric and does not speak
to the concerns of non-Western societies."[59] Issuing as they do from political theorists who believe that their discipline is capable of addressing non-
Western societies, such criticisms are accompanied by the injunction that
political theory—conceived as a universal "form"—be practiced with an ap-
propriately non-ethnocentric "content." This call has recently been answered.

Comparative Political Theory

Beginning in the 1990s, some scholars began to engage in what they termed
"comparative political theory."[60] The term is something of a misnomer, for
comparison is not a necessary feature of all work that goes under this name,[61]
which is characterized above all by the inclusion of non-Western voices and
texts in political theory in an effort to make it "genuinely global in character"[62] and "about human and not merely Western dilemmas."[63] Introducing
an edited collection on comparative political philosophy, Anthony Parel
writes that "each culture has its own basic insights about what constitutes the
good life and the good regime"[64] out of which a political philosophy emerges,

[58] Rajeev Bhargava, "Is There an Indian Political Theory?," in his *What Is Political Theory*, 59.
[59] Bhikhu Parekh, "The Poverty of Indian Political Theory," *History of Political Thought* 13:3
(Autumn 1992), 535.
[60] This subsection on comparative political theory draws upon my "Comparative Political
Theory: A Postcolonial Critique," in Leigh Jenco, Murad Idris, and Megan Thomas (eds.), *The Oxford
Handbook of Comparative Political Theory*, New York: Oxford University Press, 2020, 621–637.
[61] See Andrew March, "What Is Comparative Theory?," *Review of Politics* 71 (2009).
[62] Dallmayr, "Introduction: Toward a Comparative Political Theory," *Review of Politics* 59:3
(Summer 1997), 422.
[63] Roxanne L. Euben, *Enemy in the Mirror*, Princeton, NJ: Princeton University Press, 1999, 9. Or
in a slightly different formulation, "comparative political theory is best understood as the discursive
space carved out by immanent/internal critiques of political theory's privileging of "the West" and
its marginalization of other archives." Leigh Jenco, Murad Idris, and Megan Thomas, "Comparison,
Connectivity, and Disconnection," in Jenco, Idris, and Thomas, *Oxford Handbook of Comparative
Political Theory*, 4.
[64] Anthony J. Parel, "The Comparative Study of Political Philosophy," in Parel and Ronald Keith
(eds.), *Comparative Political Philosophy: Studies under the Upas Tree*, New Delhi: Sage, 1992, 11–12.

embodied in "texts which are recognizably political, that is, texts that consciously attempt to develop a philosophic understanding of the theory and practice of governance."[65] In a similar vein, Antony Black, introducing a study of Islamic political thought, writes, "Political thought is the study of the exercise of power, of who should exercise it, and how much power they should have; it is about justice in relationships between people, especially between those in power and those whom they rule, and the just distribution of goods in society."[66] Given these assumptions—that all times and places have "regimes" or "power" or "governance," and reflect upon "justice" and "distribution" in systematic ways—it follows that all societies and cultures "have" or "do" political theory. The practice of political theory, it would appear, is universal, even though its products, in the form of texts, ideas, and ideals, are always culturally specific. And if that is so, it is unjustifiable, indeed, outrageous, that the subdiscipline of political theory should have confined itself to the study of only European thinkers and texts. The justification and need for "comparative political theory" would appear to be self-evident.

There are two disabling objections to comparative political theory (CPT) if it is formulated in such a fashion. First, it simply assumes that the practice of political theory is a universal activity, even as a great deal of contemporary scholarship has challenged the presumption that the modern disciplines are inquiries into objects and practices that have existed everywhere at all times. Second, such a defense and elaboration of CPT is premised on the idea that there are certain "constants" or "perennial questions," which formed the stuff of political theorizing across the ages in Europe and—it is now claimed—in non-Western traditions as well. But if, as shown earlier in this chapter, the idea that an activity or practice called "political theory" has been cultivated for centuries in "the West" is an unhelpful and misleading fiction, to extend it to include the non-West is doubly so. If this were all there is to CPT, one could without further ado conclude that this is an unhistorical and thus intellectually indefensible project.

There are, however, more sophisticated elaborations of CPT. These avoid—if not always consistently—the unwarranted and unhistorical assumption that there are constants or "perennial questions" in politics, which form the subject matter of political theory. They are furthermore keenly aware of the danger of "assimilating" the texts and traditions they are engaging with, to

---

[65] Parel, "Comparative Study," 12.
[66] Antony Black, *The History of Islamic Political Thought*, New York: Routledge, 2001, 1.

modern and/or Western categories and understandings. Farah Godrej, for example, urges that any engagement with non-Western texts needs to be alert to the danger that "CPT may be vulnerable to reinscribing much of the Eurocentrism it wishes to avoid, unless it engages the radically different motivating queries of non-Western traditions."[67] She suggests that we can avoid this danger by recognizing that political theory is always and unavoidably a hermeneutical enterprise—of how to interpret texts from within a tradition—and that the crucial difference that distinguishes CPT from Eurocentric political theory is that in the former case the texts being interpreted belong to a different cultural and intellectual tradition. This being so, according to Godrej, the Gadamerian insight that "immersion in a tradition . . . allows our prejudices to be a creative force" does not apply here: "Because our prejudices operate in relation to those things that are familiar to us, using them as the lens through which we encounter otherness suggests that we may try to understand the unfamiliar by assimilating it into our own categories."[68] Comparative political theory seeks to interpret texts that do not come to us always-already interpreted, as earlier phases in the living tradition of which they are part. How then can the comparative political theorist avoid the ever-present danger of making these texts more familiar than is warranted, and engage with and interpret them while recognizing their difference?

The question as posed by Godrej and others is one of how to interpret across cultures/traditions. The details of the answer(s) need not concern us here, as this is to ask the wrong question. For it is not the abstract hermeneutical problem of interpreting texts across cultures and traditions that is at issue, but the more specific and concrete problem of interpreting non-Western texts from within a Western tradition that has become globally hegemonic. What is at issue, in other words, is not "cross-cultural" interpretation or communication, but engaging with traditions that are not Western from within a modern Western knowledge tradition that conquest, colonialism, and empire have made globally dominant. Just as the Neuer do not undertake anthropological studies of the white man, so too Hindu *pandits* do not ask themselves how to engage with Western thought and how to do so without

[67] Farah Godrej, *Cosmopolitan Political Thought: Method, Practice, Discipline*, New York: Oxford University Press, 2011, 22.

[68] Farah Godrej, "Towards a Cosmopolitan Political Thought: The Hermeneutics of Interpreting the Other," *Polity* 41:2 (2009), 142. On this question of how interpretation proceeds in an encounter with "otherness" see Walter Mignolo, *The Darker Side of the Renaissance*, 2nd ed., Ann Arbor: Ann Arbor: University of Michigan Press, 2003, especially 19.

"assimilating" it into Indic/Hindu traditions of thought. That is why the project of CPT is one of how to include and engage with non-Western traditions. It is also why the attendant problems that CPT seeks to address—such as that of not assimilating the thoughts and texts of others to "our" categories—is one in which the "our" is by definition modern and Western, irrespective of the ethnicity of the enquirer.

To argue as I have above is not tantamount, as CPT scholars sometimes suggest, to argue for "incommensurability";[69] it is not to throw up one's hands in despair and say that there is no way of engaging with texts from other traditions. Cultures and traditions are always palimpsests; the questions engaged in one tradition may also be engaged in another.[70] But a recognition that all scholarship today issues out of modern, Western knowledge, and that encounters with otherness may require (conceptual and other) translation, allows us to be attentive to that which does not translate, or does not translate easily. To become attentive to this is also potentially to become self-aware that we are working from within a tradition, and that encounters with otherness can stretch our categories beyond their limits. At its best, as in Roxanne Euben's *Enemy in the Mirror*—one of the first works that self-consciously (and successfully) sought to introduce the term "comparative political theory" and inaugurate its practice—CPT can achieve precisely this. Euben productively reads Sayyid Qutb (1906–1966) as drawing upon aspects of the Islamic tradition(s) to offer "a rebuttal of and an antidote to the perceived impoverishment of post-Enlightenment rationalist discourse."[71] Qutb, Euben points out, is not "alien" to us, for his context is also our context: "In a postcolonial world, the context is no longer peculiarly Western—although it may be Western in origin—but has come to frame the projects of the non-Western as well as the Western critics of modernity."[72] Hence why, as Euben illuminatingly shows, Qutb's themes, concerns, and anxieties have counterparts in the modern West, including anxieties and concerns that have been articulated by figures such as Hannah Arendt, Alasdair MacIntyre, Daniel Bell, and Robert Bellah. Such a reading is productive because it does not assume

---

[69] See Euben, *Enemy in the Mirror*, 10.

[70] On this see some brief but suggestive remarks in MacIntyre, *Whose Justice? Which Rationality*, 364–65.

[71] Euben, *Enemy in the Mirror*, 51. Other important works of CPT include Leigh Jenco's "'What Does Heaven Ever Say?' A Methods-Centered Approach to Cross-Cultural Engagement," *American Political Science Review* 101:4 (2007) and her *Changing Referents: Learning across Space and Time in China and the West*, New York: Oxford University Press, 2015. These are discussed in my "Comparative Political Theory."

[72] Euben, *Enemy in the Mirror*, 151.

the universality of modern Western categories and norms and "assimilate" Qutb to them. It rather discomfits them, showing us that the distinctions that we often assume to be axioms for thinking—such as the distinction be- tween the religious and the political—are in fact the presumptions of *our* thinking: "Qutb's perspective on the intimacy between religious and political concerns implicitly contests and enlarges the boundaries that . . . have de- fined political theory as a primarily Western and secular enterprise at least since the Enlightenment."[73]

These arguments, and others that cannot be discussed here, are important and insightful. But the importance and interest of Euben's engagement with Qutb lies not in any "work" that is being done by political theory, much less in treating Qutb as if he were a political theorist, but rather because Euben takes Qutb's ideas seriously, rather than treating "fundamentalism" as something irrational that is to be "explained" with reference to its sociological causes. What is at work here is good intellectual history, enabled by the fact that Qutb belongs to our temporal moment, one where debates about modernity, religion, disenchantment, and the like have achieved a global currency: the work of commensuration has already been done, by history as it were, "by the facts of Western colonialism and imperialism," in Euben's words.[74] But this very fact of Qutb's historical and intellectual contemporaneity with "us," who inhabit a globalized world—the same would be true for Gandhi and Sun Yat- sen, for instance—also ensures that this example could not license a similar retrieval of Confucius or Kautilya for CPT.

The undoubted contribution made by Euben is thus despite, rather than because, of her rather strained efforts to cast Qutb as a political theorist, and despite her claim that "the questions and categories of political theory are useful heuristic tools through which non-Western thinkers concerned with the moral foundations of political life may best be heard."[75] Given Euben is a political theorist, it is not surprising that this is her starting point. My criti- cism is not with her starting point—for in engaging with what is different we have no choice but to start with what is familiar, including our disciplinary affiliations—but rather with her desire to substantialize this "heuristic de- vice" by treating political theory as something that "others" also engage with. When Euben concludes that an engagement with Qutb helps us to "see what is distinctive about our own values, institutions and practices" and to "avoid

[73] Euben, *Enemy in the Mirror*, 53.
[74] Euben, *Enemy in the Mirror*, 91.
[75] Euben, *Enemy in the Mirror*, 158.

seeing our own cultural conventions as universal truths, thereby making possible a certain kind of distance toward what we know, or what we think we know,"[76] she is making a very important point, one that this book also seeks to make. However, the conventions that we should not see as universal practices include, it seems to me, the recently invented Western subdiscipline and practice known as political theory. If it has value as a heuristic device, its use, as with many heuristic devices, lies in providing a means by which we might eventually come to see its inappropriateness or redundancy—the ladder one kicks away.[77]

Some of the works written under the banner of CPT are valuable in illuminating aspects of non-Western intellectual traditions, but what they do not succeed in doing is "de-parochializing" political theory. They run the risk, instead, of treating as a universal practice what might just be a local Western custom. What CPT *has* successfully done, and this is all to the good, is something more "practical"—it has opened up a space where those classified or self-identifying as political theorists, and who have an interest in the non-Western world, can do serious work without having to relocate to another subdiscipline (e.g., comparative politics) or relocate disciplines altogether.

Whither Political Theory?

In 1886 Nietzsche complained that moral philosophers knew only "the morality of their environment, their class, their church, the spirit of their time, their climate and part of the world," and were "poorly informed and not even very curious about different peoples, times, and past ages."[78] Almost a hundred years later little had changed: referring to the "problems of fiendish intricacy" that arose as utilitarians and Kantians "confront[ed] each other with their ingenious casuistical exercises," the anthropologist Mary Douglas noted that for all their disagreements, the participants in these debates had one thing in common, namely, "They do not want to know about the cultural

---

[76] Euben, *Enemy in the Mirror*, 159.

[77] And in fact CPT functions somewhat like a ladder, or more aptly as scaffolding, in Euben's argument; her book is framed as a contribution to CPT, but the body of it ranges widely and freely across disciplines and is not much constrained by its introductory framing. In her subsequent *Journeys to the Other Shore*, Princeton, NJ: Princeton University Press, 2006, she continues her explorations of the Islamic and Western worlds, but now, other than a cursory reference (10), dispensing with the framing device of CPT altogether.

[78] Nietzsche, *Beyond Good and Evil*, edited by Walter Kaufmann, New York: Vintage Books, 1989, 97.

formation of moral ideas."[79] More recently John Gray has characterized the liberal political philosophers whose works dominate the subdiscipline as "struggling to confer the imprimatur of universal authority on the local practices they have inherited."[80]

The analytical and normative categories of political theory are so deeply embedded in a social imaginary that is a product of modern European (mostly West European) and North American history, in the forms and ways detailed in this chapter, that it has no purchase beyond scholars who have naturalized the idea that political philosophy is a rational-critical discussion addressed to a bourgeois public sphere on how best to reconcile and integrate the values of Atlantic liberalism. Those unwilling to add marginalia to these debates on justice, equality, liberty, and the like have—to be schematic— followed one of two options, both designed to broaden the scope of political theory. One, as seen previously, has been to expand the geographical and cultural range of political theory, in the form of CPT.

The other has been to seek analytical tools and inspiration from beyond the borders of mainstream political theory: feminism in many of its varieties, Frankfurt school-inspired critical theory, and Foucauldian genealogy have been especially prominent and productive outside sources. Such work has been premised upon and resulted in a much more capacious understanding of politics and of power than that displayed by the dominant, liberal forms of political theory. As Wendy Brown observes, political theory has always taken "its bearings from a tacit presumption of the relative autonomy and boundedness of the political. . . defining the political as distinguishable. . . from the economic, the social, the cultural, the natural, and the private/domestic/familial."[81] But if the personal is political, and if power is present in and circulates through the disciplining of bodies and knowledges, through images, and much else besides, then "politics" cannot be conceived of as a bounded space. One effect of such an enlarged conception of politics, however, is that the object of inquiry becomes too dispersed for "theorizing" it to be plausibly seen as the preserve of any particular discipline, such as political theory. That is why, even as important work continues to be

[79] Mary Douglas, "Morality and Culture," *Ethics* 93:4 (July 1983), 786.

[80] Gray, "The End of History—or of Liberalism?," in his *Post-liberalism*, 246. Elsewhere he savagely but not unjustly describes US Kantian liberal political philosophers as "trying to come up with a transcendental deduction of themselves." "Ironies of Liberal Postmodernity," in his *Endgames*, Cambridge: Polity Press, 1997, 59.

[81] Wendy Brown, *Edgework: Critical Essays on Knowledge and Politics*, Princeton, NJ: Princeton University Press, 2005, 61.

produced by political theorists who draw upon "critical theory, postcolonial theory, comparative political theory, hermeneutics, normative theory, deconstruction, cultural criticism, political ethics, genealogy [and] psychoanalytic inquiry,"[82] among other currents, much of this does not recognizably or plausibly fit under the rubric of "political theory"—except inasmuch as its authors are the "political theorists" of their political science departments. In short, if CPT runs the risk of unwarrantedly universalizing the practice of political theory, a broadened conception of politics and a correspondingly more capacious practice of theorizing has the opposite effect of *dissolving* the specificity of the subdiscipline. As Brown asks of her practice as a political theorist, "If a scholar of English literature writes brilliantly on Hobbes' *Leviathan*, if cultural anthropologists are currently the most incisive theorists of nationalism, if scholars of gender and race have developed genuinely new perspectives on social contract theory . . . then who am I and who is my constituency or reading audience?"[83] And if this rethinking of what we mean by power and politics is taken seriously—as Brown rightly insists it must be— then a difficult question arises for political theorists. As Brown formulates it, "What obscurity lies in wait for us in a world much vaster than a small cadre of colleagues whose card of entry to the order is the modest mastery of approximately two dozen great books and fluency with a small number of watchwords: justice, liberty, obligation, constitutions, equality, citizenship, action, government, rule, polity?"[84]

As Brown's question indicates, the subdiscipline is in crisis, on multiple fronts. In institutional terms, it has been marginalized within a political science discipline that has become increasingly quantitative, and where the label "theory" is being annexed by public/rational choice theory, particularly in the United States. Intellectually, its original avatar as a commentary on and continuation of an unbroken "tradition" stretching back to the Greeks has been comprehensively debunked and shown to be an uninspired

---

[82] Kaufman-Osborn, "Political Theory as Profession," 657. As the diversity of sources Kaufman-Osborn points to indicates, even to describe contemporary political theory as "an unapologetically mongrel sub-discipline," as Dryzek, Honig, and Phillips, the editors of *The Oxford Handbook of Political Theory* do ("Introduction," 5), is to ascribe far more unity to the discipline than it in fact possesses. Wendy Brown's characterization of political theory in terms of what it is *not*—"We are less a mongrel enterprise than an asylum for diverse outsiders to empirical political science"—seems a better description. Wendy Brown, "Political Theory Is Not a Luxury: A Response to Timothy Kaufman-Osborn's 'Political Theory as a Profession,'" *Political Research Quarterly* 63:3 (September 2010), 680).

[83] Brown, *Edgework*, 72–73.

[84] Brown, *Edgework*, 73.

and unproductive fiction. The dominant mainstream of the discipline since the 1970s, this chapter has argued, is premised upon and oriented toward a bourgeois public sphere, and as a result is irremediably liberal, and unwilling and incapable of mitigating its deep-rooted Eurocentrism. Those political theorists who recognize these problems—and they are many—have responded in a number of ways, most notably by seeking to expand the repertoire of political theory by including and engaging with non-Western texts, or by widening their understanding of politics, and by drawing upon other disciplines and intellectual currents. However, the first has the effect of universalizing a local practice, and the second has the effect of dissolving whatever unity the subdiscipline might possess. Lest I be misunderstood, let me make it clear that in my view these efforts have been all to the good, and that political theorists have made significant contributions to important intellectual debates; but they have done so in their individual capacities, not qua political theory. The subdiscipline itself is a minor and declining presence on the intellectual scene, and those, like Brown, who recognize this but still seek to defend it, do so on the largely strategic grounds that it is "the last outpost of nonscience in an ever more scientized field," and that it serves a crucial function as "the main portal" for the entry of the humanities into political science.[85]

Coda: On Political Science

Since the discipline of political science or politics is not an intellectually coherent discipline but rather a collection of subdisciplines, the two chapters on political science in this book have been concerned with examining the presuppositions that inform and enable the production of knowledge in international relations and political theory. Political theory, I have sought to show, does not have a referent or object that it seeks to produce knowledge of, but is instead a normative enterprise addressed to a public. However, the normative and the representational/analytical are not easily separated in any field of study, and the categories and presuppositions informing political theory are not only about what "should" be the case, but are also, as in political science more generally, presumptions about what "is" in fact the case in political life. Concepts such as those of "civil society" and the "public sphere,"

---

[85] Brown, "Not a Luxury," 681.

which I have argued are part of normative architecture of political theory, are also deployed in studies of politics that are not principally engaged in a normative endeavor but rather seek to represent and understand an object or process. Such analyses naturalize civil society and the public sphere, presuming that the objects denoted by these concepts exist everywhere, and thus that these concepts easily translate across cultures and histories. In fact, any serious student of politics in the non-Western world finds this not to be so: as one such student observes, the study of non-Western politics using the analytical vocabulary of political science continually finds that there is "a serious mismatch between the language which describes this world, and the objects which inhabit it."[86] Those seeking to understand political processes in the non-West have usually dealt with this problem by making ad hoc adjustments, bending their analytical tools to make them as fit for purpose as possible. In recent times however, there have been some sustained efforts to reflect upon this mismatch, and to develop alternative modes of analysis that do not "adapt" or "translate" in a rough-and-ready fashion. I end this chapter by briefly examining some of these: specifically, those that deploy but also problematize the concepts of "public sphere" and "civil society" that have been central to this chapter.

We saw that while Habermas treats the public sphere as a historical product, he also regards abstracted individuals engaged in rational-critical discourse as the normative rightness or "truth" contained within what are otherwise the historical and bourgeois "limitations" of this public sphere. In *Publics and Counterpublics*, Michael Warner argues that such individuals, and rational-critical discourse, are also historically produced and culturally shaped forms of selfhood and interaction, part of the "habitus" that defines and makes possible the public sphere. "To address a public or to think of oneself as belonging to a public," Warner writes, "is to be a certain kind of person, to inhabit a certain kind of social world, to have at one's disposal certain media and genres, to be motivated by a certain normative horizon, and to speak within a certain language ideology."[87]

[86] Sudipta Kaviraj, "In Search of Civil Society," in Kaviraj and Sunil Khilnani (eds.), *Civil Society: History and Possibilities*, New York: Cambridge University Press, 2001, 289. See similarly Susanne Hoeber Rudolph, "The Imperialism of Categories: Situating Knowledge in a Globalizing World," *Perspectives on Politics* 3:1 (March 2005).
[87] Warner, *Publics and Counterpublics*, 10.

Drawing upon Warner's work in his study of the *da'wa* movement in contemporary Egypt, Charles Hirschkind elaborates:

> The idea of *public* privileged within the modern social imaginary tends to exclude any recognition of the institutional and disciplinary conditions that enable it. . . . this conception of a public builds in a structural blindness to the material conditions of the discourses it produces and circulates, as well as to the pragmatics of its speech forms: the genres, stylistic elements, citational resources, gestural codes, and so on that makes a discourse intelligible to specific people inhabiting certain conditions of knowledge and learning. Such material conditions of discourse are obscured through a language ideology that circumscribes meaning to propositional content and construes the speech situation as one of rational-critical dialogue, a universal speech form unhindered by conventions of affect and expressivity or by the pragmatics of particular speech communities.[88]

In the accounts of Warner and Hirschkind, critical-rational discourse or "argument" is not the normative universality and truth contained, in potentia, within the otherwise historically particular bourgeois carapace of the public sphere. On the contrary, such critical-rational discourse has its historical source in the private readings of texts, a source that is then naturalized, illegitimately equating "the faculties of the private reader as the essential (rational-critical) faculties of man."[89] Hirschkind goes on to show that the Islamic counterpublic he studies is not a space for the formation of political opinion through intersubjective reason, but rather "is geared to the deployment of the disciplining power of ethical speech."[90] As a consequence, "The efficacy of an argument here devolves not solely on its power to gain cognitive assent on the basis of superior reasoning, as would be the case in some versions of a liberal public sphere, but also on the ability of ethical language and exemplary behavior to move human beings toward correct modes of being and acting."[91] This is why the "paradigmatic speech genre" of this counterpublic is not the text but rather the sermon, including the widely circulating cassette sermons that play a central role in Hirschkind's analysis.

---

[88] Charles Hirschkind, *The Ethical Soundscape: Cassette Sermons and Islamic Counterpublics*, New York: Columbia University Press, 2006, 106.
[89] Warner, *Publics and Counterpublics*, 116.
[90] Hirschkind, *The Ethical Soundscape*, 106.
[91] Hirschkind, *The Ethical Soundscape*, 113.

The difference is not simply one of "medium" or "technology," for the social importance of cassette sermons derives from the fact that "as opposed to the private reader, whose stillness and solitude became privileged icons of a distinct kind of critical reasoning within the imaginary of the bourgeois public, it is the figure of the ethical listener . . . that founds and inhabits the [Islamic] counterpublic."[92] If the bourgeois public sphere presupposes and naturalizes a historically produced language ideology, this counterpublic presupposes and enacts poetic, affective, and sensory modes of understanding.[93]

Those who are part of this counterpublic, adds Saba Mahmood in her study of women in the *da'wa* movement, are not liberal selves who experience authorized models of behavior and external imposition as "heteronomy," but rather subjects who view "socially prescribed forms of conduct as the potentialities, the 'scaffolding' if you will, through which the self is realized."[94] This is not a sign that they have failed to fully become selves, nor that Egyptian publics and counterpublics are deficient in some way—that they are "backward" or "underdeveloped"—but rather that they are, simply, different. The evaluative and normative judgments that are built into concepts of the rational individual, of autonomy and heteronomy, and of the public sphere come in the way of understanding this difference, by seeing in it only a lack, a deviation from the norm.

Just as Hirschkind and Mahmood find that the concepts of social and political theory are inadequate to understanding the Islamic revival movement in Egypt, Partha Chatterjee similarly argues that these concepts are inadequate to explaining the politics of India, and indeed, of the non-Western world more generally. In recent decades a seeming paradox has been widely noted in India. On the one hand, many marginalized subaltern classes and groups are no longer content to be "represented," but have mobilized and now have their own organizations, political parties, and "voice" in public affairs; to that degree, Indian democracy can be said to be more vibrant and more truly democratic than before. On the other hand, this has been accompanied by a coarsening of public life, as the norms that once underpinned public and political affairs are now routinely flouted, and politics is treated purely instrumentally rather than as the clash of values and norms. A common way of explaining this "paradox" has been to suggest that in India

<hr />

[92] Hirschkind, *The Ethical Soundscape*, 107.
[93] Hirschkind, *The Ethical Soundscape*, 113.
[94] Saba Mahmood, *Politics of Piety: The Islamic Revival and the Feminist Subject*, Princeton, NJ: Princeton University Press, 2012, 148.

formal equality and the right of suffrage preceded, rather than followed, the structural transformations that produced civil society and the public sphere. The enfranchisement of the adult population was meant to be accompanied by the efforts of a developmental state that would create the conditions for rational-critical discourse; but the advent of unscrupulous politicians willing to appeal to an unreformed popular culture, abjuring the niceties of rational public debate and, indeed, even civic decency or probity, has resulted in the entry of the unwashed masses into public and political life *before* their transformation into rational citizens, bringing into "the hallways and corridors of power some of the squalor, ugliness and violence of popular life."[95]

In this explanation it is recognized that there is mismatch "between the language which describes this world, and the objects which inhabit it," but this mismatch is taken as evidence of Indian "lack" or "incompleteness"—an insufficiently developed civil society, an overdeveloped state, a weak public sphere, and so on. This explanation accords with the inherited categories of our political language and retains the normativity built into these analytic categories. This is the explanation that Chatterjee rejects, suggesting that the mismatch lies not in the failure of Indian reality to match up to the norms implicit in this theoretical language, but rather in the fact that we lack the theoretical tools with which to talk about a domain of popular political discourse that is "far removed from the conceptual terms of liberal political theory."[96] Chatterjee is not suggesting that civil society does not exist in India; the early forms of Indian nationalism were nurtured in a newly emergent colonial civil society, and a civil society of national citizens was central to the imaginary of most currents of Indian nationalism. Furthermore, according to the Indian constitution adopted by the new nation-state in 1950, all of society is civil society, populated by rights-bearing free and equal citizens. However, as Chatterjee points out, while "Civil society as an *ideal* continues to energize an interventionist political project," as an actually existing form it is demographically limited to a relatively small number of culturally equipped citizens, and "most of the inhabitants of India are only tenuously, and even then

---

[95] Partha Chatterjee, *Politics of the Governed*, New York: Columbia University Press 2004, 74. In Chatterjee's elegant summarization of this view, "The complaint is widespread in middle-class circles today that politics has been taken over by mobs and criminals. The result is the abandonment—or so the complaint goes—of the mission of the modernizing state to change a backward society. Instead, what we see is the importation of the disorderly, corrupt, and irrational practices of unreformed popular culture into the very hallways and chambers of civic life, all because of the calculations of electoral expediency" (47–48).

[96] Chatterjee, *The Nation and Its Fragments*, New Delhi: Oxford University Press, 1995, 225.

ambiguously and contextually, rights-bearing citizens in the sense imagined by the constitution."[97]

This larger part of the population is not, however, untouched by the state and modern politics. They have been objects of state intervention since the nineteenth century, when "governmentality"—Chatterjee borrows and amends a Foucauldian concept—became an important mode of colonial government. From the second half of the nineteenth century, the colonial state classified and enumerated population groups (divided into castes, tribes, religions, and so on) for the purposes of land settlement and revenue, public health, recruitment to the army, and more generally, as targets of economic, developmental, administrative, and other policies. The postcolonial developmental state continued and greatly expanded these technologies, seeking now also to mitigate poverty and institute social reform and thereby affecting almost all the population, while civil institutions encompassed only a minority.

There are then, Chatterjee concludes, two aspects to the relation between the state and the people it governs. "One is the line connecting civil society to the nation-state founded on popular sovereignty and granting equal rights to citizens. The other is the line connecting populations to governmental agencies pursuing multiple policies of security and welfare. The first line points to a domain of politics described in great detail in democratic political theory"; the second line, Chatterjee argues, requires a theoretical innovation, namely a recognition of the existence of what he calls "political society."[98] This is the domain of those who have a political relationship to the state and who have a claim on it, including claims to welfare and benefits. Such groups include, for example, residents of the numerous illegal squatter settlements in India, who (often illegally) have access to water and electricity, and who in many cases have set up residents' associations to press their demands. These are anything but "traditional" or "primordial" groups, survivals of a premodern past; but nor are they fully part of civil society.[99] This is the domain of political society, a large and important element of everyday politics

[97] Chatterjee, *Politics of the Governed*, 38.
[98] Chatterjee, *Politics of the Governed*, 37–38.
[99] As Chatterjee writes of one of these associations, "It springs from a collective violation of property laws and civic regulations. The state cannot recognize it as having the same legitimacy as other civic associations pursuing more legitimate objectives. . . . But they make a claim to habitation and livelihood as a matter of right and use their association as the principal collective instrument to pursue that claim" (*Politics of the Governed*, 59). Such associations interact with agencies of the state and with NGOs and political parties—often through paralegal arrangements—to deliver civic services and welfare benefits to those who are not part of civil society.

in India, but one that is too often overlooked or else dismissed and decried as a deviation from the norm.

Hirschkind, Mahmood, and Chatterjee are all at pains to insist that the theoretical deficiencies that they draw attention to are not a consequence of a "category mistake," namely, of applying concepts developed to explain modern societies to premodern or nonmodern ones. This kind of explanation has for too long been a way of accounting for why there is a mismatch between what our analytical concepts lead us to expect and what we in fact find. It accounts for the explanatory shortcomings of these concepts by attributing these shortcomings to deficiencies in their objects and thereby salvages these concepts: since premodern societies are in transition to becoming modern ones, when they reach their destination, they will become adequate to their concepts. But this "salvaging" comes at a high cost: one consequence, as Achille Mbembe forcefully observes, is that African politics and economics always appear as signs of a "lack," and "The upshot is that while we feel we now know nearly everything that African states, societies and economies *are not*, we still know absolutely nothing about *what they actually are*."[100]

Mbembe, Chatterjee, Mahmood, and Hirschkind all insist that they are studying "modern" societies, integrated into the circuits of global capitalism, where the movements and phenomena they study are always obliged to forge relations of complementarity or opposition to the modern state. Chatterjee, for example, explicitly insists that the importance of political society in India and many other parts of the non-Western world is not "some pathological condition of retarded modernity, but rather part of the very process of the historical constitution of modernity in most of the world."[101] Such analyses are important, and have been briefly discussed here, precisely because they draw attention to the limitations of the categories of political science when these are pressed into service to explain the politics of the non-Western world. But because they do so while insisting that the global South is part and parcel of a globalized modernity, the import of these arguments, and the import of the critique of international relations and political theory offered in this book, is not to make a claim for non-Western "exceptionalism": it is rather to draw attention to the parochialism and the inadequacies of political science.

[100] Achille Mbembe, *On the Postcolony*, Berkeley: University of California Press, 2001, 9.
[101] Chatterjee, *Politics of the Governed*, 75.

Epilogue

Knowledge and Politics

In the early modern period in Europe a new knowledge began to emerge that was to become integral to the state formations and forms of market-based life and economic calculation that were reshaping social life in Western Europe and the Americas. Along with guns and goods, this knowledge traveled to other parts of the world, where it was used to govern colonized peoples and sometimes disseminated among their elites. It was embraced by nationalists struggling against colonial rule who, while keenly aware that this knowledge did not emerge out of their own traditions but was rather a foreign import, nonetheless came to regard it not as "Western" but simply as modern; and thus as a universal knowledge which any people who wished to fashion a modern and powerful nation needed to acquire. A knowledge born in Europe became global, and today states and universities in China, India, Nigeria, and elsewhere utilize, mobilize, produce, and disseminate it on the premise that knowledge is a subject-object relation, that the divide between nature and culture/society must be respected in all intellectual inquiry, and that to qualify as knowledge the results of all inquiries must be secular, irrespective of whether the producers of it are so or not. These presuppositions, which were once novel, hardened into unquestioned axioms and came to be seen not as the presuppositions of a particular conception and practice of knowledge, but as the premises of knowledge tout court.

Part I of this book argued that the advance of an initially European knowledge to global dominance was not a story of the forward march of intellectual progress, through the triumph of Reason over error and superstition—though it has all too often been presented as such—but rather the story of an initially Western European emic knowledge that became globally hegemonic. Chapter 1 showed that in recent times the core presumptions of this knowledge have been subjected to sustained questioning and problematization. Scholars of science studies find that picturing scientific knowledge as that which accurately "represents" some aspect of nature is a mischaracterization

Beyond Reason. Sanjay Seth, Oxford University Press (2021). © Oxford University Press.
DOI: 10.1093/oso/9780197500583.003.0008

of what science actually does, for its practice requires the mutual imbrication of subject and object and hence is better characterized as "enactment" or "assemblage" than as "representation." Some further argue that the absolute separation between nature and society/culture that underpins modern science is not a fact about the world that Western moderns "discovered"—evidence of the epistemic superiority of modern science, and of modern knowledge more generally—but rather a separation we moderns "created" and have been policing ever since. Social historians who had treated the social as the very ground of explanation began to doubt their earlier certainties; just as some scholars of science came to question the existence of "nature," so too a growing number of social historians now questioned the existence of "society" as a transhistorical entity, urging that the disciplinary skills of the historian be put into service to inquire into how human interdependence came, at a particular historical moment, to be equated or reduced to "the social." Anthropologists, long aware that the distinction between nature and culture was not one made by all peoples, are now less content to explain the "miscognitions" of their subjects in evolutionary, functional, or symbolic terms, and are more likely to treat anthropology as "our" way of translating the lifeworlds of others into our own terms. Some even suggest that the purpose of this exercise is not to produce a knowledge about others that they are incapable of arriving at themselves, but rather to unsettle our certainties, and in so doing to make it possible for us to denaturalize, critically examine, and perhaps even surpass our modes of knowing and the forms of life with which they are associated.

Such questioning, I have gone to some pains to show, has arisen in different disciplinary contexts in the social sciences, usually in the course of the production of disciplinary knowledge. It displays limited awareness of cognate problematizations in adjacent disciplines and is far from being part of a concerted "movement" with a clear intent to challenge and undermine the social sciences. And it is not an iteration of earlier challenges, such as the postmodernism debates and the "culture wars," even if it has sometimes been influenced by them. But such "local," disciplinary debates, when drawn together as they have been in chapter 1, lend credence to more general or "global" claims—the proliferation of which are part of our contemporary intellectual condition—that the social sciences, despite long-standing claims to the contrary, have not surpassed the historical and cultural circumstances of their origins.

Those who still wish to claim that our modern knowledge has some warrant to be considered superior to all others have been obliged to acknowledge that all knowledges, including our own, are shaped by their historical and cultural contexts. The most powerful of such claims seek to show that even if knowledge is contextual, the very conditions of its production presuppose context-independent, transcendental features, and that these features are recognized, incorporated into, and formalized by the modern natural and social sciences. If persuasive, such arguments would establish, in Habermas's words, that "our Occidental understanding of the world" has a legitimate "claim to universality."[1] In chapter 2 I engaged such arguments and sought to show that these were circular, presuming what they sought to prove. In doing so I rejected the claim—a claim that always takes the form of an accusation—that to question the truth and universality of modern knowledge is to lapse into "relativism."[2] To question claims to etic or universal status is not to conclude that "anything goes." It is rather to refuse a monolithic framework that defines the terms of debate such that to question that framework is deemed to be taking up a position within it: you are either with us or against us, you either accept the truth and universality of modern knowledge or you embrace relativism. In tracing the intellectual trajectory of John Rawls, I showed how one eminent neo-Kantian came to recognize that claims for the universality of Reason cannot be shored up by transcendental arguments, for practical reason is always shaped by the histories that produce it. Rawls's later work thus offers an elaboration and defense of "political liberalism" that traces the conditions for its emergence in the Reformation, the wars of religion, and the subsequent rise of religious toleration; and which therefore recognizes that political liberalism cannot be urged for all peoples.

---

[1] Jürgen Habermas, *The Theory of Communicative Action*, translated by Thomas McCarthy, vol. 1, Cambridge: Polity Press, 1984, 44.

[2] Since no scholars I have read describe themselves as relativists, relativism is, as Barbara Herrnstein Smith eloquently puts it, "a phantom position, a set of tenets without palpable adherents, an urban legend without certifiable occurrence but fearful report of which is circulated continuously"; as she goes on to note, this does not mean that the idea is without consequence, for "no matter how protean or elusive relativism may be as a doctrine, it has evident powers as a charge or anxiety." *Scandalous Knowledge*, Edinburgh: Edinburgh University Press, 2005, 18.

Contest and Reject or Anatomize?

At this point, Part II of this book could have taken a direction altogether different from the one that it in fact takes. For there are many who today argue, often in sweeping and polemical terms, that the social sciences are "ethnotheories"[3] and that "the pretension that the specific cosmic vision of a particular ethnie should be taken as universal rationality" is "to impose a provincialism as universalism."[4] Boaventura de Sousa Santos defines globalization, including the globalization of knowledge, as "the successful globalization of a given localism."[5] Anibal Quijano describes this as a form of "epistemological violence" and calls for "epistemological decolonization,"[6] while Santos calls for "global cognitive justice" through an embrace of "epistemologies of the South."[7] Since Part I of this book also argues that modern knowledge is not a culturally neutral and scientific mode of describing and comprehending the world, why then does Part II not follow Quijano, Santos, and others in seeking to develop alternatives to this knowledge, instead of engaging in a painstaking anatomization of the disciplines of history and politics? Answering this question, and distinguishing my approach and conclusions from those who would "decolonize" knowledge, will help to clarify the intellectual, and also the political, implications of this book.

Most of those who urge epistemological decolonization, an ecology of knowledges, decoloniality, and the like are engaged in an explicitly political project: in Santos's description, "The call for the epistemologies of the South is . . . intimately linked . . . to the social struggles against capitalism, colonialism and patriarchy."[8] But Santos's call is no simple project for the revival of non-Western epistemologies, for at least two reasons. First, he is well aware that there is no "pure" knowledge uncontaminated by the global hegemony of modern Western knowledge. He himself draws attention to the fact that the nowadays much-cited example of the "rights of nature" enshrined in the constitution of Ecuador is not a retrieval or reinstatement of indigenous

---

[3] Boaventura de Sousa Santos, *The End of the Cognitive Empire: The Coming of Age of Epistemologies of the South*, Durham, NC: Duke University Press, 2018, 108.

[4] Anibal Quijano, "Coloniality and Modernity/Rationality," in Walter Mignolo and Arturo Escobar (eds.), *Globalization and the Decolonial Option*, New York: Routledge, 2010, 31.

[5] Boaventura de Sousa Santos, "Human Rights as Emancipatory Script? Cultural and Political Conditions," in Santos (ed.), *Another Knowledge Is Possible*, London: Verso, 2007, 6–7.

[6] Quijano, "Coloniality and Modernity/Rationality," 31.

[7] See Santos, *Epistemologies of the South: Justice against Epistemicide*, New York: Paradigm Publishers, 2014, and *End of the Cognitive Empire*.

[8] Santos, *End of the Cognitive Empire*, 121.

cosmovisions or philosophies, but rather "a hybrid construct combining the Western notion of rights with the indigenous notion of nature/panchama," a hybrid that is "formulated in this way to be intelligible and politically effective in a society saturated with the idea of human rights."[9] Further, Santos is well aware that subaltern knowledges have their own exclusions, occlusions, and iniquities: failure to recognize this would be an egregious error, and (I would add) a political and even moral failing. Inasmuch as the aim of decolonizing epistemology has a political intent, it therefore lies in championing those occluded and marginalized knowledges conducive to a more just, and not merely a more diverse, world. Thus while Santos urges that "it is imperative to go South and learn from the South," he immediately adds that he does not mean that every knowledge emanating from the South serves struggles against inequality and injustice.[10] The project of "epistemologies of the South" is, then, less about epistemologies that correspond to geocultures than it is about epistemologies that contest the "northern epistemologies" deemed to be collaborators in, or even agents of, the suffering caused by capitalism, colonialism, and patriarchy.[11]

While I share many of Santos's political commitments, the relations of mutual complementarity, even exact correspondence, that he assumes between cognitive judgments and their social and political consequences is not plausible. To decide whether a knowledge conduces to reducing human suffering is itself a knowledge judgement—it presupposes a series of cognitive acts, such as identifying the most relevant causes of human suffering (here, "capitalism, colonialism and patriarchy"), assessing what knowledges, institutions, and practices facilitate suffering and which oppose them, and so on. Anticipating this obvious objection, Santos writes, "The objectivity presiding over the cognitive judgment of a given practice does not necessarily

---

[9] Santos, *End of the Cognitive Empire*, 11. Similarly, chapter 6 of this book notes that the "politics of the governed" makes extensive use of the modern languages of rights, law, and justice, even as this politics also draws upon other knowledges and norms; and chapter 4 shows how Hindutva reactionaries selectively draw upon indigenous modes of historicity and blend these with modern history, in a hybrid that, in this case, in no way facilitates the pursuit of justice or equality.

[10] For there is an "imperial South," and moreover the genuinely "anti-imperial South" is also to be found in the North (Santos, *Epistemologies of the South*, 223).

[11] "The anti-imperial South," Santos explains, is to be "understood as a metaphor for the global, systemic, and unjust human suffering caused by capitalism, colonialism, and patriarchy and for the resistance against the causes of such suffering" (*Epistemologies of the South*, 222–23). Thus, "The South of the epistemologies of the South is not a geographical south," but rather "a South born in struggles against the three modern forms of domination: capitalism, colonialism, and patriarchy." Santos and Meneses, "Preface" to Santos and Maria Paul Meneses (eds.), *Knowledges Born in the Struggle: Constructing the Epistemologies of the Global South*, New York: Routledge, 2020, xiv–xv.

clash with the ethical-political evaluation of such a practice."[12] A few pages later, he makes a stronger claim. Since knowledge is intervention rather than representation, the credibility we accord a knowledge or an act of cognition "is measured by the kind of intervention in the world it provides, assists, or hinders"; and since "the evaluation of such intervention always combines the cognitive and the ethicopolitical, the ecology of knowledges always starts from the compatibility between cognitive and ethicopolitical values."[13]

The problem with Santos's claim is not simply the obvious one, namely that he finds progressive politics and good knowledge to be in harmony through definitional fiat, declaring a correspondence between the two where there may, in fact, be differences and difficulties. Underlying this, and the more fundamental issue, is that knowledge and power are here fused; the slash or stroke in "power/knowledge" has been replaced by an equals sign. This is at the heart of my difference with Santos and similar projects of decoloniality and/or decolonizing epistemology, and why Part II of this book does not follow that path. For I take the Foucauldian insight that knowledge is imbricated with power and that power operates through knowledge to identify the site of an inquiry, rather than assert a correspondence between a form of knowledge and a power indissolubly tied to a given end, such as capitalism. Foucault himself uses his discussion of the confessional, a practice for the production of truth, as "an example" that the production of truth "is thoroughly imbued with relations of power."[14] But he also shows that the functions it performed "underwent a considerable transformation" as the confessional morphed from being entrenched in the Christian penitential practices of the Middle Ages to subsequently permeate a whole series of relationships, and that in the process "the motivations and effects it is expected to produce have varied."[15] In short, that there is always a relation between knowledge and power does not tell us what that relation is, let alone allow us to make sweeping judgments that equate modern Western knowledge with capitalism and colonialism, and epistemologies of the South with emancipation.

It is true, as Santos argues and as I have insisted, that knowledges do not simply serve to describe or cognize, but are a force in making that which they

---

[12] Santos, *Epistemologies of the South*, 191.
[13] Santos, *Epistemologies of the South*, 207.
[14] Michel Foucault, *The History of Sexuality: An Introduction*, translated by Robert Hurley, Harmondsworth: Penguin, 1984, 60.
[15] Foucault, *The History of Sexuality*, 63.

represent or cognize. Indeed, this is especially true of modern knowledge, which, at once cause and consequence of far-reaching transformations on a global scale, has been a force in reshaping everyone's world. But for this very reason—because modern Western knowledge is historically unprecedented in its reach and is taught and produced in schools and universities in all parts of the world, notwithstanding the many differences that otherwise characterize these parts of the world—its relations with power and with political projects is complex and variable. Further, it is a distinctive feature of this knowledge that it is divided into disciplines, a feature not attended to in sweeping assessments or condemnations of it. We saw, for example, in chapter 4 that the very ubiquity of history writing results in it being pressed into service for all manner of ends, and not only or even principally to the end of reproducing "capitalism" or producing "the modern subject"—even though its rise and functioning is undoubtedly connected to these. In the same chapter, examining the debate concerning historiography that followed the destruction of Babri Masjid, I argued that historical "truth"—as it is produced and defined via the presuppositions and protocols of modern history writing—does not necessarily reinforce liberal or leftist political commitments. Conversely, but for similar reasons, I think that the identification of modern Western knowledge with capitalism, colonialism, and patriarchy insists on correspondences where in fact there are only connections, connections that are variable and that cannot underwrite clearly defined political commitments or projects.

Thus the second part of this book, rather than taking the explicitly "political turn" of seeking alternatives to the dominant knowledge, closely examined instead the presuppositions that inform the production of historical and political knowledge. Chapters 3 and 4 examined the discipline of history. History writing is not the simple application of a method or craft to the sources bequeathed to us from the past, but rather a code that constructs its object, "the past," in particular ways. Historiography constructs the past in anthropological and humanist terms (nature and gods are not part of history), and sets itself the task of recreating the meanings that men and women once endowed their world with, and the purposes that animated them. At the same time, and in more or less equal measure, it presumes that these purposes and meanings are determined or constrained by "society"—by the web of social relations into which we are all born and which shape the ways that we, in turn, shape our world. And finally, and in sharp contrast to many others forms of historicity, history treats the past as irretrievably dead. I suggested

that as with other forms of historicity, the purpose of historiography is to establish connections between the past and the present, but that unlike other
forms of historicity, it does so by creating a divide between a dead past and a
living present, and then seeking to establish continuities between them. The
humanist and determinist presumptions are the means by which it does so.

The presumptions underlying history writing, I show in these chapters,
are not the outcome of a general and shared "human" past, but presumptions
emerging at a particular time among a particular subset of humanity. The
result is that the code of history is at once defined by its commitment to
avoiding anachronism, and yet also unavoidably engaged in anachronism
whenever it is applied to illuminate the past of those who do not share
these presumptions. This anachronism, I suggested, can be "redeemed" in
those circumstances where the application of the code to a past where its
assumptions were not shared can, nonetheless, plausibly be shown to have
provided the ground from which the code and its presuppositions emerged.
But such circumstances, I argued, do not prevail where non-Western pasts
are concerned, for modern historiography did not emerge out of and through
engagement with indigenous traditions of historicity. This led me not to a call
for retrieval of earlier or alternative forms of historicity, but rather to ask what
sort of knowledge is produced when history in the modern mode is written
about non-Western pasts. The history of pasts that were not disenchanted,
where gods had not been deprived of agency, where the past constantly bled
into the present, and where texts were not seen as the congealed remains of
the purposes and meanings of their human authors must, I suggested, be
written in recognition that such histories are translations, not better or truer
representations, and with acknowledgment and due attention to the fact that
much gets lost in translation.

The discipline of politics or political science is an archipelago of
subdisciplines, and thus my anatomization of politics took two of these, international relations and political theory, as its subject matter. International
relations constitutes itself as a discipline by defining a unique and distinct
object: namely the "anarchy" that prevails in the international domain, where
by contrast with the "domestic" realm, there is no sovereign power. In defining its object thus, it also assumes that the international order is composed
of sovereign states—either because a state ontology is built into its optic or, as
in the case of the more historically minded practitioners of the discipline, because the sovereign state is thought to have been the dominant form of polity
for many centuries. The problem, and it is a fundamental one, is that the

discipline's founding empirical assumptions are, quite simply, wrong. Until a few decades ago the number of sovereign states in the world was relatively few; most of the peoples of the world were citizens or subjects of empires. Empires covered the larger surface of the globe and included the majority of its people, and empire was neither a way station en route to the nation-state nor a "superstate," but rather an independent political form, characterized by territorial and legal complexities and ambiguities that were continually produced and reproduced. The discipline manages the extraordinary feat of either forgetting this altogether or accounting for it by dismissing it as a "survival" of an earlier era, destined to be surpassed in the inexorable teleological march toward state sovereignty that is thought to have begun with the Peace of Westphalia. But in fact the global dominance of the sovereign state emerged only in the era of decolonization, and it was thus only two decades *after* the emergence of the discipline of international relations that the world began to conform to its founding presumptions. But this "amnesia," as I have characterized it, was not thereby remedied. The failure of the discipline to accurately characterize and understand its object continues, because the imperial past, which the discipline refuses to acknowledge, shadows and shapes the contemporary international order.

Unlike history and international relations, political theory does not seek to accurately represent and explain an object, but is rather knowledge "for"— performance rather than representation. This I argued, in chapter 6, is key to understanding its governing presumptions and what it does in the world. The discipline is directed toward the public sphere, conceived as a realm of individuals possessed of their own "values," who, however, inhabit a shared world and engage in rational, critical debate about that which they hold in common. This is why political theory is an irremediably liberal enterprise and also why the discipline has so little resonance in the non-Western world, despite the fact that the global South is the site of impassioned debates about equality, freedom, justice, secularism, and other concepts and values debated in political theory. I conclude that this and the other inadequacies of political science are not a consequence of the fact that the non-West is not yet modern (the implication being that political science will be a good guide once non-Western polities have developed modern forms of civil society, public sphere, and state)—for the global South has long been a part of a globalized, if hierarchical and profoundly unequal, capitalist modernity—but that these inadequacies are, rather, evidence of the parochialism of political science. Here as elsewhere in this book, my argument is not that we should recognize non-Western exceptionalism, but rather that in the conditions of a globalized modernity, the disciplines that make up modern Western knowledge are damagingly provincial.

Why Not "Critique"?

In this book I have refused the identification of modern knowledge with Reason and progress, but also indicated, for similar reasons, that I do not think it can be reduced to a mere function or accessory of capitalism and colonialism. At this point the reader may wonder why I do not embrace the concept (one that has been available since at least the eighteenth century) of "critique" as a description of my project, instead deploying the term "anatomize" to describe the task in which I have been engaged. Kant's Copernican revolution consisted in showing that it is not the case that our knowledge must conform to its objects, but that objects must conform to our knowledge.[16] In the process he also established the limits of knowledge, of what Reason can know and of the limits it must not transgress. He labeled this exercise "critique," and at first glance, this might seem a good characterization of a book that has sought to delineate the capacities and limits of the social sciences. However whereas Kant sought to show that there were timeless and universal features of cognition, this book has argued the opposite—that our knowledge is historical and parochial, and hence a form of reasoning rather than Reason itself. If we were once confident, in David Kolb's words, that modern knowledge was "not just another in a sequence of historic constructions" but rather "the unveiling of what has been at the root of these constructions,"[17] I have argued that we no longer have good reasons for such confidence, and that we need to recognize the historicity, cultural specificity and contingency of our knowledge. I have further argued that the globalization of Western modernity does not thereby guarantee that the knowledge that accompanied it affords an understanding of all that modernity has reshaped.

---

[16] "It has hitherto been assumed that our cognition must conform to the objects; but all attempts to ascertain anything about these objects a priori, by means of conceptions, and thus to extend the range of our knowledge, have been rendered abortive by this assumption. Let us then make the experiment whether we may be more successful in metaphysics, if we assume that the objects must conform to our cognition." Immanuel Kant, preface to the second edition of the *Critique of Pure Reason*, translated by J. M. D. Meiklejohn, London: Everyman's Library, 1991, 12.

[17] David Kolb, *The Critique of Pure Modernity: Hegel, Heidegger, and After*, Chicago: University of Chicago Press, 1986, 9–10. Kolb is characterizing—rather than endorsing—Max Weber's position.

But there is another sense of critique, indebted to Foucault, which seeks "to transpose a Kantian procedure onto a historical scheme," thereby seeking not universal and timeless categories by which things may be known, but asking instead, "How is our knowledge organized by specific historical schemes ... and how do our judgments rely upon these prior organizations of knowledge?"[18] The sentence quoted comes from Judith Butler, in the course of an exchange with Talal Asad, and I will conclude with a consideration of this exchange, using it to explain why I do not fully embrace this, more historical, understanding of critique as a description of my project. In doing so I will also explain why the political implications of what I stubbornly call "anatomization" do not seem to me the same as those entailed in Butler's description of "critique."

In *On Suicide Bombing* and "Free Speech, Blasphemy and Secular Criticism"[19]—the former's subject matter indicated by its title, and the latter focused upon the various but always heated responses to the "Danish cartoons" affair—Talal Asad engages in an inquiry into the intellectual presuppositions underpinning political evaluations and moral denunciations. He does so while insisting that he is not himself interested in staking out a normative position or making moral judgments. In engaging with the first of these two texts, Butler expresses skepticism regarding the distinction Asad makes between understanding and normativity. She suggests that even if Asad eschews taking an explicitly normative position, inasmuch as *On Suicide Bombing* shows that the evaluative schemes at work in distinguishing different kinds of violence are culturally specific, he exposes as "parochialism" that which otherwise "passes itself off as universal reason,"[20] and in doing so "facilitates a *critique* of this parochial and consequential circumspection of operative evaluative frameworks."[21] In responding to Asad's second and later text on the Danish cartoons controversy, Butler expresses puzzlement over Asad's continuing efforts to make a distinction between description and evaluation, and relatedly, his "confounding protestations"[22] that his intellectual endeavors avoid normative commitments. Against this,

---

[18] Judith Butler, "The Sensibility of Critique: Response to Asad and Mahmood," in Talal Asad, Wendy Brown, Judith Butler, and Saba Mahmood, *Is Critique Secular? Blasphemy, Injury, and Free Speech*, New York: Fordham University Press, 2013, 109.

[19] Talal Asad, *On Suicide Bombing*, New York: Columbia University Press, 2007, and Talal Asad, "Free Speech, Blasphemy and Criticism," in Asad, Brown, Butler and Mahmood, *Is Critique Secular*.

[20] Butler, "Non-Thinking in the Name of the Normative," in her *Frames of War: When Is Life Grievable?*, London: Verso, 2016, 161.

[21] Butler, "The Sensibility of Critique," 101–2.

[22] Butler, "The Sensibility of Critique," 100.

Butler insists that "every description is already committed to an evaluative framework, prior to the question of any explicit or posterior judgment. We may think that we first describe a phenomenon and then later subject it to judgment, but if the very phenomenon at issue only 'exists' within certain evaluative frameworks, then norms precede description."[23]

Butler's logic is irrefutable, and in his response Asad concedes that every description includes evaluation or normativity. However—and this is what interests me most—he nonetheless continues to reject the ascription of "critique" to his writing, instead characterizing it as follows: "My effort aims at inciting the reader to consider the notions of objectionable violence and grievable death not in order to highlight the normative dispositions that have entered into evaluative frameworks but to examine what the concepts exclude and suppress, how they obscure their own indeterminacy and acquire their vitality."[24] As to what moral and political ends his problematizations are directed toward, Asad, continuing to distinguish his inquires from "critique," writes, "I think that one should be prepared for the fact that what one aims at in one's thinking may be less significant than where one ends up. By which I mean that in the process of thinking one should be open to ending up in unanticipated places—whether these produce satisfaction or desire, discomfort or horror."[25]

Suicide bombing and the Danish cartoons controversy are highly charged political topics in a way that an investigation into the epistemological status of the social sciences is not. But I read these exchanges as being highly relevant to my own inquiries and problematizations. For like Asad, I have sought to examine what the social sciences "exclude and suppress" and how they obscure their contingency and acquire their vitality. To the degree that "anatomizing" the social sciences may imply that normative (and political) frameworks and investments are absent—that one is merely engaging in description without evaluation—it is not a happy description of what I have undertaken (though alternatives, such as "understanding," are no better). Any such inquiry has political implications, and those who ardently defend the universality of modern knowledge in part because they insist that epistemological questions have normative stakes are right to insist on this, though wrong to label and condemn all questioning and criticism as relativism. But just as I reject the blackmail implicit and often explicit in

[23] Butler, "The Sensibility of Critique," 99.
[24] Asad, "Reply to Judith Butler," in *Is Critique Secular?*, 132.
[25] Asad, "Reply to Judith Butler," 132–33.

the charge of relativism,[26] nor do I, for the reasons already discussed, follow Santos and others in seeking to retrieve or reinstate knowledge-cultures of the global South. And if I am wary of navigating the difference between these alternatives by instead embracing the term "critique," it not because I think there are no normative implications to my project, but rather because I am not sure that one can know with any certainty what these implications are, let alone presume that they are bound to be emancipatory or progressive. For if, as I have argued in the preceding pages, modern Western knowledge makes some objects knowable and certain ways of living possible, but in so doing makes it difficult or even impossible to contemplate other worlds and other possibilities, then it does not seem to me that an inquiry into the presuppositions underpinning and enabling modern knowledge generally, and the social sciences more specifically, points in any one political direction. But what it does show is that like the other knowledges that have preceded it and that continue to exist in modified forms in quotidian life, our knowledge is of its time and place. It is distinctive not because it has finally arrived at the Truth, but because unlike all other knowledges it has an extraordinary global reach. All the more important, then, to know what it enables and what it obscures, what its possibilities are, and what its limits.

---

[26] In a different but not unrelated context Foucault rejects "the intellectual blackmail of 'being for or against the Enlightenment.'" "What Is Enlightenment?," in Paul Rabinow (ed.), *The Foucault Reader*, New York: Penguin, 1986, 45.

Bibliography of Works Cited

Ackerman, Bruce. *Social Justice in the Liberal State*, New Haven: Yale University Press, 1980.

Adas, Michael. *Machines as the Measure of Men: Science, Technology, and Ideologies of Western Dominance*, new ed., Ithaca, NY: Cornell University Press, 2015.

Adelman, Jeremy. "An Age of Imperial Revolutions," *American Historical Review* 113:2 (April 2008).

Agnew, John. "The Territoriality Trap: The Geographical Assumptions of International Relations Theory," *Review of International Political Economy* 1:1 (Spring 1994).

Alberti, Benjamin, Severin Fowles, Martin Holbraad, Yvonne Marshall, and Christopher Witmore. "'Worlds Otherwise': Archaeology, Anthropology, and Ontological Difference," *Current Anthropology* 52:6 (December 2011).

Alder, Ken. "The History of Science as Oxymoron: From Scientific Explanations to Episcience," *Isis* 104:1 (March 2013).

Allen, Amy. *The End of Progress: Decolonizing the Normative Foundations of Critical Theory*, New York: Columbia University Press, 2016.

Allen, Amy. "The Ethics and Politics of Progress: Dussel and the Frankfurt School," in Amy Allen and Eduardo Mendieta (eds.), *Decolonizing Ethics: The Critical Theory of Enrique Dussel*, University Park: Penn State University Press (forthcoming).

Allen, Amy. "Having One's Cake and Eating It Too: Habermas's Genealogy of Postsecular Reason," in Craig Calhoun, Eduardo Mendieta, and Jonathan VanAntwerpen (eds.), *Habermas and Religion*, Cambridge: Polity Press, 2013.

Allison, Henry. *Kant's Transcendental Idealism: An Interpretation and Defense*, rev. ed., New Haven: Yale University Press, 2004.

Almond, Gabriel A. "Political Theory and Political Science," *American Political Science Review* 60:4 (December 1966).

Almond, Gabriel A. "Separate Tables: Schools and Sects in Political Science," *PS: Political Science and Politics* 21:4 (Autumn 1988).

Alpers, Svetlana. *The Art of Describing: Dutch Art in the Seventeenth Century*, Chicago: University of Chicago Press, 1983.

Althusser, Louis. "The Errors of Classical Economics: Outline of a Concept of Historical Time," in Louis Althusser and Etienne Balibar, *Reading Capital*, translated by Ben Brewster, London: Verso, 2009.

Anderson, Benedict. *Imagined Communities*, rev. ed., London: Verso, 1991.

Anghie, Antony. *Imperialism, Sovereignty and the Making of International Law*, Cambridge: Cambridge University Press, 2004.

Apel, Karl-Otto. "Discourse Ethics, Democracy, and International Law: Towards a Globalization of Practical Reason," in Steven V. Hicks and David E. Shannon (eds.), *The Challenges of Globalization: Rethinking Nature, Culture, and Freedom*, Oxford: Blackwell, 2007.

Apel, Karl-Otto. "Globalisation and the Need for Universal Ethics," *European Journal of Social Theory* 3:2 (2000).

Apel, Karl-Otto. "Normatively Grounding 'Critical Theory' through Recourse to the Lifeworld? A Transcendental-Pragmatic Attempt to Think with Habermas against Habermas," in Axel Honneth et al. (eds.), *Philosophical Interventions in the Unfinished Project of Enlightenment*, Cambridge, MA: MIT Press, 1992.

Apel, Karl-Otto. "The Problem of Justice in a Multicultural Society," in Richard Kearney and Mark Dooley (eds.), *Questioning Ethics: Contemporary Debates in Philosophy*, New York: Routledge, 1999.

Apel, Karl-Otto. *The Response of Discourse Ethics*, Louvain-la-Neuve: Peeters, 2001.

Armitage, David. *Foundations of Modern International Thought*, New York: Cambridge University Press, 2013.

Aron, Raymond. "What Is a Theory of International Relations?," *Journal of International Affairs* 21:2 (1967).

Asad, Talal. "The Concept of Cultural Translation in British Social Anthropology," in James Clifford and George Marcus (eds.), *Writing Culture: The Poetics and Politics of Anthropology*, Berkeley: University of California Press, 1986.

Asad, Talal. "Conscripts of Western Civilization," in Christine Ward Gailey (ed.), *Civilization in Crisis: Anthropological Perspectives*, Gainesville: University of Florida Press, 1992.

Asad, Talal. "Free Speech, Blasphemy and Criticism," in Talal Asad, Wendy Brown, Judith Butler, and Saba Mahmood, *Is Critique Secular? Blasphemy, Injury, and Free Speech*, New York: Fordham University Press, 2013.

Asad, Talal. *On Suicide Bombing*, New York: Columbia University Press, 2007.

Asad, Talal. "Reply to Judith Butler," in Talal Asad, Wendy Brown, Judith Butler, and Saba Mahmood, *Is Critique Secular? Blasphemy, Injury, and Free Speech*, New York: Fordham University Press, 2013.

Ashley, Richard. "Untying the Sovereign State: A Double Reading of the Anarchy Problematique," *Millennium* 17:2 (1988).

Ashworth, Lucian. "Did the Realist-Idealist Great Debate Really Happen? A Revisionist History of International Relations," *International Relations* 16:1 (2002).

Auerbach, Eric. *Scenes from the Drama of European Literature*, Manchester: Manchester University Press, 1984.

Aydin, Cemil. *The Politics of Anti-Westernism in Asia: Visions of World Order in Pan-Islamic and Pan-Asian Thought*, New York: Columbia University Press, 2007.

Baker, Keith Michael. "Enlightenment and the Institution of Society: Notes for a Conceptual History," in William Melching and Wyger Velema (eds.), *Main Trends in Cultural History*, Amsterdam: Rodopi, 1994.

Baker, Keith Michael. "A Foucauldian French Revolution?," in Jan Goldstein (ed.), *Foucault and the Writing of History*, Oxford: Blackwell, 1994.

Ball, Terence. *Reappraising Political Theory*, Oxford: Clarendon Press, 1994.

Banerjee, Prathama. "Histories of History in South Asia," in Prasenjit Duara, Viren Murthy, and Andrew Sartori (eds.), *A Companion to Global Historical Thought*, Malden, MA: John Wiley and Sons, 2014.

Bann, Stephen. *The Clothing of Clio*, Cambridge: Cambridge University Press, 1984.

Bann, Stephen. *The Inventions of History: Essays on the Representation of the Past*, Manchester: Manchester University Press, 1990.

Barkawi, Tarak. "Empire and Order in International Relations and Security Studies," in *Oxford Research Encyclopedia of International Studies*, New York: Oxford University Press, 2010.

Barkawi, Tarak. *Soldiers of Empire: Indian and British Armies in World War II*, New York: Cambridge University Press, 2017.

Barkawi, Tarak. "War, Armed Forces and Society in Postcolonial Perspective," in Sanjay Seth (ed.), *Postcolonial Theory and International Relations: A Critical Introduction*, New York: Routledge, 2013.

Barkawi, Tarak and Mark Laffey. "Retrieving the Imperial: Empire and International Relations," *Millennium* 31:1 (2002).

Barker, Rodney. "A Tale of Three Cities: The Early Years of Political Science in Oxford, London and Manchester," in Christopher Hood, Desmond King, and Gillian Peele (eds.), *Forging a Discipline*, New York: Oxford University Press, 2014.

Barnes, Barry. *Scientific Knowledge and Sociological Theory*, London: Routledge and Kegan Paul, 1974.

Barrier, N. Gerald (ed.). *The Census in British India: New Perspectives*, New Delhi: Manohar, 1981.

Barry, Brian. *Culture and Equality*, Cambridge: Polity Press, 2001.

Barry, Brian. *The Liberal Theory of Justice: A Critical Examination of the Principal Doctrines in "A Theory of Justice" by John Rawls*, Oxford: Oxford University Press, 1973.

Barry, Brian. "The Strange Death of Political Philosophy," *Government and Opposition* 15:3–4 (July 1980).

Barry, Brian. "The Study of Politics as a Vocation," in Jack Hayward, Brian Barry, and Archie Brown (eds.), *The British Study of Politics in the Twentieth Century*, New York: Oxford University Press, 1999.

Baudrillard, Jean. *In the Shadow of the Silent Majorities, or The End of the Social*, translated by P. Fous, J. Johnston, and P. Patton, Los Angeles: Semiotext(e), 1983.

Baxandall, Michael. *The Limewood Sculptors of Renaissance Germany*, New Haven: Yale University Press, 1980.

Beaulac, Stephane. *The Power of Language in the Making of International Law*, Dordrecht: Martinus Nijhoff, 2004.

Beaulac, Stephane. "The Westphalian Legal Orthodoxy—Myth or Reality?," *Journal of the History of International Law* 2 (2000).

Bell, Duncan. *The Idea of Greater Britain: Empire and the Future of World Order, 1860–1900*, Princeton, NJ: Princeton University Press, 2007.

Belting, Hans. *Art History after Modernism*, translated by C. Saltzwedel and M. Cohen, Chicago: University of Chicago Press, 2003.

Belting, Hans. *Likeness and Presence: A History of the Image before the Era of Art*, translated by Edmond Jephcott, Chicago: University of Chicago Press, 1994.

Benjamin, Walter. "The Task of the Translator," in *Illuminations*, translated by Harry Zorn, edited by Hannah Arendt, London: Pimlico, 1999.

Bennett, Jane. *Vibrant Matter: A Political Ecology of Things*, Durham, NC: Duke University Press, 2010.

Benton, Lauren. "From International Law to Imperial Constitutions: The Problem of Quasi-Sovereignty, 1870–1900," *Law and History Review* 26:3 (Fall 2008).

Benton, Lauren. *Law and Colonial Culture: Legal Regimes in World History, 1400–1900*, New York: Cambridge University Press, 2009.

Benton, Lauren. *A Search for Sovereignty: Law and Geography in European Empires, 1400–1900*, New York: Cambridge University Press, 2010.

Berlin, Isaiah. "Does Political Theory Still Exist?," in Peter Laslett and David Runciman (eds.), *Politics, Philosophy and Society*, 2nd series, Oxford: Oxford University Press, 1962.

Berlin, Isaiah. *Four Essays on Liberty*, Oxford: Oxford University Press, 1969.

Berlin, Isaiah. "In Conversation with Steven Lukes," *Salmagundi* 120 (Fall 1998).

Berlin, Isaiah. *Vico and Herder*, London: Hogarth Press, 1976.

Berry, Christopher J. *Social Theory of the Scottish Enlightenment*, Edinburgh: Edinburgh University Press, 1997.

Bhambra, Gurminder. *Rethinking Modernity: Postcolonialism and the Sociological Imagination*, New York: Palgrave Macmillan, 2007.

Bhargava, Rajeev. *What Is Political Theory and Why Do We Need It?*, New Delhi: Oxford University Press, 2010.

Bhattacharya, Neeladri. "Myth, History and the Politics of Ramjanmabhumi," in Sarvapelli Gopal (ed.), *Anatomy of Confrontation: The Babri-Masjid–Ram Janmabhumi Issue*, New York: Penguin, 1991.

Bhattacharya, Neeladri. "Predicament of Secular Histories," *Public Culture* 20:1 (Winter 2008).

Black, Antony. *The History of Islamic Political Thought*, New York: Routledge, 2001.

Bloch, Marc. *The Historian's Craft*, translated by P. Putnam, Manchester: Manchester University Press, 1979.

Bloom, Harold. "Foreword" to Yosef Hayim Yerushalmi, *Zakhor: Jewish History and Jewish Memory*, 2nd ed., Seattle: University of Washington Press, 1996.

Bloor, David. *Knowledge and Social Imagery*, 1976, 2nd ed., Chicago: University of Chicago Press, 1991.

Bonnell, Victoria and Lynn Hunt (eds.). *Beyond the Cultural Turn: New Directions in the Study of Society and Culture*, Berkeley: University of California Press, 1999.

Branch, Jordan. *The Cartographic State: Maps, Territory, and the Origins of Sovereignty*, New York: Cambridge University Press, 2014.

Braudel, Fernand. *On History*, translated by Sarah Matthews, Chicago: University of Chicago Press, 1980.

Braver, Lee. *Groundless Grounds: A Study of Wittgenstein and Heidegger*, Cambridge, MA: MIT Press, 2012.

Braver, Lee. *A Thing of This World: A History of Continental Anti-Realism*, Evanston, IL: Northwestern University Press, 2007.

Brown, Wendy. *Edgework: Critical Essays on Knowledge and Politics*, Princeton, NJ: Princeton University Press, 2005.

Brown, Wendy. "Political Theory Is Not a Luxury: A Response to Timothy Kaufman-Osborn's 'Political Theory as a Profession,'" *Political Research Quarterly* 63:3 (September 2010).

Bujic, Bojan (ed.). *Music in European Thought, 1851–1912*, Cambridge: Cambridge University Press, 1988.

Bull, Hedley. *The Anarchical Society: A Study of Order in World Politics*, New York: Columbia University Press, 2002.

Bull, Hedley. "European States and African Political Communities," in Hedley Bull and Adam Watson (eds.), *The Expansion of International Society*, Oxford: Clarendon Press, 1984.

Bull, Hedley. "Preface" to Gerrit W. Gong, *The Standard of "Civilization" in International Society*, Oxford: Clarendon Press, 1984.

Bull, Hedley. "Society and Anarchy in International Relations," in Herbert Butterfield and Martin Wight (eds.), *Diplomatic Investigations*, Cambridge, MA: Harvard University Press, 1968.

Bull, Hedley and Adam Watson. "Introduction," in Hedley Bull and Adam Watson (eds.), *The Expansion of International Society*, Oxford: Clarendon Press, 1984.

Bungay, Stephen. *Beauty and Truth: A Study of Hegel's Aesthetics*, Oxford: Oxford University Press, 1984.

Burckhardt, Jacob. *The Civilization of the Renaissance in Italy*, translated by Samuel G. C. Middlemore, New York: Mentor, 1960.

Burguiere, Andre. *The Annales School: An Intellectual History*, translated by Jane Marie Todd, Ithaca, NY: Cornell University Press, 2009.

Burke, Peter. *The Renaissance Sense of the Past*, London: Edward Arnold, 1969.

Butler, Judith. *Frames of War: When Is Life Grievable?*, London: Verso, 2016.

Butler, Judith. "The Sensibility of Critique: Response to Asad and Mahmood," in Talal Asad, Wendy Brown, Judith Butler and Saba Mahmood, *Is Critique Secular? Blasphemy, Injury, and Free Speech*, New York: Fordham University Press, 2013.

Butt, John. *Playing with History: Historical Approaches to Musical Performance*, New York: Cambridge University Press, 2002.

Buzan, Barry and Richard Little. *International Systems and World History: Remaking the Study of International Relations*, New York: Oxford University Press, 2000.

Cabrera, Miguel A. *Postsocial History: An Introduction*, translated by Marie McMahon, Lanham, MD: Lexington Books, 2004.

Calhoun, Craig. "Introduction: Habermas and the Public Sphere," in Craig Calhoun (ed.), *Habermas and the Public Sphere*, Cambridge, MA: MIT Press, 1992.

Callahan, William A. "Nationalising International Theory: Race, Class and the English School," *Global Society* 18:4 (2004).

Carvalho, B. de, H. Leira, and J. H. Hobson. "The Big Bangs of IR: The Myths That Your Teachers Still Tell You about 1648 and 1919," *Millennium* 39:3 (2011).

Cassirer, Ernst. *The Problem of Knowledge*, translated by W. H. Woglam and C. W. Hendel, New Haven: Yale University Press, 1950.

Castoriadis, Cornelius. *The Imaginary Institution of Society*, Cambridge: Polity Press, 1987.

Castro, Eduardo Viveiros de. "Cosmological Deixis and Amerindian Perspectivism," *Journal of the Royal Anthropological Institute* 4:3 (September 1998).

Castro, Eduardo Viveiros de. "Exchanging Perspectives: The Transformation of Objects into Subjects in Amerindian Ontologies," *Common Knowledge* 10:3 (Fall 2004).

Castro, Eduardo Viveiros de. *The Relative Native: Essays on Indigenous Conceptual Worlds*, Chicago: Hau Books, 2015.

Certeau, Michel de. *Heterologies: Discourse on the Other*, translated by Brian Massumi, Manchester: Manchester University Press, 1986.

Certeau, Michel de. "History and Mysticism" (1972), in Jacques Revel and Lynn Hunt (eds.), *Histories: French Constructions of the Past*, New York: New Press, 1995.

Certeau, Michel de. *The Writing of History*, translated by Tom Conley, New York: Columbia University Press, 1988.

Chakrabarty, Dipesh. *The Calling of History: Sir Jadunath Sarkar and His Empire of Truth*, Chicago: University of Chicago Press, 2015.

Chakrabarty, Dipesh. "The Climate of History: Four Theses," *Critical Inquiry* 35 (Winter 2009).

Chakrabarty, Dipesh. "Globalisation, Democratisation and the Evacuation of History?," in J. Assayag and V. Benei (eds.), *At Home in Diaspora*, New Delhi: Permanent Black, 2003.

Chakrabarty, Dipesh. *Provincializing Europe: Postcolonial Thought and Historical Difference*, Princeton, NJ: Princeton University Press, 2000.Chakrabarty, Dipesh. "The Public Life of History: An Argument out of India," *Public Culture* 20:1 (Winter 2008).

Chandler, James. *England in 1819*, Chicago: University of Chicago Press, 1998.

Chatterjee, Kumkum. *The Culture of History in Early Modern India: Persianization and Mughal Culture in Bengal*, New Delhi: Oxford University Press, 2009.

Chatterjee, Partha. "History and the Domain of the Popular," *Seminar* 522 (February 2003).

Chatterjee, Partha. "Introduction: History and the Present," in Partha Chatterjee and Anjan Ghosh (eds.), *History and the Present*, New Delhi: Permanent Black, 2002.

Chatterjee, Partha. *Nationalist Thought and the Colonial World: A Derivative Discourse?*, Oxford: Oxford University Press, 1986.

Chatterjee, Partha. *The Nation and Its Fragments: Colonial and Postcolonial Histories*, Delhi: Oxford University Press, 1993.

Chatterjee, Partha. *The Politics of the Governed*, New York: Columbia University Press, 2004.

Ch'en, Paul. "The Treaty System and European Law in China: A Study of the Exercise of British Jurisdiction in Late Imperial China," in W. J. Mommsen and J. A. De Moor (eds.), *European Expansion and Law*, New York: Berg, 1992.

Christian, David. "The Case of 'Big History,'" *Journal of World History* 2:2 (1991).

Christian, David. *Maps of Time: An Introduction to Big History*, Berkeley: University of California Press, 2004.

Clifford, James. *The Predicament of Culture*, Cambridge, MA: Harvard University Press, 1988.

Clifford, James and George Marcus (eds.). *Writing Culture: The Poetics and Politics of Ethnography*, Berkeley: University of California Press, 1986.

Cobban, Alfred. "The Decline of Political Theory," *Political Science Quarterly* 68:3 (September 1953).

Cobban, Alfred. *The Social Interpretation of the French Revolution*, Cambridge: Cambridge University Press, 1968.

Cohen, Jean L. and Andrew Arato. *Civil Society and Political Theory*, Cambridge, MA: MIT Press, 1992.

Cohen, Sande. *Historical Culture: On the Recoding of an Academic Discipline*, Berkeley: University of California Press, 1986.

Cohn, Bernard. *An Anthropologist among the Historians and Other Essays*, New Delhi: Oxford University Press, 1987.

Collini, Stefan. "Postscript: Disciplines, Canons and Publicness: The History of the 'History of Political Thought' in Comparative Perspective," in Dario Castiglione and Iain Hampsher-Monk (eds.), *The History of Political Thought in National Context*, New York: Cambridge University Press, 2001.

Collini, Stefan. *Public Moralists: Political Thought and Intellectual Life in Britain, 1850–1930*, Oxford: Clarendon Press, 1991.

Collini, Stefan, Donald Winch, and John Burrow. *That Noble Science of Politics: A Study in Nineteenth-Century Intellectual History*, Cambridge: Cambridge University Press, 1983.

Comaroff, John and Jean Comaroff. *Ethnography and the Historical Imagination*, Boulder, CO: Westview Press, 1992.

Condren, Conal. *Argument and Authority in Early Modern England: The Presuppositions of Oaths and Offices*, New York: Cambridge University Press, 2006.

Condren, Conal. "The Death of Political Theory: The Importance of Historiographical Myth," *Politics* 11:2 (1974).

Connolly, William. "Politics and Vision," in Aryeh Botwinick and William E. Connolly (eds.), *Democracy and Vision: Sheldon Wolin and the Vicissitudes of the Political*, Princeton, NJ: Princeton University Press, 2001.

Cooper, Frederick. "Alternatives to Empire: France and Africa after World War II," in Douglas Howland and Luise White (eds.), *The State of Sovereignty: Territories, Laws, Populations*, Bloomington: Indiana University Press, 2009.

Cooper, Frederick. *Colonialism in Question: Theory, Knowledge, History*, Berkeley: University of California Press, 2005.

Croxton, Derek. "The Peace of Westphalia of 1648 and the Origins of Sovereignty," *International History Review* 21:3 (1999).

Dahlhaus, Carl. *Foundations of Music History*, translated by J. B. Robinson, Cambridge: Cambridge University Press, 1983.

Dallmayr, Fred. "Introduction: Toward a Comparative Political Theory," *Review of Politics* 59:3 (Summer 1997).

Daniel, Glyn and Colin Renfrew. *The Idea of Prehistory*, 1962, rev. ed., Edinburgh: Edinburgh University Press, 1988.

Danto, Arthur C. *After the End of Art: Contemporary Art and the Pale of History*, Princeton, NJ: Princeton University Press, 1997.

Daston, Lorraine. "Historical Epistemology," in James Chandler, Arnold Davidson, and Harry Harootunian (eds.), *Questions of Evidence*, Chicago: University of Chicago Press, 1994.

Daston, Lorraine. "The Historicity of Science," in Glenn W. Most (ed.), *Historicization-Historisierung*, Gottingen: Vendenhoek and Ruprecht, 2001.

Daston, Lorraine. "The History of Science as European Self-Portraiture," *European Review* 14:4 (October 2006).

Daston, Lorraine. "Science Studies and the History of Science," *Critical Inquiry* 35 (Summer 2009).

Dear, Peter. "Science Is Dead: Long Live Science," *Osiris* 27:1 (2012).

Dear, Peter. "What Is History of Science the History Of? Early Modern Roots of the Ideology of Modern Science," *Isis* 96:3 (September 2005).

Dear, Peter. *The Intelligibility of Nature: How Science Makes Sense of the World*, Chicago: University of Chicago Press, 2006.

Derrida, Jacques. *Learning to Live Finally: The Last Interview*, translated by Pascale-Anne Brault and Michael Naas, New York: Palgrave Macmillan, 2007.

Derrida, Jacques. *Margins of Philosophy*, translated by Alan Bass, Chicago: University of Chicago Press, 1982.

Descola, Philippe. *Beyond Nature and Culture*, translated by Janet Lloyd, Chicago: University of Chicago Press, 2013.

Descola, Philippe. "Constructing Natures: Symbolic Ecology and Social Practice," in Philippe Descola and Gisli Palsson (eds.), *Nature and Society: Anthropological Perspectives*, New York: Routledge, 1996.

Descola, Philippe. *In the Society of Nature: A Native Ecology in Amazonia*, translated by Nora Scott, New York: Cambridge University Press, 1994.

Descola, Philippe. *The Spears of Twilight: Life and Death in the Amazon Jungle*, translated by Janet Lloyd, New York: Free Press, 1996.

Deshpande, Prachi. *Creative Pasts: Historical Memory and Identity in Western India, 1700–1960*, New York: Columbia University Press, 2007.

Dirks, Nicholas. *Castes of Mind*, Princeton, NJ: Princeton University Press, 2001.

Dirks, Nicholas, Geoff Eley, and Sherry Ortner. "Introduction," in Dirks, Eley, and Ortner, (eds.), *Culture/Power/History: A Reader in Contemporary Social Theory*, Princeton, NJ: Princeton University Press, 1994.

Douglas, Mary. "Morality and Culture," *Ethics* 93:4 (July 1983).

Doyle, Michael W. *Empires*, Ithaca, NY: Cornell University Press, 1986.

Dreyfus, Laurence. "Early Music Defended against Its Devotees: A Theory of Historical Performance in the Twentieth Century," *Musical Quarterly* 69:3 (Summer 1983).

Droysen, Johann Gustav. "History and the Historical Method," in Kurt Mueller-Vollmer (ed.), *The Hermeneutics Reader*, New York: Continuum, 1997.

Dryzek, John S., Bonnie Honig, and Anne Phillips, "Introduction," in Dryzek, Honig, and Phillips (eds.), *The Oxford Handbook of Political Theory*, New York: Oxford University Press, 2006.

Duara, Prasenjit. "The Discourse of Civilization and Pan-Asianism," *Journal of World History* 12:1 (2001).

Dunn, Frederick S. "The Present Course of International Relations Research," *World Politics* 2:1 (October 1949).

Dunn, Frederick S. "The Scope of International Relations," *World Politics* 1:1 (October 1948).

Dunn, John. "The Identity of the History of Ideas," *Philosophy* 43 (1968).

Durkheim, Émile. *Montesquieu and Rousseau*, Ann Arbor: University of Michigan Press, 1970.

Dussel, Enrique. *Ethics of Liberation in the Age of Globalization and Exclusion*, translated by Eduardo Mendieta et al., Durham, NC: Duke University Press, 2013.

Eagleton, Terry. *The Ideology of the Aesthetic*, Oxford: Basil Blackwell, 1990.

Easton, David. "The Decline of Modern Political Theory," *Journal of Politics* 13:1 (February 1951).

Easton, David. "The Idea of a Political System and the Orientation of Political Research," in James Farr and Ronald Seidelman (eds.), *Discipline and History: Political Science in the United States*, Ann Arbor: University of Michigan Press, 1993.

Easton, David. "The New Revolution in Political Science," *American Political Science Review* 62:4 (December 1969).

Easton, David. "Political Science in the United States: Past and Present," in James Farr and Ronald Seidelman (eds.), *Discipline and History: Political Science in the United States*, Ann Arbor: University of Michigan Press, 1993.

Eckstein, Harry. "Political Theory and the Study of Politics: A Report of a Conference," *American Political Science Review* 50:2 (June 1956).

Eley, Geoff. *A Crooked Line: From Cultural History to the History of Society*, Ann Arbor: University of Michigan Press, 2005.

Eley, Geoff. "Is All the World a Text? From Social History to the History of Society Two Decades Later," in Terence J. McDonald (ed.), *The Historic Turn in the Human Sciences*, Ann Arbor: University of Michigan Press, 1996.

Eley, Geoff and Keith Nield. *The Future of Class in History: What's Left of the Social?*, Ann Arbor: University of Michigan Press, 2007.

Euben, Roxanne. *Enemy in the Mirror*, Princeton, NJ: Princeton University Press, 1999.

Euben, Roxanne. *Journeys to the Other Shore*, Princeton, NJ: Princeton University Press, 2006.

Fasolt, Constantine. *The Limits of History*, Chicago: University of Chicago Press, 2004.

Febvre, Lucien. *The Problem of Unbelief in the Sixteenth Century: The Religion of Rabelais*, translated by Beatrice Gottlieb, Cambridge, MA: Harvard University Press, 1982.

Fifield, Russell H. "The Introductory Course in International Relations," *American Political Science Review* 42:6 (December 1948).

Finlayson, James Gordon. *Habermas: A Very Short Introduction*, New York: Oxford University Press, 2005.

Finley, Moses. *Ancient History: Evidence and Models*, London: Chatto and Windus, 1985.

Finley, Moses. "Myth, Memory, and History," *History and Theory* 4:3 (1965).

Foucault, Michel. *The Archaeology of Knowledge*, translated by A. M. Sheridan Smith, New York: Harper Colophon Books, 1976.

Foucault, Michel. *The History of Sexuality: An Introduction*, translated by Robert Hurley, New York: Pelican, 1981.

Foucault, Michel. "On the Ways of Writing History," in James Faubion (ed.), *Michel Foucault: Aesthetics, Method, and Epistemology*, translated by Robert Hurley and others, New York: Penguin, 1998.

Foucault, Michel. *The Order of Things: An Archaeology of the Human Sciences*, New York: Vintage Books, 1994.

Foucault, Michel. "Return to History," in James Faubion (ed.), *Michel Foucault: Aesthetics, Method, and Epistemology*, translated by Robert Hurley and others, New York: Penguin, 1998.

Foucault, Michel. *Society Must Be Defended: Lectures at the College de France, 1975–1976*, translated by David Macey, New York: Picador, 2003.

Foucault, Michel. "Truth and Power," in Colin Gordon (ed.) *Power/Knowledge: Selected Interviews and Other Writings, 1972–1997*, New York: Pantheon, 1980.

Foucault, Michel. "What Is Enlightenment?," in Paul Rabinow (ed.), *The Foucault Reader*, New York: Penguin, 1986.

Fraser, Nancy. *Unruly Practices: Power, Discourse, and Gender in Contemporary Social Theory*, Minneapolis: University of Minnesota Press, 1989.

Freeman, Michael and David Robertson. "Introduction: The Rebirth of a Discipline," in Freeman and Robertson (eds.), *The Frontiers of Political Theory*, New York: Harvester Press, 1980.

Furet, François. "The French Revolution Revisited," in Gary Kates (ed.), *The French Revolution: Recent Debates and New Controversies*, 2nd ed., New York: Routledge, 2006.

Furet, François. *Interpreting the French Revolution*, translated by Elborg Foster, Cambridge: Cambridge University Press, 1981.

Furet, François. "Quantitative methods in history," in Jacques Le Goff and Pierre Nora (eds.), *Constructing the Past: Essays in Historical Methodology*, Cambridge: Cambridge University Press, 1985.

Gaukroger, Stephen. *The Collapse of Mechanism and the Rise of Sensibility*, New York: Oxford University Press, 2010.

Gaukroger, Stephen. "The Ten Modes of Aenesidemus and the Myth of Ancient Scepticism," *British Journal for the History of Philosophy* 3 (1995).

Geertz, Clifford. *Available Light: Anthropological Reflections on Philosophical Topics*, Princeton University Press, 2000.

Geertz, Clifford. *Local Knowledge*, London: Fontana Press, 1993.

Geyer, Michael and Charles Bright. "World History in a Global Age," in Bruce Mazlish and Akira Iriye (eds.), *The Global History Reader*, New York: Routledge, 2005.

Godrej, Farah. *Cosmopolitan Political Thought: Method, Practice, Discipline*, New York: Oxford University Press, 2011.

Godrej, Farah. "Towards a Cosmopolitan Political Thought: The Hermeneutics of Interpreting the Other," *Polity* 41:2 (2009).

Goehr, Lydia. *The Imaginary Museum of Musical Works: An Essay in the Philosophy of Music*, New York: Oxford University Press, 2007 (new edition).

Goehr, Lydia. "Writing Music History," *History and Theory* 31:2 (May 1992).

Goldstein, Doris. "History at Oxford and Cambridge," in Georg Iggers and James Powell (eds.), *Leopold von Ranke and the Shaping of the Historical Discipline*, Syracuse, NY: Syracuse University Press, 1990.

Goldstein, Eric. *Winning the Peace: British Diplomatic Strategy, Peace Planning, and the Paris Peace Conference, 1916–1920*, Oxford: Clarendon Press, 1991.

Golinski, Jan. "Is it Time to Forget Science?: Reflections on Singular Science and its History," *Osiris* 27:1 (2012).

Gong, Gerrit W. *The Standard of 'Civilization' in International Society*, Oxford: Clarendon Press, 1984.

Goodin, Robert E. (ed.). *The Oxford Handbook of Political Science*, New York: Oxford University Press, 2009.

Goodin, Robert E. and H. D. Klingemann. "Political Science: The Discipline," in Goodin and Klingemann (eds.), *A New Handbook of Political Science*, New York: Oxford University Press, 1996.

Gopal, Sarvapelli (ed.). *Anatomy of Confrontation: The Babri-Masjid—Ram Janmabhumi Issue*, New York: Penguin, 1991.

Gopal, Sarvapelli, Romila Thapar, et al. "The Political Abuse of History: Babri Masjid-Rama Janmabhumi Dispute," *South Asia Bulletin* 9:2 (1989).

Gossman, Lionel. *Between History and Literature*, Cambridge, MA: Harvard University Press, 1990.

Gray, John. *Endgames*, Cambridge: Polity Press, 1997.

Gray, John. *Enlightenment's Wake: Politics and Culture at the Close of the Modern Age*, New York: Routledge, 2007.

Gray, John. *Post-Liberalism: Studies in Political Thought*, New York: Routledge, 1996.

Gray, John. "Where Pluralists and Liberal Part Company," *International Journal of Philosophical Studies* 6:1 (1998).

Green, Andy. *Education and State Formation: The Rise of Educational Systems in England, France and the USA*, New York: Macmillan, 1990.

Grovogui, Siba. *Sovereigns, Quasi Sovereigns, and Africans: Race and Self-Determination in International Law*, Minneapolis: Minnesota University Press, 1996.

Guha-Thakurta, Tapati. *Monuments, Objects, Histories: Institutions of Art in Colonial and Postcolonial India*, New York: Columbia University Press, 2004.

Guignon, Charles B. *Heidegger and the Problem of Knowledge*, Indianapolis: Hackett, 1983.

Guilhot, Nicolas. "Introduction: One Discipline, Many Histories," in Nicolas Guilhot (ed.), *The Invention of IR Theory: Realism, the Rockefeller Foundation, and the 1954 Conference on Theory*, New York: Columbia University Press, 2011.

Guilhot, Nicolas. "The Realist Gambit: Postwar American Political Science and the Birth of IR Theory," *International Political Sociology* 2:4 (December 2008).

Gunnell, John. "Political Theory: The Evolution of a Sub-field," in Ada W. Finifter (ed.), *Political Science: The State of the Discipline*, New York: APSA, 1983.

Gunnell, John. *Political Theory: Tradition and Interpretation*, Cambridge, MA: Winthrop Publishers, 1979.

Gurian, Waldemar. "On the Study of International Relations," *Review of Politics* 8:3 (July 1946).

Habermas, Jürgen. *Communication and the Evolution of Society*, translated by Thomas McCarthy, London: Heinemann, 1979.

Habermas, Jürgen. *Between Naturalism and Religion: Philosophical Essays*, translated by Ciaran Cronin, Cambridge: Polity Press, 2008.

Habermas, Jürgen. *Religion and Rationality: Essays on Reason, God and Modernity*, Cambridge: Polity Press, 2002.

Habermas, Jürgen. "Discourse, Ethics, Law and *Sittlichkeit*," interview by T. Huiid Nielsen, January 1990, in Peter Dews (ed.), *Autonomy and Solidarity: Interviews with Jürgen Habermas*, rev. ed., London: Verso, 1992.

Habermas, Jürgen. *The Inclusion of the Other: Studies in Political Theory*, translated by Ciaran Cronin and Pablo De Grieff, Cambridge, MA: MIT Press, 1998.

Habermas, Jürgen. *Justice and Application: Remarks on Discourse Ethics*, translated by Ciaran Cronin, Cambridge: Polity Press, 1993.

Habermas, Jürgen. *Moral Consciousness and Communicative Action*, translated by Christian Lenhardt and Shierry Weber Nicholsen, Cambridge: Polity Press, 1990.

Habermas, Jürgen. *The Philosophical Discourse of Modernity*, translated by Frederick Lawrence, Cambridge: Polity Press, 1987.

Habermas, Jürgen. *The Postnational Constellation: Political Essays*, translated by Max Pensky, Cambridge: Polity Press, 2001.

Habermas, Jürgen. "Questions and Counterquestions," in Richard Bernstein (ed.), *Habermas and Modernity*, Cambridge: Polity Press, 1985.

Habermas, Jürgen. "Reply to my Critics," in Craig Calhoun, Eduardo Mendieta, and Jonathan VanAntwerpen (eds.), *Habermas and Religion*, Cambridge: Polity Press, 2013.

Habermas, Jürgen. *The Structural Transformation of the Bourgeois Public Sphere*, translated by Thomas Burger and Frederick Lawrence, Cambridge: Polity Press, 1989.

Habermas, Jürgen. *Theory and Practice*, translated by John Viertel, London: Heinemann, 1974.

Habermas, Jürgen. *The Theory of Communicative Action*, vol 1, translated by Thomas McCarthy, Boston: Beacon Press, 1984.

Habermas, Jürgen. *Theory of Communicative Action*, vol. 2, translated by Thomas McCarthy, Cambridge: Polity Press, 1987.

Hacking, Ian. *Representing and Intervening*, Cambridge: Cambridge University Press, 1983.

Hacking, Ian. *The Social Construction of What?*, Cambridge, MA: Harvard University Press, 1999.

Halbwachs, Maurice. *The Collective Memory*, translated by F. J. Ditter and V. Y. Ditter, New York: Harper Colophon, 1980.

Hall, Stuart. "When Was 'the Post-colonial'? Thinking at the Limit," in Iain Chambers and Lidia Curti (eds.), *The Post-colonial Question*, New York: Routledge, 1996.

Haraway, Donna. *Simians, Cyborgs, and Women: The Reinvention of Nature*, New York: Routledge, 1991.

Haskell, Harry. *The Early Music Revival: A History*, New York: Dover Publications, 1996.

Henderson, Errol A. "Hidden in Plain Sight: Racism in International Relations Theory," *Cambridge Review of International Affairs* 26:1 (2013).

Herbert, James D. "Visual Culture / Visual Studies," in Robert S. Nelson and Richard Shiff (eds.), *Critical Terms for Art History*, 2nd ed., Chicago: University of Chicago Press, 2003.

Hirschkind, Charles. *The Ethical Soundscape: Cassette Sermons and Islamic Counterpublics*, New York: Columbia University Press, 2006.

Hobbes, Thomas. *Leviathan*, edited by C. B. Macpherson, New York: Penguin, 1985.

Hobsbawm, Eric. *On History*, London: Abacus, 1998.

Hobson, John M. *The Eurocentric Conception of World Politics: Western International Theory, 1760–2010*, New York: Cambridge University Press, 2012.

Hoffman, Stanley H. "International Relations: The Long Road to Theory," *World Politics* 11:3 (April 1959).

Holbraad, Martin. *Truth in Motion: The Recursive Anthropology of Cuban Divination*, Chicago: University of Chicago Press, 2012.

Holbraad, Martin and Morton Axel Pedersen. *The Ontological Turn: An Anthropological Exposition*, New York: Cambridge University Press, 2017.

Horigan, Stephen. *Nature and Culture in Western Discourses*, New York: Routledge, 1988.

Horton, John. "Rawls, Public Reason and the Limits of Liberal Justification," *Contemporary Political Theory* 2 (2003).

Howland, Douglas and Luise S. White (eds.). *The State of Sovereignty: Territories, Laws, Populations*, Bloomington: Indiana University Press, 2009.

Hulle, Inge van. "British Protection, Extraterritoriality and the Protectorates in West Africa," in Lauren Benton, Adam Clulow, and Bain Atwood (eds.), *Protection and Empire: A Global History*, New York: Cambridge University Press, 2018.

Humboldt, Wilhelm von. "On the Historian's Task," *History and Theory* 6:1 (1967).

Hunt, Lynn (ed.). *The New Cultural History*, Berkeley: University of California Press, 1989.

Hunt, Lynn. *Writing History in the Global Era*, New York: Norton, 2014.

Ilaiah, Kancha. "Productive Labour, Consciousness and History: The Dalitbahujan Alternative," in Shahid Amin and Dipesh Chakrabarty (eds.), *Subaltern Studies IX*, Delhi: Oxford University Press, 1996.

Ingold, Tim. *The Perception of the Environment: Essays in Livelihood, Dwelling and Skill*, New York: Routledge, 2000.

Jenco, Leigh. *Changing Referents: Learning across Space and Time in China and the West*, New York: Oxford University Press, 2015.

Jenco, Leigh. "'What Does Heaven Ever Say?' A Methods-Centered Approach to Cross-Cultural Engagement," *American Political Science Review* 101:4 (2007).

Jenco, Leigh, Murad Idris, and Megan Thomas. "Comparison, Connectivity, and Disconnection," in Jenco, Idris and Thomas (eds.), *The Oxford Handbook of Comparative Political Theory*, New York: Oxford University Press, 2020.

Jones, Eric. *The European Miracle*, 3rd ed., New York: Cambridge University Press, 2003.

Joyce, Patrick. *Democratic Subjects: The Self and the Social in Nineteenth Century England*, New York: Cambridge University Press, 1994.

Joyce, Patrick. "The End of Social History?," *Social History* 20:1 (1995).

Joyce, Patrick. *Visions of the People: Industrial England and the Question of Class, 1848–1914*, New York: Cambridge University Press, 1991.

Kahler, Miles. "Inventing International Relations: International Relations Theory after 1945," in Michael W. Doyle and John Ikenberry (eds.), *New Thinking in International Relations Theory*, Boulder, CO: Westview Press, 1998.

Kant, Immanuel. "An Answer to the Question, 'What Is Enlightenment?,'" in James Schmidt (ed.), *What Is Enlightenment? Eighteenth-Century Answers and Twentieth-Century Questions*, Berkeley: University of California Press, 1996.

Kant, Immanuel. *Critique of Pure Reason*, translated by J. M. D. Meiklejohn, London: Everyman's Library, 1991.

Kateb, George. "The Condition of Political Theory," *American Behavioral Scientist* 21:1 (September–October 1977).

Katznelson, Ira and Helen Milner. "American Political Science: The Discipline's State and the State of the Discipline," in Katznelson and Milner (eds.), *Political Science: State of the Discipline*, New York: Norton and APSA, 2002.

Kaufman-Osborn, Timothy. "Political Theory as Profession and as Subfield?," *Political Research Quarterly* 63:3 (2010).

Kaviraj, Sudipta. "In Search of Civil Society," in Sudipta Kaviraj and Sunil Khilnani (eds.), *Civil Society: History and Possibilities*, New York: Cambridge University Press, 2001.

Kayaoglu, Turan. *Legal Imperialism: Sovereignty and Extraterritoriality in Japan, the Ottoman Empire, and China*, New York: Cambridge University Press, 2010.

Keane, Webb. *Christian Moderns: Freedom and Fetish in the Mission Encounter*, Berkeley: University of California Press, 2007.

Keene, Edward. *Beyond the Anarchical Society: Grotius, Colonialism and Order in World Politics*, New York: Cambridge University Press, 2002.

Kelly, P. J. "Contextual and Non-contextual Histories of Political Thought," in Jack Hayward, Brian Barry, and Archie Brown (eds.), *The British Study of Politics in the Twentieth Century*, New York: Oxford University Press, 1999.

Kerman, John. *Contemplating Music: Challenges to Musicology*, Cambridge, MA: Harvard University Press, 1985.

Keylor, William R. *Academy and Community: The Foundations of the French Historical Profession*, Cambridge, MA: Harvard University Press, 1975.

King, Ronald and Cosmin Gabriel Marian. "Defining Political Science: A Cross-National Survey," *European Political Science* 7 (2008).

Kivy, Peter. *Authenticities: Philosophical Reflections on Musical Performance*, Ithaca, NY: Cornell University Press, 1995.

Knorr, Klaus. "Economics and International Relations: A Problem in Teaching," *Political Science Quarterly* 62:4 (December 1947).

Kolb, David. *The Critique of Pure Modernity: Hegel, Heidegger, and After*, Chicago: University of Chicago Press, 1986.

Koselleck, Reinhart. *Futures Past: On the Semantics of Historical Time*, translated by Keith Tribe, New York: Columbia University Press, 2004.

Kracauer, Siegfried. *History: The Last Things before the Last*, Oxford: Oxford University Press, 1969.

Krasner, Stephen D. "Compromising Westphalia," *International Security* 20:3 (Winter 1995–96).

Krasner, Stephen D. "Rethinking the Sovereign State Model," *Review of International Studies* 27 (2001).

Krasner, Stephen D. *Sovereignty: Organized Hypocrisy*, Princeton, NJ: Princeton University Press, 1999.

Krishna, Sankaran. "Race, Amnesia, and the Education of International Relations," in Branwen Gruffydd Jones (ed.), *Decolonizing International Relations*, Lanham, MD: Rowman and Littlefield, 2006.

Kuhn, Thomas S. "Reflections on My Critics," in Imre Lakatos and Alan Musgrave (eds.), *Criticism and the Growth of Knowledge*, Cambridge: Cambridge University Press, 1970.

Kuhn, Thomas S. *The Road Since Structure*, Chicago: University of Chicago Press, 2000.

Kuhn, Thomas S. *The Structure of Scientific Revolutions*, 2nd ed., Chicago: University of Chicago Press, 1970.

Kuhn, Thomas S. *The Road since Structure*. Chicago: University of Chicago Press, 2000.

Kukathas, Chandran and Philip Pettit. *Rawls: "A Theory of Justice" and Its Critics*, Stanford, CA: Stanford University Press, 1990.

Kuper, Adam. *The Reinvention of Primitive Society: Transformations of a Myth*, New York: Routledge, 2005.

Laclau, Ernesto and Chantal Mouffe. *Hegemony and Socialist Strategy: Towards a Radical Democratic Politics*, 2nd ed., London: Verso, 2001.

Lal, Vinay. *The History of History: Politics and Scholarship in Modern India*, New Delhi: Oxford University Press, 2003.

Landes, David. *The Unbound Prometheus*, Cambridge: Cambridge University Press, 1969.

Landes, Joan. *Women and the Public Sphere in the Age of the French Revolution*, Ithaca, NY: Cornell University Press, 1988.

Langlois, Charles-Victor and Charles Seignobos. *Introduction to the Study of History*, translated by G. G. Berry, 1898, London: Frank Cass, 1966.

Laslett, Peter. "Introduction," in Laslett (ed.), *Philosophy, Politics and Society*, 1st series, Oxford: Oxford University Press, 1956.

Latour, Bruno. *Politics of Nature: How to Bring the Sciences into Democracy*, translated by Catherine Porter, Cambridge, MA: Harvard University Press, 2004.

Latour, Bruno. "The Social as Association," in Nicholas Gane (ed.), *The Future of Social Theory*, New York: Continuum, 2004.

Latour, Bruno. *We Have Never Been Modern*, translated by Catherine Porter, Harvester Wheatsheaf, 2003.

Latour, Bruno and Steve Woolgar. *Laboratory Life: The Construction of Scientific Facts*, 1979, 2nd ed., Princeton, NJ: Princeton University Press, 1986.

Leech-Wilkinson, Daniel. *The Modern Invention of Medieval Music*, New York: Cambridge University Press, 2002.

Lévi-Strauss, Claude. *The Savage Mind*, London: Weidenfeld and Nicolson, 1972.

Levine, Joseph M. *Humanism and History: Origins of Modern English Historiography*, Ithaca, NY: Cornell University Press, 1989.

Lewis, Brian. "Social History: A New *Kind* of History," in Nancy Partner and Sarah Foot (eds.), *The Sage Handbook of Historical Theory*, Thousand Oaks, CA: Sage, 2013.

Linklater, Andrew and Hidemi Suganami. *The English School of International Relations: A Contemporary Reassessment*, New York: Cambridge University Press, 2006.

Liu, Lydia H. *Translingual Practice: Literature, National Culture, and Translated Modernity—China, 1900–1937*, Stanford, CA: Stanford University Press, 1995.

Lloyd, Christopher. *The Structures of History*, Oxford: Blackwell, 1993.

Long, David and Brian C. Schmidt. "Introduction," in Long and. Schmidt (eds.), *Imperialism and Internationalism in the Discipline of International Relations*, Albany: State University of New York Press, 2005.

Louis, Wm. Roger. "The Era of the Mandates System and the Non-European World," in Hedley Bull and Adam Watson (eds.), *The Expansion of International Society*, Oxford: Clarendon Press, 1984.

Lowenthal, David. *The Past Is a Foreign Country*, Cambridge: Cambridge University Press, 1985.

Lukes, Steven. *Essays in Social Theory*, New York: Macmillan, 1977.

Lyotard, Jean-François. *The Differend: Phrases in Dispute*, translated by Georges van den Abbeele, Minneapolis: University of Minnesota Press, 1989.

Lyotard, Jean-François. *The Postmodern Condition: A Report on Knowledge*, translated by Geoff Bennington and Brian Massumi, Minneapolis: University of Minnesota Press, 1984.

Lyotard, Jean-François and Jean-Loup Thebaud. *Just Gaming*, translated by Wlad Godzich, Minneapolis: University of Minnesota Press, 1985.

MacIntyre, Alasdair. "The Relationship of Philosophy to History: Postscript to the Second Edition of *After Virtue*," in Kenneth Baynes, James Bohman, and Thomas McCarthy (eds.), *After Philosophy: End or Transformation?*, Cambridge, MA: MIT Press, 1987.

MacIntyre, Alasdair. "Some Enlightenment Projects Reconsidered," in Richard Kearney and Mark Dooley (eds.), *Questioning Ethics: Contemporary Debates in Philosophy*, New York: Routledge, 1999.

MacIntyre, Alasdair. *Whose Justice? Which Rationality?*, Notre Dame, IN: University of Notre Dame Press, 1988.

Mahmood, Saba. *Politics of Piety: The Islamic Revival and the Feminist Subject*, Princeton, NJ: Princeton University Press, 2012.

Mamdani, Mahmood. *Citizen and Subject: Contemporary Africa and the Legacy of Late Colonialism*, Princeton, NJ: Princeton University Press, 1996.

March, Andrew. "What Is Comparative Theory?," *Review of Politics* 71 (2009).

Marx, Karl. "The Eighteenth Brumaire of Louis Bonaparte," in Marx, *Surveys from Exile*, London: Verso, 2010.

Marx, Karl. *Grundrisse*, translated by Martin Nicolaus, London: Penguin and New Left Review, 1973.

Mayall, James. *Nationalism and International Society*, Cambridge: Cambridge University Press, 1990.

Mayaram, Shail. *Against History, Against State: Counterperspectives from the Margins*, New York: Columbia University Press, 2003.

Mazowar, Mark. *No Enchanted Palace: The End of Empire and the Ideological Origins of the United Nations*, Princeton, NJ: Princeton University Press, 2009.

Mbembe, Achille. *On the Postcolony*, Berkeley: University of California Press, 2001.

McCarthy, Thomas. "Enlightenment and the Idea of Public Reason," in Richard Kearney and Mark Dooley (eds.), *Questioning Ethics: Contemporary Debates in Philosophy*, New York: Routledge, 1999.

McCarthy, Thomas. *Ideals and Illusions: On Reconstruction and Deconstruction in Contemporary Critical Theory*, Cambridge, MA: MIT Press, 1991.

McCarthy, Thomas. "Part 1: Philosophy and Critical Theory: A Reprise," in David Couzens Hoy and Thomas McCarthy (eds.), *Critical Theory*, Oxford: Blackwell, 1994.

McCarthy, Thomas. "Rationality and Relativism: Habermas's 'Overcoming' of Hermeneutics," in John B. Thompson and David Held (eds.), *Habermas: Critical Debates*, New York: Macmillan Press, 1982.

McCarthy, Thomas. "Reflections on Rationalization in *The Theory of Communicative Action*," in Richard Bernstein (ed.), *Habermas and Modernity*, Cambridge: Polity Press, 1985.

McNeill, William H. "The Changing Shape of World History," *History and Theory* 34:2 (May 1995).

Meek, Ronald. *Social Science and the Ignoble Savage*, Cambridge: Cambridge University Press, 1976.

Meyer, Leonard B. *The Spheres of Music: A Gathering of Essays*, Chicago: University of Chicago Press, 2000.

Mignolo, Walter. *The Darker Side of the Renaissance*, 2nd ed., Ann Arbor: University of Michigan Press, 2003.

Mill, John Stuart. "Nature," in *Three Essays on Religion: Nature, The Utility of Religion and Theism*, London: Longmans, Green, Reader, and Dyer, 1874.

Miller, David. "The Resurgence of Political Theory," *Political Studies* 38 (1990).

Mitchell, Timothy. *Rule of Experts: Egypt, Techno-Politics, Modernity*, Berkeley: University of California Press, 2002.

Mol, Annemarie. *The Body Multiple: Ontology in Medical Practice*, Durham, NC: Duke University Press, 2002.

Mongia, Radhika. *Indian Migration and Empire: A Colonial Genealogy of the Modern State*, Durham, NC: Duke University Press, 2018.

Monroe, Kristen et al. "The Nature of Contemporary Political Science: A Roundtable Discussion," *PS: Political Science and Politics* 23:1 (March 1990).

Morefield, Jeanne. *Covenants without Swords: Idealist Liberalism and the Spirit of Empire*, Princeton, NJ: Princeton University Press, 2005.

Morgan, Robert P. "Tradition, Anxiety and the Musical Scene," in Nicholas Kenyon (ed.), *Authenticity and Early Music*, Oxford: Oxford University Press, 1988.

Morgenthau, Hans. "Reflections on the State of Political Science," *Review of Politics* 17:4 (October 1955).

Moyn, Samuel. *The Last Utopia: Human Rights in History*, Cambridge, MA: Belknap Press of Harvard University Press, 2010.

Murphy, Alexander. "The Sovereign State System as Political Territorial Ideal: Historical and Contemporary Considerations," in Thomas J. Biersteker and Cynthia Weber (eds.), *State Sovereignty as Social Construct*, New York: Cambridge University Press, 1996.

Nadel, George. "Philosophy of History before Historicism," *History and Theory* 3:6 (1964).

Nandy, Ashis. "History's Forgotten Doubles," *History and Theory* 34:2 (May 1995).

Narayan, Badri. *Women Heroes and Dalit Assertion in North India: Culture, Identity and Politics*, Thousand Oaks, CA: Sage, 2006.

Nietzsche, Friedrich. *Beyond Good and Evil*, edited by Walter Kaufmann, New York: Vintage Books, 1989.

Nietzsche, Friedrich. *The Will to Power*, translated by Walter Kaufman and R. J. Hollingdale, New York: Vintage Books, 1968.

Nigam, Sanjay. "Disciplining and Policing the 'Criminals by Birth," Parts 1 and 2, *Indian Economic and Social History Review* 27:2 and 27:3 (1990).

Nora, Pierre. "Between Memory and History: *Le Lieux de Memoire*," *Representations* 26 (Spring 1989).

Novick, Peter. *That Noble Dream: The "Objectivity Question" and the American Historical Profession*, Cambridge: Cambridge University Press, 1988.

Oakeshott, Michael. "The Activity of Being an Historian," in *Rationalism in Politics and Other Essays*, London: Methuen, 1977.

Oakeshott, Michael. *On History and Other Essays*, Indianapolis: Liberty Fund, 1999.

Orsi, Robert A. *History and Presence*, Cambridge, MA: Belknap Press of Harvard University Press, 2016.

Osiander, Andreas. "Sovereignty, International Relations, and the Westphalian Myth," *International Organization* 55:2 (2001).

Pandey, Gyanendra. "Modes of History Writing: New Hindu History of India," *Economic and Political Weekly* 29:25 (June 18, 1994).

Panikkar, K. N. "A Historical Overview," in Sarvapelli Gopal (ed.), *Anatomy of Confrontation: The Babri-Masjid–Ram Janmabhumi Issue*, New York: Penguin, 1991.

Pant, Rashmi. "The Cognitive Status of Caste in Colonial Ethnography: A Review of Some Literature on the North West Provinces and Oudh," *Indian Economic and Social History Review* 24:2, 1987.

Parekh, Bhikhu. "The Poverty of Indian Political Theory," *History of Political Thought* 13:3 (Autumn 1992).

Parel, Anthony J. "The Comparative Study of Political Philosophy," in Anthony Parel and Ronald Keith (eds.), *Comparative Political Philosophy: Studies under the Upas Tree*, New Delhi: Sage, 1992.

Philpott, Daniel. *Revolutions in Sovereignty: How Ideas Shaped Modern International Relations*, Princeton, NJ: Princeton University Press, 2001.

Philpott, Daniel. "Westphalia, Authority, and International Society," *Political Studies* 47 (1999).

Pickering, Andrew. *The Mangle of Practice: Time, Agency, and Science*, Chicago: University of Chicago Press, 1995.

Pinker, Steven. *Enlightenment Now: The Case for Reason, Science, Humanism and Progress*, London: Allen Lane, 2018.

Pippin, Robert. *Idealism as Modernism: Hegelian Variations*, New York: Cambridge University Press, 1996.

Pitts, Jennifer. "The Global in Enlightenment Historical Thought," in Prasenjit Duara, Viren Murthy, and Andrew Sartori (eds.), *A Companion to Global Historical Thought*, Malden, MA: John Wiley and Sons, 2014.

Plamenatz, John. *Man and Society*, vol. 3: *Hegel, Marx and Engels, and the Idea of Progress*, 2nd ed., London: Longman, 1992.

Pocock, John G. A. *Politics, Language and Time: Essays on Political Thought and History*, Chicago: University of Chicago Press, 1989.

Podro, Michael. *The Critical Historians of Art*, New Haven: Yale University Press, 1982.

Pollock, Sheldon. *The Language of the Gods in the World of Men: Sanskrit, Culture, and Power in Premodern India*, Berkeley: University of California Press, 2006.

Poovey, Mary. "The Liberal Civil Subject and the Social," *Public Culture* 14:1 (Winter 2002).

Poovey, Mary. *Making a Social Body: British Cultural Formation, 1830–1864*, 2nd ed., Chicago: University of Chicago Press, 1995.

Quijano, Anibal. "Coloniality and Modernity/Rationality," in Walter Mignolo and Arturo Escobar (eds.), *Globalization and the Decolonial Option*, New York: Routledge, 2010.

Quirk, Joel and Darshan Vigneswaran. "The Construction of an Edifice: The Story of a First Great Debate," *Review of International Studies* 31 (2005).

Rabinow, Paul. *Essays on the Anthropology of Reason*, Princeton, NJ: Princeton University Press, 1996.

Rai, Lajpat. *The Problem of National Education in India*, London: Allen and Unwin, 1920.

Rancière, Jacques. *The Names of History*, translated by Hassan Melehy, Minneapolis: University of Minnesota Press, 1994.

Rancière, Jacques. "Rethinking Modernity," *Diacritics* 42:3 (2014).

Rao, Velcheru Narayana, David Shulman, and Sanjay Subrahmanyam. *Textures of Time: Writing History in South India, 1600–1800*, New Delhi: Permanent Black, 2001.

Rawls, John. "Justice as Fairness: Political Not Metaphysical," *Philosophy and Public Affairs* 14:3 (Summer 1985).

Rawls, John. "The Law of Peoples," in Stephen Shute and S. L. Hurley (eds.), *On Human Rights: The Oxford Amnesty Lectures*, New York: Basic Books, 1993.

Rawls, John. *The Law of Peoples*, Cambridge, MA: Harvard University Press, 1999.

Rawls, John. *Political Liberalism*, Columbia University Press, 1996.

Rawls, John. *A Theory of Justice*, Oxford: Oxford University Press, 1972.

Raz, Joseph. "Facing Diversity: The Case of Epistemic Abstinence," *Philosophy and Public Affairs* 19:1 (January 1990).

Rheinberger, Hans-Jorg. *On Historicizing Epistemology: An Essay*, translated by David Fernbach, Stanford, CA: Stanford University Press, 2010.

Ricouer, Paul. *History and Truth*, Evanston, IL: Northwestern University Press, 1965.

Riley, Denise. *"Am I That Name"? Feminism and the Category of "Women" in History*, New York: Macmillan, 1988.

Rorty, Richard. *Philosophy and Social Hope*, New York: Penguin, 1999.

Rorty, Richard. *Objectivity, Relativism and Truth*, Cambridge: Cambridge University Press, 1991.

Rorty, Richard. *Philosophy and the Mirror of Nature*, Princeton, NJ: Princeton University Press, 1979.

Rose, Nikolas. "Governing the Social," in Nicholas Gane (ed.), *The Future of Social Theory*, New York: Continuum, 2004.

Rose, Nikolas. "Towards a Critical Sociology of Freedom," in Patrick Joyce (ed.), *Class*, New York: Oxford University Press, 1995.

Rudolph, Susanne Hoeber. "The Imperialism of Categories: Situating Knowledge in a Globalizing World," *Perspectives on Politics* 3:1 (March 2005).

Ruggie, John. "Territoriality and Beyond: Problematizing Modernity in International Relations," *International Organization* 47:1 (Winter 1993).

Sabine, George H. *A History of Political Theory*, New York: Holt, Reinhart and Winston, 1937.

Sabine, George H. "What Is a Political Theory?," *Journal of Politics* 1:1 (February 1939).

Sahlins, Marshall. *How "Natives" Think: About Captain Cook, for Example*, Chicago: University of Chicago Press, 1995.

Saikia, Yasmin. *Assam and India: Fragmented Memories, Cultural Identity, and the Tai-Ahom Struggle*, New Delhi: Permanent Black, 2005.

Santos, Boaventura de Sousa. *The End of the Cognitive Empire: The Coming of Age of Epistemologies of the South*, Durham, NC: Duke University Press, 2018.

Santos, Boaventura de Sousa. *Epistemologies of the South: Justice against Epistemicide*, New York: Paradigm Publishers, 2014.

Santos, Boaventura de Sousa. "Human Rights as Emancipatory Script? Cultural and Political Conditions," in Boaventura de Sousa Santos (ed.), *Another Knowledge is Possible*, London: Verso, 2007.

Santos, Boaventura de Sousa and Maria Meneses. "Preface" to Santos and Meneses (eds.), *Knowledges Born in the Struggle: Constructing the Epistemologies of the Global South*, New York: Routledge, 2020.

Sarkar, Sumit. *Writing Social History*, New Delhi: Oxford University Press, 1997.

Sartori, Andrew. *Bengal in Global Concept History: Culturalism in the Age of Capital*, Chicago: University of Chicago Press, 2008.

Savransky, Martin. *Around the Day in Eighty Worlds*, Durham, NC: Duke University Press (forthcoming).

Schatzki, Theodore, Karin Knorr Cetina, and Eike von Savigny (eds.). *The Practice Turn in Contemporary Theory*, New York: Routledge, 2001.

Schaffer, Simon, Lissa Roberts, Kapil Raj, and James Delbourgo (eds.). *The Brokered World: Go-Betweens and Global Intelligence, 1770–1820*, Sagamore Beach, MA: Science History Publications, 2009.

Schiffman, Zachary Sayre. *The Birth of the Past*, Baltimore: Johns Hopkins University Press, 2011.

Schiffman, Zachary Sayre. "Historicizing History / Contextualizing Context," *New Literary History* 42:3 (Summer 2011).

Schmidt, Brian C. *The Political Discourse of Anarchy: A Disciplinary History of IR*, Albany: State University of New York Press, 1997.

Schneider, David M. *A Critique of the Study of Kinship*, Ann Arbor: University of Michigan Press, 1984.

Scott, David. *Conscripts of Modernity: The Tragedy of Colonial Enlightenment*, Durham, NC: Duke University Press, 2004.

Scott, Joan W. *Gender and the Politics of History*, rev. ed., New York: Columbia University Press, 1999.

Seth, Sanjay. "Comparative Political Theory: A Postcolonial Critique," in Leigh Jenco, Murad Idris, and Megan Thomas (eds.), *The Oxford Handbook of Comparative Political Theory*, New York: Oxford University Press, 2019.

Seth, Sanjay. "Liberalism and the Politics of (Multi)culture: Or, Plurality Is Not Difference," *Postcolonial Studies* 4:1 (2001).

Seth, Sanjay. "Nationalism, Modernity and the 'Woman Question' in India and China," *Journal of Asian Studies* 72:2 (May 2013).

Seth, Sanjay. "'Once Was Blind but Now Can See': Modernity and the Social Sciences," *International Political Sociology* 7:2 (June 2013).

Seth, Sanjay. "A Postcolonial World?," in Greg Fry and Jacinta O'Hagan (eds.), *Contending Images of World Politics*, New York: Macmillan, 2000.

Seth, Sanjay. *Subject Lessons: The Western Education of Colonial India*, Durham, NC: Duke University Press, 2007.

Sewell, William H., Jr. "Geertz, Cultural Systems, and History: From Synchrony to Transformation," in Sherry B. Ortner (ed.), *The Fate of "Culture": Geertz and Beyond*, Berkeley: California University Press, 1999.

Sewell, William H., Jr. *Logics of History: Social Theory and Social Transformation*, Chicago: University of Chicago Press, 2005.

Sewell, William H., Jr. "Towards a Post-materialist Rhetoric for Labor History," in Leonard R. Berlanstein (ed.), *Rethinking Labor History*, Urbana: University of Illinois Press, 1993.

Sewell, William H., Jr. *Work and Revolution in France: The Language of Labor from the Old Regime to 1848*, Cambridge: Cambridge University Press, 1980.

Shapin, Steven. *The Scientific Revolution*, Chicago: University of Chicago Press, 1996.

Shryock, Andrew and Daniel Lord Smail et al., *Deep History: The Architecture of Past and Present*, Berkeley: University of California Press, 2011.

Sigelman, Lee. "Introduction to the Centennial Issue," *American Political Science Review* 100:4 (November 2006).

Singer, Brian C. J. *Montesquieu and the Discovery of the Social*, New York: Palgrave Macmillan, 2013.

Singer, Brian C. J. *Society, Theory and the French Revolution: Studies in the Revolutionary Imaginary*, New York: Palgrave Macmillan, 1986.

Skaria, Ajay. *Hybrid Histories: Forests, Frontiers and Wildness in Western India*, New Delhi: Oxford University Press, 1999.

Skinner, Quentin. "Meaning and Understanding in the History of Ideas," *History and Theory* 8 (1969).

Skinner, Quentin. "A Reply to My Critics," in James Tully (ed.), *Meaning and Context: Quentin Skinner and His Critics*, Cambridge: Polity Press, 1988.

Smail, Daniel Lord. *On Deep History and the Brain*, Berkeley: University of California Press, 2008.

Smith, Barbara Herrnstein. *Belief and Resistance: Dynamics of Contemporary Intellectual Controversy*, Cambridge, MA: Harvard University Press, 1997.

Smith, Barbara Herrnstein. *Scandalous Knowledge*, Edinburgh: Edinburgh University Press, 2005.

Smith, Leonard V. *Sovereignty at the Paris Peace Conference of 1919*, New York: Oxford University Press, 2018.

Smith, Richard S. "Rule-by-Records and Rule-by-Reports: Complementary Aspects of the British Imperial Rule of Law," *Contributions to Indian Sociology* 19:1 (new series), 1985.

Smith, Rogers M. "Still Blowing in the Wind: The American Quest for a Democratic, Scientific Political Science," *Daedalus* 126:1 (Winter 1997).

Somers, Margaret. *Genealogies of Citizenship: Markets, Statelessness, and the Right to Have Rights*, New York: Cambridge University Press, 2008.

Somers, Margaret. "Where Is Sociology after the Historic Turn? Knowledge Cultures, Narrativity, and Historical Epistemologies," in Terence J. McDonald (ed.), *The Historic Turn in the Human Sciences*, Ann Arbor: University of Michigan Press, 1996.

Somit, Albert and Joseph Tanehaus. *American Political Science: A Profile of a Discipline*, New York: Atherton Press, 1964.

Soper, Kate. *What Is Nature? Culture, Politics and the Non-Human*, Oxford: Blackwell, 1995.

Spiegel, Gabrielle M. "Memory and History: Liturgical Time and Historical Time," *History and Theory* 41 (May 2002).

Spivak, Gayatri Chakravorty. *A Critique of Postcolonial Reason: Toward a History of the Vanishing Present*, Cambridge, MA: Harvard University Press, 1999.

Stedman Jones, Gareth. *Languages of Class: Studies in English Working Class History, 1832–1982*, Cambridge: Cambridge University Press, 1983.

Stengers, Isabelle. *The Invention of Modern Science*, translated by David W. Smith, Minneapolis: University of Minnesota Press, 2000.

Stengers, Isabelle. *Thinking with Whitehead: A Free and Wild Creation of Concepts*, translated by Michael Chase, Cambridge, MA: Harvard University Press, 2011.

Stern, Philip J. *The Company-State: Corporate Sovereignty and the Early Modern Foundations of the British Empire in India*, New York: Oxford University Press, 2011.

Stocking, George W., Jr. *Victorian Anthropology*, New York: Free Press and London: Collier Macmillan, 1987.

Stoler, Ann Laura. "Degrees of Imperial Sovereignty," *Public Culture* 18:1 (2006).

Strathern, Marilyn. "1989 Debate: The Concept of Society Is Theoretically Obsolete," in Tim Ingold (ed.), *Key Debates in Anthropology*, New York: Routledge, 1996.

Strathern, Marilyn. *The Gender of the Gift*, Berkeley: University of California Press, 1988.

Strathern, Marilyn. *Property, Substance and Effect: Anthropological Essays on Persons and Things*, London: Athlone Press, 1999.

Strauss, Leo and Joseph Cropsey (eds.). *History of Political Philosophy*, Chicago: University of Chicago Press, 1987.

Subrahmanyam, Sanjay. "On World Historians in the Sixteenth Century," *Representations* 91:1 (Summer 2005).

Suzuki, Shogo. *Civilization and Empire: China and Japan's Encounter with European International Society*, New York: Routledge, 2009.

Taruskin, Richard. "The Authenticity Movement Can Become a Positivistic Purgatory, Literalistic and Dehumanizing," *Early Music* 12:1 (February 1984).

Taruskin, Richard. *The Danger of Music and Other Anti-Utopian Essays*, Berkeley: University of California Press, 2009.

Taruskin, Richard. "On Letting the Music Speak for Itself: Some Reflections on Musicology and Performance," *Journal of Musicology* 1:3 (July 1982).

Taruskin, Richard. *Text and Act: Essays on Music and Performance*, New York: Oxford University Press, 1995.

Taylor, Charles. *Hegel*, Cambridge: Cambridge University Press, 1975.

Taylor, Charles. *Philosophical Arguments*, Cambridge, MA: Harvard University Press, 1995.

Taylor, Charles. *Modern Social Imaginaries*, Durham, NC: Duke University Press, 2004.

Taylor, Charles. "Modes of Civil Society," *Public Culture* 3:1 (Fall 1990).

Taylor, Charles. "Overcoming Epistemology," in Kenneth Baynes, James Bohman, and Thomas McCarthy (eds.), *After Philosophy: End or Transformation?*, Cambridge, MA: MIT Press, 1987.

Taylor, Charles. "Two Theories of Modernity," *Public Culture* 11:1 (1999).

Terrier, Jean. *Visions of the Social: Society as a Political Project in France, 1750–1950*, Boston: Brill, 2011.

Tesche, Benno. *The Myth of 1648: Class, Geopolitics and the Making of Modern International Relations*, London: Verso, 2003.

Thies, Cameron. "Progress, History and Identity in International Relations Theory: The Case of the Idealist-Realist Debate," *European Journal of International Relations* 8:2 (2002).

Thompson, Kenneth W. "The Study of International Politics: A Survey of Trends and Developments," *Review of Politics* 14:4 (1952).

Touraine, Alain. "Sociology without Society," *Current Sociology* 46:2 (1998).

Treitler, Leo. "History and Music," in Ralph Cohen and Michael S. Roth (eds.), *History and Histories within the Human Sciences*, Charlottesville: University Press of Virginia, 1995.

Treitler, Leo. *Music and the Historical Imagination*, Cambridge, MA: Harvard University Press, 1989.

Tylor, Edward Burnett. *Religion in Primitive Culture*, Gloucester, MA: Peter Smith, 1970.

Veyne, Paul. *Did the Greeks Believe in Their Myths?*, translated by Paula Wissing, Chicago: University of Chicago Press, 1988.

Veyne, Paul. *Writing History*, translated by M. Moore-Rinvolucri, Middletown, CT: Wesleyan University Press, 1984.

Vitalis, Robert. "Birth of a Discipline," in David Long and Brian C. Schmidt (eds.), *Imperialism and Internationalism in the Discipline of International Relations*, Albany: State University of New York Press, 2005.

Vitalis, Robert. "The Noble American Science of Imperial Relations and Its Laws of Race Development," *Comparative Studies in Society and History* 52:4 (October 2010).

Waever, Ole. "The Rise and Fall of the Inter-paradigm Debate," in Steve Smith, Ken Booth, and Marysia Zolewski (eds.), *International Theory: Positivism and Beyond*, New York: Cambridge University Press, 1996.

Waever, Ole. "The Sociology of a Not So International Discipline: American and European Developments in International Relations," *International Organization* 52:4 (Autumn 1998).

Wagner, Peter. "An Entirely New Object of Consciousness, of Volition, of Thought," in Lorraine Daston (ed.), *Biographies of Scientific Objects*, Chicago: University of Chicago Press, 2000.

Wagner, Roy. *The Invention of Culture*, Englewood Cliffs, NJ: Prentice Hall, 1975.

Walker, R. B. J. *Inside/Outside: Political Theory as International Relations*, Cambridge: Cambridge University Press, 1992.

Walker, R. B. J. "International Relations and the Concept of the Political," in Ken Booth and Steve Smith (eds.), *International Relations Theory Today*, Cambridge: Polity Press, 1995.

Wallerstein, Immanuel et al. *Open Up the Social Sciences*, Stanford, CA: Stanford University Press, 1996.

Waltz, Kenneth. *The Theory of International Politics*, Long Grove, IL: Waveland Press, 1979.

Walzer, Michael. *Thick and Thin: Moral Argument at Home and Abroad*, Notre Dame, IN: University of Notre Dame Press, 1994.

Warner, Michael. *Publics and Counterpublics*, New York: Zone Books, 2002.

Warnke, Georgia. *Gadamer: Hermeneutics, Tradition and Reason*, Cambridge: Polity Press, 1987.

Watson, Adam. "European International Society and its Expansion," in Hedley Bull and Adam Watson (eds.), *The Expansion of International Society*, Oxford: Clarendon Press, 1984.

Watson, Adam. *The Evolution of International Society*, New York: Routledge, 1992.

Watson, Adam. "Systems of States," *Review of International Studies* 16 (1990).

Weber, Max. "Objectivity in Social Science and Social Policy," in Edward Shils and Henry Finch (eds.), *The Methodology of the Social Sciences: Max Weber*, New York: Free Press, 1949.

Weber, Max. "Politics as a Vocation," in Edward Shils and Henry Finch (eds.), *The Methodology of the Social Sciences: Max Weber*, New York: Free Press, 1949.

Wendt, Alexander. "Anarchy Is What States Make of It: The Social Construction of Power Politics," *International Politics* 46:2 (Spring 1992).

White, Hayden. *Tropics of Discourse: Essays in Cultural Criticism*, Baltimore: Johns Hopkins University Press, 1978.

White, Hayden. *Metahistory*, Baltimore: Johns Hopkins University Press, 1973.

White, Hayden. *The Practical Past*, Evanston, IL: Northwestern University Press, 2014.

White, Hayden. "The Westernization of World History," in Jörn Rüsen (ed.), *Western Historical Thinking*, New York: Berghahn Books, 2002.

White, Stephen. "Introduction: Pluralism, Platitudes, and Paradoxes: Fifty Years of Western Political Thought," *Political Theory* 30:4 (August 2002).

Wight, Martin. "Why Is There No International Theory?," in Herbert Butterfield and Martin Wight (eds.), *Diplomatic Investigations*, Cambridge, MA: Harvard University Press, 1968.

Wilder, Gary. *Freedom Time: Négritude, Decolonization, and the Future of the World*, Durham, NC: Duke University Press, 2015.

Wilson, Peter. "The Myth of the 'First Great Debate'," *Review of International Studies* 24:5 (1998).

Winch, Peter. *The Idea of a Social Science and its Relation to Philosophy*, London: Routledge and Kegan Paul, 1958.

Winichakul, Thongchai. *Siam Mapped: A History of the Geo-Body of a Nation*, Honolulu: University of Hawai'i Press, 1994.

Wittrock, B., J. Heilbron, and L. Magnusson. "The Rise of the Social Sciences and the Formation of Modernity," in Wittrock, Heilbron, and Magnusson (eds.), *The Rise of the Social Sciences and the Formation of Modernity*, Dordrecht: Kluwer, 1998.

Wolf, Eric R. "Inventing Society," *American Ethnologist* 15:4 (November 1988).

Wolff, Robert Paul. *Understanding Rawls: A Reconstruction and Critique of "A Theory of Justice"*, Princeton, NJ: Princeton University Press, 1977.

Wolin, Sheldon. *Politics and Vision*, Boston: Little, Brown, 1960.

Wolin, Sheldon. *Presence of the Past*, Baltimore: Johns Hopkins University Press, 1989.

Woodward, E. L. *The Study of International Relations at a University, an Inaugural Lecture at Oxford on 17 February 1945*, Oxford: Clarendon Press, 1945.

Woolgar, Steve. *Science: The Very Idea*, London: Ellis Horwood and Tavistock Publications, 1988.

Wright, Quincy. *Mandates under the League of Nations*, Chicago: University of Chicago Press, 1930.

Yack, Bernard. "The Significance of Isaiah Berlin's Counter-Enlightenment," *European Journal of Political Theory* 12:1 (2013).

Yerushalmi, Yosef Hayim. *Zakhor: Jewish History and Jewish Memory*, 2nd ed., Seattle: University of Washington Press, 1996.

Zastuopil, Lynn and Martin Moir (eds.). *The Great Indian Education Debate: Documents Relating to the Orientalist-Anglicist Controversy, 1781–1843*, Richmond: Curzon, 1999.

Index

For the benefit of digital users, indexed terms that span two pages (e.g., 52–53) may, on occasion, appear on only one of those pages.

4'33" (Cage), 100

Ackerman, Bruce, 189–90
Afghanistan War (2001-), 170–71
Allen, Amy, 54–55, 75
Allison, Henry, 53–54
Almond, Gabriel, 145–46, 178–80
Althusser, Louis, 89–90
American Political Science
    Association, 145–47
anachronism
    history of art and, 101–2
    history as academic discipline
        and, 17, 88, 119–26, 130, 214
    history of music and, 100–1
    history of non-Western societies
        and, 132
    history of science and, 99–100
    international relations as academic
        discipline and, 148–49, 167
    music performance and, 126–30
Anderson, Benedict, 134
animism, 42, 69–70
Annales school of history, 106–8, 111
anthropology
    animism and, 42
    epistemological privileging of Western
        knowledge in, 43–44
    etic knowledge and, 132–33
    functionalism and, 42
    nature and culture as concepts in, 41,
        44–46, 207–8
    ontology and, 47–49
    perspectivism and, 47–49
    social constructivism
        and, 43–44
    society as a concept in, 40, 45–46

structuralism and, 42, 44–45
    translation and, 132–33, 135–36
anticolonial nationalism, 10–12, 75,
    81–82, 169–73
Apel, Karl-Otto
    criticisms regarding teleology of
        Habermas by, 75
    discourse ethics and, 56–60,
        61–62, 68–69
    on the historical situatedness of
        ethics, 55–56
    on Rawls, 66–67
    universalist notions of reason defended
        by, 55, 77
Arendt, Hannah, 195–96
Aristotle, 21–22, 24
Armitage, David, 160–61, 166–67
Aron, Raymond, 150–51
art
    art history and, 96–97, 100–4, 132
    historical context shaping
        the composition of, 96–97,
        102–3, 182–83
    images contrasted with, 101–2
    ontology of, 100, 101–2
    simultaneously past and present nature
        of, 96, 103–4
    transhistorical value of, 96–97, 102–3,
        132, 175–76, 182–83
    universalist assumptions
        regarding, 101–2
    visual culture contrasted with, 102–3
    work-concept as governing principle in
        study of, 101–2
Asad, Talal, 217–18
Ashley, Richard, 151–52
Auerbach, Erich, 105, 115–16

Babri Masjid (mosque in Ayodhya, India), 138–39, 141, 142, 143, 212–13
Babur (Mughal emperor), 138–40
Bach, Johann Sebastian, 101, 129–30
Bacon, Francis, 22–23
Baker, Keith Michael, 1–2, 39–40
Barkawi, Tarak, 160, 167
Barnes, Barry, 30–31
Barry, Brian, 66–67, 177
Bartolus of Sassoferrato, 121–22
Bell, Daniel, 195–96
Bellah, Robert, 195–96
Belting, Hans, 96, 101–4
Benton, Lauren, 161, 166–67
Berlin, Isaiah, 176–77, 188–91
Bhambra, Gurminder, 9–10, 11n27
Bharatiya Janata Party (India), 141
Bhargava, Rajeev, 191–92
Black, Antony, 193
Bloch, Marc, 105–6
Bloor, David, 30–31, 97–99
Boxer Rebellion, 169
Boyle, Robert, 21–22
Braudel, Fernand, 108
British Empire
    China and, 158–59
    dominions of, 155–56
    East India Company and, 156
    extraterritoriality doctrine
        and, 158–59
    indentured labor and, 159–60
    India and, 130–32, 138, 156–57, 160
    paramountcy doctrine and, 156–57
    protectorates of, 156–57
    World Wars I and II and, 160
Brown, Wendy, 198–200
Bull, Hedley, 150–51, 162–64
Burckhardt, Jacob, 78–79
Butler, Judith, 2–3, 217–18
Buzan, Barry, 164

Cage, John, 100
Calhoun, Craig, 185–86
Cashinahua peoples, 118–19
Castro, Eduardo Viveiros de, 46–49, 132–33, 135–36
Certeau, Michel de, 92, 114–15, 119–21, 125–26

Chakrabarty, Dipesh, 6–7, 9–10, 119–21, 131n53, 135–36
Chatterjee, Bankimchandra, 131–32
Chatterjee, Partha, 81–82, 143, 171–73, 203–6
China, 81–82, 158–59, 169
Christian, David, 110
civil society, 184–85, 200–1, 204–6
Cobban, Alfred, 123–25
Cohen, Sande, 114
Collini, Stefan, 145–46, 187–88
colonialism. See empire
Comaroff, John and Jean, 5–6
comparative political theory (CPT), 18, 193–99
Condren, Conal, 12
Conring, Hermann, 121–22
Cropsey, Joseph, 176
"culture wars," 1, 15, 27–28, 208

Dahlhaus, Carl, 101
Dalit historiography, 142
Danish cartoons controversy, 217–19
Danto, Arthur, 101–2
Daston, Lorraine, 97–98, 99–100
da'wa movement (Egypt), 202–3
deep history, 109–12
Derrida, Jacques, 4–5, 115–16
Descartes, Réne, 24
Descola, Philippe, 44–45
Dewey, John, 49–50
Douglas, Mary, 197–98
Dunn, Frederick, 147–48
Dunn, John, 182–83
Durkheim, Émile, 23–24, 40

early music movement, 126–30
East India Company, 156
Easton, David, 178–80, 182–83
Egypt, 46, 133–34, 202–4
Eley, Geoff, 1–2, 37, 40–41
empire. See also British Empire
    anticolonial nationalism and, 10–12, 75, 81–82, 169–73
    extraterritoriality doctrine and, 158–59, 160–61
    international relations academic discipline, 165–68, 170–71, 214–15

mandate system after World War I and, 157–58, 160–61
nation-states and, 155–56
nonstate actors and, 156, 165–66
paramountcy doctrine and, 156–57, 162–63
protectorates and, 156–57, 162–63
sovereignty and, 156–59, 161–62, 166–67
United Nations and, 166–67
World Wars I and II and, 160
The Enlightenment
European center of, 10–11
humanity as increasing focus of history during, 104–5
introduction of society as a concept and, 39–40
Kant on, 8–9, 184–85
liberalism and, 64–65
modernity and, 8–9
natural philosophy and, 25
postmodern critiques of, 142
typologies of political systems and, 23–24
epistemological decolonization, 210–11
Euben, Roxanne, 195–97
extraterritoriality doctrine, 158–59

Fasolt, Constantine, 89–90, 114, 121–22
Febvre, Lucien, 119–20
Ferguson, Adam, 23–24
Foreign Affairs (journal), 167–68
Forst, Rainer, 53–54
Foucault, Michel, 3–5, 13–14, 107n64, 115–16, 117, 198–99, 212, 217
France, citizens and subjects of, 158–60
French revolution, historiography of, 123–26
Furet, François, 124–25

Geertz, Clifford, 105, 108–9, 172–73
Gibbon, Edward, 88
globalization, 5–6, 11–12, 116–17, 169, 217
Godrej, Farah, 193–95
Goehr, Lydia, 96–97, 100–1
Gray, John, 190–91, 197–98
Gunnell, John, 181–83

Habermas, Jürgen
anthropology and, 69–71
Axial Age and, 70–72
bourgeois public sphere and, 183–86, 201
on contradictions of universalist approaches to history, 118
criticisms regarding teleology and, 75
decentration of interpretive systems and, 70–71
on differentiation of the cognitive, moral, and aesthetic spheres, 73–76
discourse ethics and, 57–58, 68–69
on exclusion in universalistic discourses, 76–77
modern Occidental understanding of the world privileged by, 68–70, 71–77, 209
moral development of children and, 71–73
postmodernism and, 68, 75
on progress in art, 72–73
on reason and context, 52–53, 55–56, 67
on reason and transcendence, 67–69
Hacking, Ian, 32–33
Halbwachs, Maurice, 94–95
Hall, Stuart, 116–17
Hamann, Johann Georg, 25–26
Hegel, G.W.F., 67–69, 77–81, 103–4
Heidegger, Martin, 44–45, 49–50
Heilbron, Johan, 8–9
Hanslick, Eduard, 96
Herder, Johann Gottfried, 25–26, 105, 115–16
Hirschkind, Charles, 202–4, 206
history (academic discipline). *See also* social history
anachronism and, 17, 88, 119–26, 130, 214
Annales school of history and, 106–8, 111
anthropological and humanist assumptions in, 104–6, 108, 109, 111–12, 115–16, 120–21, 213–14
art history and, 96–97, 100–4, 132
cognitive emphasis of, 91–92, 113–14
collective singular humanity as a premise of, 116–19

history (academic discipline) (*cont.*)
  deep history and, 109–12
  determinism and, 115–16
  fictional forms of historicity compared
    to, 137–38
  God and the supernatural's exclusion
    from the study of, 104–5,
    119–21, 125–26
  historical memory contrasted
    with, 93–95
  history of science and, 97–100, 132
  identity formation and, 114–16
  India and, 130–36, 138, 140–42, 143–44
  instruction for life in a democratic
    society and, 113–15
  Judaism as a topic of study in,
    93–94, 119–20
  liberalism and, 142–43
  Marxist approaches to, 108, 123–26
  music history and, 96–97, 100–1, 103–4,
    126–30, 132
  natural history's exclusion from, 104–5
  nonhistorians' opinions
    regarding, 136–37
  non-Western histories and, 17,
    130–36, 214
  objectivity as an aspiration in,
    88–89, 91–92
  the past's status as dead in, 91–92, 95–
    96, 104, 116, 120–21, 213–14
  positivism and, 88–89
  prehistory and, 17, 109–11
  professionalization during nineteenth
    century of, 88–89
  public sphere and, 186–87
  The Renaissance and the origins of,
    114, 121–22
  social history and, 1–2, 36–41, 87–88,
    108–9, 208
  standard genealogy to ancient Greece
    of, 89–90
  teleology and, 88–89
  tradition contrasted with, 92, 117–19
Hobbes, Thomas, 21–22, 148–49
Hobsbawm, Eric, 36–37
Hoffman, Stanley, 150–51
Honneth, Axel, 53–54
Horton, Robin, 70–71

Humboldt, Wilhelm von, 105, 115–16
Hunt, Lynn, 38

India
  academic historical inquiry regarding,
    130–36, 138, 140–42, 143–44
  anticolonialism in, 81–82, 169
  Babri Masjid (mosque) demolition
    (1992) of, 138–41, 142, 143
  British colonialism in, 130–32, 138,
    156–57, 160
  civil society in, 204–6
  colonial censuses in, 134
  constitution (1950) in, 204–5
  contemporary political culture
    in, 203–6
  Dalit leaders and intellectuals in, 142
  Hindu Right organizations in,
    138–42, 143–44
  indentured labor in British Empire
    territories from, 159–60
  indigenous traditions of history in, 143
  myths as a form of history in, 141–42
  nationalism in, 81–82, 131–32, 135
  sectarian-produced histories in, 139–40
  Western education in, 81–82
  World War I and II and, 160
Ingold, Tim, 44–45
international relations (academic
    discipline)
  anachronism and, 167
  anarchy and, 17, 149–54, 164,
    169, 214–15
  constructivism and, 152–53
  decolonization and, 167–68
  English school of, 153, 162–64
  idealism and, 148–49, 167–68
  imperialism and, 165–68,
    170–71, 214–15
  misleading history of, 148–49
  nation-states and, 17, 152–56, 160–61,
    162–63, 167–69, 170–72, 214–15
  neoliberal institutionalism
    and, 152–53
  neorealism and, 150–51, 152–53
  origins of, 147–49, 167–68
  political theory and, 151
  realism and, 148–49

supranational organizations and, 153–54, 171
teleology in, 17, 162, 164–65
Westphalia system and, 153–55, 162–66, 214–15
Iraq War (2003-12), 170–71
Islamic political thought, 192–93, 195–97
Islamic counterpublic, 202–4

James, William, 49–50
Japan,
Meiji restoration and 81–82
extraterritoriality and, 158–59
admission to international society and, 162–63
Jews, history of, 93–94, 119–20
Joyce, Patrick, 1–2

Kant, Immanuel
aesthetics and, 103–4
categorical imperative and, 56–57, 188–89
on the Enlightenment, 8–9, 184–85
Frankfurt School and, 67
on humans' "unsocial sociability," 23–24
liberalism and, 61–62, 63
moral universalism and, 55–56, 58–59, 60
on public officials, 184–85
reading public and, 58–59
universalist notions of reason and, 68–69, 216
Kateb, George, 177
Keene, Edward, 165–67
Kivy, Peter, 126–27
Kohlberg, Lawrence, 71–72
Kolb, David, 216
Koselleck, Reinhart, 104–5, 116–17
Krasner, Stephen, 154–55
Kuhn, Thomas, 2, 28–33, 47, 55–56
Kukathas, Chandran, 66–67

Lal, Vinay, 141–42
Langlois, Charles-Victor, 113–14
Laslett, Peter, 176–77
Latour, Bruno, 2, 32–33, 34–35
League of Nations, 147–49, 157–58
Le Roy Ladurie, Emmanuel, 108

Lévi-Strauss, Claude, 89–91, 115–16
liberalism
autonomy and, 60–62, 191
discourse ethics and, 58–60
dualism of Rawls's version of, 63–65
individualism and, 60–62, 187–88, 191
pluralism and, 190–91
political theory academic discipline and, 187–92, 197–200
public sphere and, 18, 188–89
The Reformation and, 64–66, 77, 191, 209
toleration and, 64–66, 77
universalist claims on behalf of, 61–62
Little, Richard, 164
Lowenthal, David, 91–92
Lyotard, Jean-François, 15, 55–56, 118–19

Macaulay, Thomas, 88, 130–31
MacIntyre, Alasdair, 55–56, 58–59, 189–90, 195–96
Magnusson, Lars, 8–9
Mahmood, Saba, 203–4, 206
Marx, Karl, 23–24, 67, 78–79, 108
Mayall, James, 169
Mazower, Mark, 166–67
Mbembe, Achille, 5–6, 206
McCarthy, Thomas, 68–69
Meiji Restoration (Japan), 81–82
Michelet, Jules, 88
Mill, James, 135
Mill, John Stuart, 22–23, 61–62, 63–64
Mitchell, Timothy, 133–35
modernity
autonomous individualism and, 114
colonialism and, 10–11, 75
historical contingency and, 15–16
reason and, 78–79
relativism and, 18
scientific revolution and, 21–22
slavery and, 10–11
teleology in the concept of, 78
the West and, 9–12, 15–16, 52, 80
Mol, Annemarie, 33–34
Mongia, Radhika, 159–60
monism, 188–91
Montesquieu, 23–24
Morefield, Jeanne, 167–68

Morgan, Robert, 129–30
Morgenthau, Hans, 145–46,
    150–51, 178–79
Moyn, Samuel, 170–71
Murray, Gilbert, 167–68
music
    authenticity and, 126–30
    early music movement and, 126–30
    historical context shaping the
        composition and performance of,
        96–97, 129–30, 182–83
    medieval music and, 101, 126–27
    music history and, 96–97, 100–1, 103–4,
        126–30, 132
    ontology of, 100, 130
    Renaissance music and, 126–27
    simultaneously past and present nature
        of, 96, 103–4
    transhistorical value arguments
        regarding, 96–97, 132,
        175–76, 182–83
    work-concept as governing principle in
        study of, 100–1

Nandy, Ashis, 141–42
nation-states
    civil society and, 205–6
    decolonization and, 164–65, 166–67,
        169–70, 171–74
    empires and, 155–56
    Europe as initial model of, 154–55, 162–
        64, 165–66, 169, 172
    immigration and, 159–60
    international relations academic
        discipline and, 17, 152–56,
        160–61, 162–63, 167–69,
        170–72, 214–15
    self-interested character of, 153–54
    sovereignty and, 151–56, 159–61,
        165–66, 173, 214–15
    supranational organizations
        and, 153–54
    warfare and, 159–60
    Westphalia system and, 153, 154–55,
        164–66, 214–15
    World War II and, 160, 164
natural sciences
    apodictic certainty and, 25–26, 28

emergence during nineteenth century
    of category of, 99–100
ethnographic approach to the
    study of, 32
historical context shaping inquiry in,
    98, 182–83
history of science and, 97–100, 132
paradigm shifts and, 28–30
scientific revolution and, 21–22
social constructivism and, 33–34
sociology of scientific knowledge and,
    2, 30–34
transhistorical value arguments
    regarding truths in, 98–99, 132,
    175–76, 182–83
Nietzsche, Friedrich, 14–15,
    49–50, 197–98
Nora, Pierre, 94–95, 128–29, 130

Oakeshott, Michael, 89–90
Ottoman Empire, 158–59, 162–63

Parekh, Bhikhu, 191–92
perspectivism, 47–49
Pettit, Philip, 66–67
Philpott, Daniel, 164–65
Piaget, Jean, 71–72
Pickering, Andrew, 33–34
Pocock, John G., 180–81, 182–83
Podro, Michael, 96–97
political science, 145–46, 199–201, 215–
    16. See also international relations;
    political theory
political theory (academic discipline)
    comparative political theory and,
        18, 193–99
    criticisms of, 178–83, 197–200
    Egyptian politics and, 202–3
    feminism and, 198–99
    Foucaultian genealogy and, 198–99
    Frankfurt school and, 198–99
    historical context shaping,
        175–76, 181–83
    Indian politics and, 203–6
    international relations and, 151
    liberalism and, 187–92, 197–200
    public sphere and, 18, 177–78, 183–87,
        199–201

transhistorical value arguments regarding, 175–77, 180–83, 193, 200–1
Pollock, Sheldon, 5–6
Popper, Karl, 70–71
postcolonialism, 5–6, 54–55, 80
postmodernism/poststructuralism
   criticism of, 1
   The Enlightenment critiqued by, 142
   Habermas and, 68, 75
   irrationalism cited as consequence of, 142
   relativism and, 136
   social science methods criticized in, 1, 208
   universalist notions of reason critiqued in, 54–55, 80
prehistory, 17, 109–11
public sphere
   bourgeois culture and, 177–78, 183–87, 199–200, 201
   civil society and, 184–85, 200–1
   classical precedents and, 184–85
   counterpublics and, 202–3
   criticisms regarding universalizing assumptions of, 201–3
   history as academic discipline and, 186–87
   liberalism and, 18, 188–89
   normative potential of, 185–86
   political theory academic discipline and, 18, 177–78, 183–87, 199–201
   rational dialogue assumptions regarding, 177–78, 186–87, 201–3
Putnam, Hilary, 53–54

Quijano, Anibal, 210
Qutb, Sayyid, 195–97

Rabinow, Paul, 14–15
Rai, Lajpat, 81–82
Rancière, Jacques, 123–24
Ranke, Leopold von, 88–89, 91–92
Rawls, John
   historical relativism and, 55–56, 77
   on justice as fairness, 63
   liberalism and, 60–66, 191, 209
   Political Liberalism and, 60–61, 64–65

on The Reformation, 64–66, 77, 209
   on shared public life around shared conceptions of justice, 63
   A Theory of Justice and, 60–63, 65–67
   universalist concept of reason and, 53–54, 61–62, 66–67, 68–69, 77, 209
   universalist principles of justice and, 60–62, 63, 65–66
The Reformation, 64–66, 77, 191, 209
relativism
   historical situatedness of morals and, 55–56
   Kuhn on, 30
   modernity and, 18
   postmodernism viewed as a form of, 136
   sociology of scientific knowledge and, 31–32
   universalist notions of reason challenged by, 54–55, 209
The Renaissance, 114, 121–22, 126–27
Ricoeur, Paul, 105, 115–16
Rockefeller Foundation, 147–48
Rorty, Richard, 24, 49–50, 55–56, 191
Rousseau, Jean-Jacques, 61–62

Sabine, George H., 175–76
Sangh Parivar, 138–39
Santos, Boaventura de Sousa, 210–12, 218–19
Sarkar, Sumit, 140
Schneider, David, 43–44, 132–33
science. See natural sciences
Scott, Joan Wallach, 1–2
Scott, Walter, 88
Seignobos, Charles, 113–14
Sewell Jr, William, 1–2, 39–40
Skinner, Quentin, 180–81, 182–83
Smail, Daniel, 110
Smith, Adam, 23–24
Smith, Barbara Herrnstein, 59–60
Smuts, Jan, 166–67
social history, 1–2, 36–41, 87–88, 108–9, 208
sociology of scientific knowledge (SSK), 2, 30–34
Somers, Margaret, 27
Spiegel, Gabrielle, 92

Spivak, Gayatri Chakravorty, 5–6
Stedman-Jones, Gareth, 1–2, 37–38
Stern, Philip, 156
Strathern, Marilyn, 45–46, 48–49
Strauss, Leo, 176
suicide bombing, 217–19

Taruskin, Richard, 127–29, 130
Taylor, Charles, 49–50, 79, 184–85
Thapar, Romila, 141
Thompson, Kenneth, 147–48
Touraine, Alain, 40
tradition
    early music movement and, 128–30
    history as academic discipline
        contrasted with, 92, 117–19
    identity formation and, 114–15, 116
    myths and, 118
    the past's status as a living concept in,
        92, 113–14, 116
Treitler, Leo, 101
Tylor, Edward Burnett, 42

United Nations, 166–67, 171
United States, 158–59, 162–63, 170–71

Veyne, Paul, 89–91, 106–8
Vico, Giambattista, 23–24, 25–26,
    105, 115–16
Vishwa Hindu Parishad, 140

Wallerstein, Immanuel, 6–7

Waltz, Kenneth, 150–51, 152–53
Walzer, Michael, 55–56, 58–59
Warhol, Andy, 100
Warner, Michael, 186–87, 201–3
Watson, Adam, 162–64
Weber, Max
    cultural significance of Western
        rationalism and, 68–69, 74
    Frankfurt School and, 67
    on humans and meaning-making, 105
    on knowledge and values, 22–23
    on modernity and knowledge, 78–79
    on universalist aspirations of social
        science, 6
Westphalia system, 153–55,
    162–66, 214–15
White, Hayden, 89–90, 114–15
Whitehead, Alfred North, 49–50
Wight, Martin, 151
Wilder, Gary, 9–10
Winichakul, Thongchai, 133–35
Wittgenstein, Ludwig, 49–50
Wittrock, Björn, 8–9
Wolf, Eric, 40
Wolin, Sheldon, 176–77, 183–84
Woolgar, Steve, 32–33
World War I and World War II,
    160, 166–67

Yerushalmi, Yosef, 93–95, 130

Zimmern, Alfred, 167–68